Progress Chart

This chart lists the topics in the book. Once you have
completed each page, stick a star in the correct box below.

Page	Topic	Star	Page	Topic	Star	Page	Topic	Star
2	Reading and writing numbers	☆	15	Subtracting three-digit numbers	☆	28	Bar graphs	☆
3	Multiplying and dividing by 10	☆	16	Adding decimals	☆	29	Probability	☆
4	Ordering sets of large numbers	☆	17	Adding decimals	☆	30	Triangles	☆
5	Rounding numbers	☆	18	Subtracting decimals	☆	31	Expanded form	☆
6	Identifying patterns	☆	19	Subtracting decimals	☆	32	Speed trials	☆
7	Recognizing multiples of 6, 7, and 8	☆	20	Multiplying by one-digit numbers	☆	33	All the 3s	☆
8	Factors of numbers from 1 to 30	☆	21	Multiplying by one-digit numbers	☆	34	All the 3s again	☆
9	Recognizing equivalent fractions	☆	22	Division with remainders	☆	35	All the 4s	☆
10	Ordering sets of numbers	☆	23	Division with remainders	☆	36	All the 4s again	☆
11	Rounding decimals	☆	24	Real-life problems	☆	37	Speed trials	☆
12	Adding two numbers	☆	25	Real-life problems	☆	38	Some of the 6s	☆
13	Adding two numbers	☆	26	Areas of rectangles and squares	☆	39	The rest of the 6s	☆
14	Subtracting three-digit numbers	☆	27	Problems involving time	☆	40	Practise the 6s	☆

0	1	2	3	4	5	6	7	8	9	10
zero	one	two	three	four	five	six	seven	eight	nine	ten

Extra Practice Section

When you have completed the progress chart
in this book, fill in the certificate on page 202.

Ages 9-10
Grade
4
Math Workbook

Math Made Easy

Expanded Canadian Edition

Author Sean McArdle
Canadian math consultant Marilyn Wilson

Reading and writing numbers

4346 in words is	*Four thousand three hundred forty-six*
Two thousand five hundred two is	*2502*

Write each of these numbers in words.

6208

4543

701

8520

Write each of these in numbers.

Five hundred forty-two

Six thousand seven hundred eleven

Eight thousand two hundred three

Nine thousand four hundred four

Write each of these numbers in words.

7012

2390

8434

642

Write each of these in numbers.

Eight thousand two hundred fifty-one

Two thousand four hundred four

Seven thousand one hundred one

Two thousand five

Multiplying and dividing by 10

Write the answer in the box.

26 x 10 = 260

40 ÷ 10 = 4

Write the answer in the box.

76 x 10 =

43 x 10 =

93 x 10 =

66 x 10 =

13 x 10 =

47 x 10 =

147 x 10 =

936 x 10 =

284 x 10 =

364 x 10 =

821 x 10 =

473 x 10 =

Write the answer in the box.

30 ÷ 10 =

20 ÷ 10 =

70 ÷ 10 =

60 ÷ 10 =

50 ÷ 10 =

580 ÷ 10 =

310 ÷ 10 =

270 ÷ 10 =

100 ÷ 10 =

540 ÷ 10 =

890 ÷ 10 =

710 ÷ 10 =

Write the number that has been multiplied by 10.

x 10 = 370

x 10 = 640

x 10 = 740

x 10 = 810

x 10 = 100

x 10 = 830

x 10 = 7140

x 10 = 3070

x 10 = 5290

x 10 = 2640

x 10 = 8290

x 10 = 6480

Write the number that has been divided by 10.

÷ 10 = 3

÷ 10 = 2

÷ 10 = 9

÷ 10 = 42

÷ 10 = 93

÷ 10 = 74

÷ 10 = 57

÷ 10 = 38

÷ 10 = 86

Ordering sets of large numbers

Write these numbers in order, from least to greatest.

2322	526	404	32	1240	440
32	404	440	526	1240	2322

Write the numbers in each row in order, from least to greatest.

420	190	950	402	905	986
308	640	380	805	364	910
260	350	26	1000	620	100
500	820	2500	600	560	5000

Write the numbers in each row in order, from least to greatest.

4000	40 000	8900	8240	7560	5600
1550	5000	50 000	4500	1500	3150
100	70 100	7 100 000	710	710 000	7100

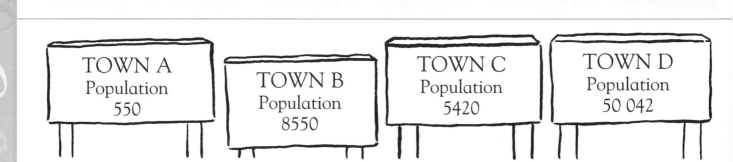

TOWN A
Population
550

TOWN B
Population
8550

TOWN C
Population
5420

TOWN D
Population
50 042

Which town has: The second-smallest population?

The largest population?   The second-largest population?

Rounding numbers

Round each number.

36 to the nearest ten   40

124 to the nearest hundred   100

4360 to the nearest thousand   4000

Remember: If a number is halfway between, round it up.

Round each number to the nearest ten.

24	91	55	73
57	68	49	35
82	37	22	52
46	26	85	99
43	51	78	29

Round each number to the nearest hundred.

386	224	825	460
539	429	378	937
772	255	549	612
116	750	618	990
940	843	172	868

Round each number to the nearest thousand.

3240	2500	9940	1051
8945	5050	5530	4850
6200	7250	8499	8450
12 501	8762	6500	3292
1499	14 836	10 650	11 241

Identifying patterns

Continue each pattern.

Steps of 9:	5	14	23	32	41	50
Steps of 14:	20	34	48	62	76	90

Continue each pattern.

21	38	55				
13	37	61				
7	25	43				
32	48	64				
12	31	50			107	
32	54	76				186
24	64	104				
4	34	64				
36	126	216		396		
12	72	132				
25	45	65			125	
22	72	122				
25	100	175				
60	165	270			585	
8	107	206				701
10	61	112				
26	127	228				733
48	100	152				

Recognizing multiples of 6, 7, and 8

Circle the multiples of 6.

8   (12)   15   (18)   20   (24)

Circle the multiples of 6.

8	22	14	18	36	40
16	38	44	25	30	60
6	21	19	54	56	24
12	48	10	20	35	26
42	39	23	28	36	32

Circle the multiples of 7.

7	17	24	59	42	55
15	20	21	46	12	70
14	27	69	36	47	49
65	19	57	28	38	63
33	34	35	37	60	56

Circle the multiples of 8.

40	26	15	25	38	56
26	8	73	41	64	12
75	58	62	24	31	72
12	80	32	46	38	78
16	42	66	28	48	68

Circle the number that is a multiple of 6 *and* 7.

18   54   42   21   28   63

Circle the numbers that are multiples of 6 *and* 8.

16   24   36   48   54   42

Circle the number that is a multiple of 7 *and* 8.

24   32   40   28   42   56

Factors of numbers from 1 to 30

The factors of 10 are   1   2   5   10

Circle the factors of 4.   ① ② 3 ④

Write all the factors of each number.

The factors of 26 are

The factors of 30 are

The factors of 9 are

The factors of 12 are

The factors of 15 are

The factors of 22 are

The factors of 20 are

The factors of 21 are

The factors of 24 are

Circle all the factors of each number.

Which numbers are factors of 14?   1 2 3 5 7 9 12 14

Which numbers are factors of 13?   1 2 3 4 5 6 7 8 9 10 11 13

Which numbers are factors of 7?   1 2 3 4 5 6 7

Which numbers are factors of 11?   1 2 3 4 5 6 7 8 9 10 11

Which numbers are factors of 6?   1 2 3 4 5 6

Which numbers are factors of 8?   1 2 3 4 5 6 7 8

Which numbers are factors of 17?   1 2 5 7 12 14 16 17

Which numbers are factors of 18?   1 2 3 4 5 6 8 9 10 12 18

Some numbers only have factors of 1 and themselves. They are called prime numbers. Write down all the prime numbers that are less than 30 in the box.

Recognizing equivalent fractions

Make each pair of fractions equal by writing a number in the box.

$$\frac{1}{2} = \frac{2}{4} \qquad\qquad \frac{1}{3} = \frac{2}{6}$$

Make each pair of fractions equal by writing a number in the box.

$$\frac{1}{2} = \frac{}{10} \qquad\qquad \frac{3}{4} = \frac{}{8} \qquad\qquad \frac{1}{3} = \frac{}{9}$$

$$\frac{2}{3} = \frac{}{12} \qquad\qquad \frac{6}{12} = \frac{}{6} \qquad\qquad \frac{4}{8} = \frac{}{2}$$

$$\frac{1}{5} = \frac{}{10} \qquad\qquad \frac{4}{12} = \frac{}{6} \qquad\qquad \frac{3}{5} = \frac{}{10}$$

$$\frac{1}{4} = \frac{}{8} \qquad\qquad \frac{6}{18} = \frac{}{3} \qquad\qquad \frac{3}{12} = \frac{}{4}$$

$$\frac{3}{9} = \frac{1}{} \qquad\qquad \frac{4}{10} = \frac{2}{} \qquad\qquad \frac{3}{4} = \frac{9}{}$$

$$\frac{4}{16} = \frac{1}{} \qquad\qquad \frac{15}{20} = \frac{3}{} \qquad\qquad \frac{6}{12} = \frac{1}{}$$

$$\frac{3}{5} = \frac{6}{} \qquad\qquad \frac{3}{6} = \frac{1}{} \qquad\qquad \frac{9}{12} = \frac{3}{}$$

Make each row of fractions equal by writing a number in each box.

$$\frac{1}{2} = \frac{}{4} = \frac{3}{} = \frac{}{8} = \frac{}{10} = \frac{6}{}$$

$$\frac{1}{4} = \frac{2}{} = \frac{}{12} = \frac{4}{} = \frac{5}{} = \frac{}{24}$$

$$\frac{3}{4} = \frac{6}{} = \frac{}{12} = \frac{12}{} = \frac{}{20} = \frac{18}{}$$

$$\frac{1}{3} = \frac{}{6} = \frac{3}{} = \frac{4}{} = \frac{}{15} = \frac{12}{}$$

$$\frac{1}{5} = \frac{}{10} = \frac{}{15} = \frac{4}{} = \frac{5}{} = \frac{}{30}$$

$$\frac{2}{3} = \frac{}{6} = \frac{}{9} = \frac{8}{} = \frac{10}{} = \frac{14}{}$$

Ordering sets of numbers

Write the numbers in order, from least to greatest.

$$2 \qquad 1\frac{1}{4} \qquad \frac{3}{4} \qquad \frac{1}{4} \qquad 1\frac{3}{4}$$

$$\boxed{\frac{1}{4}} \qquad \boxed{\frac{3}{4}} \qquad \boxed{1\frac{1}{4}} \qquad \boxed{1\frac{3}{4}} \qquad \boxed{2}$$

Write each row of numbers in order, from least to greatest.

$4 \qquad 2\frac{1}{4} \qquad 1\frac{3}{4} \qquad 1\frac{1}{4} \qquad 3\frac{1}{4}$

$2 \qquad 1\frac{1}{2} \qquad 1 \qquad 2\frac{1}{2} \qquad 3$

$2 \qquad 1\frac{1}{4} \qquad 3\frac{1}{2} \qquad 1\frac{1}{2} \qquad 2\frac{1}{2}$

$7\frac{1}{2} \qquad 3\frac{1}{4} \qquad 1\frac{1}{2} \qquad 1\frac{1}{4} \qquad 2\frac{3}{4}$

$4\frac{1}{4} \qquad 3\frac{1}{2} \qquad 2\frac{3}{4} \qquad 2\frac{1}{2} \qquad 3\frac{1}{4}$

$3\frac{3}{4} \qquad 3\frac{1}{3} \qquad 4\frac{1}{4} \qquad 3\frac{2}{3} \qquad 3\frac{1}{2}$

$4\frac{2}{3} \qquad 4\frac{1}{2} \qquad 4\frac{3}{4} \qquad 4\frac{1}{3} \qquad 5\frac{1}{4}$

$7\frac{1}{2} \qquad 6\frac{2}{3} \qquad 7\frac{3}{4} \qquad 7\frac{1}{4} \qquad 6\frac{1}{2}$

$14\frac{1}{2} \qquad 15\frac{3}{4} \qquad 15\frac{1}{2} \qquad 14\frac{3}{4} \qquad 13\frac{3}{4}$

$7\frac{1}{3} \qquad 8\frac{1}{2} \qquad 7\frac{3}{4} \qquad 8\frac{1}{5} \qquad 7\frac{2}{3}$

$10\frac{1}{5} \qquad 9\frac{3}{4} \qquad 10\frac{1}{2} \qquad 9\frac{1}{5} \qquad 9\frac{1}{2}$

Rounding decimals

Round each decimal to the nearest whole number.

3.4   *3*

5.7   *6*

4.5   *5*

If the whole number has 5 after it, round it to the whole number above.

Round each decimal to the nearest whole number.

6.2		2.5		1.5		3.8
5.5		2.8		3.2		8.5
5.4		7.9		3.7		2.3
1.1		8.6		8.3		9.2
4.7		6.3		7.3		8.7

Round each decimal to the nearest whole number.

14.4		42.3		74.1		59.7
29.9		32.6		63.5		96.4
18.2		37.5		39.6		76.3
40.1		28.7		26.9		12.5
29.5		38.5		87.2		41.6

Round each decimal to the nearest whole number.

137.6		423.5		426.2		111.8
641.6		333.5		805.2		246.8
119.5		799.6		562.3		410.2
682.4		759.6		531.5		829.9
743.4		831.1		276.7		649.3

Adding two numbers

Find each sum.

```
  271          483
+ 524        + 571
─────        ─────
  795         1054
```

Remember to regroup if you need to.

Find each sum.

```
  334          352          723          843
+ 265        + 127        + 345        + 291
─────        ─────        ─────        ─────
```

```
  385          363          535          392
+ 606        + 147        + 187        + 488
─────        ─────        ─────        ─────
```

Write the answer in the box.

213 + 137 =   535 + 167 =

Write the missing number in the box.

```
  3 6 2        2   6        7   1        7 3 9
+ 4 1 9      + 5 8 1      + 2 6 4      + 2 4
─────────    ─────────    ─────────    ─────────
  7   1        8 3 7        9 8            7 9
```

Find each sum.

One jar contains 204 candies, and another contains 148 candies. How many candies are there altogether?

A boy has 136 baseball cards, and his sister has 159. How many cards do they have altogether?

Adding two numbers

Find each sum.

```
  4321          ¹ ¹
+ 2465        3794
  6786      + 5325
              9119
```

Remember to carry if you need to.

Find each sum.

```
  2642          4325          2471
+ 3241        + 2653        + 4238
_____        _____        _____


  3749          5764          8482
+ 2471        + 3915        + 1349
_____        _____        _____
```

Write the answer in the box.

1342 + 1264   =   2531 + 4236   =

2013 + 3642   =   1738 + 4261   =

Write the missing number in the box.

```
    7 4 1            6 5 2            3 6 4 2
  + 2 9 4          + 3 2  4        +     8 3
  ─────────        ─────────        ─────────
    6 6 8 4          4 9 2 6          8 4 7 3
```

Find each sum.

5621 people saw the local soccer team play on Saturday, and 3246 people watched the midweek match. How many people saw the soccer team play that week?

6214 people went to the rock concert on Saturday night, and 3471 people went on Sunday night. How many people saw the rock concert that weekend?

Subtracting three-digit numbers

Write the difference between the lines.

$$
\begin{array}{r} 364 \\ -\ 223 \\ \hline 141 \end{array}
\qquad
\begin{array}{r} 4\overset{6\ 11}{7\!\!/1} \text{ cm} \\ -\ 252 \text{ cm} \\ \hline 219 \text{ cm} \end{array}
$$

Write the difference between the lines.

$$
\begin{array}{r} 263 \\ -\ 151 \\ \hline \end{array}
\qquad
\begin{array}{r} 478 \\ -\ 234 \\ \hline \end{array}
\qquad
\begin{array}{r} 845 \\ -\ 624 \\ \hline \end{array}
\qquad
\begin{array}{r} 793 \\ -\ 581 \\ \hline \end{array}
$$

$$
\begin{array}{r} 580 \text{ cm} \\ -230 \text{ cm} \\ \hline \end{array}
\qquad
\begin{array}{r} 659 \text{ m} \\ -\ 318 \text{ m} \\ \hline \end{array}
\qquad
\begin{array}{r} 850 \text{ cm} \\ -\ 740 \text{ cm} \\ \hline \end{array}
\qquad
\begin{array}{r} 372 \text{ m} \\ -\ 262 \text{ m} \\ \hline \end{array}
$$

Write the difference in the box.

$365\ -\ 123\ =$ ⬚ $\qquad 799\ -\ 354\ =$ ⬚

$\$876\ -\ \$515\ =$ ⬚ $\qquad \$940\ -\ \$730\ =$ ⬚

$\$684\ -\ \$574\ =$ ⬚ $\qquad \$220\ -\ \$120\ =$ ⬚

Write the difference between the lines.

$$
\begin{array}{r} 363 \\ -\ 145 \\ \hline \end{array}
\qquad
\begin{array}{r} 484 \\ -\ 237 \\ \hline \end{array}
\qquad
\begin{array}{r} 561 \\ -\ 342 \\ \hline \end{array}
\qquad
\begin{array}{r} 394 \\ -\ 185 \\ \hline \end{array}
$$

$$
\begin{array}{r} 937 \\ -\ 719 \\ \hline \end{array}
\qquad
\begin{array}{r} 568 \\ -\ 209 \\ \hline \end{array}
\qquad
\begin{array}{r} 225 \\ -\ 116 \\ \hline \end{array}
\qquad
\begin{array}{r} 752 \\ -\ 329 \\ \hline \end{array}
$$

Find the answer to each problem.

A grocer has 234 apples. He sells 127. How many apples does he have left?

A store has 860 videos to rent. 420 are rented. How many are left in the store?

There are 572 children in a school. 335 are girls. How many are boys?

14

Subtracting three-digit numbers

Write the difference between the lines.

$$\begin{array}{r} {\scriptstyle 3\ 11} \\ 4\!\!\!/15 \\ -\ 152 \\ \hline 263 \end{array}$$

$$\begin{array}{r} {\scriptstyle\ \ \ 10} \\ {\scriptstyle 6\ \emptyset\ 11} \\ 7\!\!\!/1\!\!\!/1\ \text{m} \\ -392\ \text{m} \\ \hline 319\ \text{m} \end{array}$$

Write the difference between the lines.

524 m	319 m	647 cm	915 cm
− 263 m	− 137 m	−456 cm	−193 cm

714	926	421	815
− 407	− 827	− 355	− 786

Write the difference in the box.

512 − 304 =

648 − 239 =

831 − 642 =

377 − 198 =

Write the difference between the lines.

423	615	312	924
− 136	− 418	− 113	− 528

Write the missing number in the box.

$$\begin{array}{r} 7\ 2\ 3 \\ -\ 1\ 2\ \square \\ \hline 5\ 9\ 5 \end{array}$$

$$\begin{array}{r} 5\ \square\ 2 \\ -\ 3\ 1\ 7 \\ \hline 2\ 4\ 5 \end{array}$$

$$\begin{array}{r} 8\ 3\ \square \\ -\ 2\ 5\ 7 \\ \hline 5\ 7\ 7 \end{array}$$

$$\begin{array}{r} 5\ 3\ 2 \\ -\ \square\ \square\ 5 \\ \hline 3\ 4\ 7 \end{array}$$

Find the answer to each problem.

A theatre holds 645 people. 257 people buy tickets. How many seats are empty?

There are 564 people in a park. 276 are boating on the lake. How many are taking part in other activities?

Adding decimals

Write the answer between the lines.

$5.25	2.25 m
+ $2.40	+ 3.50 m
$7.65	5.75 m

Write the answer between the lines.

$2.25	$7.50	$3.35
+ $4.50	+ $2.25	+ $1.50

$6.45	$3.15	$1.50
+ $2.35	+ $4.75	+ $3.95

5.50 m	3.60 m	7.30 m
+ 2.35 m	+ 4.15 m	+ 1.65 m

6.15 m	3.30 m	5.20 m
+ 2.20 m	+ 6.55 m	+ 1.75 m

Write the answer in the box.

$5.25 + $3.30 =   6.15 m + 1.50 m = $6.35 + $2.30 =

$5.20 + $2.55 =   2.45 m + 5.10 m = $7.45 + $1.50 =

Find the answer to each problem.

Lorna has $2.50. Her brother has $2.75. How much do they have together?

Max has 9.50 m of track for a model train. His friend has 7.75 m of track. If they joined their tracks, how long would the new track be?

Adding decimals

Write the answer between the lines.

$$\begin{array}{r} \overset{1}{}\$3.35 \\ + \quad \$5.55 \\ \hline \$8.90 \end{array} \qquad \begin{array}{r} \overset{1}{}3.45 \text{ m} \\ + \quad 1.25 \text{ m} \\ \hline 4.70 \text{ m} \end{array}$$

Write the answer between the lines.

$$\begin{array}{r} \$3.60 \\ + \$2.25 \\ \hline \\ \hline \end{array} \qquad \begin{array}{r} \$1.25 \\ + \$4.55 \\ \hline \\ \hline \end{array} \qquad \begin{array}{r} \$7.45 \\ + \$2.35 \\ \hline \\ \hline \end{array}$$

$$\begin{array}{r} \$3.60 \\ + \$3.25 \\ \hline \\ \hline \end{array} \qquad \begin{array}{r} \$7.35 \\ + \$1.45 \\ \hline \\ \hline \end{array} \qquad \begin{array}{r} \$5.25 \\ + \$2.65 \\ \hline \\ \hline \end{array}$$

$$\begin{array}{r} 3.45 \text{ m} \\ + 4.35 \text{ m} \\ \hline \\ \hline \end{array} \qquad \begin{array}{r} 8.55 \text{ m} \\ + 1.35 \text{ m} \\ \hline \\ \hline \end{array} \qquad \begin{array}{r} 1.75 \text{ m} \\ + 5.20 \text{ m} \\ \hline \\ \hline \end{array}$$

$$\begin{array}{r} 2.40 \text{ m} \\ + 1.45 \text{ m} \\ \hline \\ \hline \end{array} \qquad \begin{array}{r} 7.15 \text{ m} \\ + 1.35 \text{ m} \\ \hline \\ \hline \end{array} \qquad \begin{array}{r} 3.85 \text{ m} \\ + 4.10 \text{ m} \\ \hline \\ \hline \end{array}$$

Write the answer in the box.

$2.75 + \$4.15 =$ 　　　 $3.75 \text{ m} + 2.75 \text{ m} =$ 　　　 $\$3.65 + \$1.50 =$

$6.25 + \$1.50 =$ 　　　 $8.65 \text{ m} + 2.55 \text{ m} =$ 　　　 $\$3.45 + \$1.55 =$

Work out the answer to each sum.

George buys two magazines that cost $2.55 and $1.75. How much does he spend?

Jennifer buys two rolls of tape. One is 7.75 m long, and the other is 6.75 m. How much tape does she have altogether?

Subtracting decimals

Write the difference between the lines.

$$
\begin{array}{r} \$\,6.55 \\ -\ \$\,3.20 \\ \hline \$3.35 \end{array}
\qquad
\begin{array}{r} 4.70\ \text{m} \\ -\ 2.50\ \text{m} \\ \hline 2.20\ \text{m} \end{array}
$$

Write the difference between the lines.

$$
\begin{array}{r} \$7.45 \\ -\ \$3.30 \\ \hline \end{array}
\qquad
\begin{array}{r} \$9.60 \\ -\ \$7.20 \\ \hline \end{array}
\qquad
\begin{array}{r} \$5.55 \\ -\ \$2.40 \\ \hline \end{array}
$$

$$
\begin{array}{r} \$8.35 \\ -\ \$3.25 \\ \hline \end{array}
\qquad
\begin{array}{r} \$3.95 \\ -\ \$1.75 \\ \hline \end{array}
\qquad
\begin{array}{r} \$6.55 \\ -\ \$2.40 \\ \hline \end{array}
$$

Write the difference between the lines.

$$
\begin{array}{r} 3.90\ \text{m} \\ -\ 1.40\ \text{m} \\ \hline \end{array}
\qquad
\begin{array}{r} 4.75\ \text{m} \\ -\ 3.35\ \text{m} \\ \hline \end{array}
\qquad
\begin{array}{r} 9.20\ \text{m} \\ -\ 2.20\ \text{m} \\ \hline \end{array}
$$

$$
\begin{array}{r} 7.55\ \text{m} \\ -\ 1.15\ \text{m} \\ \hline \end{array}
\qquad
\begin{array}{r} 2.15\ \text{m} \\ -\ 1.00\ \text{m} \\ \hline \end{array}
\qquad
\begin{array}{r} 3.35\ \text{m} \\ -\ 2.20\ \text{m} \\ \hline \end{array}
$$

Write the difference in the box.

$\$4.15\ -\ \$1.10\ =$ $\qquad\qquad$ $\$3.55\ -\ \$2.50\ =$

$\$9.75\ -\ \$4.30\ =$ $\qquad\qquad$ $\$8.85\ -\ \$6.05\ =$

$7.55\ \text{m} - 2.30\ \text{m} =$ $\qquad\qquad$ $6.15\ \text{m} - 4.05\ \text{m} =$

Find the answer to each problem.

Mei-ling has $4.65 to spend. She buys a book for $3.45. How much money does she have left?

Shawn is given $9.50 for his birthday. If he spends $3.20 at the mall, how much money will he have left?

Subtracting decimals

Write the difference between the lines.

4 13	6 13
$5.35	7.35 m
– $2.40	– 1.65 m
$2.95	5.70 m

Write the difference between the lines.

$6.55	$7.45	$8.65
– $2.75	– $3.65	– $4.75

$3.15	$5.70	$4.15
– $1.25	– $2.90	– $1.75

Write the difference between the lines.

5.35 m	7.25 m	4.15 m
– 2.55 m	– 2.55 m	– 2.25 m

5.45 m	8.15 m	7.30 m
– 2.55 m	– 2.20 m	– 3.50 m

Write the difference in the box.

$6.25 – $2.50 =

$5.20 – $3.30 =

6.45 m – 2.55 m =

$4.35 – $2.55 =

$7.40 – $3.80 =

7.35 m – 3.55 m =

Find the answer to each problem.

Keisha has a piece of wood 4.55 m long. She cuts off a piece
1.65 m long. How long a piece of wood is left?

Eli's long-jump result is 2.35 m. Steven's is 1.40 m. How much
longer is Eli's jump than Steven's?

Multiplying by one-digit numbers

Find each product.

32	26	34
x 2	x 3	x 4
64	78	136

Find each product.

27	32	16	19
x 2	x 3	x 4	x 2

22	25	18	33
x 3	x 4	x 6	x 5

39	26	41	38
x 2	x 2	x 2	x 3

29	45	28	16
x 3	x 2	x 3	x 6

10	40	20	50
x 5	x 2	x 4	x 3

Find the answer to each problem.

Laura has 36 marbles, and Sarah has twice as many. How many marbles does Sarah have?

A ruler is 30 cm long. How long will 4 rulers be?

Multiplying by one-digit numbers

Find each product.

$$
\begin{array}{r} 53 \\ \times\ 3 \\ \hline 159 \end{array}
\qquad
\begin{array}{r} \overset{3}{76} \\ \times\ 6 \\ \hline 456 \end{array}
\qquad
\begin{array}{r} \overset{3}{25} \\ \times\ 7 \\ \hline 175 \end{array}
$$

Find each product.

56	48	46	32	36
x 8	x 5	x 7	x 6	x 9
45	33	73	96	58
x 4	x 6	x 5	x 3	x 7
81	24	19	64	52
x 3	x 9	x 8	x 4	x 6
37	40	50	30	20
x 7	x 8	x 3	x 7	x 9

Find the answer to each problem.

A school bus holds 36 children.
How many children can travel in
6 busloads?

Each of 28 children brings
7 drawings to school. How
many drawings do they have
altogether?

Division with remainders

Find each quotient.

$$3\overline{)16}$$ 5 r 1
15
1

$$4\overline{)26}$$ 6 r 2
24
2

Find each quotient.

$$2\overline{)35}$$ $$4\overline{)46}$$ $$3\overline{)22}$$ $$5\overline{)49}$$

$$4\overline{)58}$$ $$5\overline{)63}$$ $$5\overline{)37}$$ $$4\overline{)50}$$

$$3\overline{)76}$$ $$4\overline{)59}$$ $$5\overline{)94}$$ $$5\overline{)83}$$

$$2\overline{)99}$$ $$4\overline{)75}$$ $$5\overline{)77}$$ $$2\overline{)37}$$

Write the answer in the box.

What is 27 divided by 4?   Divide 78 by 5.

What is 46 divided by 3?   Divide 63 by 2.

22

Division with remainders

Find each quotient.

$$6\overline{)34}$$ 5 r 4
30
4

$$7\overline{)50}$$ 7 r 1
49
1

Find each quotient.

$$6\overline{)99}$$

$$6\overline{)43}$$

$$9\overline{)30}$$

$$8\overline{)76}$$

$$7\overline{)52}$$

$$7\overline{)83}$$

$$9\overline{)52}$$

$$6\overline{)91}$$

$$7\overline{)66}$$

$$8\overline{)63}$$

$$6\overline{)27}$$

$$8\overline{)46}$$

$$9\overline{)93}$$

$$7\overline{)85}$$

$$8\overline{)67}$$

$$7\overline{)26}$$

Write the answer in the box.

What is 87 divided by 7?

Divide 84 by 8.

What is 75 divided by 6?

Divide 73 by 9.

Real-life problems

Write the answer in the box.

Yasmin has $4.60 and she is given another $1.20.
How much money does she have?

$5.80

$$\begin{array}{r} \$4.60 \\ +\ \$1.20 \\ \hline \$5.80 \end{array}$$

David has 120 marbles.
He divides them equally among his 5 friends.
How many marbles
does each get?   24

$$\begin{array}{r} 24 \\ 5\overline{)120} \\ 10 \\ \hline 20 \\ 20 \\ \hline 0 \end{array}$$

Write the answer in the box.

Michael buys a ball for $5.50 and a flashlight for $3.65.
How much does he spend?

How much does he have left from $10?

The 32 children of a class bring in $5 each for a school trip.
What is the total of the amount brought in?

A set of 5 shelves can be made from a piece of wood 4 metres
long. What fraction of a metre will each shelf be?

Each of 5 children has $16.
How much do they have altogether?

If the above total were shared among 8 children, how much would
each child have?

Real-life problems

Find the answer to each problem.

A box is 16 cm wide. How wide will 6 boxes side by side be?

96 cm

```
    3
  16 cm
 x 6
  96 cm
```

Josh is 1.20 m tall. His sister is 1.55 m tall. How much taller than Josh is his sister?

0.35 m

```
   1.55 m
 - 1.20 m
   0.35 m
```

Find the answer to each problem.

A can contains 56 g of lemonade mix. If 12 g are used, how much is left?

A large jar of coffee weighs 280 g. A smaller jar weighs 130 g. How much heavier is the larger jar than the smaller jar?

There are 7 shelves of books. 5 shelves are 1.2 m long. 2 shelves are 1.5 m long. What is the total length of the 7 shelves?

A rock star can sign 36 photographs in a minute. How many can he sign in 30 seconds?

Shana has read 5 pages of a 20-page comic book. If it has taken her 9 minutes, how long is it likely to take her to read the whole comic book?

25

Areas of rectangles and squares

Find the area of this rectangle.

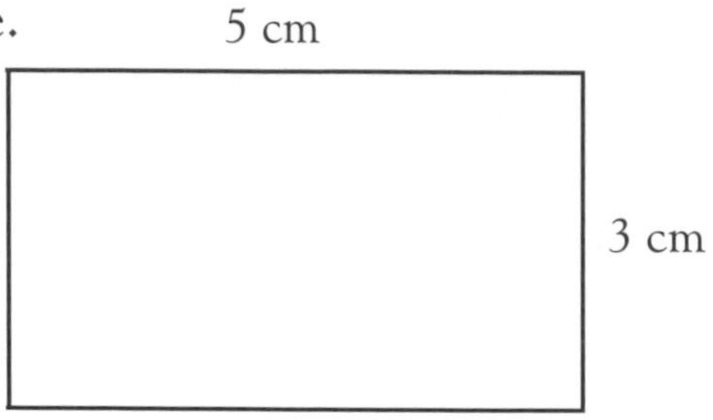

5 cm

15 cm²

3 cm

To find the area of a rectangle or square, multiply length (*l*) by width (*w*).
Area → *l* x *w* → 5 cm x 3 cm = 15 cm²

Find the area of each rectangle and square.

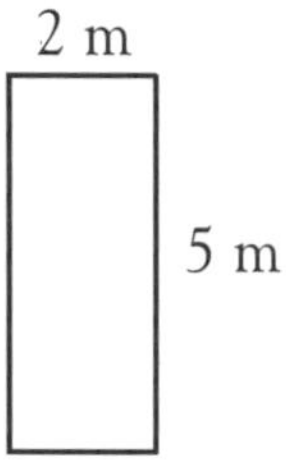

3 m

2 m

5 m

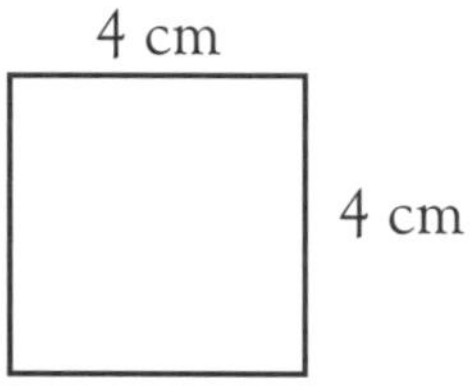

4 cm

4 cm

8 m

___ m²

___ cm²

___ m²

2 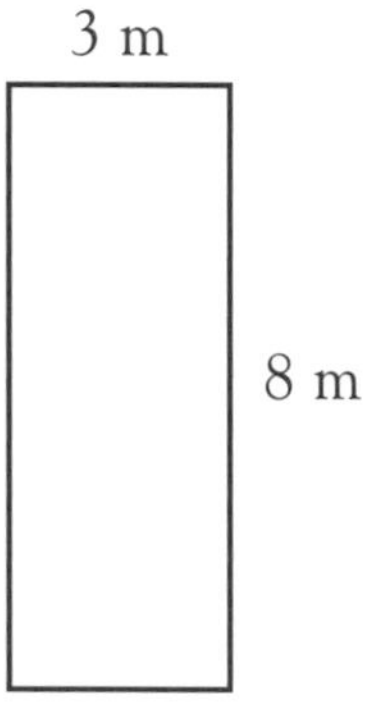 m

2 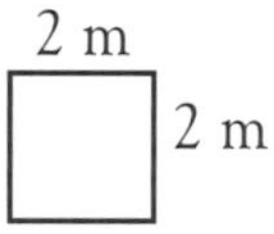 m

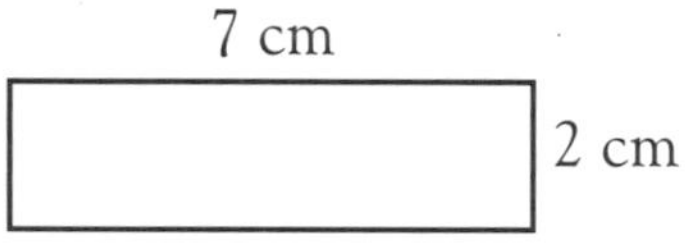

7 cm

2 cm

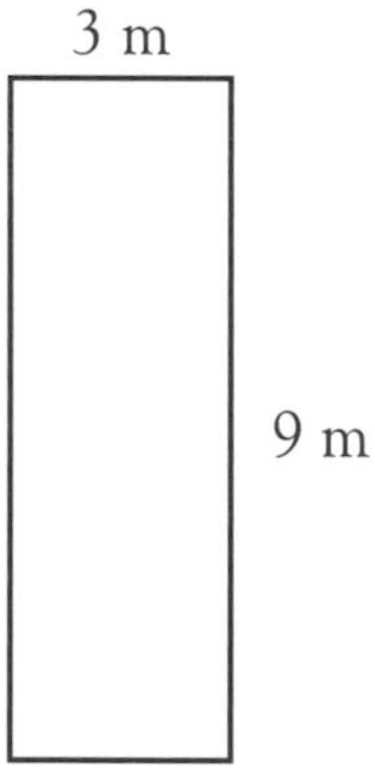

3 m

9 m

___ m²

___ cm²

___ m²

6 cm

4 cm

5 m

4 m

5 cm

5 cm

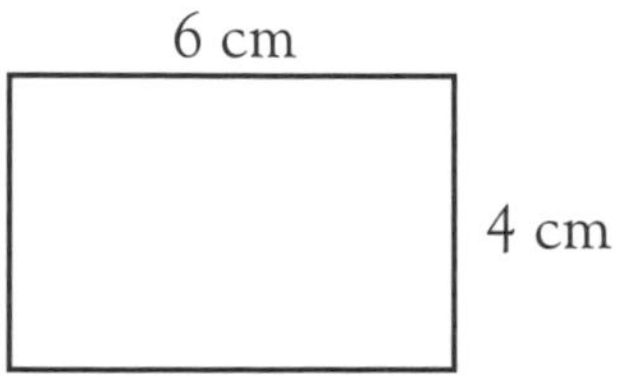

___ cm²

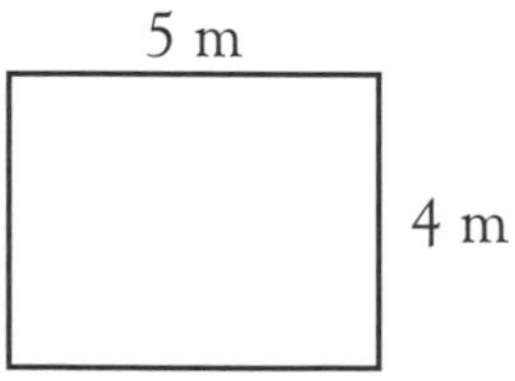

___ m²

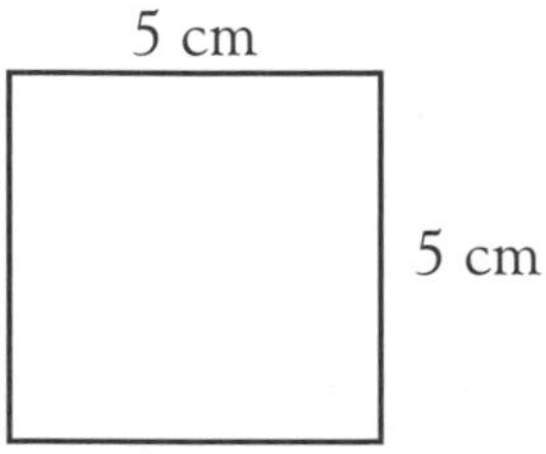

___ cm²

Problems involving time

Find the answer to this problem.

A train leaves the station at 7:30 A.M. and arrives at the end of the line at 10:45 A.M. How long did the journey take?

3 hours 15 minutes

7:30 → 10:30 = 3 h
10:30 → 10:45 = 15 min
Total = 3 h 15 min

Find the answer to each problem.

A film starts at 7:00 P.M. and finishes at 8:45 P.M. How long is the film?

A cake takes 2 hours 25 minutes to bake. If it begins baking at 1:35 P.M., at what time will the cake be done?

Sanjay needs to clean his bedroom and wash the car. It takes him 1 hour 10 minutes to clean his room and 45 minutes to clean the car. If he starts at 10:00 A.M., at what time will he finish?

A car is taken in for repair at 7:00 A.M. It is finished at 1:50 P.M. How long did the repairs take?

Claire has to be at school by 8:50 A.M. If she takes 1 hour 30 minutes to get ready, and the trip takes 35 minutes, at what time does she need to get up?

A bus leaves the bus station at 8:45 A.M. and arrives back at 10:15 A.M. How long has its trip taken?

Bar graphs

Use this bar graph to answer each question.

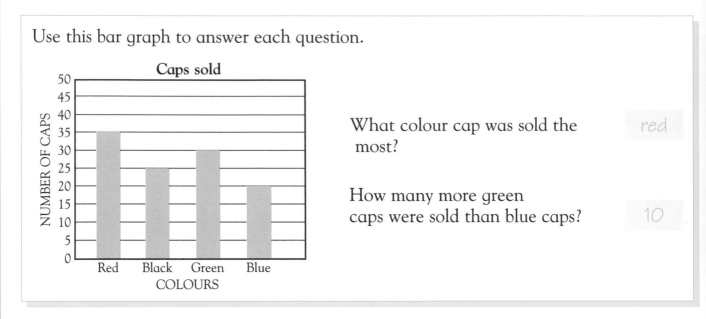

What colour cap was sold the most?   red

How many more green caps were sold than blue caps?   10

Use this bar graph to answer each question.

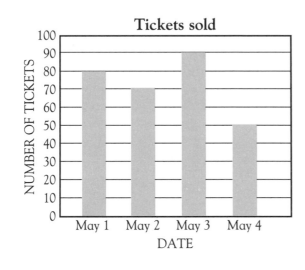

How many tickets were sold on May 1?

How many more tickets were sold on May 2 than on May 4?

On which date were 90 tickets sold?

Use this bar graph to answer each question.

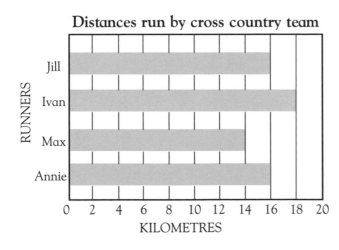

Which runner ran 14 kilometres?

Which runner ran the same distance as Annie?

How much farther did Ivan run than Max?

Probability

Mark each event on the probability line.

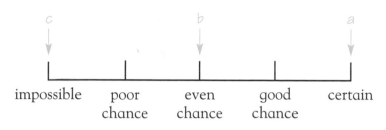

impossible   poor chance   even chance   good chance   certain

a) It will get dark tonight.
b) When I toss a coin, it will land showing heads.
c) Abraham Lincoln will come for lunch.

Mark each event on the probability line.

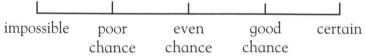

impossible   poor chance   even chance   good chance   certain

a) Snow will fall in August.
b) The sun will come up tomorrow.
c) A new baby will be a boy.
d) A dog will speak English.
e) I will watch some television tonight.

Mark each event on the probability line.

impossible   poor chance   even chance   good chance   certain

a) I will roll a 6 on a number cube.
b) I will not roll a 6 on a number cube.
c) I will roll a number between 1 and 6 on a number cube.
d) I will roll a 7 on a number cube.
e) I will roll a 1, a 2, or a 3 on a number cube.

Mark each event on the probability line.

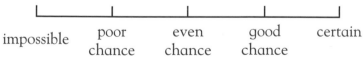

impossible   poor chance   even chance   good chance   certain

a) I will drink something today.
b) If I drop my book, it will fall face down.
c) The next book I read will have exactly 100 pages.
d) It will rain orange juice tomorrow.
e) I will see a white car today.

Triangles

Look at these different triangles.

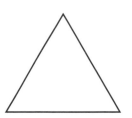  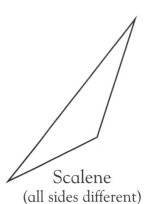

Equilateral
(all sides equal;
is also isosceles)

Isosceles
(two sides equal)

Scalene
(all sides different)

Right angle
(may be isosceles or
scalene, but one angle
must be a right angle)

1 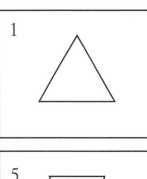	2 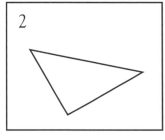	3 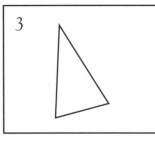	4 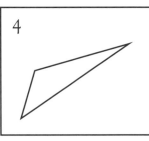
5 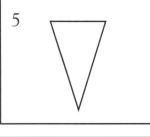	6 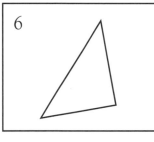	7 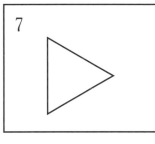	8 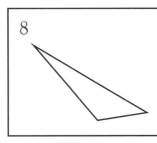
9 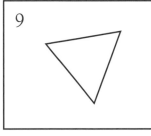	10 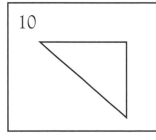	11 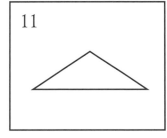	12 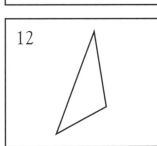

List the triangles that are:

Equilateral _____

Isosceles _____

Scalene _____

Right angle _____

Expanded form

What is the value of 3 in 2308?   300

Write 3417 in expanded form.

(3 x 1000) + (4 x 100) + (1 x 10) +(7 x 1)

3000 + 400 + 10 + 7

What is the value of 5 in each of these numbers?

25   5904   52   2512   805

What is the value of 8 in each of these numbers?

8300   982   1805   768   19 873

Circle each number in which 7 has the value of 70.

7682   927   870   372   707

171   767   875   7057   70 000

Write each number in expanded form.

3897   24 098

50 810   8945

6098   14 003

31

Speed trials

Write the answers as fast as you can, but get them right!

3 x 2 =	0 x 5 =	3 x 10 =	0 x 3 =
5 x 2 =	10 x 5 =	5 x 10 =	10 x 3 =
1 x 2 =	8 x 5 =	1 x 10 =	8 x 3 =
4 x 2 =	6 x 5 =	4 x 10 =	6 x 3 =
7 x 2 =	2 x 5 =	7 x 10 =	2 x 3 =
2 x 2 =	7 x 5 =	2 x 10 =	7 x 3 =
6 x 2 =	4 x 5 =	6 x 10 =	4 x 3 =
8 x 2 =	1 x 5 =	8 x 10 =	1 x 3 =
10 x 2 =	5 x 5 =	10 x 10 =	5 x 3 =
0 x 2 =	3 x 5 =	0 x 10 =	3 x 3 =
9 x 2 =	5 x 3 =	9 x 10 =	6 x 4 =
2 x 7 =	5 x 8 =	10 x 7 =	3 x 4 =
2 x 1 =	5 x 6 =	10 x 1 =	7 x 4 =
2 x 4 =	5 x 9 =	10 x 4 =	4 x 4 =
3 x 7 =	5 x 7 =	10 x 7 =	10 x 4 =
2 x 5 =	5 x 4 =	10 x 5 =	8 x 4 =
2 x 9 =	5 x 1 =	10 x 9 =	0 x 4 =
2 x 6 =	4 x 7 =	10 x 6 =	9 x 4 =
2 x 8 =	5 x 10 =	10 x 8 =	5 x 4 =
2 x 3 =	5 x 2 =	10 x 3 =	2 x 4 =

All the 3s

You will need to know these:

$1 \times 3 = 3$ $2 \times 3 = 6$ $3 \times 3 = 9$ $4 \times 3 = 12$ $5 \times 3 = 15$ $10 \times 3 = 30$

How many altogether?

6 sets of three are   six threes are $6 \times 3 =$

How many altogether?

7 sets of three are   seven threes are $7 \times 3 =$

How many altogether?

8 sets of three are   eight threes are $8 \times 3 =$

How many altogether?

9 sets of three are   nine threes are $9 \times 3 =$

All the 3s again

You should know all of the three times table by now.

1 x 3 = 3	2 x 3 = 6	3 x 3 = 9	4 x 3 = 12	5 x 3 = 15
6 x 3 = 18	7 x 3 = 21	8 x 3 = 24	9 x 3 = 27	10 x 3 = 30

Say these to yourself a few times.

Cover the three times table with a sheet of paper so you can't see the numbers.
Write the answers. Be as fast as you can, but get them right!

1 x 3 =	5 x 3 =	6 x 3 =
2 x 3 =	7 x 3 =	9 x 3 =
3 x 3 =	9 x 3 =	4 x 3 =
4 x 3 =	4 x 3 =	5 x 3 =
5 x 3 =	6 x 3 =	3 x 7 =
6 x 3 =	8 x 3 =	3 x 4 =
7 x 3 =	10 x 3 =	2 x 3 =
8 x 3 =	1 x 3 =	10 x 3 =
9 x 3 =	3 x 3 =	3 x 9 =
10 x 3 =	2 x 3 =	3 x 6 =
3 x 1 =	3 x 5 =	3 x 5 =
3 x 2 =	3 x 7 =	3 x 8 =
3 x 3 =	3 x 9 =	7 x 3 =
3 x 4 =	3 x 4 =	3 x 2 =
3 x 5 =	3 x 6 =	3 x 10 =
3 x 6 =	3 x 8 =	8 x 3 =
3 x 7 =	3 x 10 =	3 x 0 =
3 x 8 =	3 x 1 =	1 x 3 =
3 x 9 =	3 x 0 =	3 x 3 =
3 x 10 =	3 x 2 =	3 x 9 =

All the 4s

You should know these:

1 x 4 = 4   2 x 4 = 8   3 x 4 = 12   4 x 4 = 16   5 x 4 = 20   10 x 4 = 40

How many altogether?

6 sets of four are   six fours are   6 x 4 =

How many altogether?

7 sets of four are   seven fours are   7 x 4 =

How many altogether?

8 sets of four are   eight fours are   8 x 4 =

How many altogether?

9 sets of four are   nine fours are   9 x 4 =

All the 4s again

You should know all of the four times table by now.

$1 \times 4 = 4$	$2 \times 4 = 8$	$3 \times 4 = 12$	$4 \times 4 = 16$	$5 \times 4 = 20$
$6 \times 4 = 24$	$7 \times 4 = 28$	$8 \times 4 = 32$	$9 \times 4 = 36$	$10 \times 4 = 40$

Say these to yourself a few times.

Cover the four times table with a sheet of paper so you can't see the numbers.
Write the answers. Be as fast as you can, but get them right!

$1 \times 4 =$	$5 \times 4 =$	$6 \times 4 =$
$2 \times 4 =$	$7 \times 4 =$	$9 \times 4 =$
$3 \times 4 =$	$9 \times 4 =$	$4 \times 1 =$
$4 \times 4 =$	$3 \times 4 =$	$5 \times 4 =$
$5 \times 4 =$	$6 \times 4 =$	$4 \times 7 =$
$6 \times 4 =$	$8 \times 4 =$	$3 \times 4 =$
$7 \times 4 =$	$10 \times 4 =$	$2 \times 4 =$
$8 \times 4 =$	$1 \times 4 =$	$10 \times 4 =$
$9 \times 4 =$	$4 \times 4 =$	$4 \times 3 =$
$10 \times 4 =$	$2 \times 4 =$	$4 \times 6 =$
$4 \times 1 =$	$4 \times 5 =$	$4 \times 5 =$
$4 \times 2 =$	$4 \times 7 =$	$4 \times 8 =$
$4 \times 3 =$	$4 \times 9 =$	$7 \times 4 =$
$4 \times 4 =$	$4 \times 4 =$	$4 \times 2 =$
$4 \times 5 =$	$4 \times 6 =$	$4 \times 10 =$
$4 \times 6 =$	$4 \times 8 =$	$8 \times 4 =$
$4 \times 7 =$	$4 \times 10 =$	$4 \times 0 =$
$4 \times 8 =$	$4 \times 1 =$	$1 \times 4 =$
$4 \times 9 =$	$4 \times 0 =$	$4 \times 4 =$
$4 \times 10 =$	$4 \times 2 =$	$4 \times 9 =$

Speed trials

You should know all of the 1, 2, 3, 4, 5, and 10 times tables by now, but how quickly can you do them?
Ask someone to time you as you do this page.
Remember, you must be fast but also correct.

4 x 2 =	6 x 3 =	9 x 5 =
8 x 3 =	3 x 4 =	8 x 10 =
7 x 4 =	7 x 5 =	7 x 2 =
6 x 5 =	3 x 10 =	6 x 3 =
8 x 10 =	1 x 2 =	5 x 4 =
8 x 2 =	7 x 3 =	4 x 5 =
5 x 3 =	4 x 4 =	3 x 10 =
9 x 4 =	6 x 5 =	2 x 2 =
5 x 5 =	4 x 10 =	1 x 3 =
7 x 10 =	6 x 2 =	0 x 4 =
0 x 2 =	5 x 3 =	10 x 5 =
4 x 3 =	8 x 4 =	9 x 2 =
6 x 4 =	0 x 5 =	8 x 3 =
3 x 5 =	2 x 10 =	7 x 4 =
4 x 10 =	7 x 2 =	6 x 5 =
7 x 2 =	8 x 3 =	5 x 10 =
3 x 3 =	9 x 4 =	4 x 0 =
2 x 4 =	5 x 5 =	3 x 2 =
7 x 5 =	7 x 10 =	2 x 8 =
9 x 10 =	5 x 2 =	1 x 9 =

Some of the 6s

You should already know parts of the 6 times table because they are parts of the 1, 2, 3, 4, 5, and 10 times tables.

1 x 6 = 6   2 x 6 = 12   3 x 6 = 18
4 x 6 = 24   5 x 6 = 30   10 x 6 = 60

Find out if you can remember them quickly and correctly.

Cover the six times table with paper so you can't see the numbers.
Write the answers as quickly as you can.

What is three sixes?   What is ten sixes?

What is two sixes?   What is four sixes?

What is one six?   What is five sixes?

Write the answers as quickly as you can.

How many sixes make 12?   How many sixes make 6?

How many sixes make 30?   How many sixes make 18?

How many sixes make 24?   How many sixes make 60?

Write the answers as quickly as you can.

Multiply six by three.   Multiply six by ten.

Multiply six by two.   Multiply six by five.

Multiply six by one.   Multiply six by four.

Write the answers as quickly as you can.

4 x 6 =   2 x 6 =   10 x 6 =

5 x 6 =   1 x 6 =   3 x 6 =

Write the answers as quickly as you can.

A box contains six eggs. A man buys five boxes. How many eggs does he have?

A pack contains six sticks of gum.
How many sticks will there be in 10 packs?

The rest of the 6s

You need to learn these:

$6 \times 6 = 36$ $7 \times 6 = 42$ $8 \times 6 = 48$ $9 \times 6 = 54$

This work will help you remember the 6 times table.

Complete these sequences.

6   12   18   24   30

$5 \times 6 = 30$ so $6 \times 6 = 30$ plus another 6 =

18   24   30

$6 \times 6 = 36$ so $7 \times 6 = 36$ plus another 6 =

6   12   18   48   60

$7 \times 6 = 42$ so $8 \times 6 = 42$ plus another 6 =

6   18   24   30

$8 \times 6 = 48$ so $9 \times 6 = 48$ plus another 6 =

24   42   60

Test yourself on the rest of the 6 times table.
Cover the above part of the page with a sheet of paper.

What is six sixes?   What is seven sixes?

What is eight sixes?   What is nine sixes?

$8 \times 6 =$ $7 \times 6 =$ $6 \times 6 =$ $9 \times 6 =$

Practise the 6s

You should know all of the 6 times table now, but how quickly can you remember it?
Ask someone to time you as you do this page.
Remember, you must be fast but also correct.

1 x 6 =	2 x 6 =	7 x 6 =
2 x 6 =	4 x 6 =	3 x 6 =
3 x 6 =	6 x 6 =	9 x 6 =
4 x 6 =	8 x 6 =	6 x 4 =
5 x 6 =	10 x 6 =	1 x 6 =
6 x 6 =	1 x 6 =	6 x 2 =
7 x 6 =	3 x 6 =	6 x 8 =
8 x 6 =	5 x 6 =	0 x 6 =
9 x 6 =	7 x 6 =	6 x 3 =
10 x 6 =	9 x 6 =	5 x 6 =
6 x 1 =	6 x 3 =	6 x 7 =
6 x 2 =	6 x 5 =	2 x 6 =
6 x 3 =	6 x 7 =	6 x 9 =
6 x 4 =	6 x 9 =	4 x 6 =
6 x 5 =	6 x 2 =	8 x 6 =
6 x 6 =	6 x 4 =	10 x 6 =
6 x 7 =	6 x 6 =	6 x 5 =
6 x 8 =	6 x 8 =	6 x 0 =
6 x 9 =	6 x 10 =	6 x 1 =
6 x 10 =	6 x 0 =	6 x 6 =

Speed trials

You should know all of the 1, 2, 3, 4, 5, 6, and 10 times tables by now, but how quickly can you remember them?
Ask someone to time you as you do this page.
Remember, you must be fast but also correct.

4 x 6 =	6 x 3 =	9 x 6 =
5 x 3 =	8 x 6 =	8 x 6 =
7 x 3 =	6 x 6 =	7 x 3 =
6 x 5 =	3 x 10 =	6 x 6 =
6 x 10 =	6 x 2 =	5 x 4 =
8 x 2 =	7 x 3 =	4 x 6 =
5 x 3 =	4 x 6 =	3 x 6 =
9 x 6 =	6 x 5 =	2 x 6 =
5 x 5 =	6 x 10 =	6 x 3 =
7 x 6 =	6 x 2 =	0 x 6 =
0 x 2 =	5 x 3 =	10 x 5 =
6 x 3 =	8 x 4 =	6 x 2 =
6 x 6 =	0 x 6 =	8 x 3 =
3 x 5 =	5 x 10 =	7 x 6 =
4 x 10 =	7 x 6 =	6 x 5 =
7 x 10 =	8 x 3 =	5 x 10 =
3 x 6 =	9 x 6 =	6 x 0 =
2 x 4 =	5 x 5 =	3 x 10 =
6 x 9 =	7 x 10 =	2 x 8 =
9 x 10 =	5 x 6 =	1 x 8 =

41

Some of the 7s

You should already know parts of the 7 times table because they are parts of the 1, 2, 3, 4, 5, 6 and 10 times tables.

$1 \times 7 = 7$ $2 \times 7 = 14$ $3 \times 7 = 21$ $4 \times 7 = 28$
$5 \times 7 = 35$ $6 \times 7 = 42$ $10 \times 7 = 70$

Find out if you can remember them quickly and correctly.

Cover the seven times table with paper and write the answers to these questions as quickly as you can.

What is three sevens?   What is ten sevens?

What is two sevens?   What is four sevens?

What is six sevens?   What is five sevens?

Write the answers as quickly as you can.

How many sevens make 14?   How many sevens make 42?

How many sevens make 35?   How many sevens make 21?

How many sevens make 28?   How many sevens make 70?

Write the answers as quickly as you can.

Multiply seven by three.   Multiply seven by ten.

Multiply seven by two.   Multiply seven by five.

Multiply seven by six.   Multiply seven by four.

Write the answers as quickly as you can.

$4 \times 7 =$ $2 \times 7 =$ $10 \times 7 =$

$5 \times 7 =$ $1 \times 7 =$ $3 \times 7 =$

Write the answers as quickly as you can.

A bag has seven candies. Ann buys five bags. How many candies does she have?

How many days are there in six weeks?

The rest of the 7s

You should now know all of the 1, 2, 3, 4, 5, 6, and 10 times tables.

You need to learn only these parts of the seven times table.
7 x 7 = 49   8 x 7 = 56   9 x 7 = 63

This work will help you remember the 7 times table.

Complete these sequences.

7   14   21   28   35   42

6 x 7 = 42   so   7 x 7 = 42 plus another 7 =

21   28   35

7 x 7 = 49   so   8 x 7 = 49 plus another 7 =

7   14   21   56   70

8 x 7 = 56   so   9 x 7 = 56 plus another 7 =

7   21   28   35

Test yourself on the rest of the 7 times table.
Cover the section above with a sheet of paper.

What is seven sevens?   What is eight sevens?

What is nine sevens?   What is ten sevens?

8 x 7 =   7 x 7 =   9 x 7 =   10 x 7 =

How many days are there in eight weeks?

A package contains seven pens.
How many pens will there be in nine packets?

How many sevens make 56?

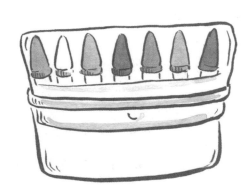

43

Practise the 7s

You should know all of the 7 times table now, but how quickly can you remember it?
Ask someone to time you as you do this page.
Remember, you must be fast but also correct.

1 x 7 =	2 x 7 =	7 x 6 =
2 x 7 =	4 x 7 =	3 x 7 =
3 x 7 =	6 x 7 =	9 x 7 =
4 x 7 =	8 x 7 =	7 x 4 =
5 x 7 =	10 x 7 =	1 x 7 =
6 x 7 =	1 x 7 =	7 x 2 =
7 x 7 =	3 x 7 =	7 x 8 =
8 x 7 =	5 x 7 =	0 x 7 =
9 x 7 =	7 x 7 =	7 x 3 =
10 x 7 =	9 x 7 =	5 x 7 =
7 x 1 =	7 x 3 =	7 x 7 =
7 x 2 =	7 x 5 =	2 x 7 =
7 x 3 =	7 x 7 =	7 x 9 =
7 x 4 =	7 x 9 =	4 x 7 =
7 x 5 =	7 x 2 =	8 x 7 =
7 x 6 =	7 x 4 =	10 x 7 =
7 x 7 =	7 x 6 =	7 x 5 =
7 x 8 =	7 x 8 =	7 x 0 =
7 x 9 =	7 x 10 =	7 x 1 =
7 x 10 =	7 x 0 =	6 x 7 =

Speed trials

You should know all of the 1, 2, 3, 4, 5, 6, 7, and 10 times tables by now, but how quickly can you remember them?
Ask someone to time you as you do this page.
Remember, you must be fast but also correct.

4 x 7 =	7 x 3 =	9 x 7 =
5 x 10 =	8 x 7 =	7 x 6 =
7 x 5 =	6 x 6 =	8 x 3 =
6 x 5 =	5 x 10 =	6 x 6 =
6 x 10 =	6 x 3 =	7 x 4 =
8 x 7 =	7 x 5 =	4 x 6 =
5 x 8 =	4 x 6 =	3 x 7 =
9 x 6 =	6 x 5 =	2 x 8 =
5 x 7 =	7 x 10 =	7 x 3 =
7 x 6 =	6 x 7 =	0 x 6 =
0 x 5 =	5 x 7 =	10 x 7 =
6 x 3 =	8 x 4 =	6 x 2 =
6 x 7 =	0 x 7 =	8 x 7 =
3 x 5 =	5 x 8 =	7 x 7 =
4 x 7 =	7 x 6 =	6 x 5 =
7 x 10 =	8 x 3 =	5 x 10 =
7 x 8 =	9 x 6 =	7 x 0 =
2 x 7 =	7 x 7 =	3 x 10 =
4 x 9 =	9 x 10 =	2 x 7 =
9 x 10 =	5 x 6 =	7 x 8 =

Some of the 8s

You should already know some of the 8 times table because it is part of the 1, 2, 3, 4, 5, 6, 7, and 10 times tables.

1 x 8 = 8	2 x 8 = 16	3 x 8 = 24	4 x 8 = 32
5 x 8 = 40	6 x 8 = 48	7 x 8 = 56	10 x 8 = 80

Find out if you can remember them quickly and correctly.

Cover the 8 times table with paper so you can't see the numbers.
Write the answers as quickly as you can.

What is three eights?   What is ten eights?

What is two eights?   What is four eights?

What is six eights?   What is five eights?

Write the answers as quickly as you can.

How many eights equal 16?   How many eights equal 40?

How many eights equal 32?   How many eights equal 24?

How many eights equal 56?   How many eights equal 48?

Write the answers as quickly as you can.

Multiply eight by three.   Multiply eight by ten.

Multiply eight by two.   Multiply eight by five.

Multiply eight by six.   Multiply eight by four.

Write the answers as quickly as you can.

6 x 8 =   2 x 8 =   10 x 8 =

5 x 8 =   7 x 8 =   3 x 8 =

Write the answers as quickly as you can.
A pizza has eight slices. John buys six pizzas.

How many slices does he have?

Which number multiplied by 8 gives the answer 56?

The rest of the 8s

You need to learn only these parts of the eight times table.
8 x 8 = 64   9 x 8 = 72

This work will help you remember the 8 times table.

Complete these sequences.

| 8 | 16 | 24 | 32 | 40 | 48 |

7 x 8 = 56   so   8 x 8 = 56 plus another 8 =

| 24 | 32 | 40 |

8 x 8 = 64   so   9 x 8 = 64 plus another 8 =

| 8 | 16 | 24 | | | 64 | | 80 |

| 8 | | 24 | | 40 |

Test yourself on the rest of the 8 times table.
Cover the section above with a sheet of paper.

What is seven eights?   What is eight eights?

What is nine eights?   What is eight nines?

8 x 8 =   9 x 8 =   8 x 9 =   10 x 8 =

What number multiplied by 8 gives the answer 72?

A number multiplied by 8 gives the answer 80. What is the number?

David puts out building bricks in piles of 8.
How many bricks will there be in 10 piles?

What number multiplied by 5 gives the answer 40?

How many 8s make 72?

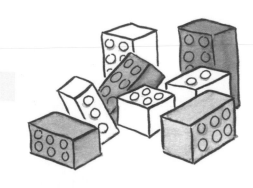

47

Practise the 8s

You should know all of the 8 times table now, but how quickly can you remember it?
Ask someone to time you as you do this page.
Be fast but also correct.

1 x 8 =	2 x 8 =	8 x 6 =
2 x 8 =	4 x 8 =	3 x 8 =
3 x 8 =	6 x 8 =	9 x 8 =
4 x 8 =	8 x 8 =	8 x 4 =
5 x 8 =	10 x 8 =	1 x 8 =
6 x 8 =	1 x 8 =	8 x 2 =
7 x 8 =	3 x 8 =	7 x 8 =
8 x 8 =	5 x 8 =	0 x 8 =
9 x 8 =	7 x 8 =	8 x 3 =
10 x 8 =	9 x 8 =	5 x 8 =
8 x 1 =	8 x 3 =	8 x 8 =
8 x 2 =	8 x 5 =	2 x 8 =
8 x 3 =	8 x 8 =	8 x 9 =
8 x 4 =	8 x 9 =	4 x 8 =
8 x 5 =	8 x 2 =	8 x 6 =
8 x 6 =	8 x 4 =	10 x 8 =
8 x 7 =	8 x 6 =	8 x 5 =
8 x 8 =	8 x 8 =	8 x 0 =
8 x 9 =	8 x 10 =	8 x 1 =
8 x 10 =	8 x 0 =	6 x 8 =

Speed trials

You should know all of the 1, 2, 3, 4, 5, 6, 7, 8, and 10 times tables now,
but how quickly can you remember them?
Ask someone to time you as you do this page.
Be fast but also correct.

4 x 8 =	7 x 8 =	9 x 8 =
5 x 10 =	8 x 7 =	7 x 6 =
7 x 8 =	6 x 8 =	8 x 3 =
8 x 5 =	8 x 10 =	8 x 8 =
6 x 10 =	6 x 3 =	7 x 4 =
8 x 7 =	7 x 7 =	4 x 8 =
5 x 8 =	5 x 6 =	3 x 7 =
9 x 8 =	6 x 7 =	2 x 8 =
8 x 8 =	7 x 10 =	7 x 3 =
7 x 6 =	6 x 9 =	0 x 8 =
7 x 5 =	5 x 8 =	10 x 8 =
6 x 8 =	8 x 4 =	6 x 2 =
6 x 7 =	0 x 8 =	8 x 6 =
5 x 7 =	5 x 9 =	7 x 8 =
8 x 4 =	7 x 6 =	6 x 5 =
7 x 10 =	8 x 3 =	8 x 10 =
2 x 8 =	9 x 6 =	8 x 7 =
4 x 7 =	8 x 6 =	5 x 10 =
6 x 9 =	9 x 10 =	8 x 2 =
9 x 10 =	6 x 6 =	8 x 9 =

Some of the 9s

You should already know nearly all of the 9 times table because it is part of the 1, 2, 3, 4, 5, 6, 7, 8, and 10 times tables.

$1 \times 9 = 9$	$2 \times 9 = 18$	$3 \times 9 = 27$	$4 \times 9 = 36$	$5 \times 9 = 45$
$6 \times 9 = 54$	$7 \times 9 = 63$	$8 \times 9 = 72$	$10 \times 9 = 90$	

Find out if you can remember them quickly and correctly.

Cover the nine times table so you can't see the numbers.
Write the answers as quickly as you can.

What is three nines?   What is ten nines?

What is two nines?   What is four nines?

What is six nines?   What is five nines?

What is seven nines?   What is eight nines?

Write the answers as quickly as you can.
How many nines equal 18?   How many nines equal 54?

How many nines equal 90?   How many nines equal 27?

How many nines equal 72?   How many nines equal 36?

How many nines equal 45?   How many nines equal 63?

Write the answers as quickly as you can.
Multiply nine by seven.   Multiply nine by ten.

Multiply nine by two.   Multiply nine by five.

Multiply nine by six.   Multiply nine by four.

Multiply nine by three.   Multiply nine by eight.

Write the answers as quickly as you can.

$6 \times 9 =$ $2 \times 9 =$ $10 \times 9 =$

$5 \times 9 =$ $3 \times 9 =$ $8 \times 9 =$

$0 \times 9 =$ $7 \times 9 =$ $4 \times 9 =$

The rest of the 9s

You need to learn only this part of the nine times table.

9 x 9 = 81

This work will help you remember the 9 times table.

Complete these sequences.

9   18   27   36   45   54

8 x 9 = 72   so   9 x 9 = 72 plus another 9 =

27   36   45

9   18   27   72   90

9   27   45

Look for a pattern in the nine times table.

1	x	9	=	09
2	x	9	=	18
3	x	9	=	27
4	x	9	=	36
5	x	9	=	45
6	x	9	=	54
7	x	9	=	63
8	x	9	=	72
9	x	9	=	81
10	x	9	=	90

Write down any patterns you can see. (There is more than one.)

Practise the 9s

You should know all of the 9 times table now, but how quickly can you remember it?
Ask someone to time you as you do this page.
Be fast and correct.

1 x 9 =	2 x 9 =	9 x 6 =
2 x 9 =	4 x 9 =	3 x 9 =
3 x 9 =	6 x 9 =	9 x 9 =
4 x 9 =	9 x 7 =	9 x 4 =
5 x 9 =	10 x 9 =	1 x 9 =
6 x 9 =	1 x 9 =	9 x 2 =
7 x 9 =	3 x 9 =	7 x 9 =
8 x 9 =	5 x 9 =	0 x 9 =
9 x 9 =	7 x 9 =	9 x 3 =
10 x 9 =	9 x 9 =	5 x 9 =
9 x 1 =	9 x 3 =	9 x 9 =
9 x 2 =	9 x 5 =	2 x 9 =
9 x 3 =	0 x 9 =	8 x 9 =
9 x 4 =	9 x 1 =	4 x 9 =
9 x 5 =	9 x 2 =	9 x 7 =
9 x 6 =	9 x 4 =	10 x 9 =
9 x 7 =	9 x 6 =	9 x 5 =
9 x 8 =	9 x 8 =	9 x 0 =
9 x 9 =	9 x 10 =	9 x 1 =
9 x 10 =	9 x 0 =	6 x 9 =

Speed trials

You should know all of the times tables by now, but how quickly can you remember them?
Ask someone to time you as you do this page.
Be fast and correct.

6 x 8 =	4 x 8 =	8 x 10 =
9 x 10 =	9 x 8 =	7 x 9 =
5 x 8 =	6 x 6 =	8 x 5 =
7 x 5 =	8 x 9 =	8 x 7 =
6 x 4 =	6 x 4 =	7 x 4 =
8 x 8 =	7 x 3 =	4 x 9 =
5 x 10 =	5 x 9 =	6 x 7 =
9 x 8 =	6 x 8 =	4 x 6 =
8 x 3 =	7 x 7 =	7 x 8 =
7 x 7 =	6 x 9 =	6 x 9 =
9 x 5 =	7 x 8 =	10 x 8 =
4 x 8 =	8 x 4 =	6 x 5 =
6 x 7 =	0 x 9 =	8 x 8 =
2 x 9 =	10 x 10 =	7 x 6 =
8 x 4 =	7 x 6 =	6 x 8 =
7 x 10 =	8 x 7 =	9 x 10 =
2 x 8 =	9 x 6 =	8 x 4 =
4 x 7 =	8 x 6 =	7 x 10 =
6 x 9 =	9 x 9 =	5 x 8 =
9 x 9 =	6 x 7 =	8 x 9 =

Times tables for division

Knowing the times tables can also help with division problems. Look at these examples.

3 x 6 = 18 which means that 18 ÷ 3 = 6 and that 18 ÷ 6 = 3
4 x 5 = 20 which means that 20 ÷ 4 = 5 and that 20 ÷ 5 = 4
9 x 3 = 27 which means that 27 ÷ 3 = 9 and that 27 ÷ 9 = 3

Use your knowledge of the times tables to work these division problems.

3 x 8 = 24 which means that 24 ÷ 3 =   and that 24 ÷ 8 =

4 x 7 = 28 which means that 28 ÷ 4 =   and that 28 ÷ 7 =

3 x 5 = 15 which means that 15 ÷ 3 =   and that 15 ÷ 5 =

4 x 3 = 12 which means that 12 ÷ 3 =   and that 12 ÷ 4=

3 x 10 = 30 which means that 30 ÷ 3 =   and that 30 ÷ 10 =

4 x 8 = 32 which means that 32 ÷ 4 =   and that 32 ÷ 8 =

3 x 9 = 27 which means that 27 ÷ 3 =   and that 27 ÷ 9 =

4 x 10 = 40 which means that 40 ÷ 4 =   and that 40 ÷ 10 =

These division problems help practise the 3 and 4 times tables.

20 ÷ 4 =	15 ÷ 3 =	16 ÷ 4 =
24 ÷ 4 =	27 ÷ 3 =	30 ÷ 3 =
12 ÷ 3 =	18 ÷ 3 =	28 ÷ 4 =
24 ÷ 3 =	32 ÷ 4 =	21 ÷ 3 =

How many fours in 36?   Divide 27 by three.

Divide 28 by 4.   How many threes in 21?

How many fives in 35?   Divide 40 by 5.

Divide 15 by 3.   How many eights in 48?

Times tables for division

This page will help you remember times tables by dividing by 2, 3, 4, 5, and 10.

20 ÷ 5 = 4   18 ÷ 3 = 6   60 ÷ 10 = 6

Complete the problems.

40 ÷ 10 =   14 ÷ 2 =   32 ÷ 4 =

25 ÷ 5 =   21 ÷ 3 =   16 ÷ 4 =

24 ÷ 4 =   28 ÷ 4 =   12 ÷ 2 =

45 ÷ 5 =   35 ÷ 5 =   12 ÷ 3 =

10 ÷ 2 =   40 ÷ 10 =   12 ÷ 4 =

20 ÷ 10 =   20 ÷ 2 =   20 ÷ 2 =

6 ÷ 2 =   18 ÷ 3 =   20 ÷ 4 =

24 ÷ 3 =   32 ÷ 4 =   20 ÷ 5 =

30 ÷ 5 =   40 ÷ 5 =   20 ÷ 10 =

30 ÷ 10 =   80 ÷ 10 =   18 ÷ 2 =

40 ÷ 5 =   6 ÷ 2 =   18 ÷ 3 =

21 ÷ 3 =   15 ÷ 3 =   15 ÷ 3 =

14 ÷ 2 =   24 ÷ 4 =   15 ÷ 5 =

27 ÷ 3 =   15 ÷ 5 =   24 ÷ 3 =

90 ÷ 10 =   10 ÷ 10 =   24 ÷ 4 =

15 ÷ 5 =   4 ÷ 2 =   50 ÷ 5 =

15 ÷ 3 =   9 ÷ 3 =   50 ÷ 10 =

20 ÷ 5 =   4 ÷ 4 =   30 ÷ 3 =

20 ÷ 4 =   10 ÷ 5 =   30 ÷ 5 =

16 ÷ 2 =   100 ÷ 10 =   30 ÷ 10 =

Times tables for division

Complete the problems.

$18 \div 6 =$	$27 \div 3 =$	$48 \div 6 =$
$30 \div 10 =$	$18 \div 6 =$	$35 \div 5 =$
$14 \div 2 =$	$20 \div 2 =$	$36 \div 4 =$
$18 \div 3 =$	$24 \div 6 =$	$24 \div 3 =$
$20 \div 4 =$	$24 \div 3 =$	$20 \div 2 =$
$15 \div 5 =$	$24 \div 4 =$	$30 \div 6 =$
$36 \div 6 =$	$30 \div 10 =$	$25 \div 5 =$
$50 \div 10 =$	$18 \div 2 =$	$32 \div 4 =$
$8 \div 2 =$	$18 \div 3 =$	$27 \div 3 =$
$15 \div 3 =$	$36 \div 4 =$	$16 \div 2 =$
$16 \div 4 =$	$36 \div 6 =$	$42 \div 6 =$
$25 \div 5 =$	$40 \div 5 =$	$5 \div 5 =$
$6 \div 6 =$	$100 \div 10 =$	$4 \div 4 =$
$10 \div 10 =$	$16 \div 4 =$	$28 \div 4 =$
$42 \div 6 =$	$42 \div 6 =$	$14 \div 2 =$
$24 \div 4 =$	$48 \div 6 =$	$24 \div 6 =$
$54 \div 6 =$	$54 \div 6 =$	$18 \div 6 =$
$90 \div 10 =$	$60 \div 6 =$	$54 \div 6 =$
$30 \div 6 =$	$60 \div 10 =$	$60 \div 6 =$
$30 \div 5 =$	$30 \div 6 =$	$40 \div 5 =$

Times tables for division

This page will help you remember times tables by dividing by 2, 3, 4, 5, 6, and 7.

14 ÷ 7 =   2   28 ÷ 7 =   4   70 ÷ 7 =   10

Complete the problems.

21 ÷ 7 =   18 ÷ 6 =   49 ÷ 7 =

35 ÷ 5 =   28 ÷ 7 =   35 ÷ 5 =

14 ÷ 2 =   24 ÷ 6 =   35 ÷ 7 =

18 ÷ 6 =   24 ÷ 4 =   24 ÷ 6 =

20 ÷ 5 =   24 ÷ 2 =   21 ÷ 3 =

15 ÷ 3 =   21 ÷ 7 =   70 ÷ 7 =

36 ÷ 4 =   42 ÷ 7 =   42 ÷ 7 =

56 ÷ 7 =   18 ÷ 3 =   32 ÷ 4 =

18 ÷ 2 =   49 ÷ 7 =   27 ÷ 3 =

15 ÷ 5 =   36 ÷ 4 =   16 ÷ 4 =

49 ÷ 7 =   36 ÷ 6 =   42 ÷ 6 =

25 ÷ 5 =   40 ÷ 5 =   45 ÷ 5 =

 7 ÷ 7 =   70 ÷ 7 =   40 ÷ 4 =

63 ÷ 7 =   24 ÷ 3 =   24 ÷ 3 =

42 ÷ 7 =   42 ÷ 6 =   14 ÷ 7 =

24 ÷ 6 =   48 ÷ 6 =   24 ÷ 4 =

54 ÷ 6 =   54 ÷ 6 =   18 ÷ 3 =

28 ÷ 7 =   60 ÷ 6 =   56 ÷ 7 =

30 ÷ 6 =   63 ÷ 7 =   63 ÷ 7 =

35 ÷ 7 =   25 ÷ 5 =   48 ÷ 6 =

Times tables for division

Complete the problems.

$42 \div 6 =$	$81 \div 9 =$	$56 \div 7 =$
$32 \div 8 =$	$56 \div 7 =$	$45 \div 5 =$
$14 \div 7 =$	$72 \div 9 =$	$35 \div 7 =$
$18 \div 9 =$	$24 \div 8 =$	$18 \div 9 =$
$63 \div 7 =$	$27 \div 9 =$	$21 \div 3 =$
$72 \div 9 =$	$72 \div 9 =$	$28 \div 7 =$
$72 \div 8 =$	$42 \div 6 =$	$64 \div 8 =$
$56 \div 7 =$	$27 \div 3 =$	$32 \div 8 =$
$18 \div 6 =$	$14 \div 7 =$	$27 \div 9 =$
$81 \div 9 =$	$36 \div 4 =$	$16 \div 8 =$
$63 \div 9 =$	$36 \div 6 =$	$42 \div 6 =$
$45 \div 5 =$	$48 \div 8 =$	$45 \div 9 =$
$54 \div 9 =$	$21 \div 7 =$	$40 \div 4 =$
$70 \div 7 =$	$24 \div 3 =$	$24 \div 8 =$
$42 \div 7 =$	$40 \div 8 =$	$63 \div 7 =$
$30 \div 5 =$	$45 \div 9 =$	$24 \div 6 =$
$54 \div 6 =$	$54 \div 6 =$	$18 \div 6 =$
$56 \div 8 =$	$42 \div 7 =$	$56 \div 8 =$
$30 \div 5 =$	$63 \div 9 =$	$63 \div 9 =$
$35 \div 7 =$	$50 \div 5 =$	$48 \div 8 =$

Times tables practice grids

This is a times tables grid.

X	3	4	5
7	21	28	35
8	24	32	40

Complete each times tables grid.

X	1	3	5	7	9
2					
3					

X	4	6
6		
7		
8		

X	6	7	8	9	10
3					
4					
5					

X	10	7	8	4
3				
5				
7				

X	6	2	4	7
5				
10				

X	8	7	9	6
9				
7				

Times tables practice grids

Here are more times tables grids.

X	2	4	6
5			
7			

X	8	3	9	2
5				
6				
7				

X	2	3	4	5
8				
9				

X	10	9	8	7
6				
5				
4				

X	3	8
2		
3		
4		
5		
6		
7		

X	2	4	6	8
1				
3				
5				
7				
9				
0				

60

Times tables practice grids

Here are some other times tables grids.

X	8	9
7		
8		

X	9	8	7	6	5	4
9						
8						
7						

X	2	5	9
4			
7			
8			

X	2	3	4	5	7
4					
6					
8					

X	3	5	7
2			
8			
6			
0			
4			
7			

X	8	7	9	6
7				
9				
0				
10				
8				
6				

Speed trials

Try this final test.

27 ÷ 3 =

7 x 9 =

64 ÷ 8 =

90 ÷ 10 =

6 x 8 =

45 ÷ 9 =

3 x 7 =

9 x 5 =

48 ÷ 6 =

7 x 7 =

3 x 9 =

56 ÷ 8 =

36 ÷ 4 =

24 ÷ 3 =

36 ÷ 9 =

6 x 7 =

4 x 4 =

32 ÷ 8 =

49 ÷ 7 =

25 ÷ 5 =

56 ÷ 7 =

4 x 9 =

18 ÷ 2 =

6 x 8 =

21 ÷ 3 =

9 x 7 =

36 ÷ 4 =

4 x 6 =

45 ÷ 5 =

8 x 5 =

42 ÷ 6 =

7 x 4 =

35 ÷ 7 =

9 x 3 =

24 ÷ 8 =

8 x 2 =

36 ÷ 9 =

6 x 10 =

80 ÷ 10 =

6 x 9 =

16 ÷ 2 =

54 ÷ 9 =

14 ÷ 2 =

9 x 9 =

15 ÷ 3 =

8 x 8 =

24 ÷ 4 =

7 x 8 =

30 ÷ 5 =

6 x 6 =

42 ÷ 6 =

9 x 5 =

49 ÷ 7 =

8 x 6 =

72 ÷ 8 =

9 x 7 =

54 ÷ 9 =

7 x 6 =

10 ÷ 10 =

7 x 7 =

16 ÷ 8 =

7 x 9 =

63 ÷ 7 =

Addition, multiplication, and division

Write the missing number in the box.

4 + [ ] = 4   12 x [ ] = 12   [ ] x 9 = 9   6 + [ ] = 6

3 + [ ] = 15   17 + [ ] = 25   [ ] + 8 = 19   [ ] + 17 = 26

4 + [ ] = 9   12 + [ ] = 17   35 ÷ [ ] = 5   25 + [ ] = 40

[ ] + 60 = 75   14 + [ ] = 20   [ ] + 32 = 53   [ ] + 9 = 58

5 x [ ] = 30   12 ÷ [ ] = 3   50 ÷ [ ] = 5   8 x [ ] = 48

[ ] x 6 = 54   100 ÷ [ ] = 5   63 x [ ] = 630   [ ] ÷ 9 = 4

Rewrite each equation, and fill in the missing number.

3 x (6 x 4) = (3 x ?) x 4   (7 x 9) x 3 = 7 x (? x 3)

(2 x 5) x 9 = ? x (5 x 9)   8 x (8 x 7) = (8 x 8) x ?

5 x (10 + 3) = (5 x 10) + (? x 3)   (8 + 6) x 7 = (8 x 7) + (6 x ?)

(3 + 7) x 2 = (? x 2) + (7 x 2)   9 x (5 + 12) = (? x 5) + (? x 12)

Place value to 10 000

How many hundreds are there in 7000?	*70*	hundreds (70 × 100 = 7000)
What is the value of the 9 in 694?	*90*	(because the 9 is in the tens column)

Write how many tens there are in:

400	tens	600	tens	900	tens
200	tens	1300	tens	4700	tens
4800	tens	1240	tens	1320	tens
2630	tens	5920	tens	4350	tens

What is the value of the 7 in these numbers?

76	720	137
7122	7430	724

What is the value of the 3 in these numbers?

3241	2731	4623
4320	3999	4372

Write how many hundreds there are in:

6400	hundreds	8500	hundreds
1900	hundreds	6200	hundreds
4600	hundreds	2400	hundreds

What is the value of the 8 in these numbers?

2148	9814	6384
8703	1189	5428

Multiplying and dividing by 10

Write the answer in the box.

37 x 10 = 370   58 ÷ 10 = 5.8

Write the product in the box.

94 x 10 =   13 x 10 =   37 x 10 =

36 x 10 =   47 x 10 =   54 x 10 =

236 x 10 =   419 x 10 =   262 x 10 =

531 x 10 =   674 x 10 =   801 x 10 =

Write the quotient in the box.

92 ÷ 10 =   48 ÷ 10 =   37 ÷ 10 =

18 ÷ 10 =   29 ÷ 10 =   54 ÷ 10 =

345 ÷ 10 =   354 ÷ 10 =   723 ÷ 10 =

531 ÷ 10 =   262 ÷ 10 =   419 ÷ 10 =

Find the missing factor.

x 10 = 230   x 10 = 750   x 10 = 990

x 10 = 480   x 10 = 130   x 10 = 250

x 10 = 520   x 10 = 390   x 10 = 270

x 10 = 620   x 10 = 860   x 10 = 170

Find the dividend.

÷ 10 = 4.7   ÷ 10 = 6.8   ÷ 10 = 12.4

÷ 10 = 25.7   ÷ 10 = 36.2   ÷ 10 = 31.4

÷ 10 = 40.8   ÷ 10 = 67.2   ÷ 10 = 80.9

÷ 10 = 92.4   ÷ 10 = 32.7   ÷ 10 = 56.3

Ordering sets of measures

Write these measures in order, from least to greatest.

| 3100 km | 24 km | 1821 km | 247 km | 4 km | 960 km |

| 4 km | 24 km | 247 km | 960 km | 1821 km | 3100 km |

Write these measures in order, from least to greatest.

| $526 | $15 940 | $1504 | $826 | $37 532 |

| 720 km | 7200 km | 27 410 km | 15 km | 247 km |

| 70 000 litres | 650 litres | 26 000 litres | 6500 litres | 7000 litres |

| 656 kg | 9565 kg | 22 942 kg | 752 247 kg | 1327 kg |

| 9520 yrs | 320 yrs | 4681 yrs | 8940 yrs | 20 316 yrs |

| 217 846 kg | 75 126 kg | 8940 kg | 14 632 kg | 175 kg |

| 9420 km | 764 km | 25 811 km | 114 243 km | 7240 km |

| $37 227 | $1 365 240 | $143 820 | $950 | $4212 |

| 24 091 m | 59 473 m | 1237 m | 426 m | 837 201 m |

| 47 632 g | 847 g | 9625 g | 103 427 g | 2330 g |

| 7340 m | 249 m | 12 746 m | 32 m | 17 407 321 m |

Appropriate units of measure

Choose the best units to measure the length of each item.

millimetres	centimetres	metres
desk	tooth	swimming pool
centimetres	millimetres	metres

Choose the best units to measure the length of each item.

centimetres	metres	kilometres

bed   bicycle   toothbrush   football field

shoe   driveway   sailboat   highway

The height of a door is about 2 _____ .

The length of a pencil is about 17 _____ .

The height of a flagpole is about 7 _____ .

Choose the best units to measure the mass of each item.

grams	kilograms	tonnes

train   kitten   watermelon   tennis ball

shoe   bag of potatoes   elephant   washing machine

The mass of a hamburger is about 26 _____ .

The mass of a bag of apples is about 1 _____ .

The mass of a truck is about 4 _____ .

Identifying patterns

Continue each pattern.

Intervals of 6:	1	7	13	19	25	31	37
Intervals of 3:	27	24	21	18	15	12	9

Continue each pattern.

0	10	20				
15	20	25				
5	7	9				
2	9	16				
4	7	10			19	
2	10	18		34		

Continue each pattern.

44	38	32				
33	29	25				
27	23	19				
56	48	40			16	
49	42	35				
28	25	22				10

Continue each pattern.

36	30	24		12		
5	14	23				
3	8	13				
47	40	33			12	
1	4	7				

Recognizing multiples

Circle the multiples of 10.

14   (20)   25   (30)   47   (60)

Circle the multiples of 6.

| 20 | 48 | 56 | 72 | 25 | 35 |
| 1 | 3 | 6 | 16 | 26 | 36 |

Circle the multiples of 7.

| 14 | 24 | 35 | 27 | 47 | 49 |
| 63 | 42 | 52 | 37 | 64 | 71 |

Circle the multiples of 8.

| 25 | 31 | 48 | 84 | 32 | 8 |
| 18 | 54 | 64 | 35 | 72 | 28 |

Circle the multiples of 9.

17	81	27	35	92	106
45	53	108	90	33	95
64	9	28	18	36	98

Circle the multiples of 10.

| 15 | 35 | 20 | 46 | 90 | 100 |
| 44 | 37 | 30 | 29 | 50 | 45 |

Circle the multiples of 5.

25	110	125	54	35	48
45	33	87	98	99	120
43	44	65	55	21	20

Circle the multiples of 4.

18	12	45	66	30	72
24	36	58	68	48	60
35	29	82	74	84	94

Using information in tables

Use the table to answer the questions.

Students' favourite sports

Sport	Number of votes
Basketball	4
Soccer	10
Softball	5
Swimming	6

How many students voted for softball? 5

What is the most popular sport? *soccer*

Use the table to answer the questions.

Pieces made by pottery club

Name	Cups	Bowls	Plates
Carl	5	9	11
Marta	7	2	9
Assam	3	1	12
Colin	8	8	10
Renee	6	9	2

How many plates did Colin make?

Who made 7 cups?

Who made the same
number of bowls as Renee?

Complete the table, and answer the questions.

Olympic medals 1998

Country	Gold	Silver	Bronze	Total
Austria	3	5	9	17
Canada	6	5	4	
Germany	12	9	8	
Norway	10	10	5	
Russia	9	6	3	
United States	6	3	4	

How many more gold medals
did Russia win than bronze medals?

Which country won
the most silver medals?

Which country won
three times as many
bronze medals as gold medals?

Coordinate graphs

Write the coordinates for each point.
Remember to write the coordinate for
the x-axis first.

A   (2, 4)

B   (3, 2)

C   (5, 3)

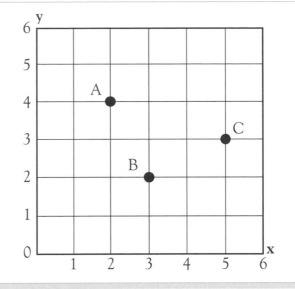

Write the coordinates for each symbol.

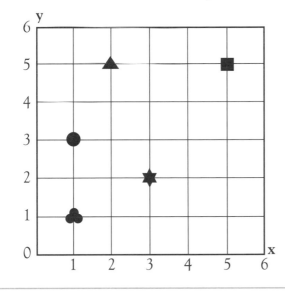

Place each of the points on the graph.

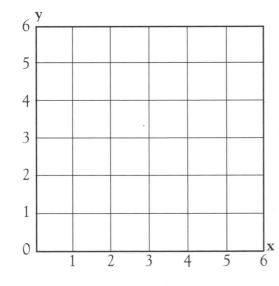

A   (2, 3)

B   (5, 4)

C   (2, 4)

D   (5, 3)

E   (4, 4)

Fraction models

Write the missing numbers to show what part is shaded.

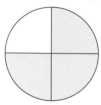

$\dfrac{3 \text{ shaded parts}}{4 \text{ parts}} = \dfrac{3}{4}$

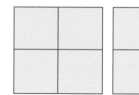

$\dfrac{4}{4} = 1$ and $\dfrac{2}{4} = \dfrac{1}{2}$

So, shaded part $= 1\dfrac{1}{2}$

Write the missing numbers to show what part is shaded.

$\dfrac{}{9}$ $\dfrac{1}{}$ $\dfrac{}{}$ $\dfrac{}{}$

Write the fraction for the part that is shaded.

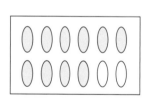

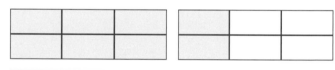

$\dfrac{}{}$ or $\dfrac{}{}$ $\dfrac{}{}$ or $\dfrac{}{}$ $\dfrac{}{}$ or $\dfrac{}{}$

Write the fraction for the part that is shaded.

$\dfrac{}{}$ or $\dfrac{}{}$ $\dfrac{}{}$ or $\dfrac{}{}$ $\dfrac{}{}$

Converting fractions and decimals

Write these fractions as decimals.   Write these fractions as decimals.

$\frac{7}{10}$ = 0.7   0.2 = $\frac{2}{10}$ = $\frac{1}{5}$

$\frac{3}{100}$ = 0.03   0.47 = $\frac{47}{100}$

Write these fractions as decimals.

$\frac{3}{10}$ = $\frac{7}{10}$ = $\frac{9}{10}$ =

$\frac{2}{10}$ = $\frac{1}{10}$ = $\frac{6}{10}$ =

$\frac{1}{2}$ =   = $\frac{8}{10}$ = $\frac{4}{10}$ =

Write these decimals as fractions.

0.1 = $\frac{1}{\quad}$ 0.2 = $\frac{2}{\quad}$ = $\frac{1}{\quad}$ 0.3 = $\frac{3}{\quad}$

0.4 = $\frac{4}{\quad}$ = $\frac{2}{\quad}$ 0.5 = $\frac{5}{\quad}$ = $\frac{1}{\quad}$ 0.6 = $\frac{6}{\quad}$ = $\frac{3}{\quad}$

0.7 = $\frac{7}{\quad}$ 0.8 = $\frac{8}{\quad}$ = $\frac{4}{\quad}$ 0.9 = $\frac{9}{\quad}$

Change these fractions to decimals.

$\frac{1}{100}$ = $\frac{3}{100}$ = $\frac{7}{100}$ =

$\frac{15}{100}$ = $\frac{25}{100}$ = $\frac{49}{100}$ =

$\frac{24}{100}$ = $\frac{56}{100}$ = $\frac{72}{100}$ =

Change these decimals to fractions.

0.39 =   0.47 =   0.21 =

0.83 =   0.91 =   0.73 =

0.51 =   0.43 =   0.17 =

Factors of numbers from 31 to 65

The factors of 40 are   1   2   4   5   8   10   20   40

Circle the factors of 56.

(1)   (2)   3   (4)   5   6   (7)   (8)   (14)   (28)   32   (56)

Find all the factors of each number.

The factors of 31 are

The factors of 47 are

The factors of 60 are

The factors of 50 are

The factors of 42 are

The factors of 32 are

The factors of 48 are

The factors of 35 are

The factors of 52 are

Circle all the factors of each number.

Which numbers are factors of 39?

  1   2   3   4   5   8   9   10   13   14   15   20   25   39

Which numbers are factors of 45?

  1   3   4   5   8   9   12   15   16   21   24   36   40   44   45

Which numbers are factors of 61?

  1   3   4   5   6   10   15   16   18   20   26   31   40   61

Which numbers are factors of 65?

  1   2   4   5   6   8   9   10   12   13   14   15   30   60   65

Some numbers have only factors of 1 and themselves. They are called prime numbers. Write all the prime numbers between 31 and 65 in the box.

Writing equivalent fractions

Make these fractions equal by writing a number in the box.

$$\frac{10}{100} = \frac{\square}{10} \qquad \frac{8}{100} = \frac{\square}{25} \qquad \frac{4}{100} = \frac{\square}{25}$$

$$\frac{2}{20} = \frac{\square}{10} \qquad \frac{5}{100} = \frac{\square}{20} \qquad \frac{6}{20} = \frac{\square}{10}$$

$$\frac{3}{5} = \frac{\square}{20} \qquad \frac{5}{6} = \frac{\square}{12} \qquad \frac{2}{8} = \frac{\square}{24}$$

$$\frac{2}{3} = \frac{\square}{24} \qquad \frac{2}{18} = \frac{\square}{9} \qquad \frac{4}{50} = \frac{\square}{25}$$

$$\frac{11}{12} = \frac{\square}{36} \qquad \frac{12}{15} = \frac{\square}{5} \qquad \frac{8}{20} = \frac{\square}{5}$$

$$\frac{2}{12} = \frac{1}{\square} \qquad \frac{5}{20} = \frac{1}{\square} \qquad \frac{5}{8} = \frac{10}{\square}$$

$$\frac{7}{8} = \frac{21}{\square} \qquad \frac{15}{100} = \frac{3}{\square} \qquad \frac{6}{24} = \frac{1}{\square}$$

$$\frac{5}{25} = \frac{1}{\square} \qquad \frac{8}{20} = \frac{2}{\square} \qquad \frac{15}{20} = \frac{3}{\square}$$

$$\frac{5}{30} = \frac{1}{\square} \qquad \frac{12}{14} = \frac{6}{\square} \qquad \frac{1}{5} = \frac{4}{\square}$$

$$\frac{9}{18} = \frac{1}{\square} \qquad \frac{24}{30} = \frac{4}{\square} \qquad \frac{25}{30} = \frac{5}{\square}$$

$$\frac{1}{8} = \frac{\square}{16} = \frac{3}{\square} = \frac{\square}{32} = \frac{\square}{40} = \frac{6}{\square}$$

$$\frac{20}{100} = \frac{\square}{25} = \frac{2}{\square} = \frac{1}{\square} = \frac{\square}{50} = \frac{\square}{200}$$

$$\frac{2}{5} = \frac{6}{\square} = \frac{\square}{20} = \frac{10}{\square} = \frac{\square}{50} = \frac{40}{\square}$$

$$\frac{1}{6} = \frac{\square}{12} = \frac{3}{\square} = \frac{4}{\square} = \frac{5}{\square} = \frac{6}{\square}$$

$$\frac{2}{3} = \frac{\square}{24} = \frac{\square}{36} = \frac{\square}{21} = \frac{6}{\square} = \frac{\square}{300}$$

Properties of polygons

Circle the polygon that has two pairs of parallel sides.

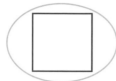 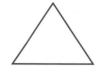 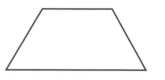

Read the description, and circle the polygon.

All the angles are right angles, but not all the sides are the same length.

Exactly three pairs of sides parallel.

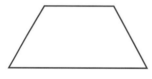 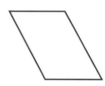

Exactly one pair of sides is parallel.

 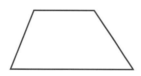 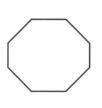

All the sides are the same length, and all the angles are right angles.

   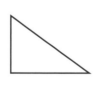

All the sides are the same length, and all the angles are the same.

 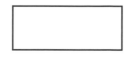 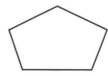 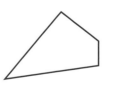

Naming polygons

Polygons are named for the number of sides they have.

triangle　　　quadrilateral　　　pentagon　　　hexagon　　　octagon

Quadrilaterals, which have four sides, can be different shapes.

rectangle　　　rhombus　　　square　　　parallelogram　　　trapezoid

Circle the quadrilaterals.

Write the name of each polygon in the box.

Adding decimals

Find each sum. Remember to regroup.

$$\begin{array}{r} 1 \\ \$7.49 \\ +\ \$1.36 \\ \hline \$8.85 \end{array}$$

$$\begin{array}{r} 1 \\ 4.18 \\ +\ 5.59 \\ \hline 9.77 \end{array}$$

Find each sum.

$$\begin{array}{r} \$5.22 \\ +\ \$3.49 \\ \hline \end{array}$$

$$\begin{array}{r} 4.34 \\ +\ 2.56 \\ \hline \end{array}$$

$$\begin{array}{r} \$8.21 \\ +\ \$4.49 \\ \hline \end{array}$$

$$\begin{array}{r} 3.28 \\ +\ 9.22 \\ \hline \end{array}$$

Find each sum.

$$\begin{array}{r} 2.77\ m \\ +\ 4.59\ m \\ \hline \end{array}$$

$$\begin{array}{r} 6.58\ km \\ +\ 3.54\ km \\ \hline \end{array}$$

$$\begin{array}{r} 7.37\ cm \\ +\ 2.76\ cm \\ \hline \end{array}$$

$$\begin{array}{r} 8.09\ m \\ +\ 4.96\ m \\ \hline \end{array}$$

Write each sum in the box.

$3.39 + \$5.52 =$

$\$6.37 + \$5.09 =$

$7.46 + \$9.53 =$

$\$8.22 + \$1.19 =$

$3.77\ km + 1.99\ km =$

$5.24\ m + 8.37\ m =$

Solve each problem.

Sandra has saved $3.99. Her mom gives her $1.62. How much does she now have?

Mrs. Jones's car is 4.53 m long. Mr. Jones's car is 5.24 m long. How long must their driveway be in order to fit both cars end to end?

Adding decimals

Find each sum. Remember to regroup.

```
  1
  $4.96          7.92 km
+ $2.83        + 1.68 km
─────          ─────────
  $7.79          9.60 km
```

Find each sum.

```
  8.94          $9.57          $7.96          5.73
+ 5.88        + $9.99        + $4.78        + 9.97
─────         ──────         ──────         ─────
```

```
  6.43 m         7.34 cm        8.62 km        3.04
+ 8.57 m       + 9.99 cm      + 8.08 km      + 5.76
───────        ─────────      ─────────      ─────
```

Write each sum in the box.

$5.03 + $6.49 =   2.74 + 9.61 =

$8.32 + $9.58 =   1.29 + 4.83 =

5.26 km + 9.19 km =   2.04 m + 9.97 m =

Solve each problem.

Anna buys a can of soda for 45¢ and a sandwich for $1.39. How much does she pay?

Mr. Bailey buys two wardrobes. One is 1.29 m wide and the other is 96 cm wide. How much space will they take up if he puts them side by side?

Subtracting decimals

Find each difference. Remember to regroup.

$$\begin{array}{r} 8.23 \\ -\ 4.78 \\ \hline 3.45 \end{array} \qquad \begin{array}{r} 2.64 \\ -\ 1.77 \\ \hline 0.87 \end{array}$$

Find each difference.

$$\begin{array}{r} 8.24 \\ -\ 5.36 \\ \hline \end{array} \qquad \begin{array}{r} \$6.27 \\ -\ \$3.48 \\ \hline \end{array} \qquad \begin{array}{r} 3.12 \\ -\ 1.23 \\ \hline \end{array} \qquad \begin{array}{r} \$9.47 \\ -\ \$4.79 \\ \hline \end{array}$$

Find each difference.

$$\begin{array}{r} 5.21 \\ -\ 2.99 \\ \hline \end{array} \qquad \begin{array}{r} 3.64 \text{ m} \\ -\ 1.99 \text{ m} \\ \hline \end{array} \qquad \begin{array}{r} 9.12 \text{ km} \\ -\ 3.99 \text{ km} \\ \hline \end{array} \qquad \begin{array}{r} 6.63 \text{ cm} \\ -\ 2.94 \text{ cm} \\ \hline \end{array}$$

Write each difference in the box.

$2.22 \quad - \quad \$1.63 \quad = \qquad\qquad 8.14 \quad - \quad 3.25 \quad =$

$9.76 \quad - \quad \$3.87 \quad = \qquad\qquad 5.71 \quad - \quad 1.92 \quad =$

$7.71 \quad - \quad 1.99 \quad = \qquad\qquad 3.55 \quad - \quad 1.89 \quad =$

Solve each problem.

Kofi's mother gave him $5.75 to spend at the store.
He came back with $1.87.
How much did he spend?

The end of Mrs. Brophy's hose was damaged.
The hose was 4 m 32 cm long, and she cut off 1 m 49 cm.
How much did she have left?

Subtracting decimals

Find each difference. Remember to regroup.

$$\begin{array}{r} \$8.31 \\ - \ \$2.94 \\ \hline \$5.37 \end{array} \qquad \begin{array}{r} 6.23 \text{ m} \\ - \ 2.84 \text{ m} \\ \hline 3.39 \text{ m} \end{array}$$

Find each difference.

$$\begin{array}{r} \$5.31 \\ - \ \$1.89 \\ \hline \end{array} \qquad \begin{array}{r} 8.24 \\ - \ 2.87 \\ \hline \end{array} \qquad \begin{array}{r} 7.23 \\ - \ 3.44 \\ \hline \end{array} \qquad \begin{array}{r} \$6.23 \\ - \ \$1.24 \\ \hline \end{array} \qquad \begin{array}{r} \$4.11 \\ - \ \$1.12 \\ \hline \end{array}$$

Find each difference.

$$\begin{array}{r} 8.14 \text{ m} \\ - \ 2.97 \text{ m} \\ \hline \end{array} \qquad \begin{array}{r} 6.33 \text{ km} \\ - \ 2.94 \text{ km} \\ \hline \end{array} \qquad \begin{array}{r} 9.11 \text{ cm} \\ - \ 1.32 \text{ cm} \\ \hline \end{array} \qquad \begin{array}{r} 6.23 \\ - \ 2.24 \\ \hline \end{array} \qquad \begin{array}{r} 7.48 \text{ m} \\ - \ 3.49 \text{ m} \\ \hline \end{array}$$

Write each difference in the box.

$7.14 \ - \ 3.17 \ =$ 　　　　$\$3.39 \ - \ \$1.47 \ =$

$8.51 \ - \ 6.59 \ =$ 　　　　$\$6.23 \ - \ \$5.34 \ =$

$8.14 \ - \ 3.46 \ =$ 　　　　$7.42 \text{ m} \ - \ 4.57 \text{ m} =$

Solve each problem.

Suzanne goes to the park with $5.13 to spend. She buys a hot dog for $2.49. How much does she have left?

Gita's garden is 7.43 m long. Josh's garden is 9.21 m long. How much longer is Josh's garden than Gita's?

Multiplying by one-digit numbers

Find each product. Remember to regroup.

```
  11                3                 34
 465              391               278
x   3           x   4             x   5
 1395            1564              1390
```

Find each product.

```
    563              910              437              812
x     3          x     2          x     3          x     2
_____          _____          _____          _____
```

```
    572              831              406              394
x     4          x     3          x     5          x     6
_____          _____          _____          _____
```

Find each product.

```
    318              223              542              217
x     3          x     4          x     4          x     3
_____          _____          _____          _____
```

```
    127              275              798              365
x     4          x     5          x     6          x     6
_____          _____          _____          _____
```

```
    100              372              881              953
x     5          x     4          x     4          x     3
_____          _____          _____          _____
```

Solve each problem.

A middle school has 255 students. A high school has 6 times as many students. How many children are there at the high school?

A train can carry 365 passengers. How many could it carry on

four trips?

six trips?

Multiplying by one-digit numbers

Find each product. Remember to regroup.

```
    33              12              44
   456             823             755
 x   6           x   8           x   9
  2736            6584            6795
```

Find each product.

```
   394             736             827             943
 x   7           x   7           x   8           x   9
```

```
   643             199             821             547
 x   6           x   6           x   7           x   8
```

```
   501             377             843             222
 x   7           x   8           x   8           x   9
```

```
   471             223             606             513
 x   9           x   8           x   6           x   7
```

```
   500             800             900             200
 x   9           x   9           x   8           x   9
```

Solve each problem.

A crate holds 550 apples. How many
apples are there in 8 crates?

Keyshawn swims 760 laps each week. How many
laps does he swim in 5 weeks?

Division with remainders

Find each quotient.

$$
\begin{array}{r}
180 \text{ r } 1 \\
2\overline{)3\,6\,1} \\
2 \\
\overline{1\,6} \\
1\,6 \\
\overline{1}
\end{array}
\qquad
\begin{array}{r}
141 \text{ r } 1 \\
3\overline{)4\,2\,4} \\
3 \\
\overline{1\,2} \\
1\,2 \\
\overline{4} \\
3 \\
\overline{1}
\end{array}
\qquad
\begin{array}{r}
58 \text{ r } 3 \\
4\overline{)2\,3\,5} \\
2\,0 \\
\overline{3\,5} \\
3\,2 \\
\overline{3}
\end{array}
$$

Find each quotient.

$2\overline{)4\,1\,3}$ $4\overline{)6\,4\,3}$ $3\overline{)5\,7\,2}$

$4\overline{)9\,5\,1}$ $2\overline{)3\,6\,5}$ $3\overline{)2\,0\,0}$

$4\overline{)7\,3\,7}$ $3\overline{)8\,5\,1}$ $4\overline{)2\,0\,3}$

Write the answer in the box.

What is 563 divided by 2?   Divide 293 by 5.

What is 374 divided by 3?   Divide 767 by 4.

Division with remainders

Find each quotient.

```
7)4 0 3          8)6 5 5          9)2 0 5
```

```
9)5 7 4          6)4 3 1          7)1 2 1
```

```
9)2 1 7          9)4 0 4          6)7 7 7
```

Write the answer in the box.

What is 759 divided by 7?   Divide 941 by 9.

What is 463 divided by 8?   Divide 232 by 6.

Real-life problems

Find the answer to each problem.

Jacob spent $4.68 at the store and had $4.77 left.
How much did he have to start with?

$9.45

$$\begin{array}{r} \overset{1\ \ 1}{4.77} \\ +\ 4.68 \\ \hline 9.45 \end{array}$$

Tracy receives a weekly allowance of $3.00 a week.
How much will she have if she saves all of it for 8 weeks?

$24.00

$$\begin{array}{r} 3.00 \\ \times\ \ \ \ 8 \\ \hline 24.00 \end{array}$$

Find the answer to each problem.

A theatre charges $4 for each matinee ticket. If it sells
360 tickets for a matinee performance, how much does
it take in?

David has saved $9.59. His sister
has $3.24 less. How much does
she have?

The cost for 9 children to go to a
theme park is $72. How much does
each child pay? If only 6 children
go, what will the cost be?

Paul has $3.69. His sister gives him
another $5.25, and he goes out and
buys a CD single for $3.99. How
much does he have left?

Ian has $20 in savings. He
decides to spend $\frac{1}{4}$ of it.
How much will he have left?

86

Real-life problems

Find the answer to each problem.

Nina has an hour to do her homework. She plans to spend $\frac{1}{3}$ of her time on math. How many minutes will she spend doing math?

20 minutes

1 hour is 60 minutes

$$3\overline{)60} \quad \begin{array}{c} 20 \end{array}$$

In gym class, David makes 2 long jumps of 1.78 m and 2.19 m. How far does he jump altogether?

3.97 m

$$\begin{array}{r} 1 \\ 1.78\,m \\ +\ 2.19\,m \\ \hline 3.97\,m \end{array}$$

Find the answer to each problem.

Moishe has a can of lemonade containing 400 ml. He drinks $\frac{1}{4}$ of it. How much is left?

David ran 40 m in 8 seconds. At that speed, how far did he run in 1 second?

A large jar of coffee contains 1.75 kg. If 1.48 kg is left in the jar, how much has been used?

A worker can fill 145 boxes of tea in 15 minutes. How many boxes can he fill in 1 hour?

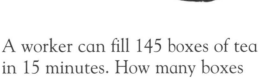

Jennifer's computer is 41.63 cm wide and her printer is 48.37 cm wide. How much space does she have for books if her desk is 1.5 m wide?

Perimeters of squares and rectangles

Find the perimeter of this rectangle.

To find the perimeter of a rectangle or a square, add the lengths of the four sides.

6 cm + 6 cm + 4 cm + 4 cm = 20 cm

You can also do this with multiplication.

(2 x 6) cm + (2 x 4) cm
= 12 cm + 8 cm = 20 cm

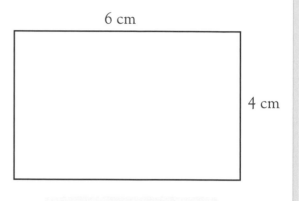

6 cm

4 cm

20 cm

Find the perimeters of these rectangles and squares.

4 cm

1 cm

cm

3 m

3 m

m

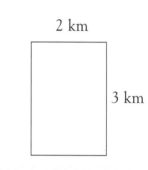

2 km

3 km

km

3 cm

2 cm

1 m

1 m

4 km

2 km

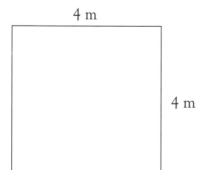

4 m

4 m

4 cm

3 cm

2 km

2 km

Problems involving time

Find the answer to each problem.

Caitlin spends 35 minutes on her homework each day. How many minutes does she spend on her homework in one week from Monday through Friday?

175 minutes

$$\begin{array}{r} \overset{2}{35} \\ \times \quad 5 \\ \hline 175 \end{array}$$

Jenny spends 175 minutes on her homework from Monday through Friday. How much time does she spend on homework each day?

35 minutes

$$5\overline{)175} \quad 35$$

Find the answer to each problem.

Amy works from 9 A.M. until 5 P.M. She has a lunch break from noon until 1 P.M. How many hours does she work in a 5-day week?

School children have a 15-minute break in the morning and a 10-minute break in the afternoon. How many minutes of break do they have in a week?

It takes 2 hours for one person to do a job. If John shares the work with 3 of his friends, how long will it take?

Mr. Tambo spent 7 days building a patio. If he worked a total of 56 hours and he divided the work evenly among the seven days, how long did he work each day?

It took Ben 45 hours to build a remote-controlled airplane. If he spent 5 hours a day working on it:

How many days did it take?

How many hours per day would he have needed to finish it in 5 days?

Using bar graphs

Use the graph to answer the questions.

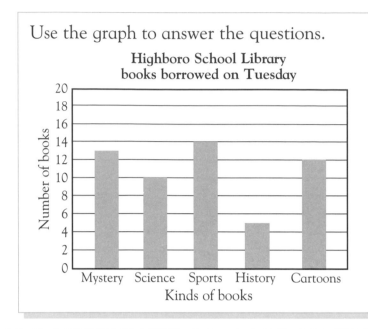

**Highboro School Library
books borrowed on Tuesday**

How many science books
were borrowed on Tuesday? 10

How many more sports books
were borrowed than history books?

14 − 5 = 9

Use the graphs to answer the questions.

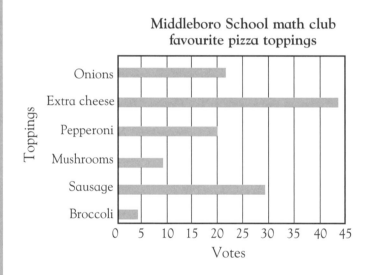

**Middleboro School math club
favourite pizza toppings**

Which topping is
the most popular?

Which topping got 8 votes?

About how many more votes did
sausage receive than pepperoni?

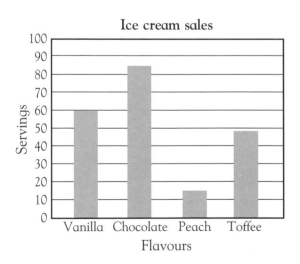

Ice cream sales

About how many servings
of toffee ice cream were sold?

About how many more servings of
chocolate were sold than vanilla?

Which flavour sold more than
40 servings but fewer than 50?

Congruency

Congruent triangles are triangles that are exactly the same shape and size. Triangles are congruent if the corresponding sides are the same and the three corresponding angles are the same.

Which triangles are congruent?

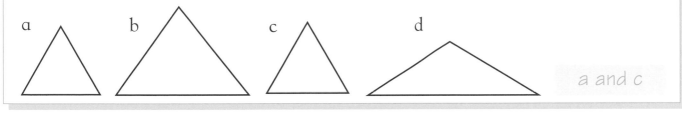

a   b   c   d

a and c

Which triangles are congruent?

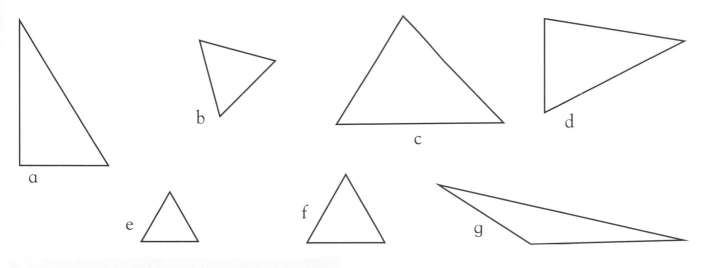

a   b   c   d   e   f   g

Which triangles are congruent?

a   b   c   d   e   f   g

Lines of symmetry

How many lines of
symmetry does this figure have?   6

Six lines can be drawn each of
which divide the figure exactly in half.

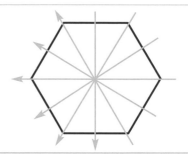

How many lines of symmetry do these figures have?

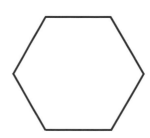
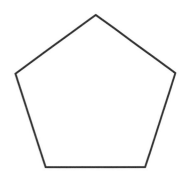

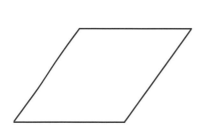
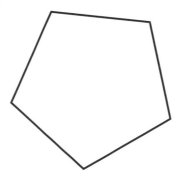
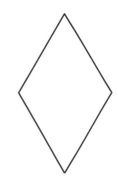

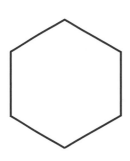
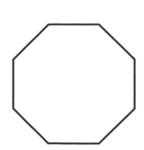
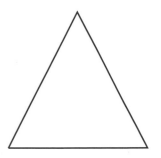

Writing equivalent number sentences

Write a multiplication sentence that goes with $24 \div 6 = 4$.

$6 \times 4 = 24$ or $4 \times 6 = 24$

Write a related subtraction sentence for $5 + 12 = 17$.

$17 - 5 = 12$ or $17 - 12 = 5$

Write a related subtraction sentence for each sentence.

$25 + 12 = 37$

$35 + 8 = 43$

$13 + 9 = 22$

Write a related addition sentence for each sentence.

$35 - 24 = 11$

$82 - 23 = 59$

$45 - 20 = 25$

Write a related multiplication sentence for each sentence.

$36 \div 4 = 9$

$32 \div 2 = 16$

$72 \div 9 = 8$

Write a related division sentence for each sentence.

$8 \times 6 = 48$

$7 \times 12 = 84$

$9 \times 5 = 45$

Multiplying and dividing

Write the product in the box.

33 x 10 =	21 x 10 =	42 x 10 =
94 x 100 =	36 x 100 =	81 x 100 =
416 x 10 =	204 x 10 =	513 x 10 =
767 x 100 =	821 x 100 =	245 x 100 =

Write the quotient in the box.

120 ÷ 10 =	260 ÷ 10 =	470 ÷ 10 =
300 ÷ 100 =	800 ÷ 100 =	400 ÷ 100 =
20 ÷ 10 =	30 ÷ 10 =	70 ÷ 10 =
500 ÷ 100 =	100 ÷ 100 =	900 ÷ 100 =

Write the number that has been multiplied by 100.

x 100 = 5900   x 100 = 71 400

x 100 = 72 100   x 100 = 23 400

x 100 = 1100   x 100 = 47 000

x 100 = 8400   x 100 = 44 100

Write the number that has been divided by 100.

÷ 100 = 2   ÷ 100 = 8

÷ 100 = 21   ÷ 100 = 18

÷ 100 = 86   ÷ 100 = 21

÷ 100 = 10   ÷ 100 = 59

Ordering sets of measures

Write these amounts in order, from least to greatest.

70 cm	300 mm	2 km	6 m	500 mm
300 mm	*500 mm*	*70 cm*	*6 m*	*2 km*

Write these amounts in order, from least to greatest.

500¢	$4.00	$5.50	350¢	640¢

2 ml	1 litre	12 ml	2 litres	10 ml

125 min	2 h	$3\frac{1}{2}$ h	200 min	$\frac{3}{4}$ h

2500 m	2 km	1000 cm	20 m	1000 m

$240	3500¢	$125.00	4600¢	$50.00

1 m	9 cm	24 mm	72 mm	7 cm

6 ml	8 litres	3 litres	1 ml	4 ml

2 h	75 min	$1\frac{1}{2}$ h	100 min	150 min

44 mm	4 cm	4 m	4 km	40 cm

4 m	36 cm	2 mm	20 cm	2 m

Decimal models

Fill in the grid to show the decimal.

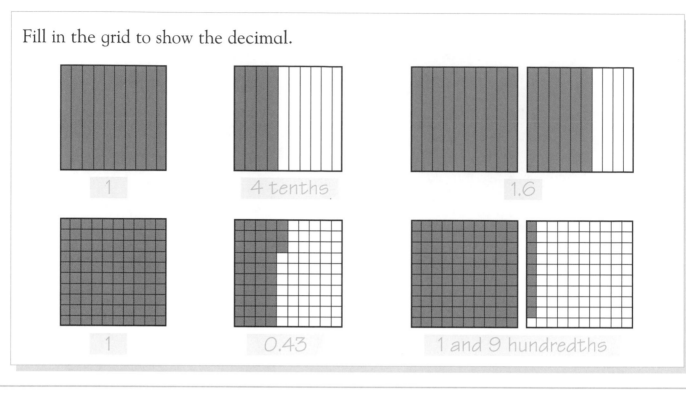

1

4 tenths

1.6

1

0.43

1 and 9 hundredths

Fill in the grid to show the decimal.

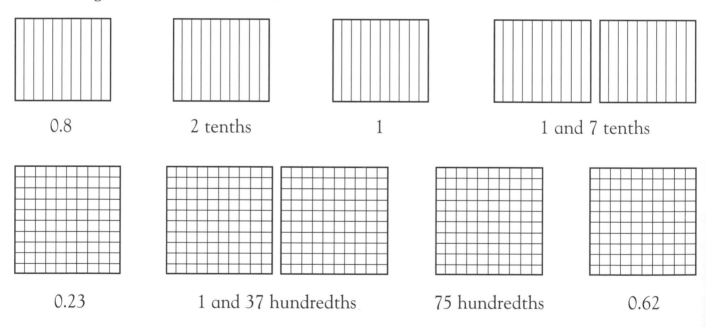

0.8   2 tenths   1   1 and 7 tenths

0.23   1 and 37 hundredths   75 hundredths   0.62

Write the decimal represented by the grid.

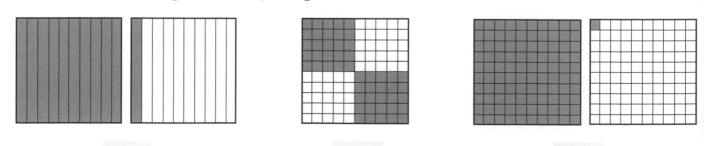

Identifying patterns

Continue each pattern.

Steps of 2: $\frac{1}{2}$ $2\frac{1}{2}$ $4\frac{1}{2}$ $6\frac{1}{2}$ $8\frac{1}{2}$ $10\frac{1}{2}$

Steps of 5:   3.5   8.5   13.5   18.5   23.5   28.5

Continue each pattern.

$5\frac{1}{2}$	$10\frac{1}{2}$	$15\frac{1}{2}$			
$1\frac{1}{4}$	$3\frac{1}{4}$	$5\frac{1}{4}$			
$8\frac{1}{3}$	$9\frac{1}{3}$	$10\frac{1}{3}$		$12\frac{1}{3}$	
$55\frac{3}{4}$	$45\frac{3}{4}$	$35\frac{3}{4}$			
$42\frac{1}{2}$	$38\frac{1}{2}$	$34\frac{1}{2}$			$22\frac{1}{2}$
7.5	6.5	5.5			
28.4	25.4	22.4		16.4	
81.6	73.6	65.6			
6.3	10.3	14.3			
12.1	13.1	14.1			17.1
14.6	21.6	28.6			
$11\frac{1}{2}$	$10\frac{1}{2}$	$9\frac{1}{2}$			
8.4	11.4	14.4		20.4	
$7\frac{3}{4}$	$13\frac{3}{4}$	$19\frac{3}{4}$			$37\frac{3}{4}$
57.5	48.5	39.5			

97

Products with odd and even numbers

Find the products of these numbers.

3 and 4   The product of 3 and 4 is 12.   6 and 8   The product of 6 and 8 is 48.

Find the products of these odd and even numbers.

5 and 6 _____   3 and 2 _____

7 and 4 _____   8 and 3 _____

6 and 3 _____   2 and 9 _____

10 and 3 _____   12 and 5 _____

What do you notice about your answers? _____

_____

Find the products of these odd numbers.

5 and 7 _____   3 and 9 _____

5 and 11 _____   7 and 3 _____

9 and 5 _____   11 and 7 _____

13 and 3 _____   1 and 5 _____

What do you notice about your answers? _____

_____

Find the products of these even numbers.

2 and 4 _____   4 and 6 _____

6 and 2 _____   4 and 8 _____

10 and 2 _____   4 and 10 _____

6 and 10 _____   6 and 8 _____

What do you notice about your answers? _____

_____

Can you write a rule for the products with odd and even numbers?

_____

Squares of numbers

Find the square of 2.

$$2 \times 2 = 4$$

What is the area of this square?

2 cm
2 cm

$2 \times 2 = 4$
Area = 4 cm²

Find the square of these numbers.

3   1   6

7   8   5

9   4   10

Now try these.

13   20   40

11   12   30

What are the areas of these squares?

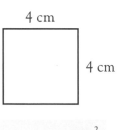

4 cm
4 cm

cm²

5 m
5 m

m²

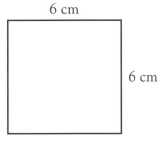

6 cm
6 cm

cm²

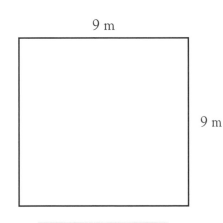

7 cm
7 cm

cm²

9 m
9 m

m²

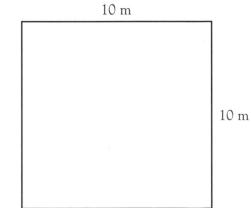

10 m
10 m

m²

Factors of numbers from 66 to 100

The factors of 66 are   1   2   3   6   11   22   33   66

Circle the factors of 94.   (1)   (2)   28   32   43   (47)   71   86   (94)

Write the factors of each number in the box.

The factors of 70 are

The factors of 85 are

The factors of 69 are

The factors of 83 are

The factors of 75 are

The factors of 96 are

The factors of 63 are

The factors of 99 are

The factors of 72 are

Circle the factors of 68.

    1   2   3   4   5   6   7   8   9   11   12   17   34   35   62   68

Circle the factors of 95.

    1   2   3   4   5   15   16   17   19   24   37   85   90   95   96

Circle the factors of 88.

    1   2   3   4   5   6   8   10   11   15   22   25   27   44   87   88

Circle the factors of 73.

    1   2   4   5   6   8   9   10   12   13   14   15   30   60   73

A prime number only has two factors, 1 and itself.
Write all the prime numbers between 66 and 100 in the box.

Renaming fractions

Rename these improper fractions as mixed numbers in simplest form.

$$\frac{17}{10} = 1\frac{7}{10} \qquad\qquad \frac{25}{6} = 4\frac{1}{6}$$

Rename this improper fraction as a mixed number in simplest form.

$$\frac{16}{10} = 1\frac{\overset{3}{\cancel{6}}}{\underset{5}{\cancel{10}}} = 1\frac{3}{5}$$

Rename these improper fractions as mixed numbers in simplest form.

$\dfrac{15}{4} =$ $\qquad$ $\dfrac{13}{10} =$ $\qquad$ $\dfrac{29}{5} =$

$\dfrac{19}{12} =$ $\qquad$ $\dfrac{22}{9} =$ $\qquad$ $\dfrac{17}{6} =$

$\dfrac{19}{6} =$ $\qquad$ $\dfrac{24}{5} =$ $\qquad$ $\dfrac{13}{3} =$

$\dfrac{13}{4} =$ $\qquad$ $\dfrac{21}{2} =$ $\qquad$ $\dfrac{14}{9} =$

$\dfrac{9}{8} =$ $\qquad$ $\dfrac{11}{6} =$ $\qquad$ $\dfrac{15}{7} =$

$\dfrac{17}{8} =$ $\qquad$ $\dfrac{43}{4} =$ $\qquad$ $\dfrac{11}{5} =$

$\dfrac{16}{10} =$ $\qquad$ $\dfrac{36}{8} =$ $\qquad$ $\dfrac{18}{8} =$

$\dfrac{45}{10} =$ $\qquad$ $\dfrac{22}{6} =$ $\qquad$ $\dfrac{24}{20} =$

$\dfrac{26}{8} =$ $\qquad$ $\dfrac{20}{8} =$ $\qquad$ $\dfrac{16}{12} =$

$\dfrac{25}{15} =$ $\qquad$ $\dfrac{18}{4} =$ $\qquad$ $\dfrac{20}{14} =$

$\dfrac{28}{24} =$ $\qquad$ $\dfrac{32}{6} =$ $\qquad$ $\dfrac{26}{10} =$

$\dfrac{18}{12} =$ $\qquad$ $\dfrac{46}{4} =$ $\qquad$ $\dfrac{30}{9} =$

Ordering sets of decimals

Write these decimals in order, from least to greatest.

| 0.45 | 0.21 | 2.07 | 1.45 | 3.62 | 2.17 |

| 0.21 | 0.45 | 1.45 | 2.07 | 2.17 | 3.62 |

Write these decimals in order, from least to greatest.

| 5.63 | 2.14 | 5.6 | 3.91 | 1.25 | 4.63 |

| 9.39 | 0.24 | 7.63 | 8.25 | 7.49 | 9.40 |

| 1.05 | 2.36 | 1.09 | 2.41 | 7.94 | 1.50 |

| 3.92 | 5.63 | 2.29 | 4.62 | 5.36 | 2.15 |

| 28.71 | 21.87 | 27.18 | 21.78 | 28.17 | 27.81 |

Write these measures in order, from least to greatest.

| $56.25 | $32.40 | $11.36 | $32.04 | $55.26 | $36.19 |

| 94.21 km | 87.05 km | 76.91 km | 94.36 km | 65.99 km | 110.75 km |

| $26.41 | $47.23 | $26.14 | $35.23 | $49.14 | $35.32 |

| 19.51 m | 16.15 m | 15.53 m | 12.65 m | 24.24 m | 16.51 m |

| 7.35 l | 8.29 l | 5.73 l | 8.92 l | 10.65 l | 4.29 l |

Symmetry

How many lines of symmetry does each figure have?

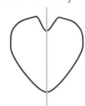  

1   2   5   0

Is the dashed line a line symmetry? Write yes or no.

 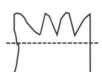

Draw the lines of symmetry. Write how many there are.

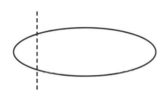 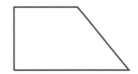

Draw the lines of symmetry. Write how many there are.

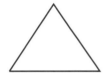

Draw the lines of symmetry. Write how many there are.

  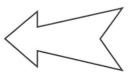

Comparing areas

Write how many units are in each figure.

18 units   16 units

Which figure has the greater area?   The figure on the left
has the greater area.

Write how many units are in each figure. Then circle the figure with the greatest area in each group.

Probability

Use the table to answer the questions.

**Pairs of socks in
Mr. O' Neill's drawer**

colour	number
red	2
blue	5
green	3
yellow	2
black	6

If Mr. O' Neill picks a pair of socks without looking, which colour is he most likely to pick? black

Which colour is Mr. O' Neill as likely to pick as red? yellow

Use the table to answer the questions.

Marbles in Margaret's bag

orange	blue	white	yellow
𝍸𝍸𝍸	𝍸 II	𝍸𝍸	𝍸𝍸𝍸𝍸

If Margaret picks a marble without looking, is she more likely to pick an orange marble or a yellow marble?

Which colour is she least likely to pick?

Use the graph to answer the questions.

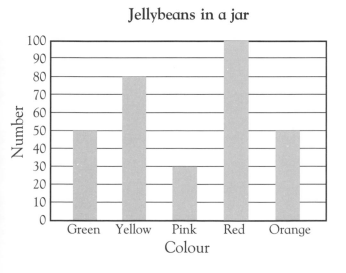

If you pick a jellybean without looking, which colour will you most probably pick?

Are you more likely to pick a pink jellybean or a yellow jellybean?

Which colour jellybean are you as likely to pick as an orange one?

Column addition

Find these sums.

```
    1 1                    1 2 1
    $327                   1374 km
    $644                   2362 km
    $923                   1690 km
 +  $455                +  4216 km
   $2349                   9642 km
```

Find these sums.

```
    539 m          206 m          481 m          735 m
    965 m          812 m          604 m          234 m
    774 m          619 m          274 m          391 m
 +  347 m       +  832 m       +  976 m       +  863 m
```

```
    746 kg         817 kg         944 kg         763 kg
    201 kg         591 kg         835 kg         861 kg
    432 kg         685 kg         391 kg         608 kg
 +  309 kg      +  245 kg      +  105 kg      +  671 kg
```

```
   6329 m         5245 m         6431 m         8690 m
   3251 m         2845 m         7453 m         5243 m
   2642 m         1937 m         4650 m         6137 m
 + 4823 m       + 5610 m       + 3782 m       + 5843 m
```

```
   $4721          $3654          $8172          $4352
   $1711          $5932          $1475          $3920
   $8342          $6841          $7760          $8439
 + $2365        + $4736        + $8102        + $1348
```

```
   1573 km        4902 km        3756 km        8010 km
   6231 km        7547 km        1150 km        7793 km
   2112 km        8463 km        5535 km        1641 km
 + 2141 km      + 6418 km      + 3852 km      + 7684 km
```

Column addition

Find these sums.

$$\begin{array}{r} {}^{1\ 1\ 1} \\ 3461 \text{ km} \\ 2100 \text{ km} \\ 3522 \text{ km} \\ 4159 \text{ km} \\ +\ 3614 \text{ km} \\ \hline 16\ 856 \text{ km} \end{array} \qquad \begin{array}{r} {}^{2\ 2\ 1} \\ \$3645 \\ \$4231 \\ \$8560 \\ \$7213 \\ +\ \$9463 \\ \hline \$33\ 112 \end{array}$$

Find these sums.

$$\begin{array}{r} 3144 \text{ m} \\ 2345 \text{ m} \\ 8479 \text{ m} \\ 1004 \text{ m} \\ +\quad 6310 \text{ m} \\ \hline \end{array} \qquad \begin{array}{r} 2510 \text{ m} \\ 1734 \text{ m} \\ 5421 \text{ m} \\ 3205 \text{ m} \\ +\quad 2365 \text{ m} \\ \hline \end{array} \qquad \begin{array}{r} 3276 \text{ m} \\ 1593 \text{ m} \\ 6837 \text{ m} \\ 1769 \text{ m} \\ +\quad 3846 \text{ m} \\ \hline \end{array} \qquad \begin{array}{r} 1475 \text{ m} \\ 2653 \text{ m} \\ 2765 \text{ m} \\ 3742 \text{ m} \\ +\quad 5905 \text{ m} \\ \hline \end{array}$$

$$\begin{array}{r} \$1480 \\ \$6366 \\ \$1313 \\ \$3389 \\ +\quad \$4592 \\ \hline \end{array} \qquad \begin{array}{r} \$4527 \\ \$8309 \\ \$6235 \\ \$4487 \\ +\quad \$4065 \\ \hline \end{array} \qquad \begin{array}{r} \$3063 \\ \$8460 \\ \$2712 \\ \$3756 \\ |\quad \$5650 \\ \hline \end{array} \qquad \begin{array}{r} \$8741 \\ \$6334 \\ \$3231 \\ \$6063 \\ +\quad \$4096 \\ \hline \end{array}$$

$$\begin{array}{r} 8644 \text{ km} \\ 3353 \text{ km} \\ 6400 \text{ km} \\ 5768 \text{ km} \\ +\ 1092 \text{ km} \\ \hline \end{array} \qquad \begin{array}{r} 3823 \text{ km} \\ 9275 \text{ km} \\ 3669 \text{ km} \\ 2998 \text{ km} \\ +\ 7564 \text{ km} \\ \hline \end{array} \qquad \begin{array}{r} 8636 \text{ km} \\ 8986 \text{ km} \\ 5367 \text{ km} \\ 6863 \text{ km} \\ +\ 3605 \text{ km} \\ \hline \end{array} \qquad \begin{array}{r} 8618 \text{ km} \\ 3453 \text{ km} \\ 4404 \text{ km} \\ 4361 \text{ km} \\ +\ 5641 \text{ km} \\ \hline \end{array}$$

$$\begin{array}{r} \$3742 \\ \$2785 \\ \$7326 \\ \$1652 \\ +\quad \$5753 \\ \hline \end{array} \qquad \begin{array}{r} \$8596 \\ \$5430 \\ \$8379 \\ \$2943 \\ +\quad \$1081 \\ \hline \end{array} \qquad \begin{array}{r} \$2739 \\ \$6517 \\ \$6014 \\ \$7115 \\ +\quad \$2704 \\ \hline \end{array} \qquad \begin{array}{r} \$8463 \\ \$5641 \\ \$9430 \\ \$8204 \\ +\quad \$6326 \\ \hline \end{array}$$

Adding fractions

Write the sum in simplest form.

$\frac{1}{3} + \frac{1}{3} = \underline{}$

$\frac{2}{9} + \frac{4}{9} = \underline{} = \underline{}$

$\frac{1}{4} + \frac{1}{4} = \underline{} = \underline{}$

$\frac{5}{7} + \frac{1}{7} = \underline{}$

$\frac{2}{3} + \frac{2}{3} = \underline{} = \underline{}$

$\frac{1}{12} + \frac{3}{12} = \underline{} = \underline{}$

$\frac{3}{7} + \frac{5}{7} = \underline{} = \underline{}$

$\frac{5}{11} + \frac{9}{11} = \underline{} = \underline{}$

$\frac{2}{5} + \frac{4}{5} = \underline{} = \underline{}$

$\frac{5}{18} + \frac{4}{18} = \underline{} = \underline{}$

$\frac{5}{16} + \frac{7}{16} = \underline{} = \underline{}$

$\frac{5}{9} + \frac{5}{9} = \underline{} = \underline{}$

$\frac{3}{8} + \frac{5}{8} = \underline{} =$

$\frac{4}{15} + \frac{7}{15} = \underline{}$

$\frac{7}{13} + \frac{8}{13} = \underline{} = \underline{}$

$\frac{2}{5} + \frac{1}{5} = \underline{}$

$\frac{5}{16} + \frac{7}{16} = \underline{} = \underline{}$

$\frac{1}{6} + \frac{5}{6} = \underline{} =$

$\frac{9}{10} + \frac{7}{10} = \underline{} = \underline{} = \underline{}$

$\frac{3}{4} + \frac{3}{4} = \underline{} = \underline{} = \underline{}$

$\frac{4}{5} + \frac{3}{5} = \underline{} = \underline{}$

$\frac{1}{8} + \frac{5}{8} = \underline{} = \underline{}$

$\frac{7}{12} + \frac{5}{12} = \underline{} =$

$\frac{3}{10} + \frac{9}{10} = \underline{} = \underline{} = \underline{}$

$\frac{3}{11} + \frac{5}{11} = \underline{}$

$\frac{9}{15} + \frac{11}{15} = \underline{} = \underline{} = \underline{}$

$\frac{8}{14} + \frac{5}{14} = \underline{}$

$\frac{1}{20} + \frac{6}{20} = \underline{}$

Adding fractions

Write the sum in simplest form.

$$\frac{1}{12} + \frac{3}{4} = \frac{1}{12} + \frac{9}{12} = \frac{10}{12} = \frac{5}{6} \qquad\qquad \frac{3}{5} + \frac{7}{10} = \frac{6}{10} + \frac{7}{10} = \frac{13}{10} = 1\frac{3}{10}$$

Write the sum in simplest form.

$$\frac{1}{6} + \frac{2}{3} = \frac{\ \ }{\ } + \frac{\ \ }{\ } = \frac{\ \ }{\ } \qquad\qquad \frac{7}{12} + \frac{7}{36} = \frac{\ \ }{\ } + \frac{\ \ }{\ } = \frac{\ \ }{\ } = \frac{\ \ }{\ }$$

$$\frac{1}{3} + \frac{2}{6} = \frac{\ \ }{\ } + \frac{\ \ }{\ } = \frac{\ \ }{\ } = \frac{\ \ }{\ } \qquad\qquad \frac{6}{10} + \frac{7}{30} = \frac{\ \ }{\ } + \frac{\ \ }{\ } = \frac{\ \ }{\ } = \frac{\ \ }{\ }$$

$$\frac{8}{12} + \frac{5}{24} = \frac{\ \ }{\ } + \frac{\ \ }{\ } = \frac{\ \ }{\ } = \frac{\ \ }{\ } \qquad\qquad \frac{7}{12} + \frac{5}{6} = \frac{\ \ }{\ } + \frac{\ \ }{\ } = \frac{\ \ }{\ } = \ \ \frac{\ \ }{\ }$$

$$\frac{5}{7} + \frac{7}{14} = \frac{\ \ }{\ } + \frac{\ \ }{\ } = \frac{\ \ }{\ } = \ \ \frac{\ \ }{\ } \qquad\qquad \frac{9}{25} + \frac{1}{5} = \frac{\ \ }{\ } + \frac{\ \ }{\ } = \frac{\ \ }{\ }$$

$$\frac{5}{6} + \frac{9}{12} = \frac{\ \ }{\ } + \frac{\ \ }{\ } = \frac{\ \ }{\ } = \qquad\qquad \frac{6}{16} + \frac{1}{4} = \frac{\ \ }{\ } + \frac{\ \ }{\ } = \frac{\ \ }{\ } = \frac{\ \ }{\ }$$

$$\frac{4}{5} + \frac{3}{10} = \frac{\ \ }{\ } + \frac{\ \ }{\ } = \frac{\ \ }{\ } = \ \ \frac{\ \ }{\ } \qquad\qquad \frac{5}{15} + \frac{5}{30} = \frac{\ \ }{\ } + \frac{\ \ }{\ } = \frac{\ \ }{\ } = \frac{\ \ }{\ }$$

$$\frac{3}{8} + \frac{5}{24} = \frac{\ \ }{\ } + \frac{\ \ }{\ } = \frac{\ \ }{\ } = \frac{\ \ }{\ } \qquad\qquad \frac{7}{8} + \frac{1}{2} = \frac{\ \ }{\ } + \frac{\ \ }{\ } = \frac{\ \ }{\ } = \ \ \frac{\ \ }{\ }$$

$$\frac{4}{9} + \frac{2}{3} = \frac{\ \ }{\ } + \frac{\ \ }{\ } = \frac{\ \ }{\ } = \ \ \frac{\ \ }{\ } \qquad\qquad \frac{2}{3} + \frac{7}{15} = \frac{\ \ }{\ } + \frac{\ \ }{\ } = \frac{\ \ }{\ } = \ \ \frac{\ \ }{\ }$$

$$\frac{7}{8} + \frac{3}{16} = \frac{\ \ }{\ } + \frac{\ \ }{\ } = \frac{\ \ }{\ } = \ \ \frac{\ \ }{\ } \qquad\qquad \frac{5}{14} + \frac{9}{28} = \frac{\ \ }{\ } + \frac{\ \ }{\ } = \frac{\ \ }{\ }$$

$$\frac{3}{10} + \frac{7}{20} = \frac{\ \ }{\ } + \frac{\ \ }{\ } = \frac{\ \ }{\ } \qquad\qquad \frac{3}{33} + \frac{5}{11} = \frac{\ \ }{\ } + \frac{\ \ }{\ } = \frac{\ \ }{\ } = \frac{\ \ }{\ }$$

Subtracting fractions

Write the answer in simplest form.

$$\frac{5}{6} - \frac{4}{6} = \frac{1}{6} \qquad\qquad \frac{5}{8} - \frac{3}{8} = \frac{\overset{1}{\cancel{2}}}{\underset{4}{\cancel{8}}} = \frac{1}{4}$$

Write the answer in simplest form.

$$\frac{2}{3} - \frac{1}{3} = \underline{}$$

$$\frac{1}{4} - \frac{1}{4} =$$

$$\frac{7}{12} - \frac{5}{12} = \underline{} = \underline{}$$

$$\frac{6}{7} - \frac{5}{7} = \underline{}$$

$$\frac{18}{30} - \frac{15}{30} = \underline{} = \underline{}$$

$$\frac{3}{6} - \frac{1}{6} = \underline{} = \underline{}$$

$$\frac{11}{16} - \frac{7}{16} = \underline{} = \underline{}$$

$$\frac{7}{13} - \frac{5}{13} = \underline{}$$

$$\frac{12}{13} - \frac{8}{13} = \underline{}$$

$$\frac{9}{10} - \frac{7}{10} = \underline{} = \underline{}$$

$$\frac{8}{17} - \frac{4}{17} = \underline{}$$

$$\frac{4}{5} - \frac{3}{5} = \underline{}$$

$$\frac{9}{11} - \frac{5}{11} = \underline{}$$

$$\frac{7}{8} - \frac{5}{8} = \underline{} = \underline{}$$

$$\frac{3}{16} - \frac{2}{16} = \underline{}$$

$$\frac{7}{9} - \frac{4}{9} = \underline{} = \underline{}$$

$$\frac{5}{7} - \frac{1}{7} = \underline{}$$

$$\frac{5}{11} - \frac{3}{11} = \underline{}$$

$$\frac{9}{12} - \frac{5}{12} = \underline{} = \underline{}$$

$$\frac{4}{5} - \frac{2}{5} = \underline{}$$

$$\frac{7}{8} - \frac{1}{8} = \underline{} = \underline{}$$

$$\frac{5}{9} - \frac{2}{9} = \underline{} = \underline{}$$

$$\frac{14}{15} - \frac{4}{15} = \underline{} = \underline{}$$

$$\frac{4}{5} - \frac{1}{5} = \underline{}$$

$$\frac{5}{6} - \frac{1}{6} = \underline{} = \underline{}$$

$$\frac{11}{18} - \frac{8}{18} = \underline{} = \underline{}$$

$$\frac{7}{12} - \frac{1}{12} = \underline{} = \underline{}$$

$$\frac{8}{14} - \frac{5}{14} = \underline{}$$

$$\frac{9}{10} - \frac{3}{10} = \underline{} = \underline{}$$

$$\frac{17}{20} - \frac{7}{20} = \underline{} = \underline{}$$

Subtracting fractions

Write the answer in simplest form.

$$\frac{3}{4} - \frac{1}{12} = \frac{9}{12} - \frac{1}{12} = \frac{8}{12} = \frac{2}{3}$$

$$\frac{3}{5} - \frac{4}{10} = \frac{6}{10} - \frac{4}{10} = \frac{2}{10} = \frac{1}{5}$$

Write the answer in simplest form.

$\dfrac{5}{6} - \dfrac{9}{12} = \underline{\quad} - \underline{\quad} = \underline{\quad}$

$\dfrac{6}{10} - \dfrac{7}{30} = \underline{\quad} - \underline{\quad} = \underline{\quad}$

$\dfrac{6}{14} - \dfrac{9}{28} = \underline{\quad} - \underline{\quad} = \underline{\quad}$

$\dfrac{1}{3} - \dfrac{2}{6} = \underline{\quad} - \underline{\quad} =$

$\dfrac{7}{8} - \dfrac{6}{16} = \underline{\quad} - \underline{\quad} = \underline{\quad} = \underline{\quad}$

$\dfrac{5}{15} - \dfrac{5}{30} = \underline{\quad} - \underline{\quad} = \underline{\quad} = \underline{\quad}$

$\dfrac{1}{2} - \dfrac{5}{12} = \underline{\quad} - \underline{\quad} = \underline{\quad}$

$\dfrac{8}{9} - \dfrac{2}{3} = \underline{\quad} - \underline{\quad} = \underline{\quad}$

$\dfrac{6}{16} - \dfrac{1}{4} = \underline{\quad} - \underline{\quad} = \underline{\quad} = \underline{\quad}$

$\dfrac{6}{7} - \dfrac{7}{14} = \underline{\quad} - \underline{\quad} = \underline{\quad}$

$\dfrac{7}{9} - \dfrac{7}{36} = \underline{\quad} - \underline{\quad} - \underline{\quad} - \underline{\quad}$

$\dfrac{2}{5} - \dfrac{4}{15} = \underline{\quad} - \underline{\quad} = \underline{\quad}$

$\dfrac{8}{12} - \dfrac{3}{24} = \underline{\quad} - \underline{\quad} = \underline{\quad}$

$\dfrac{3}{10} - \dfrac{3}{20} = \underline{\quad} - \underline{\quad} = \underline{\quad}$

$\dfrac{7}{8} - \dfrac{1}{2} = \underline{\quad} - \underline{\quad} = \underline{\quad}$

$\dfrac{7}{12} - \dfrac{2}{6} = \underline{\quad} - \underline{\quad} = \underline{\quad} = \underline{\quad}$

$\dfrac{5}{7} - \dfrac{1}{21} = \underline{\quad} - \underline{\quad} = \underline{\quad} = \underline{\quad}$

$\dfrac{14}{18} - \dfrac{5}{9} = \underline{\quad} - \underline{\quad} = \underline{\quad} = \underline{\quad}$

$\dfrac{3}{4} - \dfrac{3}{20} = \underline{\quad} - \underline{\quad} = \underline{\quad} = \underline{\quad}$

$\dfrac{1}{2} - \dfrac{3}{8} = \underline{\quad} - \underline{\quad} = \underline{\quad}$

$\dfrac{8}{21} - \dfrac{2}{7} = \underline{\quad} - \underline{\quad} = \underline{\quad}$

$\dfrac{3}{5} - \dfrac{6}{15} = \underline{\quad} - \underline{\quad} = \underline{\quad} = \underline{\quad}$

Multiplying

Write the product for each problem.

$$
\begin{array}{r}
\overset{1}{5}6 \\
\times\ 2 \\
\hline
112
\end{array}
\qquad
\begin{array}{r}
\overset{1}{4}5 \\
\times\ 3 \\
\hline
135
\end{array}
$$

Write the product for each problem.

$$
\begin{array}{r}
56 \\
\times\ 3 \\
\hline
\end{array}
\qquad
\begin{array}{r}
23 \\
\times\ 4 \\
\hline
\end{array}
\qquad
\begin{array}{r}
47 \\
\times\ 5 \\
\hline
\end{array}
\qquad
\begin{array}{r}
84 \\
\times\ 2 \\
\hline
\end{array}
$$

$$
\begin{array}{r}
73 \\
\times\ 4 \\
\hline
\end{array}
\qquad
\begin{array}{r}
52 \\
\times\ 5 \\
\hline
\end{array}
\qquad
\begin{array}{r}
64 \\
\times\ 3 \\
\hline
\end{array}
\qquad
\begin{array}{r}
51 \\
\times\ 2 \\
\hline
\end{array}
$$

Write the product for each problem.

$$
\begin{array}{r}
41 \\
\times\ 2 \\
\hline
\end{array}
\qquad
\begin{array}{r}
65 \\
\times\ 4 \\
\hline
\end{array}
\qquad
\begin{array}{r}
72 \\
\times\ 8 \\
\hline
\end{array}
\qquad
\begin{array}{r}
84 \\
\times\ 1 \\
\hline
\end{array}
$$

$$
\begin{array}{r}
92 \\
\times\ 3 \\
\hline
\end{array}
\qquad
\begin{array}{r}
57 \\
\times\ 2 \\
\hline
\end{array}
\qquad
\begin{array}{r}
38 \\
\times\ 4 \\
\hline
\end{array}
\qquad
\begin{array}{r}
26 \\
\times\ 5 \\
\hline
\end{array}
$$

Multiplying

Write the product for each problem.

$$\begin{array}{r} \overset{6}{39} \\ \times\ 7 \\ \hline 273 \end{array} \qquad \begin{array}{r} \overset{6}{68} \\ \times\ 8 \\ \hline 544 \end{array}$$

Write the product for each problem.

$$\begin{array}{r} 87 \\ \times\ 8 \\ \hline \end{array} \qquad \begin{array}{r} 76 \\ \times\ 8 \\ \hline \end{array} \qquad \begin{array}{r} 99 \\ \times\ 9 \\ \hline \end{array} \qquad \begin{array}{r} 85 \\ \times\ 8 \\ \hline \end{array}$$

$$\begin{array}{r} 88 \\ \times\ 5 \\ \hline \end{array} \qquad \begin{array}{r} 67 \\ \times\ 6 \\ \hline \end{array} \qquad \begin{array}{r} 94 \\ \times\ 9 \\ \hline \end{array} \qquad \begin{array}{r} 89 \\ \times\ 7 \\ \hline \end{array}$$

Write the product for each problem.

$$\begin{array}{r} 87 \\ \times\ 9 \\ \hline \end{array} \qquad \begin{array}{r} 46 \\ \times\ 7 \\ \hline \end{array} \qquad \begin{array}{r} 58 \\ \times\ 9 \\ \hline \end{array} \qquad \begin{array}{r} 73 \\ \times\ 8 \\ \hline \end{array}$$

$$\begin{array}{r} 95 \\ \times\ 7 \\ \hline \end{array} \qquad \begin{array}{r} 58 \\ \times\ 8 \\ \hline \end{array} \qquad \begin{array}{r} 78 \\ \times\ 7 \\ \hline \end{array} \qquad \begin{array}{r} 96 \\ \times\ 9 \\ \hline \end{array}$$

Dividing by one-digit numbers

Find the quotient. Estimate your answer first.

$257 \div 3$

$3 \times 100 = 300$, so the quotient will be less than 100.
$3 \times 80 = 240$ and $3 \times 90 = 270$,
so the quotient will be between 80 and 90.

85 r 2

$$\begin{array}{r} 85\ r\ 2 \\ 3)\overline{257} \\ \underline{24} \\ 17 \\ \underline{15} \\ 2 \end{array}$$

Find the quotients. Remember to estimate your answers first.

$2)\overline{571}$ $4)\overline{823}$ $3)\overline{604}$ $4)\overline{925}$

$2)\overline{147}$ $3)\overline{259}$ $4)\overline{725}$ $5)\overline{811}$

$2)\overline{593}$ $4)\overline{406}$ $3)\overline{739}$ $5)\overline{591}$

Dividing by one-digit numbers

Find the quotient. Estimate your answer first.

$$845 \div 8$$

8 x 100 = 800, so the quotient will be more than 100.
8 x 110 = 880, so the quotient will be
between 100 and 110.

105 r 5

$$
\begin{array}{r}
105 \text{ r } 5 \\
8\overline{)845} \\
8 \\
\hline
04 \\
0 \\
\hline
45 \\
40 \\
\hline
5
\end{array}
$$

Find the quotients. Remember to estimate your answers first.

6)833   7)465   8)941   9)812

7)566   7)499   8)532   8)321

7)635   9)365   6)598   9)184

115

Real-life problems

Find the answer to each problem.

Tim spends $26.54 on holiday gifts for his family. His sister spends $32.11. How much more does she spend than Tim?

$5.57

$$\begin{array}{r} {}^{1\,1}\,{}^{10} \\ 2\not{8}\not{0}\,11 \\ \not{3}\not{2}.\not{X}\not{X} \\ -\;26.54 \\ \hline 5.57 \end{array}$$

A school spends $99 per class on new books. If there are 16 classes in the school, how much is spent?

$1584

$$\begin{array}{r} 99 \\ \times\;\;16 \\ \hline 594 \\ 990 \\ \hline 1584 \end{array}$$

Mr. Brown has $4762 in stocks and $2247 in his bank. How much does he have altogether?

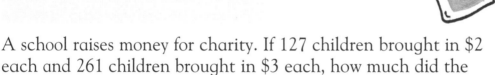

A shop in Calgary takes in $9651 on a Saturday. A smaller branch in Edmonton takes in $3247. How much more does the Calgary shop take in?

A school raises money for charity. If 127 children brought in $2 each and 261 children brought in $3 each, how much did the school raise altogether?

David has to fill a pond that holds 66 litres. If his bucket holds 3 litres, how many buckets of water will he need to fill the pond?

Samantha has $25. She spends $14.25 on an aquarium, $3.75 on gravel, and $2.50 on aquarium ornaments. How much did she spend? How much money does she have left?

A man regularly saves $1200 each year. How much will he save in 5 years?

Real-life problems

Find the answer to each problem.

Jaime runs round a field 8 times.
If he runs a total of 944 metres,
what is the perimeter of the field?

118 m

$$\begin{array}{r} 118 \\ 8\overline{)944} \\ \underline{8} \\ 14 \\ \underline{8} \\ 64 \\ \underline{64} \\ 0 \end{array}$$

Mr. and Mrs. Green's living room is 5.75 m
long and their dining room is 4.37 m long.
If they knock out the wall between them to
make one room, how long will it be?

10.12 m

$$\begin{array}{r} {\scriptstyle 1\ 1} \\ 5.75 \\ + 4.37 \\ \hline 10.12 \end{array}$$

A family's car trip took 5 hours. If they travelled 50 kilometres
each hour, how far did they travel?

Two men weigh $90\frac{1}{2}$ kilograms and 79 kilograms.
What is the difference between their masses?

An electrician uses 480 metres of wire in 6 apartments. If he uses
the same amount in each, how much does he use per house?

A jar of coffee weighs 2.5 kilograms.
How much will 7 jars weigh?

A box of pencils is 5 centimetres wide. How many can be stored
on a shelf 1 metre long?

Maria spends 32 hours working on a school project. If she spreads the
work evenly over 8 days, how many hours does she work each day?

Sean runs 143.26 m in 40 seconds. Malik runs 97.92 m in the
same time. How much farther does Sean run than Malik?

Problems involving time

Find the answer to each problem.

A yard sale began at 12 P.M. and ended at 4:35 P.M. How long did it last?

```
12:00 → 4:00 = 4 h
4:00 → 4:35 = 35 min
Total = 4 h 35 min
```

4 h 35 min

Fred's watch says 2:27. What time will it say in 1 h 26 min?

```
2:27 + 1 h = 3:27
3.27 + 26 min = 3:53
```

3:53

Rachel begins painting fences at 12:15 P.M. and finishes at 4:45 P.M. If she paints 3 fences, how long does each one take?

Joy works from 9 A.M. until 5 P.M. every day. If she takes an hour's lunch break, how many hours does she work altogether from Monday through Friday?

A train leaves at 2:29 P.M. and arrives at 10:47 P.M. How long does the trip take?

A castle has a 24-hour guard on the gate. Three soldiers share the work equally. If the first soldier starts his duty at 2:30 P.M., what times will the other two soldiers start their duties?

Soldier 2

Soldier 3

Kobe wants to videotape a program that starts at 3:30 P.M. and finishes at 5 P.M. If the program is on every day for the next five days, how many hours will he videotape?

Looking at graphs

Derek recorded the temperature in his garden during one day.
At what time was the temperature at its highest? *noon*

By how much did the temperature fall between 6 P.M. and midnight? *6°C*

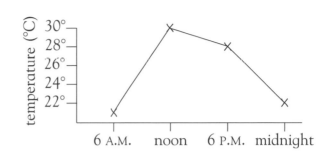

Kate keeps a record of her last 10 spelling test scores.

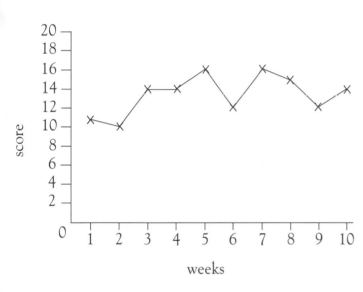

What was Kate's score in week 3?

In which 2 consecutive weeks did Kate's score stay the same?

What was Kate's best score?

How much did her score improve between weeks 4 and 5?

The local tourist board produced a graph to show the maximum temperatures in Charleston between April and August.

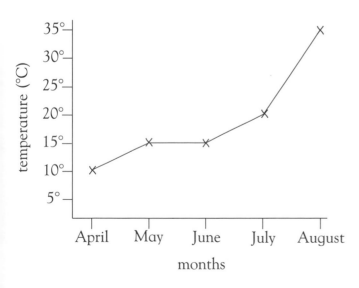

What was the maximum temperature in April?

Overall, what is happening to the temperature between April and August?

How much did the temperature rise between May and July?

Which two months had the same maximum temperature?

Place value for whole numbers

Write the value of 7 in 573 in standard form and word form.

70   seventy

What happens to the value of 247 if you change the 2 to a 3?

The value of the number increases by 100.

Write the value of the 6 in these numbers in standard form and word form.

26   162   36 904   12 612

Circle the numbers that have a 7 with a value of seventy.

457 682   67 974   870 234   372 987

177 079   767 777   79 875   16 757

Write what happens to the value of each number.

Change the 6 in 3586 to 3.

Change the 9 in 1921 to 8.

Change the 7 in 7246 to 9.

Change the 1 in 817 to 9.

Change the 5 in 50 247 to 1.

Change the 2 in 90 205 to 9.

Place value for decimals

Write the value of 5 in 7.53 in standard form and word form.

    0.5   5 tenths

What happens to the value of 2.48 if you change the 8 to a 1?

    The value of the number decreases by 0.07.

Write the value of the 9 in these numbers in standard form and written form.

2.9   0.19   975.04   9.12

0.89   591.65   19.85   3.96

Write what happens to the value of each number.

Change the 8 in 35.86 to 7.

Change the 2 in 1.02 to 6.

Change the 3 in 3460 to 9.

Change the 1 in 8.17 to 6.

Change the 5 in 8.35 to 1.

Circle the numbers that have an 8 with a value of 8 tenths.

457.68   1.8   8.09   35.85   388.1

Circle the numbers that have a 5 with a value of 5 hundredths.

550.7   5.25   99.95   16.53   68.95

Circle the numbers that have a 3 with a value of 3 tenths.

3603.3   0.93   32.45   5.33   23.53

Reading tally charts

Use the chart to answer the questions.

Club members' pets

Pet	Number
dog	ЖН ЖН IIII
cat	ЖН ЖН ЖН I
fish	ЖН III

What is the most popular pet for club members? cats

How many more club members have cats than have fish?

16 – 8 = 8,   8 members

Use the chart to answer the questions.

Birds seen at feeder

sparrow	junco	blue jay	chickadee
ЖН ЖН ЖН IIII	ЖН II	ЖН ЖН I	ЖН ЖН ЖН ЖН

What kinds of birds were seen
at the feeder more than 12 times?

What is the total number of
sparrows and chickadees seen at the feeder?

How many more blue jays than juncos were seen?

Use the chart to answer the questions.

Snacks chosen by students

carrots	chips	cookies	pretzels
IIII	ЖН ЖН III	ЖН ЖН ЖН II	ЖН ЖН ЖН II

What snack did fewer than 10 students choose?

What is the most popular snack for students?

Was the total number of students who chose chips and cookies greater than
or less than the total number who chose carrots and pretzels?

Volumes of cubes

This cube is 1 cm long, 1 cm high, and 1 cm wide. We say it has a volume of 1 cubic centimetre (1 cm³).

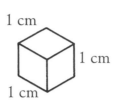

If we put 4 of these cubes together the new shape has a volume of 4 cm³.

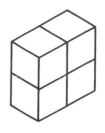

These shapes are made of 1 cm³ cubes. What are their volumes?

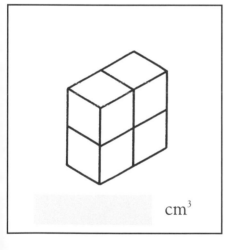
cm³

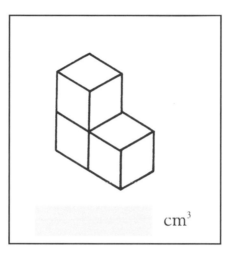
cm³

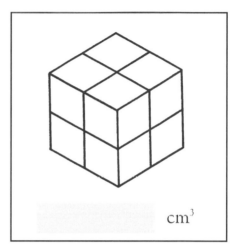
cm³

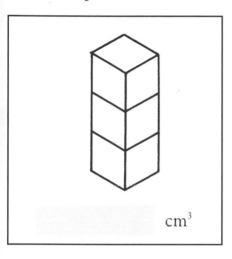
cm³

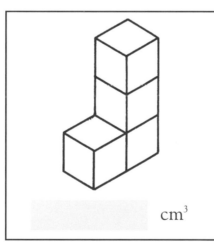
cm³

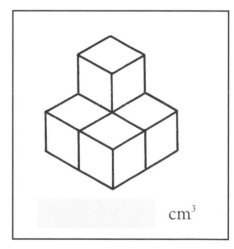
cm³

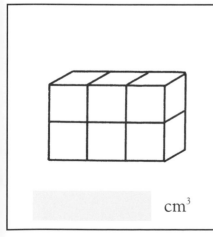
cm³

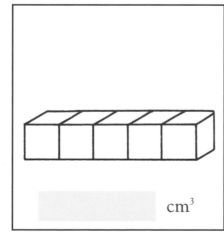
cm³

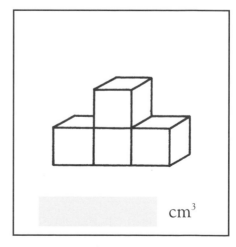
cm³

Acute and obtuse angles

A right angle forms
a square corner.

An obtuse angle is greater
than a right angle.

An acute angle is less
than a right angle.

Look at these angles.

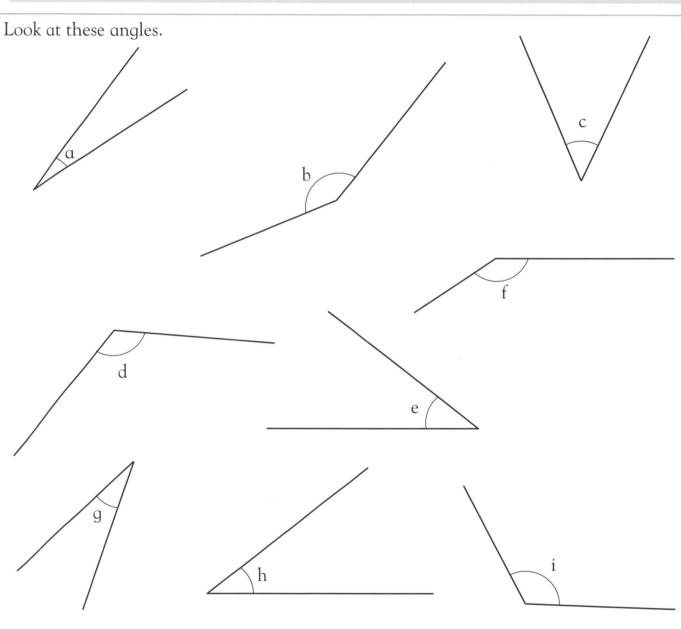

Which of the angles are acute?

Which of the angles are obtuse?

Acute and obtuse angles

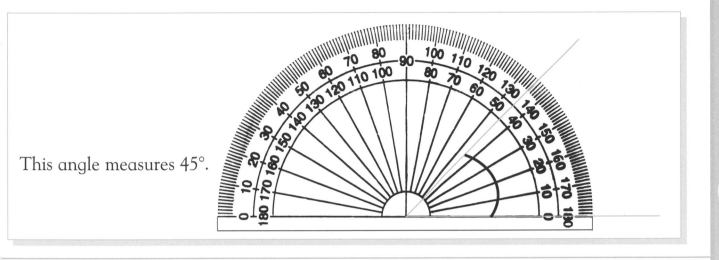

This angle measures 45°.

Use a protractor to measure these angles.

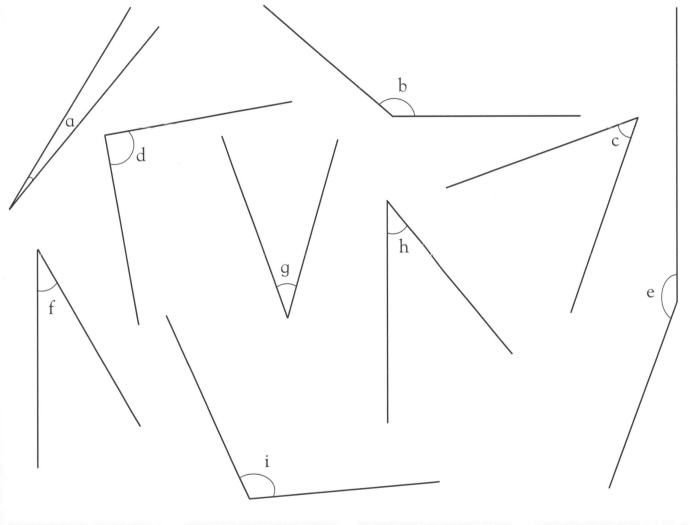

Addition fact families

Circle the number sentence that is in the same fact family.

$12 - 5 = 7$
$5 + 7 = 12$ $12 - 4 = 8$ $(7 + 5 = 12)$ $12 + 12 = 24$

$10 - 8 = 2$
$8 + 2 = 10$ $8 - 6 = 2$ $(2 + 8 = 10)$ $8 - 2 = 6$

Circle the number sentence that is in the same fact family.

$7 + 8 = 15$
$8 + 7 = 15$ $7 + 5 = 12$ $15 - 8 = 7$ $8 - 7 = 1$

$17 - 6 = 11$
$11 + 6 = 17$ $17 - 11 = 6$ $17 + 6 = 23$ $5 + 6 = 11$

$14 - 5 = 9$
$14 - 9 = 5$ $9 - 3 = 6$ $14 + 9 = 23$ $5 + 9 = 14$

$9 + 7 = 16$
$7 + 9 = 16$ $16 - 9 = 7$ $16 + 7 = 23$ $9 - 7 = 2$

$19 - 9 = 10$
$19 - 10 = 9$ $9 + 3 = 12$ $9 + 10 = 19$ $18 - 8 = 10$

$4 + 7 = 11$
$11 - 4 = 7$ $11 + 4 = 15$ $7 + 4 = 11$ $7 + 7 = 14$

Write the fact family for each group of numbers.

5, 6, 11   6, 10, 4   5, 13, 8

Odds and evens

Write the answer in the box.

3 + 3 = 6   4 + 6 = 10   7 + 3 = 10   2 + 6 = 8

Add the even numbers to the even numbers.

4 + 8 =   12 + 6 =   10 + 6 =   8 + 14 =

20 + 14 =   14 + 12 =   16 + 10 =   30 + 20 =

14 + 16 =   18 + 6 =   22 + 8 =   20 + 40 =

What do you notice about each answer? _____

Add the odd numbers to the odd numbers.

7 + 9 =   5 + 7 =   11 + 5 =   9 + 5 =

7 + 7 =   9 + 3 =   15 + 5 =   13 + 7 =

11 + 3 =   17 + 9 =   15 + 9 =   13 + 15 =

What do you notice about each answer? _____

Add the odd numbers to the even numbers.

3 + 8 =   9 + 12 =   5 + 18 =   7 + 14 =

11 + 4 =   13 + 10 =   15 + 6 =   21 + 4 =

7 + 20 =   13 + 30 =   11 + 16 =   17 + 6 =

What do you notice about each answer? _____

Add the even numbers to the odd numbers.

6 + 7 =   8 + 5 =   10 + 9 =   2 + 17 =

10 + 29 =   14 + 3 =   8 + 13 =   12 + 5 =

14 + 7 =   8 + 51 =   16 + 9 =   30 + 17 =

What do you notice about each answer? _____

Word problems

Write the answer in the box.

I multiply a number by 6 and the answer is 24.

What number did I begin with? 4

Write the answer in the box.

A number multiplied by 7 equals 35. What is the number?

I divide a number by 10 and the answer is 3. What number did I divide?

I multiply a number by 4 and the answer is 20. What is the number I multiplied?

After dividing a piece of wood into four equal sections, each section is
4 cm long. How long was the piece of wood I started with?

A number multiplied by 6 gives the answer 24. What is the number?

Some money is divided into five equal amounts. Each amount is 10 cents.
How much money was there before it was divided?

I multiply a number by 9 and the result is 45. What number was multiplied?

A number divided by 6 is 3. What number was divided?

Three children share 18 peanuts equally among themselves.
How many peanuts does each child receive?

A number divided by 4 is 8. What is the number?

I multiply a number by 6 and the answer is 30. What is the number?

Four sets of a number equal 16. What is the number?

A number divided by 5 is 5. What is the number?

A child divides a number by 8 and gets 2. What number was divided?

Three groups of a number equal 27. What is the number?

I multiply a number by 10 and the result is 100. What is the number?

Word problems

Write the answer in the box.

A child is given four dimes. How much money does she have altogether? 40¢

Write the answer in the box.

A box contains 6 eggs. How many boxes would I need to buy to have 18 eggs?

A boy is given three bags of candy. There are 20 pieces in each bag. How many pieces of candy does the boy have in total?

Four lifeboats carry a total of 100 people. How many people are in each boat?

A shepherd had 200 sheep but 70 were lost in a snowstorm. How many sheep does the shepherd have left?

Three women win the lottery and share $900 equally among themselves. How much does each woman receive?

A truck contains 50 barrels of oil. It delivers 27 barrels to one garage. How many barrels are left on the truck?

Andrej has a collection of 150 baseball cards. He sells 30 of them to a friend. How many cards does he have left?

When Peter multiplies his apartment number by 3, the result is 75. What is his apartment number?

One photograph costs $1.80. How much will two photographs cost?

A dog buries 20 bones on Monday, 30 bones on Tuesday, and 40 bones on Wednesday. How many bones has the dog buried altogether?

A car trip is supposed to be 70 kilometres long but the car breaks down half-way. How far has the car gone when it breaks down?

A teacher has 32 children in her class. 13 children are out with the flu. How many children are left in class?

Multiples

Circle the multiples of 3.

4   7   ⑨   14   20   ㉔

Circle the multiples of 3.

4	7	10	15	21	30	35	50
2	4	6	8	10	12	14	16
1	3	5	7	9	11	13	15
2	5	8	11	14	17	20	23
5	10	15	20	25	30	35	40
0	3	6	9	12	15	18	21
10	20	30	40	50	60	70	80
5	8	11	14	17	20	23	26
2	7	13	17	21	25	33	60

Circle the multiples of 4.

2	7	11	15	19	23	28	31
2	4	6	8	10	12	14	16
1	3	5	7	9	11	13	15
3	6	9	12	15	18	21	24
4	12	14	18	22	24	28	34
5	10	15	20	25	30	35	40
3	5	12	17	24	26	32	80
1	5	9	13	18	20	60	100
10	20	30	40	50	60	70	80

Factors

Write the factors of each number.

6   1, 2, 3, 6   8   1, 2, 4, 8

Write the factors of each number.

4	10	14
9	3	12
7	15	17
5	20	19
2	24	11
13	30	16

Write the factors of each number.

1	4	16
25	36	49
64	81	100

Do you notice anything about the number of factors each of the numbers has?

_____

Do you know the name for these special numbers? _____

Write the factors of each number.

2	3	5
7	11	13
17	19	23
29	31	37

Do you notice anything about the number of factors each of the numbers has?

_____

Do you know the name for these special numbers? _____

131

Fractions

Write the answer in the box.

$1\frac{1}{2} + \frac{1}{4} = \boxed{1\frac{3}{4}}$ $2\frac{1}{2} + 3\frac{1}{2} = \boxed{6}$ $1\frac{1}{4} + 2\frac{1}{2} = \boxed{3\frac{3}{4}}$

Write the answer in the box.

$2\frac{1}{4} + 1\frac{1}{4} =$ $1\frac{1}{2} + 1\frac{1}{2} =$ $1\frac{1}{4} + \frac{1}{4} =$

$3\frac{1}{2} + 1 =$ $3\frac{1}{2} + 1\frac{1}{4} =$ $2\frac{1}{4} + 4 =$

$4\frac{1}{2} + 1\frac{1}{4} =$ $2\frac{1}{2} + 1\frac{1}{2} =$ $5 + 1\frac{1}{2} =$

$3\frac{1}{4} + 1\frac{1}{2} =$ $2 + 3\frac{1}{2} =$ $7 + \frac{1}{2} =$

$3 + \frac{1}{4} =$ $4\frac{1}{4} + \frac{1}{4} =$ $5 + 4\frac{1}{2} =$

Write the answer in the box.

$1\frac{1}{3} + 2\frac{1}{3} =$ $3\frac{1}{3} + 4\frac{2}{3} =$ $1\frac{2}{3} + 5 =$

$3\frac{2}{3} + 2 =$ $4\frac{1}{3} + 1\frac{2}{3} =$ $2\frac{2}{3} + 1\frac{2}{3} =$

$1\frac{2}{3} + 1\frac{2}{3} =$ $4\frac{1}{3} + 2\frac{1}{3} =$ $3 + 2\frac{1}{3} =$

$6 + 2\frac{2}{3} =$ $2\frac{1}{3} + 3\frac{2}{3} =$ $3\frac{1}{3} + 1\frac{1}{3} =$

$5\frac{2}{3} + 2\frac{2}{3} =$ $7 + \frac{1}{3} =$ $2\frac{2}{3} + 5\frac{2}{3} =$

Write the answer in the box.

$2\frac{1}{5} + 2\frac{2}{5} =$ $3\frac{1}{5} + 2\frac{3}{5} =$ $1\frac{4}{5} + 6 =$

$3\frac{1}{5} + 3\frac{2}{5} =$ $4 + 2\frac{2}{5} =$ $5\frac{3}{5} + 1\frac{1}{5} =$

$\frac{3}{5} + \frac{3}{5} =$ $3\frac{2}{5} + \frac{4}{5} =$ $3\frac{2}{5} + \frac{2}{5} =$

Fractions and decimals

Write each fraction as a decimal.

$1\frac{1}{10}$ = 1.1 $1\frac{2}{10}$ = 1.2 $1\frac{7}{10}$ = 1.7

Write each decimal as a fraction.

2.5 = $2\frac{1}{2}$ 1.9 = $1\frac{9}{10}$ 3.2 = $3\frac{2}{10}$

Write each fraction as a decimal.

$2\frac{1}{2}$ $3\frac{1}{10}$ $4\frac{3}{10}$ $1\frac{1}{2}$

$5\frac{1}{10}$ $2\frac{3}{10}$ $8\frac{1}{10}$ $5\frac{1}{2}$

$7\frac{8}{10}$ $2\frac{4}{10}$ $6\frac{1}{2}$ $8\frac{1}{2}$

$7\frac{6}{10}$ $9\frac{1}{2}$ $6\frac{7}{10}$ $10\frac{1}{2}$

Write each decimal as a fraction.

3.2   4.5   1.7   1.2

6.5   2.7   5.2   5.5

7.2   8.5   9.7   10.2

11.5   12.7   13.2   14.5

15.7   16.2   17.5   18.7

Write each fraction as a decimal.

$\frac{1}{2}$ = $\frac{2}{10}$ = $\frac{3}{10}$ =

Write each decimal as a fraction.

0.5 = —   0.2 = —   0.7 = —

Real-life problems

Write the answer in the box.

A number multiplied by 8 is 56.
What is the number?

7

I divide a number by 9 and the result is 6.
What is the number?

54

Write the answer in the box.

A number multiplied by 6 is 42.
What is the number?

I divide a number by 4 and the
result is 7. What is the number?

I divide a number by 8 and the
result is 6. What number did I
begin with?

A number multiplied by itself
gives the answer 25. What is
the number?

I divide a number by 7 and the
result is 7. What number did I
begin with?

A number multiplied by itself
gives the answer 49. What is
the number?

When I multiply a number by 7
I end up with 56. What
number did I begin with?

Seven times a number is 63.
What is the number?

What do I have to multiply 8
by to get the result 72?

Nine times a number is 81.
What is the number?

When 6 is multiplied by a
number the result is 42. What
number was 6 multiplied by?

A number divided by 8 gives
the answer 10. What was the
starting number?

I multiply a number by 9 and
end up with 45. What number
did I multiply?

I multiply a number by 9 and
the result is 81. What number
did I begin with?

Symmetry

The dotted line is a mirror line. Complete each shape.

Complete each shape.

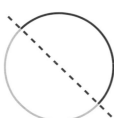

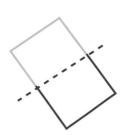

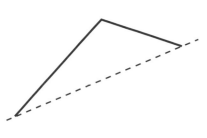

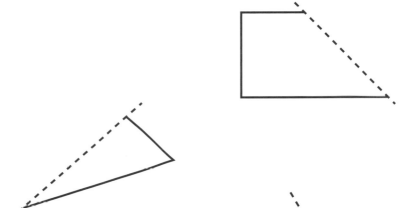

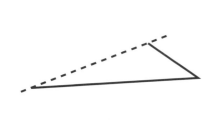

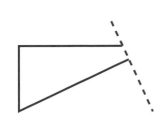

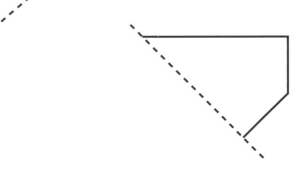

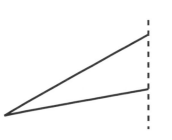

Fractions and decimals

Write each fraction as a decimal.

$\frac{1}{2}$ = 0.5 $\qquad$ $\frac{1}{10}$ = 0.1

Write each decimal as a fraction.

0.25 = $\frac{1}{4}$ $\qquad$ 0.4 = $\frac{4}{10}$

Write each fraction as a decimal.

$\frac{1}{10}$	$\frac{1}{2}$	$\frac{3}{10}$	$\frac{5}{10}$
$\frac{2}{10}$	$\frac{9}{10}$	$\frac{6}{10}$	$\frac{1}{10}$
$\frac{2}{10}$	$\frac{3}{10}$	$\frac{4}{10}$	$\frac{5}{10}$
$\frac{6}{10}$	$\frac{7}{10}$	$\frac{8}{10}$	$\frac{9}{10}$

Write each decimal as a fraction.

0.8	0.5	0.3	0.4
0.25	0.7	0.2	0.75
0.2	0.6	0.5	0.8
0.1	0.4	0.6	0.9

Write the answer in the box.

Which two of the fractions above are the same as 0.5?

Which two of the fractions above are the same as 0.8?

Which two of the fractions above are the same as 0.6?

Which two of the fractions above are the same as 0.2?

Which two of the fractions above are the same as 0.4?

Fractions of shapes

Shade $\frac{3}{5}$ of each shape.

Shade $\frac{4}{5}$ of each shape.

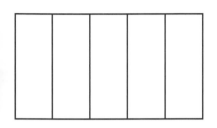

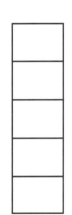

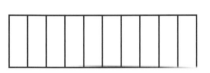

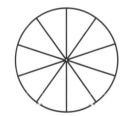

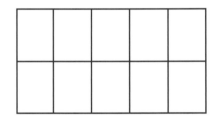

Shade the fraction shown of each shape.

$\frac{4}{10}$

$\frac{8}{10}$

$\frac{3}{10}$

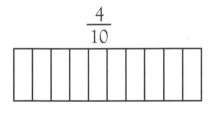

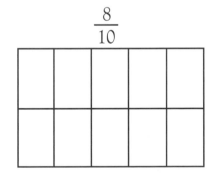

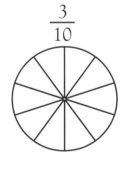

$\frac{7}{10}$

$\frac{6}{10}$

$\frac{9}{10}$

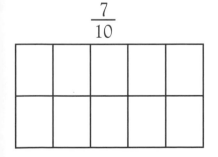

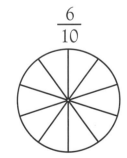

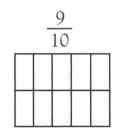

Fractions

Colour $\frac{3}{4}$ of each shape.

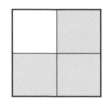 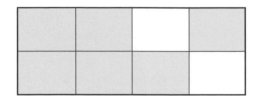

Colour $\frac{2}{3}$ of each shape.

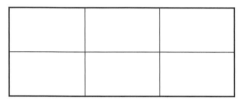 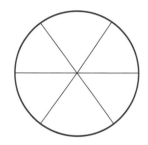 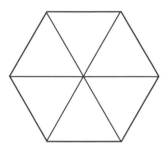

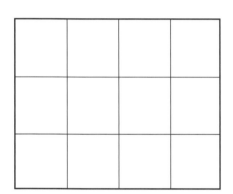 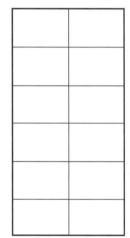 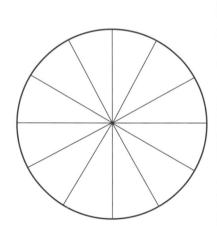

Colour $\frac{3}{4}$ of each shape.

 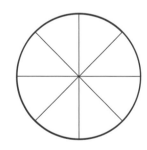 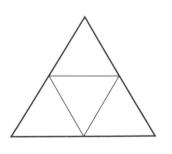

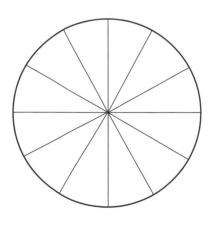 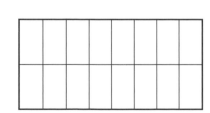 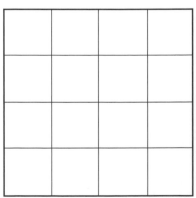

Reading timetables

	Frostburg	Elmhurst	Badger Farm	Winchester
Redline bus	8:00	8:05	8:15	8:25
Blueline bus	8:05	No stop	8:12	8:20
City taxi	8:30	8:35	8:45	8:55
Greenline bus	8:07	No stop	No stop	8:15

The timetable shows the times it takes to travel using different transport companies between Frostburg and Winchester.

Write the answer in the box.

How long does the Redline bus take between Frostburg and Winchester?

When does the Blueline bus arrive at Badger Farm?

Where does the Greenline bus not stop?

Where is City taxi at 8.35?

Does the Blueline bus stop at Elmhurst?

How long does the Redline bus take to travel between Badger Farm and Winchester?

Which is the fastest trip between Frostburg and Winchester?

Which service arrives at five minutes to nine?

How long does City taxi take between Frostburg and Badger Farm?

Where is the Blueline bus at twelve minutes past eight?

Averages

Write the average of this row in the box.

| 4 | 2 | 2 | 2 | 6 | 3 | 2 |

The average is 3 .

Write the average of each row in the box.

2	3	7	4	2	7	2	5
7	4	5	4	8	5	3	4
5	3	5	3	5	2	4	5
7	5	9	7	2	4	8	6
4	3	4	3	4	3	4	7
1	4	2	7	3	8	2	5
3	2	1	2	2	3	2	1
8	3	6	3	8	2	8	2

Write the average of each row in the box.

4	8	6	3	9	6	6
5	9	2	6	9	1	3
6	3	8	6	1	5	6
3	8	6	7	5	9	4
1	8	3	4	2	6	4
9	5	8	7	4	7	9
1	3	2	3	1	2	2
6	3	7	4	5	8	2

Multiplying larger numbers by ones

Write the product for each problem.

¹³   ¹ ³¹
529   1273
x   4   x   5
2116   6365

Write the product for each problem.

724	831	126	455
x 2	x 3	x 3	x 4

161	282	349	253
x 4	x 5	x 5	x 6

328	465	105	562
x 6	x 6	x 4	x 4

Write the product for each problem.

4261	1582	3612	4284
x 3	x 3	x 4	x 4

5907	1263	1303	1467
x 5	x 5	x 6	x 6

6521	8436	1599	3761
x 6	x 6	x 6	x 6

5837	6394	8124	3914
x 4	x 5	x 6	x 6

Multiplying larger numbers by ones

Write the product for each problem.

```
    1 4              1 7 4
    417              2185
  x   7            x    9
   2919            19 665
```

Write the product for each problem.

```
    419              604              715              327
  x   7            x   7            x   8            x   7
  _____            _____            _____            _____


    425              171              682              246
  x   8            x   9            x   8            x   8
  _____            _____            _____            _____


    436              999              319              581
  x   8            x   9            x   9            x   9
  _____            _____            _____            _____
```

Write the product for each problem.

```
   4331             2816             1439             2617
  x   7            x   7            x   8            x   8
  _____            _____            _____            _____


   3104             4022             3212             2591
  x   8            x   8            x   9            x   9
  _____            _____            _____            _____


   1710             3002             2468             1514
  x   9            x   8            x   7            x   8
  _____            _____            _____            _____


   4624             2993             3894             4361
  x   7            x   8            x   8            x   9
  _____            _____            _____            _____
```

Real-life multiplication problems

There are 157 apples in a box.
How many will there be in three boxes?

471 apples

```
  12
 157
x   3
-----
 471
```

A stamp album can hold 550 stamps.
How many stamps will 5 albums hold?

A train can take 425 passengers.
How many can it take in four trips?

Mr Jenkins puts $256 a month into the bank.
How much will he have put in after six months?

A theatre can seat 5524 people. If a play runs for 7 days, what is
the maximum number of people who will be able to see it?

A car costs $9956. How much will it cost a
company to buy nine cars for its people?

Installing a new window for a house costs $435. How
much will it cost to install 8 windows of the same size?

An airplane flies at a steady speed of
550 kilometres per hour. How far will it
travel in 7 hours?

Area of rectangles and squares

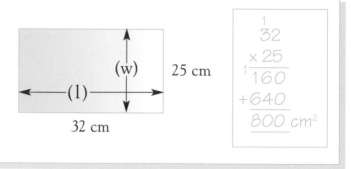

Find the area of this rectangle.

To find the area of a rectangle or square, we multiply length (l) by width (w).

Area = *800 cm²*

(w) 25 cm

(l)

32 cm

$$
\begin{array}{r}
{}^{1}32 \\
\times\ 25 \\
\hline
^{1}160 \\
+640 \\
\hline
800\ cm² \\
\end{array}
$$

Find the area of these rectangles and squares.
You may need to do your work on a separate sheet.

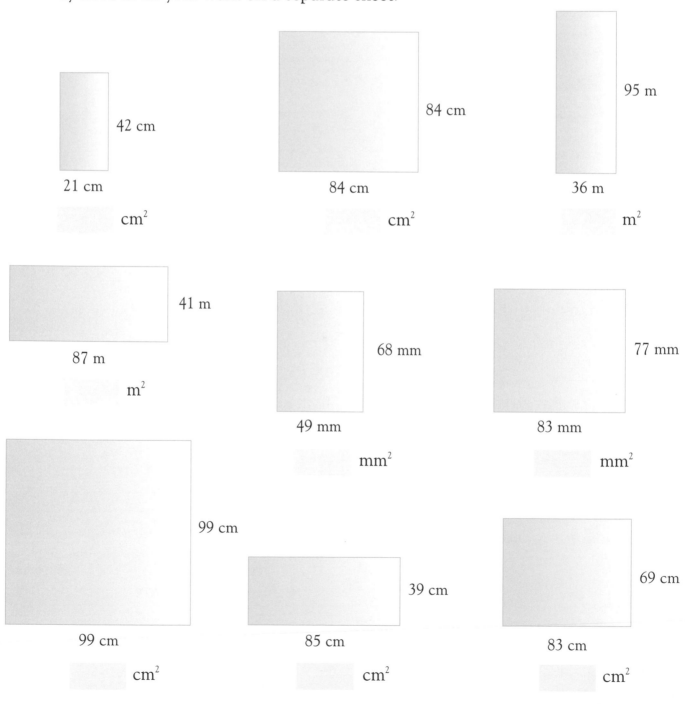

42 cm

21 cm

_____ cm²

84 cm

84 cm

_____ cm²

95 m

36 m

_____ m²

41 m

87 m

_____ m²

68 mm

49 mm

_____ mm²

77 mm

83 mm

_____ mm²

99 cm

99 cm

_____ cm²

39 cm

85 cm

_____ cm²

69 cm

83 cm

_____ cm²

Perimeter of shapes

Find the perimeter of this rectangle.

To find the perimeter of
a rectangle or square, we
add the two lengths and
the two widths together.

12.4 cm

27.3 cm

```
  1 1
 27.3 cm
 27.3 cm
 12.4 cm
+12.4 cm
 79.4 cm
```
79.4 cm

Find the perimeter of these rectangles and squares.
You may need to do your work on a separate sheet.

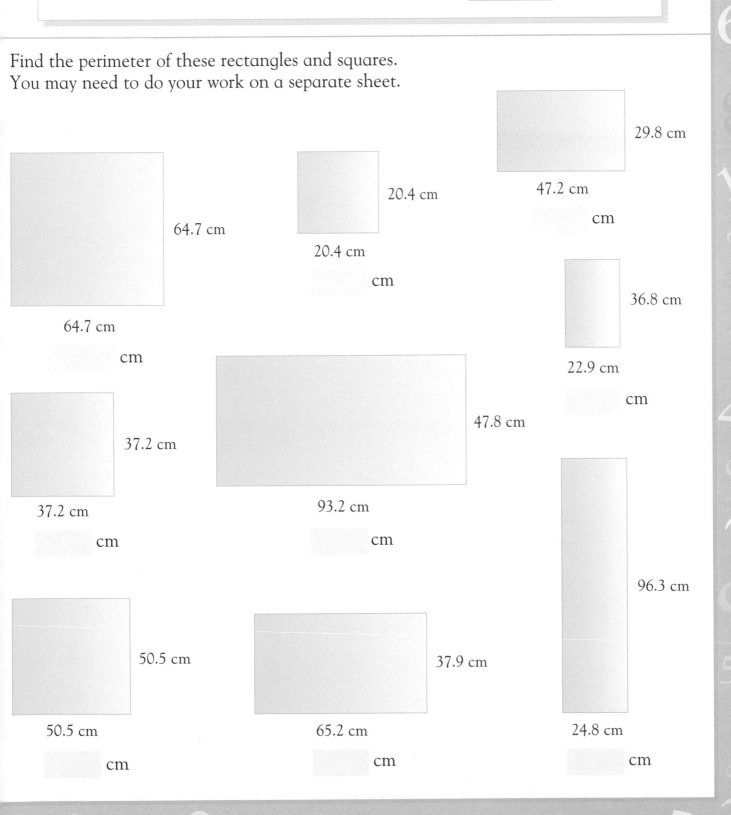

64.7 cm

64.7 cm

_____ cm

20.4 cm

20.4 cm

_____ cm

29.8 cm

47.2 cm

_____ cm

36.8 cm

22.9 cm

_____ cm

37.2 cm

37.2 cm

_____ cm

47.8 cm

93.2 cm

_____ cm

96.3 cm

24.8 cm

_____ cm

50.5 cm

50.5 cm

_____ cm

37.9 cm

65.2 cm

_____ cm

145

Adding fractions

Work out the answer to the problem.

$$\frac{1}{5} + \frac{3}{5} = \boxed{\frac{4}{5}} \qquad \frac{4}{9} + \frac{2}{9} = \boxed{\frac{{}^2\cancel{6}}{\cancel{9}_3}} = \boxed{\frac{2}{3}}$$

Remember to reduce to simplest form if you need to.

Work out the answer to each sum. Reduce to simplest form if you need to.

$\frac{2}{7} + \frac{3}{7} = \frac{}{7}$ $\qquad$ $\frac{2}{9} + \frac{5}{9} = \frac{}{9}$ $\qquad$ $\frac{1}{3} + \frac{1}{3} = \frac{}{3}$

$\frac{3}{10} + \frac{4}{10} = \frac{}{10}$ $\qquad$ $\frac{1}{8} + \frac{2}{8} = \frac{}{8}$ $\qquad$ $\frac{2}{9} + \frac{3}{9} = \frac{}{9}$

$\frac{2}{5} + \frac{1}{5} = \underline{}$ $\qquad$ $\frac{1}{7} + \frac{5}{7} = \underline{}$ $\qquad$ $\frac{4}{9} + \frac{1}{9} = \frac{}{9}$

$\frac{3}{20} + \frac{4}{20} = \underline{}$ $\qquad$ $\frac{3}{100} + \frac{8}{100} = \underline{}$ $\qquad$ $\frac{7}{10} + \frac{2}{10} = \underline{}$

$\frac{1}{6} + \frac{2}{6} = \underline{} = \underline{}$ $\qquad$ $\frac{31}{100} + \frac{19}{100} = \underline{} = \underline{}$ $\qquad$ $\frac{11}{20} + \frac{4}{20} = \underline{} = \underline{}$

$\frac{3}{10} + \frac{3}{10} = \underline{} = \underline{}$ $\qquad$ $\frac{1}{12} + \frac{5}{12} = \underline{} = \underline{}$ $\qquad$ $\frac{2}{6} + \frac{2}{6} = \underline{} = \underline{}$

$\frac{3}{8} + \frac{3}{8} = \underline{} = \underline{}$ $\qquad$ $\frac{3}{8} + \frac{1}{8} = \underline{} = \underline{}$ $\qquad$ $\frac{5}{12} + \frac{3}{12} = \underline{} = \underline{}$

$\frac{1}{4} + \frac{1}{4} = \underline{} = \underline{}$ $\qquad$ $\frac{3}{20} + \frac{2}{20} = \underline{} = \underline{}$ $\qquad$ $\frac{2}{6} + \frac{2}{6} = \underline{} = \underline{}$

$\frac{2}{7} + \frac{4}{7} = \underline{}$ $\qquad$ $\frac{2}{9} + \frac{2}{9} = \underline{}$ $\qquad$ $\frac{13}{20} + \frac{5}{20} = \underline{} = \underline{}$

$\frac{81}{100} + \frac{9}{100} = \underline{} = \underline{}$ $\qquad$ $\frac{7}{20} + \frac{6}{20} = \underline{}$ $\qquad$ $\frac{3}{8} + \frac{2}{8} = \underline{}$

$\frac{6}{10} + \frac{2}{10} = \underline{} = \underline{}$ $\qquad$ $\frac{29}{100} + \frac{46}{100} = \underline{} = \underline{}$ $\qquad$ $\frac{73}{100} + \frac{17}{100} = \underline{} = \underline{}$

Adding fractions

Write the answer to each problem.

$$\frac{3}{8} + \frac{5}{8} = \frac{8}{8} = 1 \qquad \frac{3}{4} + \frac{3}{4} = \frac{\cancel{6}}{\cancel{4}} = \frac{3}{2} = 1\frac{1}{2}$$

Write the answer to each problem.

$$\frac{7}{10} + \frac{6}{10} = \frac{}{10} = 1\frac{}{10} \qquad \frac{6}{7} + \frac{5}{7} = \frac{}{7} = 1\frac{}{7} \qquad \frac{2}{3} + \frac{2}{3} = \frac{}{3} = 1\frac{}{3}$$

$$\frac{5}{10} + \frac{6}{10} = \frac{}{} = \frac{}{} \qquad \frac{8}{13} + \frac{5}{13} = \frac{}{} = \qquad \frac{7}{8} + \frac{4}{8} = \frac{}{} = \frac{}{}$$

$$\frac{7}{8} + \frac{5}{8} = \frac{}{} = \frac{}{} = \frac{}{} \qquad \frac{2}{5} + \frac{3}{5} = \frac{}{} = \qquad \frac{5}{8} + \frac{5}{8} = \frac{}{} = \frac{}{} = \frac{}{}$$

$$\frac{10}{20} + \frac{15}{20} = \frac{}{} = \frac{}{} = \frac{}{} \qquad \frac{2}{3} + \frac{1}{3} = \frac{}{} = \qquad \frac{5}{6} + \frac{5}{6} = \frac{}{} = \frac{}{} = \frac{}{}$$

$$\frac{5}{6} + \frac{3}{6} = \frac{}{} = \frac{}{} = \frac{}{} \qquad \frac{6}{12} + \frac{7}{12} = \frac{}{} = \frac{}{} \qquad \frac{8}{10} + \frac{6}{10} = \frac{}{} = \frac{}{} = \frac{}{}$$

$$\frac{12}{20} + \frac{10}{20} = \frac{}{} = \frac{}{} = \frac{}{} \qquad \frac{3}{10} + \frac{7}{10} = \frac{}{} = \qquad \frac{75}{100} + \frac{75}{100} = \frac{}{} = \frac{}{} = \frac{}{}$$

$$\frac{10}{20} + \frac{16}{20} = \frac{}{} = \frac{}{} = \frac{}{} \qquad \frac{4}{5} + \frac{4}{5} = \frac{}{} = \frac{}{} \qquad \frac{11}{21} + \frac{17}{21} = \frac{}{} = \frac{}{} = \frac{}{}$$

Subtracting fractions

Write the answer to each problem.

$$\frac{4}{5} - \frac{2}{5} = \frac{2}{5} \qquad\qquad \frac{8}{9} - \frac{5}{9} = \frac{\cancel{3}^{1}}{\cancel{9}_{3}} = \frac{1}{3}$$

Reduce to simplest form if you need to.

Write the answer to each problem. Reduce to simplest form if you need to.

$$\frac{3}{5} - \frac{1}{5} = \frac{}{5} \qquad\qquad \frac{6}{7} - \frac{3}{7} = \frac{}{7} \qquad\qquad \frac{9}{10} - \frac{6}{10} = \frac{}{10}$$

$$\frac{7}{10} - \frac{4}{10} = \frac{}{} \qquad\qquad \frac{5}{9} - \frac{4}{9} = \frac{}{} \qquad\qquad \frac{2}{3} - \frac{1}{3} = \frac{}{}$$

$$\frac{7}{8} - \frac{3}{8} = \frac{}{} = \frac{}{} \qquad\qquad \frac{14}{20} - \frac{10}{20} = \frac{}{} = \frac{}{} \qquad\qquad \frac{5}{6} - \frac{1}{6} = \frac{}{} = \frac{}{}$$

$$\frac{11}{12} - \frac{5}{12} = \frac{}{} = \frac{}{} \qquad\qquad \frac{17}{20} - \frac{12}{20} = \frac{}{} = \frac{}{} \qquad\qquad \frac{9}{12} - \frac{3}{12} = \frac{}{} = \frac{}{}$$

$$\frac{8}{10} - \frac{6}{10} = \frac{}{} = \frac{}{} \qquad\qquad \frac{12}{12} - \frac{2}{12} = \frac{}{} = \frac{}{} \qquad\qquad \frac{9}{10} - \frac{3}{10} = \frac{}{} = \frac{}{}$$

$$\frac{8}{9} - \frac{2}{9} = \frac{}{} = \frac{}{} \qquad\qquad \frac{7}{8} - \frac{1}{8} = \frac{}{} = \frac{}{} \qquad\qquad \frac{9}{12} - \frac{3}{12} = \frac{}{} = \frac{}{}$$

$$\frac{3}{4} - \frac{2}{4} = \frac{}{} \qquad\qquad \frac{6}{8} - \frac{3}{8} = \frac{}{} \qquad\qquad \frac{18}{20} - \frac{8}{20} = \frac{}{} = \frac{}{}$$

$$\frac{4}{6} - \frac{2}{6} = \frac{}{} = \frac{}{} \qquad\qquad \frac{5}{12} - \frac{4}{12} = \frac{}{} \qquad\qquad \frac{3}{8} - \frac{2}{8} = \frac{}{}$$

$$\frac{5}{7} - \frac{1}{7} = \frac{}{} \qquad\qquad \frac{5}{16} - \frac{1}{16} = \frac{}{} = \frac{}{} \qquad\qquad \frac{90}{100} - \frac{80}{100} = \frac{}{} = \frac{}{}$$

Showing decimals

Write the decimals on the number line.

$$0.4, \ 0.5, \ 0.6, \ 0.8, \ 0.9, \ 0.25, \ 0.45, \ 0.63$$

Write the decimals on the number line.

$$0.56, \ 0.2, \ 0.87, \ 0.45, \ 0.98, \ 0.6, \ 0.1$$

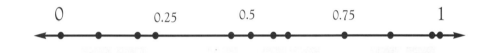

Write the decimals on the number line.

$$1.41, \ 1.8, \ 1.3, \ 1.98, \ 1.68, \ 1.2$$

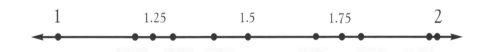

Write these decimals on the number line.

$$2.5, \ 3.75, \ 2.25, \ 3.1, \ 3.68, \ 4.2$$

Conversions: length

Units of length	
10 millimetres	1 centimetre
100 centimetres	1 metre
1000 metres	1 kilometre

This conversion table shows how to convert millimetres, centimetres, metres, and kilometres.

Neilika's rope is 3 metres long. How many millimetres long is it?

$3 \times 100 = 300$
$300 \times 10 = 3000$

300 centimetres long
3000 millimetres long

Brian's rope is 1000 centimetres long. How many metres long is it?

$1000 \div 100 = 10$ 10 metres long

Convert each measurement to metres.

500 centimetres	6 kilometres	300 centimetres	550 centimetres

6000 centimetres	1000 centimetres	14 kilometres	10 kilometres

Convert each measurement to centimetres.

14 metres	6 metres	10 metres	$10\frac{1}{2}$ metres

12 metres	1400 millimetres	7 metres	5 metres

Convert each measurement to kilometres.

1600 metres	2500 metres	100 metres	3700 metres

1200 metres	31 000 metres	10 000 metres	100 000 metres

Conversions: capacity

Units of capacity	
1000 millilitres	1 litre

This conversion table shows how to convert millilitres and litres.

Katya's thermos holds 8 litres. How many millilitres does it hold?

Hannah's thermos holds 6000 millilitres. How many litres does it hold?

8 x 1000 = 8000   8000 millilitres   6000 ÷ 1000 = 6   6 litres

Convert each measurement to millilitres.

4 litres	2 litres	7 litres	10 litres

$\frac{1}{4}$ litre	3 litres	1.5 litres	$\frac{1}{4}$ litre

5 litres	9 litres	$2\frac{1}{2}$ litres	10 litres

Convert each measurement to litres.

1000 millilitres	6000 millilitres	2500 millilitres	500 millilitres

3000 millilitres	3500 millilitres	9000 millilitres	10 000 millilitres

5500 millilitres	250 millilitres	4000 millilitres	5000 millilitres

Rounding money

Round to the nearest dollar.	Round to the nearest ten dollars.
$3.95 rounds to $4	$15.50 rounds to $20
$2.25 rounds to $2	$14.40 rounds to $10

Round to the nearest dollar.

$2.60 rounds to	$8.49 rounds to	$3.39 rounds to
$9.55 rounds to	$1.75 rounds to	$4.30 rounds to
$7.15 rounds to	$6.95 rounds to	$2.53 rounds to

Round to the nearest ten dollars.

$37.34 rounds to	$21.75 rounds to	$85.03 rounds to
$71.99 rounds to	$66.89 rounds to	$52.99 rounds to
$55.31 rounds to	$12.79 rounds to	$15.00 rounds to

Round to the nearest hundred dollars.

$307.12 rounds to	$175.50 rounds to	$115.99 rounds to
$860.55 rounds to	$417.13 rounds to	$650.15 rounds to
$739.10 rounds to	$249.66 rounds to	$367.50 rounds to

Estimating sums of money

Round to the leading digit. Estimate the sum.

$52.61 →
+ $27.95 → ____
is about   ____

$19.20 →
+ $22.13 → ____
is about   ____

$70.75 →
+ $12.49 → ____
is about   ____

$701.34 →
+ $100.80 → ____
is about   ____

$339.50 →
+ $422.13 → ____
is about   ____

$160.07 →
+ $230.89 → ____
is about   ____

$25.61 →
+ $72.51 → ____
is about   ____

$61.39 →
+ $19.50 → ____
is about   ____

$18.32 →
+ $13.90 → ____
is about   ____

$587.35 →
+ 251.89 → ____
is about   ____

$109.98 →
+ $210.09 → ____
is about   ____

$470.02 →
+ $203.17 → ____
is about   ____

Round to the leading digit. Estimate the sum.

$75.95 + $17.95 →

$41.67 + $20.35 →

$49.19 + $38.70 →

$784.65 + $101.05 →

$516.50 + $290.69 →

$58.78 + $33.25 →

$82.90 + $11.79 →

$90.09 + $14.50 →

Estimating differences of money

Round the numbers to the leading digit. Estimate the differences.

$8.75 →	$9		$61.47 →	$60
− $5.10 →	− $5		− $35.64 →	− $40
is about	$4		is about	$20

Round the numbers to the leading digit. Estimate the differences.

$17.90 →		$6.40 →		$87.45 →
− $12.30 → ____		− $3.75 → ____		− $54.99 → ____
is about ____		is about ____		is about ____

$34.90 →		$8.68 →		$363.24 →
− $12.60 → ____		− $4.39 → ____		− $127.66 → ____
is about ____		is about ____		is about ____

$78.75 →		$64.21 →		$723.34 →
− $24.99 → ____		− $28.56 → ____		− $487.12 → ____
is about ____		is about ____		is about ____

Round the numbers to the leading digit. Estimate the differences.

$8.12 − $1.35 $49.63 − $27.85

→   =   →   =

$7.50 − $3.15 $85.15 − $42.99

→   =   →   =

$5.85 − $4.75 $634.60 − $267.25

→   =   →   =

$37.35 − $16.99 $842.17 − $169.54

→   =   →   =

$56.95 − $20.58 $628.37 − $252.11

→   =   →   =

Estimating sums and differences

Round the numbers to the leading digit. Estimate the sum or difference.

$$
\begin{array}{r}
3576 \rightarrow 4000 \\
+ 1307 \rightarrow +1000 \\
\hline
\text{is about} \quad 5000
\end{array}
\qquad
\begin{array}{r}
198\ 248 \rightarrow 200\ 000 \\
- 116\ 431 \rightarrow -100\ 000 \\
\hline
\text{is about} \quad 100\ 000
\end{array}
$$

Round the numbers to the leading digit. Estimate the sum or difference.

$$
\begin{array}{r}
685 \rightarrow \\
+ 489 \rightarrow \\
\hline
\text{is about}
\end{array}
\qquad
\begin{array}{r}
21\ 481 \rightarrow \\
- 12\ 500 \rightarrow \\
\hline
\text{is about}
\end{array}
\qquad
\begin{array}{r}
7834 \rightarrow \\
+ 3106 \rightarrow \\
\hline
\text{is about}
\end{array}
$$

$$
\begin{array}{r}
682\ 778 \rightarrow \\
+ 130\ 001 \rightarrow \\
\hline
\text{is about}
\end{array}
\qquad
\begin{array}{r}
58\ 499 \rightarrow \\
- 22\ 135 \rightarrow \\
\hline
\text{is about}
\end{array}
\qquad
\begin{array}{r}
902\ 276 \rightarrow \\
- 615\ 999 \rightarrow \\
\hline
\text{is about}
\end{array}
$$

$$
\begin{array}{r}
46\ 801 \rightarrow \\
+ 34\ 700 \rightarrow \\
\hline
\text{is about}
\end{array}
\qquad
\begin{array}{r}
9734 \rightarrow \\
- 8306 \rightarrow \\
\hline
\text{is about}
\end{array}
\qquad
\begin{array}{r}
65\ 606 \rightarrow \\
+ 85\ 943 \rightarrow \\
\hline
\text{is about}
\end{array}
$$

$$
\begin{array}{r}
5218 \rightarrow \\
- 3673 \rightarrow \\
\hline
\text{is about}
\end{array}
\qquad
\begin{array}{r}
745 \rightarrow \\
+ 451 \rightarrow \\
\hline
\text{is about}
\end{array}
\qquad
\begin{array}{r}
337\ 297 \rightarrow \\
- 168\ 931 \rightarrow \\
\hline
\text{is about}
\end{array}
$$

Write < or > for each problem.

$329 + 495 \qquad 800$ 　　　　　　　　　$11\ 569 - 6146 \qquad 6000$

$563 - 317 \qquad 300$ 　　　　　　　　　$8193 - 6668 \qquad 1000$

$41\ 924 - 12\ 445 \qquad 50\ 000$ 　　　　　$634\ 577 + 192\ 556 \qquad 800\ 000$

$18\ 885 + 12\ 691 \qquad 30\ 000$ 　　　　　$713\ 096 - 321\ 667 \qquad 400\ 000$

Conversion tables

Draw a table to convert dollars to cents.

$	cents
1	100
2	200
3	300

Complete the conversion chart below.

Weeks	Days
1	7
2	
	28
10	70

If there are 60 minutes in 1 hour, make a conversion chart for up to 10 hours.

Hours	Minutes

Extra Practice

This section gives children a chance to further practice what they've learned, helping to reinforce the core skills developed while working through this book.

Content

In this section, children will review:

- representing, comparing, and ordering whole numbers up to 4 digits
- representing, comparing, and ordering decimal numbers and fractions
- rounding numbers to the nearest 10 or 100, and decimals to the nearest whole number
- developing fluency with multiplication and division
- applying mathematics to solve problems in real-life situations
- solving money and time problems
- calculating perimeters of 2-D shapes and classifying the properties of 3-D shapes
- identifying and measuring angles
- representing and interpreting data
- converting metric units of measurement

The "Keeping skills sharp" pages can act as a test to see how well children are learning the material. Further parents' notes are found in the answer section at the back of the book.

When your child has completed this book, fill out the certificate of achievement and congratulate him or her on a job well done!

These are large numbers, be careful how you read and write them.

Write the number in words.

6124   Six thousand one hundred twenty-four

5102

7034

1638

7400

2805

3967

7452

Write the number.

One thousand forty-nine   1049

Nine hundred eighty-four

Four hundred seventeen

Four hundred seventy-six

One hundred six

Three thousand ninety-seven

One thousand six hundred twenty-four

One thousand three

Completing sequences

Some answers have negative values.

Complete each sequence.

12	24	36	48	60	72		
24	32	40	48	56			
18	27	36	45	54			
45	50	55	60	65			
−40	−35	−30	−25	−20			
−18	−15	−12	−9	−6			
−36	−32	−28	−24	−20			
−70	−60	−50	−40	−30			
63	52	41	30	19			
80	71	62	53	44			
26	21	16	11	6			
−8	−12	−16	−20	−24			
13	26	39	52	65			
−31	−25	−19	−13	−7			
12	18	24	30	36			

Complete this sequence but be careful, this is a bit trickier.

| 2 | 4 | 8 | 16 | | | |

Write the odd numbers that are missing in each sequence.

3	5				13
17					27
41					51
79					89

Write the even numbers that are missing in each sequence.

8					18
26					36
50					60
92					102

Strike out the numbers that are **not** odd.

~~650~~   179   231

538   792

705   163   196

Strike out the numbers that are **not** even.

~~979~~   488   297

406   135

584   753   322

Circle the correct answer.

Adding two odd numbers together will always give an   **odd number**   **even number**

Adding two even numbers together will always give an   **odd number**   **even number**

Try to answer these questions as quickly as possible—but still be correct!

58 + 10 = 68   71 + 10 =   92 + 10 =   46 + 10 =

10 + 31 =   10 + 19 =   10 + 42 =   10 + 56 =

73 + 10 =   66 + 10 =   82 + 10 =   79 + 10 =

100 + 48 =   100 + 67 =   100 +39 =   100 + 14 =

76 + 100 =   98 + 100 =   34 + 100 =   9 + 100 =

100 + 42 =   66 + 100 =   100 + 56 =   31 + 100 =

Write the answers.

76 – 10 =   93 – 10 =   48 – 10 =   60 – 10 =

113 – 10 =   156 – 10 =   231 – 10 =   400 – 10 =

261 – 10 =   200 – 10 =   403 – 10 =   601 – 10 =

250 – 100 =   134 – 100 =   700 – 100 =   106 – 100 =

327 – 100 =   708 – 100 =   1000 – 100 =   853 – 100 =

564 – 100 =   100 – 100 =   1242 – 100 =   1067 – 100 =

Try to answer these questions as quickly as possible—but still be correct!

3 x 10 = 30   7 x 10 =   9 x 10 =   10 x 10 =

12 x 10 =   0 x 10 =   14 x 10 =   1 x 10 =

15 x 10 =   17 x 10 =   21 x 10 =   30 x 10 =

10 x 2 =   10 x 6 =   10 x 0 =   10 x 8 =

10 x 13 =   10 x 24 =   10 x 50 =   10 x 22 =

10 x 15 =   10 x 36 =   10 x 100 =   10 x 6 =

Write the answers.

2 x 100 =   4 x 100 =   6 x 100 =   11 x 100 =

0 x 100 =   5 x 100 =   14 x 100 =   15 x 100 =

1 x 100 =   7 x 100 =   9 x 100 =   19 x 100 =

100 x 8 =   100 x 14 =   100 x 3 =   100 x 10 =

100 x 18 =   100 x 23 =   100 x 61 =   100 x 32 =

100 x 0 =   100 x 55 =   100 x 82 =   100 x 16 =

Write the answers.

$\frac{1}{2}$ x 10 = $\frac{1}{5}$ x 10 =   100 x $\frac{1}{2}$ = $\frac{1}{5}$ x 100 =

Divide each number by 10.

20 [2]   50 [   ]   90 [   ]   10 [   ]   100 [   ]

30 [   ]   60 [   ]   70 [   ]   80 [   ]   40 [   ]

Write the answer.

60 ÷ 10 = [   ]   80 ÷ 10 = [   ]   10 ÷ 10 = [   ]   40 ÷ 10 = [   ]

70 ÷ 10 = [   ]   20 ÷ 10 = [   ]   90 ÷ 10 = [   ]   50 ÷ 10 = [   ]

Divide each amount by 10.

120 ¢ [   ]   170 cm [   ]   200 mL [   ]   90 ¢ [   ]

250 cm [   ]   400 kg [   ]   110 m [   ]   30 litres [   ]

50 km [   ]   180 m [   ]   500 kg [   ]   230 g [   ]

Write the answer.

140 kg ÷ 10 = [   ]   70 ¢ ÷ 10 = [   ]   80 g ÷ 10 = [   ]

280 m ÷ 10 = [   ]   330 ¢ ÷ 10 = [   ]   560 m ÷ 10 = [   ]

400 kg ÷ 10 = [   ]   780 g ÷ 10 = [   ]   20 mL ÷ 10 = [   ]

Divide each number by 100.

400 [   ]   600 [   ]   800 [   ]   100 [   ]

Write the answers.

4500 ÷ 100 = [   ]   2800 ÷ 100 = [   ]   6400 ÷ 100 = [   ]

Write each row in order, beginning with the smallest number.

0.4	0.1	0.5	0.2	0.9	0.1	0.2	0.4	0.5	0.9
0.8	1.0	0.1	0.3	0.6					
2.3	1.3	2.1	3.1	3.2					

Write each row in order, beginning with the smallest value.

2.6 m	1.9 m	2.3 m	2.0 m	1.8 m					
12.8 kg	4.8 kg	20.0 kg	6.3 kg	9.7 kg					
5.2 g	2.5 g	5.0 g	2.0 g	2.2 g					

Write each row in order, beginning with the smallest number.

2.31	3.12	1.32	1.23	2.13					
8.75	7.85	7.58	8.57	5.78					
4.63	6.34	6.43	4.36	3.64					

Write each row in order, beginning with the smallest value.

4.72 km	7.05 km	6.31 km	4.02 km	8.13 km
12.45 cm	10.86 cm	14.64 cm	9.07 cm	11.64 cm
16.67 kg	15.67 kg	15.76 kg	17.56 kg	16.76 kg

Round each amount to the nearest 10.

46 [50]   59 [ ]   42 [ ]   85 [ ]   34 [ ]

9 [ ]   27 [ ]   91 [ ]   53 [ ]   88 [ ]

Round each amount to the nearest 100.

126 [ ]   141 [ ]   139 [ ]   184 [ ]   155 [ ]

212 [ ]   268 [ ]   193 [ ]   237 [ ]   165 [ ]

112 [ ]   350 [ ]   278 [ ]   490 [ ]   135 [ ]

466 [ ]   885 [ ]   327 [ ]   70 [ ]   751 [ ]

206 [ ]   650 [ ]   180 [ ]   263 [ ]   505 [ ]

Round each amount to the nearest whole number.

0.85 [ ]   1.34 [ ]   2.51 [ ]   2.02 [ ]   1.05 [ ]

3.56 [ ]   2.75 [ ]   4.19 [ ]   2.38 [ ]   4.52 [ ]

6.4 [ ]   8.3 [ ]   12.1 [ ]   8.2 [ ]   4.9 [ ]

6.5 [ ]   11.7 [ ]   3.6 [ ]   8.8 [ ]   10.5 [ ]

3.45 [ ]   2.06 [ ]   3.01 [ ]   4.08 [ ]   5.09 [ ]

Circle the larger number or amount each time.

(0.5) or 0.3   0.5 kg or 600 g $\frac{1}{2}$ or 0.3

1.2 or 2.1   70 cm or 0.5 m $2.40 or 189 ¢

5.6 m or 600 cm   0.3 or 0.4 $1.90 or $5.00

Circle the smaller number or amount each time.

0.8 or $\frac{1}{2}$ 3.5 m or 290 cm   4.2 or 2.4

3.5 or 5.3   625 cm or 6.2 m   130 g or 1.2 kg

3.5 litres or $3\frac{1}{3}$ litres $3.50 or 250 ¢   65 cm or 1 m

Circle the larger number or amount each time.

6 x 7 or 40   2 x 12 or 22   double 150 or 295

3.5 km or half of 5 km   3 x 8 or 6 x 3 $2.50 or 300 ¢

400 mL or 0.5 L   40 x 2 or 10 x 7   4 m or 54 cm

Circle the smaller number or amount each time.

6 kg or 53 g   6.72 or 6.27 $7.00 or 1000 ¢

12 km or half of 14 km   4.01 or 4.1   2 km or 1600 m

2.65 km or 2.56 km   7.54 m or 7.45 m   3.6 m or 400 cm

Circle the larger number each time.

10 x 11 or 12 x 10   8 x 7 or 6 x 9   7 x 4 or 6 x 5

4 x 11 or 6 x 7   6 x 4 or 9 x 3   11 x 3 or 9 x 8

5 x 8 or 7 x 5   6 x 6 or 8 x 4   10 x 5 or 5 x 5

These are the units we might use sometimes.
millimetres (mm), centimetres (cm), metres (m), grams (g), kilograms (kg), millilitres (mL), litres (L), kilometres (km)

Write the most sensible unit to measure each of these.

.... Metres ....

....

....

....

....

....

Write two things that you can measure with each unit.

metres (m)   Tree, wall ....   kilograms (kg)   ....

centimetres (cm)   ....   kilometres (km)   ....

grams (g)   ....   millilitres (mL)   ....

litres (L)   ....   millimetres (mm)   ....

What is half ($\frac{1}{2}$) of each amount? (US)

| $3.00 $1.50 | $5.00 | 6 kg | 3 g | 60 m |
| $1.20 | $1.50 | 12 mL | $2.50 | 6 m |

What is two-thirds ($\frac{2}{3}$) of each amount?

| 12 m | 21 kg | 15 g | $6.00 | 30 m |
| 18 g | $3.00 | 21 km | 24 kg | 15 m |

What is a quarter ($\frac{1}{4}$) of each amount?

| $1.00 | 60 cm | 2 m | 48 g | $4.00 |
| 120 cm | 80 g | 12 kg | 32 ¢ | 56 g |

What is one-fifth ($\frac{1}{5}$) of each amount?

| 20 ¢ | 50 ¢ | 10 ¢ | 25 cm | $20.00 |
| 60 cm | 10 m | 40 km | 35 g | 45 kg |

What is two-fifths ($\frac{2}{5}$) of each amount?

| 30 ¢ | $20.00 | 10 cm | 5 m | 20 mm |
| 40 ¢ | 50 g | 60 kg | 55 ¢ | 25 ¢ |

Fractions and decimals

Write each fraction as a decimal.

$\frac{1}{2}$ 0.5 $\frac{1}{4}$ ___ $\frac{1}{10}$ ___ $\frac{2}{10}$ ___

$\frac{3}{10}$ ___ $\frac{4}{10}$ ___ $\frac{1}{5}$ ___ $\frac{24}{100}$ ___

$\frac{5}{10}$ ___ $\frac{15}{100}$ ___ $\frac{6}{10}$ ___ $\frac{35}{100}$ ___

$\frac{7}{10}$ ___ $\frac{8}{10}$ ___ $\frac{50}{100}$ ___ $\frac{9}{10}$ ___

Write each decimal as a fraction in its simplest form.

0.2 ___   0.4 ___   0.6 ___   0.8 ___

0.5 ___   0.7 ___   0.25 ___   0.75 ___

0.1 ___   0.3 ___   0.9 ___   0.15 ___

How many tenths are equivalent to $\frac{20}{100}$? ___

How many hundredths are equivalent to $\frac{6}{10}$? ___

Which of these is the same as 20 305? Circle the correct answer.

Twenty thousand three hundred fifty   Twenty-three thousand five

Twenty thousand three hundred five   Twenty thousand thirty-five

---

Complete each sequence.

18	14						−10
−14	−9						21
12	10						−2

Write the answers.

$$45 \times 10$$ $$100 \times 27$$ $$100 \times 0.5$$ $$78 \times 100$$

Find the answer to each problem.

The temperature at the South Pole is −16°C and during a storm goes down by another 12°C. What is the temperature during the storm?

Peter has $36 and is given another $15 but then goes shopping and spends $25. How much does Peter have left after his shopping trip?

Place the amounts in order, starting with the smallest.

$6.50	560 ¢	$6.05	$65.00	680 ¢	$5.06

These are some of the ingredients for a cake.

Round each amount to the nearest whole gram.

14.2 g of salt ....

225.3 g of flour ....

130.4 g of cherries ....

90.7 g of almonds ....

A class usually has 33 children but two-thirds
are away on a trip.
How many children did not go on the trip?

How many tenths are equivalent to one half?

How many thirds are equivalent to one whole?

How many quarters are equivalent to 2?

Write each decimal as a fraction.

0.5 ——   0.2 ——   0.75 ——   0.9 ——

Write each fraction as a decimal.

$\frac{4}{10}$ $\frac{7}{10}$ $\frac{37}{100}$ $\frac{12}{100}$

⭐ Adding

Write the answers.

46 + 20 = 66   21 + 30 =   54 + 40 =   53 + 10 =

73 + 30 =   69 + 40 =   45 + 70 =   95 + 20 =

67 + 50 =   70 + 60 =   90 + 90 =   40 + 80 =

49 + 13 =   52 + 18 =   62 + 12 =   37 + 16 =

46 + 32 =   53 + 27 =   38 + 43 =   74 + 17 =

76 + 28 =   44 + 66 =   12 + 73 =   55 + 23 =

Write the answers.

| 73 | 56 | 39 | 52 | 51 |
| + 15 | + 17 | + 24 | + 38 | + 26 |

| 25 | 67 | 48 | 90 | 85 |
| + 45 | + 44 | + 28 | + 23 | + 17 |

Write the answers.

$8 + $80 + $4 = $45 + $25 + $15 =

60 cm + 6 cm + 12 cm =   12 ¢ + 24 ¢ + 36 ¢ =

32 cm + 64 cm + 8 cm =   35 ¢ + 45 ¢ + 16 ¢ =

21 cm + 20 cm + 19 cm =   12 ¢ + 13 ¢ + 14 ¢ =

Write the answers.

40 – 12 = 28   50 – 17 =   60 – 11 =   80 – 19 =

90 – 18 =   30 – 10 =   100 – 15 =   60 – 45 =

26 – 14 =   39 – 16 =   42 – 11 =   63 – 22 =

76 – 34 =   96 – 45 =   54 – 40 =   59 – 28 =

46 – 17 =   52 – 16 =   73 – 19 =   25 – 17 =

34 – 18 =   48 – 29 =   40 – 26 =   81 – 44 =

Write the answers.

$$
\begin{array}{r} 35 \\ -12 \\ \hline \end{array}
\qquad
\begin{array}{r} 41 \\ -20 \\ \hline \end{array}
\qquad
\begin{array}{r} 57 \\ -25 \\ \hline \end{array}
\qquad
\begin{array}{r} 63 \\ -41 \\ \hline \end{array}
\qquad
\begin{array}{r} 44 \\ -34 \\ \hline \end{array}
$$

$$
\begin{array}{r} 27 \\ -19 \\ \hline \end{array}
\qquad
\begin{array}{r} 32 \\ -14 \\ \hline \end{array}
\qquad
\begin{array}{r} 54 \\ -26 \\ \hline \end{array}
\qquad
\begin{array}{r} 70 \\ -37 \\ \hline \end{array}
\qquad
\begin{array}{r} 36 \\ -17 \\ \hline \end{array}
$$

Write the answers.

47 cm – 34 cm =   59 ¢ – 28 ¢ =   70 m – 32 m =

$40 – $26 =   61 ¢ – 34 ¢ =   73 cm – 48 cm =

64 m – 49 m =   53 ¢ – 49 ¢ =   25 ¢ – 24 ¢ =

21 ¢ – 17 ¢ =   41 ¢ – 38 ¢ = $98 – $45 =

Circle the multiples of 9.

4   19   29   (18)

39   36   27

90   108

Circle the multiples of 8.

8   26   16   34

32   55   54

64   50

Circle the multiples of 7.

21   24   35   37

42   46   70

14   39

Circle the numbers that are multiples of both 7 and 9.

35   36   49   42

28   56   63

45   42

Circle the numbers that are multiples of both 6 and 8.

12   18   24   40

8   48   60

80   96

Circle the numbers that are multiples of both 4 and 8.

4   8   12   36

20   24   30

40   48

Circle the numbers that are multiples of both 5 and 10.

5   10   15   40

30   35   25

55   60

Circle the numbers that are multiples of both 4 and 6.

4   6   12   8

20   32   24

48   22

Factors are numbers that divide exactly into another number.
For example, factors of 6 are 1, 2, 3, and 6.

Write the factors of each number.

4 1, 2, and 4 ....   5 ....   6 ....

7 ....   8 ....   9 ....

10 ....   12 ....   14 ....

15 ....   16 ....   17 ....

26 ....   21 ....   22 ....

23 ....   27 ....   25 ....

20 ....   24 ....

36 ....   28 ....

30 ....   32 ....

Of which number are these factors?

(1, 3, 9)   (1, 3, 5, 15)   (1, 2, 4, 8)

What do you notice about the factors of these numbers?	What do you notice about the factors of these numbers?
4 9 16 25 36	3 5 7 11 13
49 81 64 100	17 19 23 29
....	....

Can you be correct and quick?

Write the answers.

3 x 6 = 18	4 x 7 =	3 x 8 =	4 x 9 =
10 x 6 =	7 x 7 =	1 x 8 =	0 x 9 =
6 x 0 =	7 x 10 =	8 x 8 =	7 x 9 =
0 x 6 =	5 x 9 =	8 x 9 =	9 x 0 =
6 x 9 =	7 x 8 =	6 x 8 =	9 x 5 =
6 x 4 =	7 x 6 =	8 x 0 =	9 x 9 =
1 x 6 =	1 x 7 =	5 x 8 =	9 x 6 =
2 x 6 =	0 x 7 =	8 x 4 =	2 x 9 =
6 x 6 =	7 x 5 =	8 x 7 =	9 x 8 =
5 x 6 =	2 x 7 =	2 x 8 =	3 x 9 =
8 x 6 =	3 x 7 =	10 x 8 =	5 x 0 =
6 x 7 =	7 x 9 =	8 x 5 =	9 x 10 =

Write the answers.

3 x 5 =	1 x 5 =	0 x 5 =	5 x 3 =
10 x 5 =	6 x 5 =	2 x 5 =	8 x 5 =
5 x 5 =	5 x 9 =	5 x 4 =	5 x 7 =

Write the answers.

35 x 3 = 105   42 x 3 =   38 x 5 =   74 x 3 =

69 x 2 =   71 x 3 =   56 x 4 =   73 x 3 =

67 x 4 =   58 x 2 =   14 x 6 =   23 x 6 =

44 x 3 =   52 x 6 =   46 x 3 =   32 x 4 =

Write the answers.

29	36	45	54	62
x 3	x 4	x 5	x 6	x 7

71	86	93	73	64
x 4	x 3	x 4	x 5	x 2

59	43	23	38	40
x 4	x 5	x 6	x 4	x 6

56	63	76	41	67
x 3	x 4	x 2	x 5	x 7

78	89	37	48	59
x 8	x 10	x 5	x 6	x 7

★ Dividing with remainders

Write the answers. Some of these answers may have remainders.

27 ÷ 4 = 6 r3   24 ÷ 4 =   47 ÷ 4 =   44 ÷ 4 =

29 ÷ 3 =   14 ÷ 3 =   17 ÷ 3 =   21 ÷ 3 =

12 ÷ 7 =   56 ÷ 7 =   77 ÷ 7 =   23 ÷ 7 =

15 ÷ 5 =   6 ÷ 5 =   12 ÷ 5 =   34 ÷ 5 =

10 ÷ 8 =   57 ÷ 8 =   84 ÷ 8 =   24 ÷ 8 =

48 ÷ 6 =   38 ÷ 6 =   44 ÷ 6 =   19 ÷ 6 =

90 ÷ 9 =   52 ÷ 9 =   70 ÷ 9 =   40 ÷ 9 =

70 ÷ 10 =   100 ÷ 10 =   130 ÷ 10 =   26 ÷ 10 =

44 ÷ 11 =   120 ÷ 11 =   82 ÷ 11 =   211 ÷ 11 =

Write the answers.

$$2 \overline{)\ 19}\quad \begin{array}{r} 9\ r1 \\ -18 \\ \hline 1 \end{array}$$

$2 \overline{)\ 23}$ $2 \overline{)\ 41}$ $2 \overline{)\ 30}$ $2 \overline{)\ 26}$

$3 \overline{)\ 32}$ $3 \overline{)\ 41}$ $3 \overline{)\ 13}$ $3 \overline{)\ 17}$ $3 \overline{)\ 21}$

Write the answers. Some of these answers may have remainders.

$$6$$
$$8\,)\,\overline{48}$$
$$-\,48$$
$$\overline{0}$$

$$9\,)\,\overline{57}$$

$$6\,)\,\overline{32}$$

$$11\,)\,\overline{77}$$

$$10\,)\,\overline{90}$$

$$4\,)\,\overline{41}$$

$$4\,)\,\overline{5}$$

$$7\,)\,\overline{56}$$

$$5\,)\,\overline{27}$$

$$7\,)\,\overline{32}$$

Write the answers.

$18 \div 3 =$ $26 \div 9 =$ $53 \div 2 =$ $76 \div 10 =$

$49 \div 7 =$ $41 \div 10 =$ $14 \div 8 =$ $75 \div 6 =$

$69 \div 7 =$ $37 \div 8 =$ $7 \div 7 =$ $78 \div 11 =$

What is the remainder each time?

6 divided by 5   28 divided by 10   17 divided by 11

42 divided by 6   50 divided by 11   25 divided by 8

53 divided by 6   19 divided by 7   26 divided by 3

100 divided by 9   87 divided by 2   60 divided by 7

Choosing the operation

Which operation makes the number sentence correct?

14 ÷ 2 = 7   25 ▢ 2 = 27   32 ▢ 4 = 8

15 ▢ 3 = 45   2 ▢ 20 = 40   50 ▢ 10 = 60

12 ▢ 12 = 24   16 ▢ 2 = 32   40 ▢ 8 = 5

6 ▢ 2 = 12   6 ▢ 2 = 3   14 ▢ 7 = 2

40 ▢ 10 = 50   14 ▢ 5 = 9   12 ▢ 6 = 18

20 ▢ 2 = 10   36 ▢ 12 = 48   4 ▢ 5 = 20

7 ▢ 8 = 56   10 ▢ 10 = 1   34 ▢ 2 = 17

50 ▢ 10 = 60   56 ▢ 7 = 8   100 ▢ 60 = 40

40 ▢ 8 = 32   72 ▢ 2 = 74   30 ▢ 3 = 10

50 ▢ 20 = 30   2 ▢ 2 = 1   24 ▢ 6 = 4

42 ▢ 6 = 7   24 ▢ 12 = 2   32 ▢ 20 = 12

1 ▢ 2 = 3   21 ▢ 3 = 63   12 ▢ 12 = 0

10 ▢ 5 = 15   16 ▢ 2 = 14   14 ▢ 3 = 42

60 ▢ 3 = 20   60 ▢ 10 = 6   35 ▢ 7 = 5

Use the box for your working out if needed.

A package contains 12 chocolate cookies. Barbara buys four packages for a party. How many cookies will Barbara have?

48 cookies

```
  12
×  4
────
  48
```

Ann runs 2000 metres around the school field each day for five days. How far has Ann run in total over the five days?

Songs can be downloaded from a website for 50 ¢ each. Kenny has $1.70 to spend on downloads. How many songs can Kenny download and how much will he have left?

Harris shares 50 bananas equally between 8 monkeys and gives the remainder to a giraffe. How many bananas does the giraffe receive?

Mark has $20. He shares this with his two sisters and gives the remainder to charity. How much does Mark give to charity?

Children earn $15 a week delivering newspapers. Three children put their weekly earnings together. How much do the children have in total?

Write the answers.

30 ¢ + 50 ¢ = 80 ¢	25 ¢ + 35 ¢ =	50 ¢ + 70 ¢ =
15 ¢ + 25 ¢ =	12 ¢ + 17 ¢ =	23 ¢ + 40 ¢ =
42 ¢ + 13 ¢ =	60 ¢ + 29 ¢ =	32 ¢ + 17 ¢ =
18 ¢ + 23 ¢ =	54 ¢ + 17 ¢ =	45 ¢ + 18 ¢ =
34 ¢ + 26 ¢ =	52 ¢ + 18 ¢ =	67 ¢ + 16 ¢ =
25 ¢ + 27 ¢ =	48 ¢ + 56 ¢ =	72 ¢ + 19 ¢ =
60 ¢ – 15 ¢ =	70 ¢ – 50 ¢ =	85 ¢ – 35 ¢ =
40 ¢ – 12 ¢ =	32 ¢ – 11 ¢ =	50 ¢ – 27 ¢ =
75 ¢ – 32 ¢ =	56 ¢ – 19 ¢ =	95 ¢ – 65 ¢ =

Round to the nearest dollar.

$2.34	$15.25	$0.78
$1.50	$3.50	$5.01
$1.20	$1.80	$2.65
$0.37	$0.84	$6.20
$1.54	$2.60	$4.50
$4.65	$1.90	$2.30
$18.00	$12.00	$17.42

Use the box for working out if you need to.

John earns $12 a week gardening for a neighbour.
He works for six weeks. How much has John earned
in the six weeks?

$72

```
  12
 ×6
 ──
  72
```

Jo has saved $15 to spend on her vacation.
Her vacation will last two weeks. How much
will Jo spend each week if she spends the
same amount each week?

Yasir saves 25 ¢ coins to spend on
toys. He has saved twenty 25 ¢ coins.
How much has Yasir saved?

It costs Esther $5.50 a week to buy
food for her dog. How much will
the dog's food cost in total for
eight weeks?

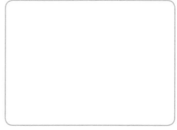

Konrad is given $10 to spend at a fair
and actually spends $8.45. How much
does Konrad have left?

Mirka saves $6 a month for a new
mp3 player. How much will Mirka
have saved after one year?

Units of measurement

Write each length in metres.

8 km 8000 m	15 km	60 km	100 km
2.5 km	1.34 km	6.13 km	12.7 km
7.056 km	1.008 km	5.030 km	8.44 km

Write each length in centimetres.

2 m	12 m	50 m	9.2 m
2.1 m	5.5 m	4.85 m	1.94 m
9.06 m	6.04 m	0.65 m	2.07 m

Write each weight in grams.

7 kg	18 kg	23 kg	2.1 kg
8.4 kg	12.7 kg	3.9 kg	5.98 kg
9.56 kg	2.06 kg	1.08 kg	0.67 kg

Write each weight in kilograms.

50 g	180 g	4 g	39 g
546 g	3005 g	14 000 g	20 000 g
1500 g	700 g	7905 g	3456 g

Write each amount in litres.

900 mL	100 mL	2450 mL	4780 mL

Use the box for your working out.

The workmen have laid 562 m of blacktop for a new path. The path has to be 640 m long. How much further do the workmen need to go? **78 m**

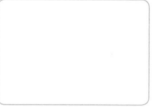
```
  640
 -562
 ----
   78
```

 Eleanor has to put 20 litres of orange juice into 40 glasses. How much should Eleanor put in each glass?

Matt needs 450 grams of flour for a cake recipe but only has 400 grams. How much more flour does Matt need?

Richard has to cut a length of wood to be exactly 53 centimetres long. He begins with a piece of wood 60 centimetres long. How much wood does Richard need to cut off?

A large parcel weighs 8 kg. Parcels cost $1.30 per kg to post. How much will the parcel cost to post?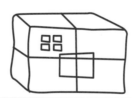

A family travels by car from Matheson City to Elliot Lake. The distance between the cities is about 136 kilometres. After 72 kilometres, the car runs out of gas. How much farther is there still to go?

 A tortoise can travel 25 centimetres in 5 minutes. If the tortoise can keep up the same speed, how far will it travel in one hour?

Three children put their money together to buy some flowers.

$2.55 $1.80 $3.20

How much money do they have in total to spend on flowers?

A family drives to Kelowna on vacation. The journey is 285 kilometres. After 192 kilometres, they stop for a break. How much further does the family have to travel?

A teacher gives a test with 25 questions to a class of 9 children. How many total questions will the teacher have to mark?

In a raffle, only tickets with numbers that were multiples of 9 won a prize. Circle the tickets that won a prize.

12   57   180   27   100

15   13   24

96   90   18   44

Write all the factors of each number.

45 ....   36 ....

A builder puts bricks in piles of 12. A load of 100 bricks is delivered. How many piles will the builder make and how many bricks will be left over?

Complete each problem, by filling in the missing operation.

7 ☐ 5 = 35   20 ☐ 4 = 5   16 ☐ 4 = 20

4 ☐ 3 ☐ 2 = 14   10 ☐ 2 ☐ 3 = 8   36 ☐ 4 ☐ 1 = 10

Darius works filling shelves in a supermarket. He is paid $7.85 per hour and works for eight hours a day. How much will Darius earn each day?

In a sponsored bike ride, each rider is sponsored $1 per kilometre. These are the distances three riders cycled.

27 kilometres   23.4 kilometres   9.6 kilometres

How much did each rider raise on the cycle ride?

Change each length to millimetres.

3 cm ☐   40 cm ☐   4.2 cm ☐   7.5 cm ☐

Look at this train timetable.

Southport	8:42	9:05	9:14	9:45	10:02	10:24
Westham	9:02	9:25	9:34	10:05	10:22	10:44
Northdon	9:27	9:50	9:59	10:30	10:47	11:09
Eastpool	10:15	10:38	10:47	11:18	11:35	11:57

What time is the first train to leave Southport after 9:00?

9:05

What time does the 9:14 from Southport arrive at Eastpool?

How long does the journey between Westham and Northdon take?

If the train arrives at Northdon at 10:30, what time did it leave Southport?

How long is the journey from Southport to Eastpool?

If I miss the 9:02 from Westham, how long will I have to wait until the next train?

Which part of the journey between Southport and Eastpool takes 20 minutes?

....

What time does the train leaving Southport at 10:24 arrive at Northdon?

Darius and Amy go to the movie theatre to watch a movie. The movie begins at 7:15 and lasts two and a half hours. What time does the movie end?

9:45

It will take a delivery lady 55 minutes to go from the warehouse to a customer. The delivery has to be made by 10:00 a.m. What is the latest time the lady can leave the warehouse?

Each half of a soccer match lasts 45 minutes. The first half of a match had four minutes added for injuries. The second half had 3 minutes added for injuries. How long was the match in total?

Barbara is going on a fast ferry. The journey takes 4 hours and 20 minutes. If the ferry leaves at 8:30 a.m., what time will it arrive?

Kasim is very fussy about how long to boil his egg. He likes his egg boiled for exactly 210 seconds. How long is 210 seconds in minutes and seconds?

In the morning, Olly wakes up at 8:00 a.m. He spends 8 minutes getting dressed, 20 minutes having breakfast, 5 minutes washing and cleaning his teeth, and he is then ready to go to school. At what time is Olly ready to go to school?

An exam is supposed to last one and a half hours but Clara finishes it with 12 minutes to spare. How long does Clara take to complete the exam?

★ Measuring weight

1000 grams (g) are the same as 1 kilogram (kg).

Write the answers.

4 kg = 4000 g   6 kg =   g   8 kg =   g

9 kg =   g   10 kg =   g   12 kg =   g

2000 g =   kg   3000 g =   kg   5000 g =   kg

1000 g =   kg   7000 g =   kg   10 000 g =   kg

Match the object to its weight. Draw a line.

20 mg

200 g

3 kg

Match the object to its weight. Draw a line.

120 g

1 kg

15 g

What amount is shown on these measuring cups?

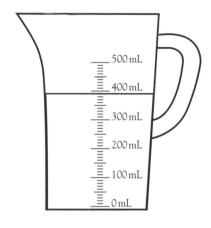

390 mL

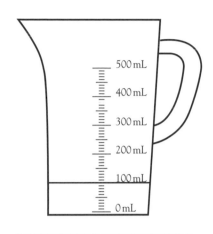

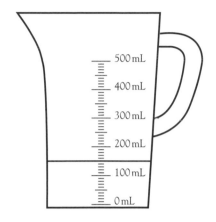

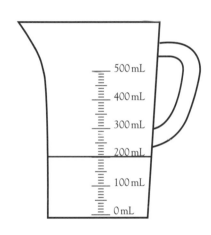

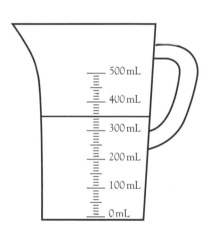

This measuring cup holds 500 millilitres (mL) of water. How many cups will be needed to fill a bowl that can take the following amounts?

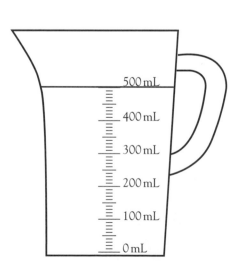

5 litres

10 litres

15 litres

Grade 4 children were asked about the foreign language they would like to study. Look at the bar graph and then answer the questions.

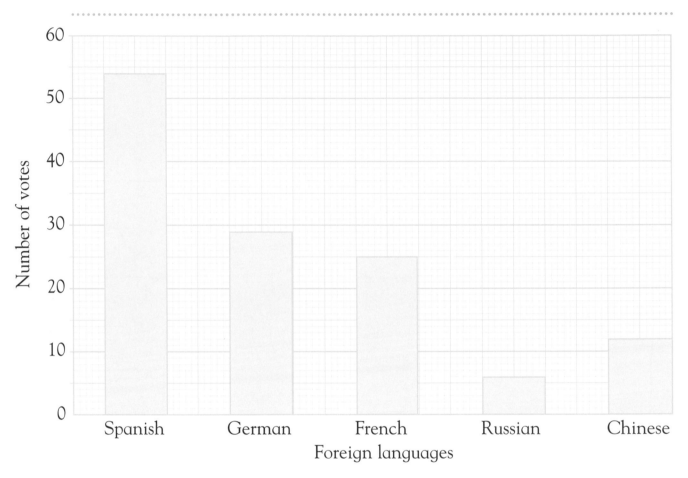

The chart does not have a title—write a title for the chart.

Write inside each bar the number of children who voted for the language.

What was the total number of children asked?

Which languages have less than 20 votes?

Which was the most popular language to learn?

Which was the least popular language to learn?

The school decided not to teach Russian and these children were taught French instead. How many children will now study French?

David is going to record his test scores over one term. These are David's scores out of 20.

Week	1	2	3	4	5	6	7	8	9	10	11	12
Score	12	7	13	12	11	14	14	16	13	17	18	20

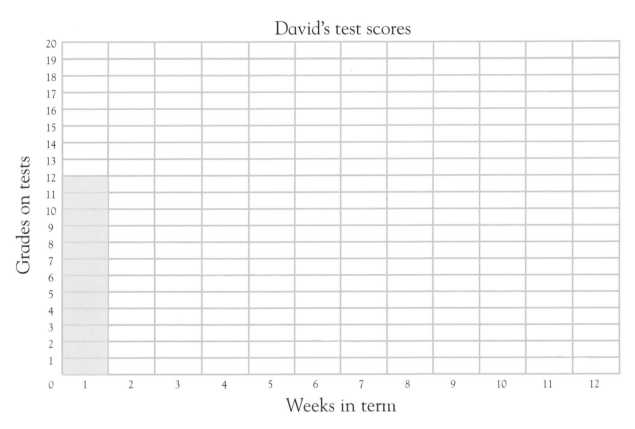

Show David's scores on the graph paper. Use crayons.

What was David's lowest score?

What was David's highest score?

By how many points did David improve
from week 1 to week 12?

By how many points did David's
score rise from week 5 to week 6?

In which weeks did David's score
remain the same?

Between which weeks did David
make the most improvement?

What is the perimeter of each shape?

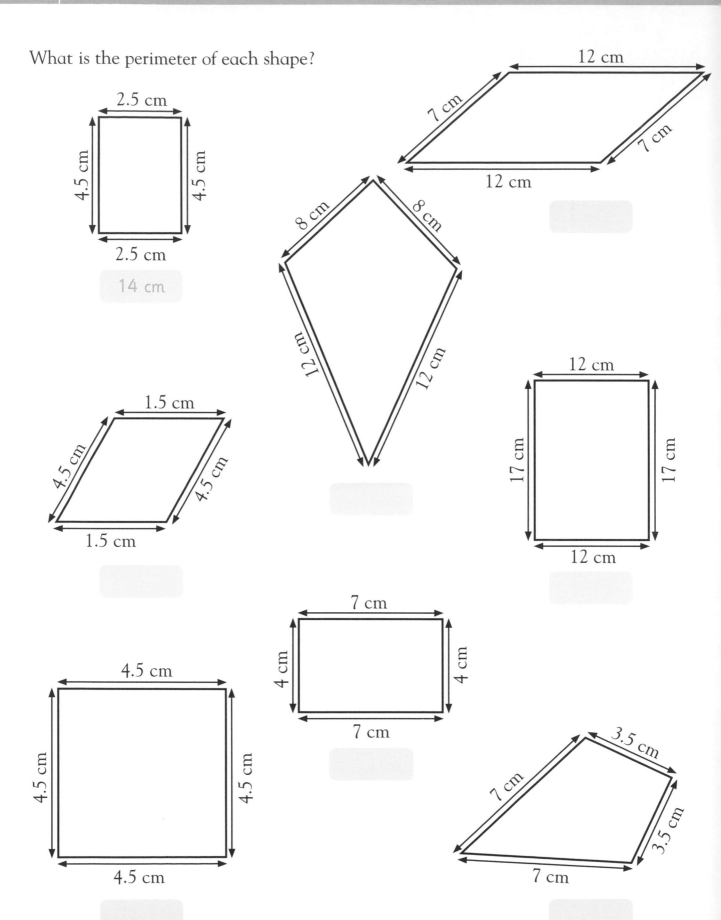

2.5 cm

4.5 cm   4.5 cm

2.5 cm

14 cm

12 cm

7 cm   7 cm

12 cm

8 cm   8 cm

12 cm   12 cm

1.5 cm

4.5 cm   4.5 cm

1.5 cm

12 cm

17 cm   17 cm

12 cm

4.5 cm

4.5 cm   4.5 cm

4.5 cm

7 cm

4 cm   4 cm

7 cm

3.5 cm

7 cm

3.5 cm

7 cm

Is the dotted line a line of symmetry?

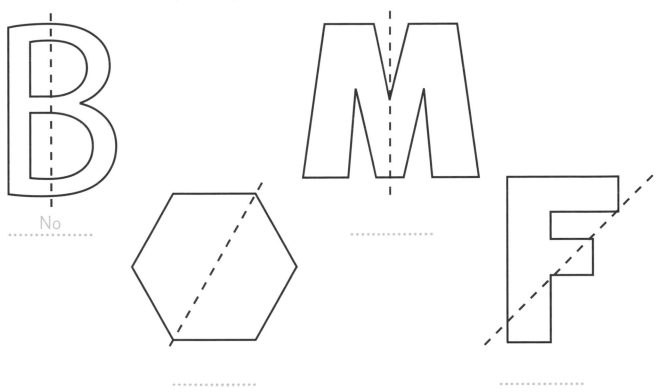

No

....

....

....

....

Complete each drawing.

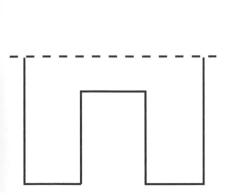

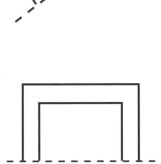

Use a protractor to carefully measure each angle.

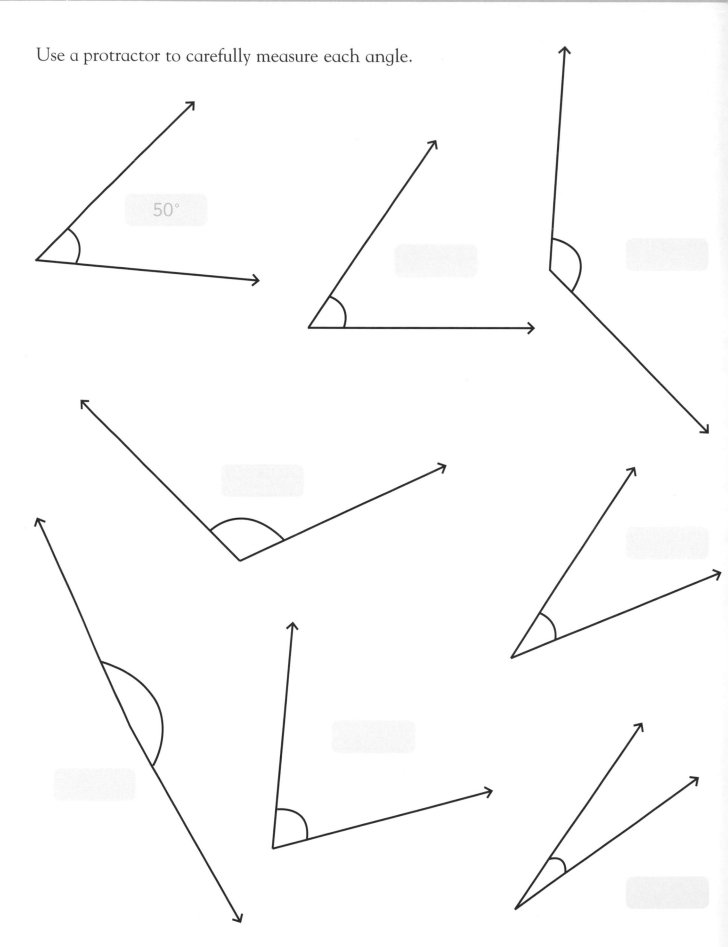

50°

Use a protractor to measure more angles.

Now use your protractor to draw these same angles.

Look at the shapes. Name two differences between a square and a rectangle.

Look at the shapes. Name two differences between a rectangle and a trapezoid.

Look at the shapes. Name two similarities between a rhombus and a square.

Look at the shapes. Name two similarities between a rectangle and a parallelogram.

Properties of 3-D shapes

Look at the shapes.

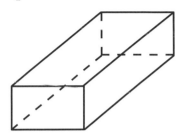

Name of shape   Rectangular prism

Number of faces   6

Number of edges   12

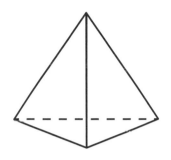

Name of shape

Number of faces

Number of edges

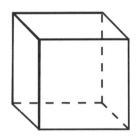

Name of shape

Number of faces

Number of edges

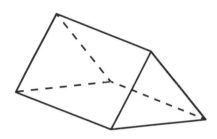

Name of shape

Number of faces

Number of edges

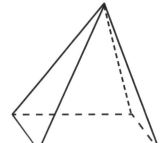

Name of shape

Number of faces

Number of edges

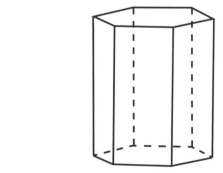

Name of shape

Number of faces

Number of edges

Barbara finds out her rail journey will take 3 hours 25 minutes. If Barbara's train journey begins at 9:42 a.m., what time will it end?

A playing field is 320 m long and 250 m across. What is the perimeter of the field?

Ann runs these distances to get fitter.

1300 m   2000 m   2300 m   3600 m

What is Ann's mean (average) distance?

Give the remainder each time.

20 divided by 3   14 divided by 5   13 divided by 6

24 ÷ 4 =   30 ÷ 4 =   17 ÷ 2 =

How many edges does a triangular prism have?

What shape am I?

I am a quadrilateral.

I have opposite sides parallel.

Only the opposite angles are equal.

A bricklayer builds a wall around a garden. This is a plan of the garden.

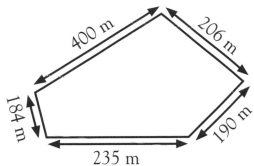

What is the perimeter of the wall that has been built?

A flat piece of rectangular plastic has a square hole cut out.

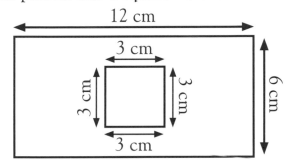

What is the perimeter of the rectangle?

What is the perimeter of the square?

Draw an angle of 65°.

Measure and write down the size of each angle in this triangle.

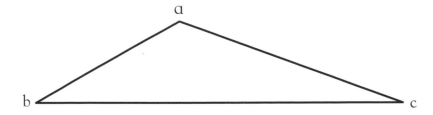

a.

b.

c.

Certificate

Congratulations to

....

for successfully finishing this book.

Grade **4**

WELL DONE!

You're a star.

Date

....

Answer Section with Parents' Notes

Grade 4
ages 9–10
Workbook

This section provides answers to all the activities in the book. These pages will enable you to mark your children's work, or they can be used by your children if they prefer to do their own marking.

The notes for each page help to explain common errors and problems and, where appropriate, indicate the kind of practice needed to ensure that your children understand where and how they have made errors.

☆ Reading and writing numbers

4346 in words is	Four thousand three hundred forty-six
Two thousand five hundred two is	2502

Write each of these numbers in words.

6208	Six thousand two hundred eight
4543	Four thousand five hundred forty-three
701	Seven hundred one
8520	Eight thousand five hundred twenty

Write each of these in numbers.

Five hundred forty-two	542
Six thousand seven hundred eleven	6711
Eight thousand two hundred three	8203
Nine thousand four hundred four	9404

Write each of these numbers in words.

7012	Seven thousand twelve
2390	Two thousand three hundred ninety
8434	Eight thousand four hundred thirty-four
642	Six hundred forty-two

Write each of these in numbers.

Eight thousand two hundred fifty-one	8251
Two thousand four hundred four	2404
Seven thousand one hundred one	7101
Two thousand five	2005

Children may use zeros incorrectly in numbers. In word form, zeros are omitted, but children should take care to include them when writing numbers in standard form.

Multiplying and dividing by 10 ☆

Write the answer in the box.

26 x 10 = 260
40 ÷ 10 = 4

Write the answer in the box.

76 x 10 = 760	43 x 10 = 430	93 x 10 = 930
66 x 10 = 660	13 x 10 = 130	47 x 10 = 470
147 x 10 = 1470	936 x 10 = 9360	284 x 10 = 2840
364 x 10 = 3640	821 x 10 = 8210	473 x 10 = 4730

Write the answer in the box.

30 ÷ 10 = 3	20 ÷ 10 = 2	70 ÷ 10 = 7
60 ÷ 10 = 6	50 ÷ 10 = 5	580 ÷ 10 = 58
310 ÷ 10 = 31	270 ÷ 10 = 27	100 ÷ 10 = 10
540 ÷ 10 = 54	890 ÷ 10 = 89	710 ÷ 10 = 71

Write the number that has been multiplied by 10.

37 x 10 = 370	64 x 10 = 640	74 x 10 = 740
81 x 10 = 810	10 x 10 = 100	83 x 10 = 830
714 x 10 = 7140	307 x 10 = 3070	529 x 10 = 5290
264 x 10 = 2640	829 x 10 = 8290	648 x 10 = 6480

Write the number that has been divided by 10.

30 ÷ 10 = 3	20 ÷ 10 = 2	90 ÷ 10 = 9
420 ÷ 10 = 42	930 ÷ 10 = 93	740 ÷ 10 = 74
570 ÷ 10 = 57	380 ÷ 10 = 38	860 ÷ 10 = 86

Children should realize that multiplying a whole number by 10 means writing a zero at the end of it. To divide a multiple of 10 by 10, simply take the final zero off the number. The two final sections can be solved by using the inverse operation.

☆ Ordering sets of large numbers

Write these numbers in order, from least to greatest.

2322	526	404	32	1240	440
32	404	440	526	1240	2322

Write the numbers in each row in order, from least to greatest.

420	190	950	402	905	986
190	402	420	905	950	986
308	640	380	805	364	910
308	364	380	640	805	910
260	350	26	1000	620	100
26	100	260	350	620	1000
500	820	2500	600	560	5000
500	560	600	820	2500	5000

Write the numbers in each row in order, from least to greatest.

4000	40 000	8900	8240	7560	5600
4000	5600	7560	8240	8900	40 000
1550	5000	50 000	4500	1500	3150
1500	1550	3150	4500	5000	50 000
100	70 100	7 100 000	710	710 000	7100
100	710	7100	70 100	710 000	7 100 000

TOWN A Population 550	TOWN B Population 8550	TOWN C Population 5420	TOWN D Population 50 042

Which town has:

The largest population? Town D

The second-smallest population? Town C

The second-largest population? Town B

Some children may need help to identify the value of the significant digit of each number in a set. If the numbers are close in value, it will be necessary to compare the digits to the right of the significant digit.

Rounding numbers

Round each number.

36 to the nearest ten	40
124 to the nearest hundred	100
4360 to the nearest thousand	4000

Remember: If a number is halfway between, round it up.

Round each number to the nearest ten.

24	20	91	90	55	60	73	70
57	60	68	70	49	50	35	40
82	80	37	40	22	20	52	50
46	50	26	30	85	90	99	100
43	40	51	50	78	80	29	30

Round each number to the nearest hundred.

386	400	224	200	825	800	460	500
539	500	429	400	378	400	937	900
772	800	255	300	549	500	612	600
116	100	750	800	618	600	990	1000
940	900	843	800	172	200	868	900

Round each number to the nearest thousand.

3240	3000	2500	3000	9940	10 000	1051	1000
8945	9000	5050	5000	5530	6000	4850	5000
6200	6000	7250	7000	8499	8000	8450	8000
12 501	13 000	8762	9000	6500	7000	3292	3000
1499	1000	14 836	15 000	10 650	11 000	11 241	11 000

Children may have difficulty with numbers that have final digits of 5 or greater—for example, they may round 429 to 500 rather than 400. Make sure children understand which digit determines how to round the number.

Identifying patterns

Continue each pattern.

Steps of 9:	5	14	23	32	41	50
Steps of 14:	20	34	48	62	76	90

Continue each pattern.

21	38	55	72	89	106	123	140
13	37	61	85	109	133	157	181
7	25	43	61	79	97	115	133
32	48	64	80	96	112	128	144
12	31	50	69	88	107	126	145
32	54	76	98	120	142	164	186
24	64	104	144	184	224	264	304
4	34	64	94	124	154	184	214
36	126	216	306	396	486	576	666
12	72	132	192	252	312	372	432
25	45	65	85	105	125	145	165
22	72	122	172	222	272	322	372
25	100	175	250	325	400	475	550
60	165	270	375	480	585	690	795
8	107	206	305	404	503	602	701
10	61	112	163	214	265	316	367
26	127	228	329	430	531	632	733
48	100	152	204	256	308	360	412

Children should determine what number to add to the first number to make the second number, and double-check that adding the same number turns the second number into the third. They can then repeat the operation to continue the pattern.

Recognizing multiples of 6, 7, and 8

Circle the multiples of 6.

8 (12) 15 (18) 20 (24)

Circle the multiples of 6.

8	22	14	(18)	(36)	40
16	38	44	25	(30)	(60)
(6)	21	19	(54)	56	(24)
(12)	(48)	10	20	35	26
(42)	39	23	28	(36)	32

Circle the multiples of 7.

(7)	17	24	59	(42)	55
15	20	(21)	46	12	(70)
(14)	27	69	36	47	(49)
65	19	57	(28)	38	(63)
33	34	(35)	37	60	(56)

Circle the multiples of 8.

(40)	26	15	25	38	(56)
26	(8)	73	41	(64)	12
75	58	62	(24)	31	(72)
12	(80)	(32)	46	38	78
(16)	42	66	28	(48)	68

Circle the number that is a multiple of 6 and 7.

18 54 (42) 21 28 63

Circle the numbers that are multiples of 6 and 8.

16 (24) 36 (48) 54 42

Circle the number that is a multiple of 7 and 8.

24 32 40 28 42 (56)

Success on this page will basically depend on a knowledge of multiplication tables. Where children experience difficulty, multiplication table practice should be encouraged.

Factors of numbers from 1 to 30

The factors of 10 are	1 2 5 10
Circle the factors of 4.	(1) (2) 3 (4)

Write all the factors of each number.

The factors of 26 are	1, 2, 13, 26
The factors of 30 are	1, 2, 3, 5, 6, 10, 15, 30
The factors of 9 are	1, 3, 9
The factors of 12 are	1, 2, 3, 4, 6, 12
The factors of 15 are	1, 3, 5, 15
The factors of 22 are	1, 2, 11, 22
The factors of 20 are	1, 2, 4, 5, 10, 20
The factors of 21 are	1, 3, 7, 21
The factors of 24 are	1, 2, 3, 4, 6, 8, 12, 24

Circle all the factors of each number.

Which numbers are factors of 14? (1) (2) 3 5 (7) 9 12 (14)
Which numbers are factors of 13? (1) 2 3 4 5 6 7 8 9 10 11 (13)
Which numbers are factors of 7? (1) 2 3 4 5 6 (7)
Which numbers are factors of 11? (1) 2 3 4 5 6 7 8 9 10 (11)
Which numbers are factors of 6? (1) (2) (3) 4 5 (6)
Which numbers are factors of 8? (1) (2) 3 (4) 5 6 7 (8)
Which numbers are factors of 17? (1) 2 5 7 12 14 16 (17)
Which numbers are factors of 18? (1) (2) (3) 4 5 (6) 8 (9) 10 12 (18)

Some numbers only have factors of 1 and themselves. They are called prime numbers. Write down all the prime numbers that are less than 30 in the box.

2, 3, 5, 7, 11, 13, 17, 19, 23, 29

Encourage a systematic approach such as starting at 1 and working toward the number that is half of the number in question. Children often forget that 1 and the number itself are factors. You may need to point out that 1 is not a prime number.

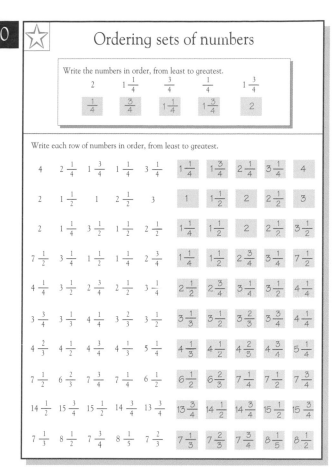
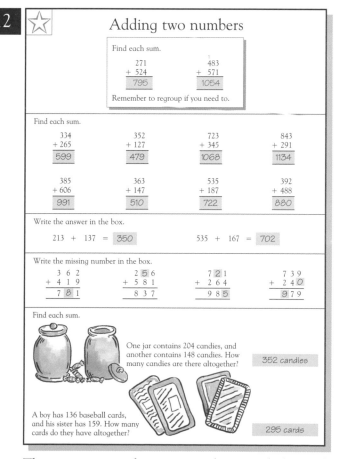

Recognizing equivalent fractions ☆

Make each pair of fractions equal by writing a number in the box.

$$\frac{1}{2} = \frac{2}{4} \qquad \frac{1}{3} = \frac{2}{6}$$

Make each pair of fractions equal by writing a number in the box.

$$\frac{1}{2} = \frac{5}{10} \qquad \frac{3}{4} = \frac{6}{8} \qquad \frac{1}{3} = \frac{3}{9}$$

$$\frac{2}{3} = \frac{8}{12} \qquad \frac{6}{12} = \frac{3}{6} \qquad \frac{4}{8} = \frac{1}{2}$$

$$\frac{1}{5} = \frac{2}{10} \qquad \frac{4}{12} = \frac{2}{6} \qquad \frac{3}{5} = \frac{6}{10}$$

$$\frac{1}{4} = \frac{2}{8} \qquad \frac{6}{18} = \frac{1}{3} \qquad \frac{3}{12} = \frac{1}{4}$$

$$\frac{3}{9} = \frac{1}{3} \qquad \frac{4}{10} = \frac{2}{5} \qquad \frac{3}{4} = \frac{9}{12}$$

$$\frac{4}{16} = \frac{1}{4} \qquad \frac{15}{20} = \frac{3}{4} \qquad \frac{6}{12} = \frac{1}{2}$$

$$\frac{3}{5} = \frac{6}{10} \qquad \frac{3}{6} = \frac{1}{2} \qquad \frac{9}{12} = \frac{3}{4}$$

Make each row of fractions equal by writing a number in each box.

$$\frac{1}{2} = \frac{2}{4} = \frac{3}{6} = \frac{4}{8} = \frac{5}{10} = \frac{6}{12}$$

$$\frac{1}{4} = \frac{2}{8} = \frac{3}{12} = \frac{4}{16} = \frac{5}{20} = \frac{6}{24}$$

$$\frac{3}{4} = \frac{6}{8} = \frac{9}{12} = \frac{12}{16} = \frac{15}{20} = \frac{18}{24}$$

$$\frac{1}{3} = \frac{2}{6} = \frac{3}{9} = \frac{4}{12} = \frac{5}{15} = \frac{12}{36}$$

$$\frac{1}{5} = \frac{2}{10} = \frac{3}{15} = \frac{4}{20} = \frac{5}{25} = \frac{6}{30}$$

$$\frac{2}{3} = \frac{4}{6} = \frac{6}{9} = \frac{8}{12} = \frac{10}{15} = \frac{14}{21}$$

If children have problems with this page, point out that fractions remain the same as long as you multiply the numerator and denominator by the same number, or divide the numerator and denominator by the same number.

☆ Ordering sets of numbers

Write the numbers in order, from least to greatest.

$$2 \qquad 1\frac{1}{4} \qquad \frac{3}{4} \qquad \frac{1}{4} \qquad 1\frac{3}{4}$$

$$\boxed{\frac{1}{4}} \quad \boxed{\frac{3}{4}} \quad \boxed{1\frac{1}{4}} \quad \boxed{1\frac{3}{4}} \quad \boxed{2}$$

Write each row of numbers in order, from least to greatest.

4	$2\frac{1}{4}$	$1\frac{3}{4}$	$1\frac{1}{4}$	$3\frac{1}{4}$	$1\frac{1}{4}$	$1\frac{3}{4}$	$2\frac{1}{4}$	$3\frac{1}{4}$	4
2	$1\frac{1}{2}$	1	$2\frac{1}{2}$	3	1	$1\frac{1}{2}$	2	$2\frac{1}{2}$	3
2	$1\frac{1}{4}$	$3\frac{1}{2}$	$1\frac{1}{2}$	$2\frac{1}{2}$	$1\frac{1}{4}$	$1\frac{1}{2}$	2	$2\frac{1}{2}$	$3\frac{1}{2}$
$7\frac{1}{2}$	$3\frac{1}{4}$	$1\frac{1}{2}$	$1\frac{1}{4}$	$2\frac{3}{4}$	$1\frac{1}{4}$	$1\frac{1}{2}$	$2\frac{3}{4}$	$3\frac{1}{4}$	$7\frac{1}{2}$
$4\frac{1}{4}$	$3\frac{1}{2}$	$2\frac{3}{4}$	$2\frac{1}{2}$	$3\frac{1}{4}$	$2\frac{1}{2}$	$2\frac{3}{4}$	$3\frac{1}{4}$	$3\frac{1}{2}$	$4\frac{1}{4}$
$3\frac{3}{4}$	$3\frac{1}{3}$	$4\frac{1}{4}$	$3\frac{2}{3}$	$3\frac{1}{2}$	$3\frac{1}{3}$	$3\frac{1}{2}$	$3\frac{2}{3}$	$3\frac{3}{4}$	$4\frac{1}{4}$
$4\frac{2}{3}$	$4\frac{1}{2}$	$4\frac{3}{4}$	$4\frac{1}{3}$	$5\frac{1}{4}$	$4\frac{1}{3}$	$4\frac{1}{2}$	$4\frac{2}{3}$	$4\frac{3}{4}$	$5\frac{1}{4}$
$7\frac{1}{2}$	$6\frac{2}{3}$	$7\frac{3}{4}$	$7\frac{1}{4}$	$6\frac{1}{2}$	$6\frac{1}{2}$	$6\frac{2}{3}$	$7\frac{1}{4}$	$7\frac{1}{2}$	$7\frac{3}{4}$
$14\frac{1}{2}$	$15\frac{3}{4}$	$15\frac{1}{2}$	$14\frac{3}{4}$	$13\frac{3}{4}$	$13\frac{3}{4}$	$14\frac{1}{2}$	$14\frac{3}{4}$	$15\frac{1}{2}$	$15\frac{3}{4}$
$7\frac{1}{3}$	$8\frac{1}{2}$	$7\frac{3}{4}$	$8\frac{1}{5}$	$7\frac{2}{3}$	$7\frac{1}{3}$	$7\frac{2}{3}$	$7\frac{3}{4}$	$8\frac{1}{5}$	$8\frac{1}{2}$

The most likely area of difficulty will be ordering fractions such as $\frac{3}{4}$ and $\frac{2}{3}$. If children experience difficulty, refer to the previous page or use two index cards, cut into quarters and into thirds, to allow comparison.

Rounding decimals ☆

Round each decimal to the nearest whole number.

3.4	3
5.7	6
4.5	5

If the whole number has 5 after it, round it to the whole number above.

Round each decimal to the nearest whole number.

6.2	6	2.5	3	1.5	2	3.8	4
5.5	6	2.8	3	3.2	3	8.5	9
5.4	5	7.9	8	3.7	4	2.3	2
1.1	1	8.6	9	8.3	8	9.2	9
4.7	5	6.3	6	7.3	7	8.7	9

Round each decimal to the nearest whole number.

14.4	14	42.3	42	74.1	74	59.7	60
29.9	30	32.6	33	63.5	64	96.4	96
18.2	18	37.5	38	39.6	40	76.3	76
40.1	40	28.7	29	26.9	27	12.5	13
29.5	30	38.5	39	87.2	87	41.6	42

Round each decimal to the nearest whole number.

137.6	138	423.5	424	426.2	426	111.8	112
641.6	642	333.5	334	805.2	805	246.8	247
119.5	120	799.6	800	562.3	562	410.2	410
682.4	682	759.6	760	531.5	532	829.9	830
743.4	743	831.1	831	276.7	277	649.3	649

If children experience difficulty, you might want to use a number line showing tenths. Errors often occur when a number with 9 in the ones column is rounded up. Children also often neglect to alter the tens digit in a number such as 19.7.

☆ Adding two numbers

Find each sum.

$$\begin{array}{r} 271 \\ + 524 \\ \hline 795 \end{array} \qquad \begin{array}{r} 483 \\ + 571 \\ \hline 1054 \end{array}$$

Remember to regroup if you need to.

Find each sum.

$$\begin{array}{r} 334 \\ + 265 \\ \hline 599 \end{array} \quad \begin{array}{r} 352 \\ + 127 \\ \hline 479 \end{array} \quad \begin{array}{r} 723 \\ + 345 \\ \hline 1068 \end{array} \quad \begin{array}{r} 843 \\ + 291 \\ \hline 1134 \end{array}$$

$$\begin{array}{r} 385 \\ + 606 \\ \hline 991 \end{array} \quad \begin{array}{r} 363 \\ + 147 \\ \hline 510 \end{array} \quad \begin{array}{r} 535 \\ + 187 \\ \hline 722 \end{array} \quad \begin{array}{r} 392 \\ + 488 \\ \hline 880 \end{array}$$

Write the answer in the box.

$$213 + 137 = 350 \qquad 535 + 167 = 702$$

Write the missing number in the box.

$$\begin{array}{r} 3\;6\;2 \\ + 4\;1\;9 \\ \hline 7\;8\;1 \end{array} \quad \begin{array}{r} 2\;5\;6 \\ + 5\;8\;1 \\ \hline 8\;3\;7 \end{array} \quad \begin{array}{r} 7\;2\;1 \\ + 2\;6\;4 \\ \hline 9\;8\;5 \end{array} \quad \begin{array}{r} 7\;3\;9 \\ + 2\;4\;0 \\ \hline 9\;7\;9 \end{array}$$

Find each sum.

One jar contains 204 candies, and another contains 148 candies. How many candies are there altogether?

352 candies

A boy has 136 baseball cards, and his sister has 159. How many cards do they have altogether?

295 cards

The questions on this page involve straightforward addition work. If children have difficulty with the horizontal sums, suggest that they rewrite them in vertical form. Some errors may result from neglecting to regroup.

Adding two numbers

Find each sum.

```
    4321         ¹ ¹
  + 2465        3794
  ------       + 5325
   6786        ------
                9119
```

Remember to carry if you need to.

Find each sum.

```
   2642          4325          2471
 + 3241        + 2653        + 4238
 ------        ------        ------
  5883          6978          6709

   3749          5764          8482
 + 2471        + 3915        + 1349
 ------        ------        ------
  6220          9679          9831
```

Write the answer in the box.

1342 + 1264 = 2606   2531 + 4236 = 6767

2013 + 3642 = 5655   1738 + 4261 = 5999

Write the missing number in the box.

```
   3 7 4 1        1 6 5 2        3 6 4 2
 + 2 9 4 3      + 3 2 7 4      + 4 8 3 1
 ---------      ---------      ---------
   6 6 8 4        4 9 2 6        8 4 7 3
```

Find each sum.

5621 people saw the local soccer team play on Saturday, and 3246 people watched the midweek match. How many people saw the soccer team play that week?

8867 people

6214 people went to the rock concert on Saturday night, and 3471 people went on Sunday night. How many people saw the rock concert that weekend?

9685 people

This page is similar to the previous page, with larger numbers. If children have difficulty with the section on missing numbers, have them try various digits until they find the correct one.

Subtracting three-digit numbers

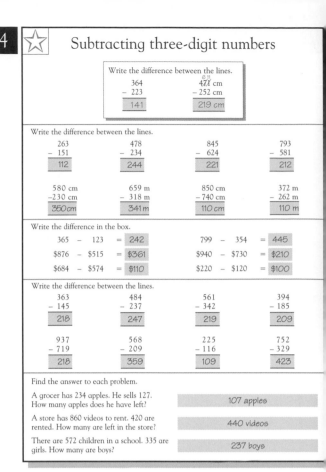

Write the difference between the lines.

```
                ⁶ ¹¹
    364         4̶7̶1̶ cm
  - 223        - 252 cm
  ------       --------
   141          219 cm
```

Write the difference between the lines.

```
    263          478          845          793
  - 151        - 234        - 624        - 581
  ------       ------       ------       ------
   112          244          221          212

    580 cm       659 m        850 cm       372 m
  - 230 cm     - 318 m      - 740 cm     - 262 m
  --------     ------       --------     ------
   350 cm       341 m        110 cm       110 m
```

Write the difference in the box.

365 - 123 = 242   799 - 354 = 445

$876 - $515 = $361 $940 - $730 = $210

$684 - $574 = $110 $220 - $120 = $100

Write the difference between the lines.

```
    363          484          561          394
  - 145        - 237        - 342        - 185
  ------       ------       ------       ------
   218          247          219          209

    937          568          225          752
  - 719        - 209        - 116        - 329
  ------       ------       ------       ------
   218          359          109          423
```

Find the answer to each problem.

A grocer has 234 apples. He sells 127. How many apples does he have left?

107 apples

A store has 860 videos to rent. 420 are rented. How many are left in the store?

440 videos

There are 572 children in a school. 335 are girls. How many are boys?

237 boys

In some of these problems, children may incorrectl subtract the smaller digit from the larger one, when they should be subtracting the larger digit from the smaller one. In such cases, point out that children should regroup.

Subtracting three-digit numbers

Write the difference between the lines.

```
    ³ ¹¹          ¹⁰
    4̶1̶5          6̶0̶ 1
                 7̶ 1̶ 1̶ m
  - 152        - 392 m
  ------       ------
   263          319 m
```

Write the difference between the lines.

```
    524 m        319 m        647 cm       915 cm
  - 263 m      - 137 m      - 456 cm     - 193 cm
  ------       ------       --------     --------
   261 m        182 m        191 cm       722 cm

    714          926          421          815
  - 407        - 827        - 355        - 786
  ------       ------       ------       ------
   307           99           66           29
```

Write the difference in the box.

512 - 304 = 208   648 - 239 = 409

831 - 642 = 189   377 - 198 = 179

Write the difference between the lines.

```
    423          615          312          924
  - 136        - 418        - 113        - 528
  ------       ------       ------       ------
   287          197          199          396
```

Write the missing number in the box.

```
   7 2 3        5 6 2        8 3 4        5 3 2
 - 1 2 8      - 3 1 7      - 2 5 7      - 1 8 5
 -------      -------      -------      -------
   5 9 5        2 4 5        5 7 7        3 4 7
```

Find the answer to each problem.

A theatre holds 645 people. 257 people buy tickets. How many seats are empty?

388 seats

There are 564 people in a park. 276 are boating on the lake. How many are taking part in other activities?

288 people

Some children may have difficulty with the section on missing numbers. Have them use trial and error until they find the correct number, or encourage them to use addition and subtraction fact families to find the number.

Adding decimals

Write the answer between the lines.

```
    $5.25          2.25 m
  + $2.40        + 3.50 m
  -------        --------
    $7.65          5.75 m
```

Write the answer between the lines.

```
    $2.25          $7.50          $3.35
  + $4.50        + $2.25        + $1.50
  -------        -------        -------
    $6.75          $9.75          $4.85

    $6.45          $3.15          $1.50
  + $2.35        + $4.75        + $3.95
  -------        -------        -------
    $8.80          $7.90          $5.45

   5.50 m         3.60 m         7.30 m
 + 2.35 m       + 4.15 m       + 1.65 m
 -------        -------        -------
   7.85 m         7.75 m         8.95 m

   6.15 m         3.30 m         5.20 m
 + 2.20 m       + 6.55 m       + 1.75 m
 -------        -------        -------
   8.35 m         9.85 m         6.95 m
```

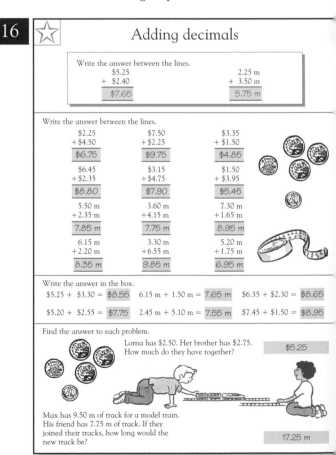

Write the answer in the box.

$5.25 + $3.30 = $8.55   6.15 m + 1.50 m = 7.65 m $6.35 + $2.30 = $8.65

$5.20 + $2.55 = $7.75   2.45 m + 5.10 m = 7.55 m $7.45 + $1.50 = $8.95

Find the answer to each problem.

Lorna has $2.50. Her brother has $2.75. How much do they have together?

$5.25

Max has 9.50 m of track for a model train. His friend has 7.75 m of track. If they joined their tracks, how long would the new track be?

17.25 m

Children may place the decimal point incorrectly in problems that are presented horizontally. Have them rewrite the problems in vertical form, lining up the decimal points. You may also need to remind children to regroup when necessary.

Adding decimals

Write the answer between the lines.

$3.35 + $5.55	3.45 m + 1.25 m
$8.90	4.70 m

Write the answer between the lines.

$3.60 + $2.25	$1.25 + $4.55	$7.45 + $2.35
$5.85	$5.80	$9.80
$3.60 + $3.25	$7.35 + $1.45	$5.25 + $2.65
$6.85	$8.80	$7.90
3.45 m + 4.35 m	8.55 m + 1.35 m	1.75 m + 5.20 m
7.80 m	9.90 m	6.95 m
2.40 m + 1.45 m	7.15 m + 1.35 m	3.85 m + 4.10 m
3.85 m	8.50 m	7.95 m

Write the answer in the box.

$2.75 + $4.15 = $6.90   3.75 m + 2.75 m = 6.50 m $3.65 + $1.50 = $5.15

$6.25 + $1.50 = $7.75   8.65 m + 2.55 m = 11.20 m $3.45 + $1.55 = $5.00

Work out the answer to each sum.

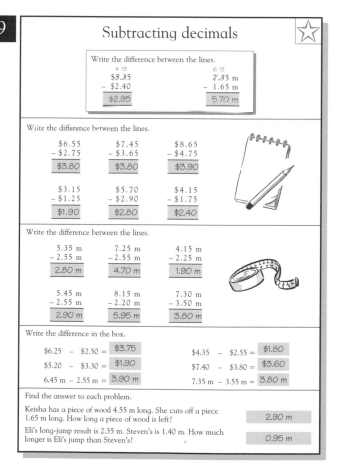

George buys two magazines that cost $2.55 and $1.75. How much does he spend? $4.30

Jennifer buys two rolls of tape. One is 7.75 m long, and the other is 6.75 m. How much tape does she have altogether?   14.5 m

You may wish to discuss with children that when the final decimal place of a sum is zero, it can be written, but it can also be omitted—unless the sum is an amount of dollars.

Subtracting decimals

Write the difference between the lines.

$6.55 − $3.20	4.70 m − 2.50 m
$3.35	2.20 m

Write the difference between the lines.

$7.45 − $3.30	$9.60 − $7.20	$5.55 − $2.40
$4.15	$2.40	$3.15
$8.35 − $3.25	$3.95 − $1.75	$6.55 − $2.40
$5.10	$2.20	$4.15

Write the difference between the lines.

3.90 m − 1.40 m	4.75 m − 3.35 m	9.20 m − 2.20 m
2.50 m	1.40 m	7.00 m
7.55 m − 1.15 m	2.15 m − 1.00 m	3.35 m − 2.20 m
6.40 m	1.15 m	1.15 m

Write the difference in the box.

$4.15 − $1.10 = $3.05 $3.55 − $2.50 = $1.05

$9.75 − $4.30 = $5.45 $8.85 − $6.05 = $2.80

7.55 m − 2.30 m = 5.25 m   6.15 m − 4.05 m = 2.10 m

Find the answer to each problem.

Mei-ling has $4.65 to spend. She buys a book for $3.45. How much money does she have left? $1.20

Shawn is given $9.50 for his birthday. If he spends $3.20 at the mall, how much money will he have left? $6.30

Some children are confused about subtracting decimals. Show them that once they line up the decimal points, they can simply subtract the digits, lining up the decimal point of the answer as well.

Subtracting decimals

Write the difference between the lines.

⁴ ¹³ $5.35 − $2.40	⁶ ¹³ 7.35 m − 1.65 m
$2.95	5.70 m

Write the difference between the lines.

$6.55 − $2.75	$7.45 − $3.65	$8.65 − $4.75
$3.80	$3.80	$3.90
$3.15 − $1.25	$5.70 − $2.90	$4.15 − $1.75
$1.90	$2.80	$2.40

Write the difference between the lines.

5.35 m − 2.55 m	7.25 m − 2.55 m	4.15 m − 2.25 m
2.80 m	4.70 m	1.90 m
5.45 m − 2.55 m	8.15 m − 2.20 m	7.30 m − 3.50 m
2.90 m	5.95 m	3.80 m

Write the difference in the box.

$6.25 − $2.50 = $3.75 $4.35 − $2.55 = $1.80

$5.20 − $3.30 = $1.90 $7.40 − $3.80 = $3.60

6.45 m − 2.55 m = 3.90 m   7.35 m − 3.55 m = 3.80 m

Find the answer to each problem.

Keisha has a piece of wood 4.55 m long. She cuts off a piece 1.65 m long. How long a piece of wood is left?   2.90 m

Eli's long-jump result is 2.35 m. Steven's is 1.40 m. How much longer is Eli's jump than Steven's?   0.95 m

This page follows from the previous page, but the subtraction involves regrouping. You may need to remind children that they can regroup across a decimal point in the same way as they would if the decimal point were not there.

Multiplying by one-digit numbers

Find each product.

32 × 2	26 × 3	34 × 4
64	78	136

Find each product.

27 × 2	32 × 3	16 × 4	19 × 2
54	96	64	38
22 × 3	25 × 4	18 × 6	33 × 5
66	100	108	165
39 × 2	26 × 2	41 × 2	38 × 3
78	52	82	114
29 × 3	45 × 2	28 × 3	16 × 6
87	90	84	96
10 × 5	40 × 2	20 × 4	50 × 3
50	80	80	150

Find the answer to each problem.

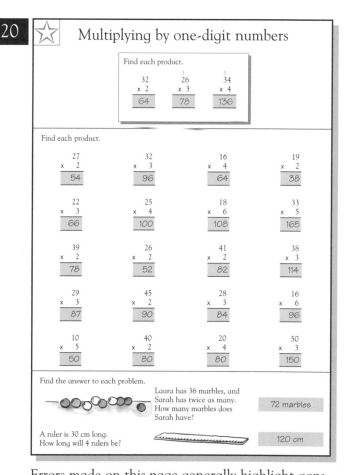

Laura has 36 marbles, and Sarah has twice as many. How many marbles does Sarah have?   72 marbles

A ruler is 30 cm long. How long will 4 rulers be?   120 cm

Errors made on this page generally highlight gaps in children's knowledge of the 2, 3, 4, 5 and 6 multiplication tables. Other errors can result from neglecting to regroup.

Multiplying by one-digit numbers

Find each product.

$$
\begin{array}{r} 53 \\ \times\ 3 \\ \hline 159 \end{array}
\qquad
\begin{array}{r} {\scriptstyle 3} \\ 76 \\ \times\ 6 \\ \hline 456 \end{array}
\qquad
\begin{array}{r} {\scriptstyle 3} \\ 25 \\ \times\ 7 \\ \hline 175 \end{array}
$$

Find each product.

56 × 8 = 448	48 × 5 = 240	46 × 7 = 322	32 × 6 = 192	36 × 9 = 324
45 × 4 = 180	33 × 6 = 198	73 × 5 = 365	96 × 3 = 288	58 × 7 = 406
81 × 3 = 243	24 × 9 = 216	19 × 8 = 152	64 × 4 = 256	52 × 6 = 312
37 × 7 = 259	40 × 8 = 320	50 × 3 = 150	30 × 7 = 210	20 × 9 = 180

Find the answer to each problem.

A school bus holds 36 children.
How many children can travel in
6 busloads?   216 children

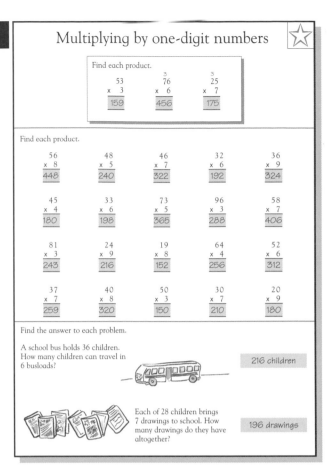

Each of 28 children brings
7 drawings to school. How
many drawings do they have
altogether?   196 drawings

Errors made on this page generally highlight gaps
in children's knowledge of the 6, 7, 8, and 9 times
tables. As on the previous page, errors may result
from neglecting to regroup.

Division with remainders

Find each quotient.

$$
\begin{array}{r} 5\ r\ 1 \\ 3\overline{)16} \\ \underline{15} \\ 1 \end{array}
\qquad
\begin{array}{r} 6\ r\ 2 \\ 4\overline{)26} \\ \underline{24} \\ 2 \end{array}
$$

Find each quotient.

17 r 1 — 2)35, 2, 15, 14, 1	11 r 2 — 4)46, 4, 6, 4, 2	7 r 1 — 3)22, 21, 1	9 r 4 — 5)49, 45, 4
14 r 2 — 4)58, 4, 18, 16, 2	12 r 3 — 5)63, 5, 13, 10, 3	7 r 2 — 5)37, 35, 2	12 r 2 — 4)50, 4, 10, 8, 2
25 r 1 — 3)76, 6, 16, 15, 1	14 r 3 — 4)59, 4, 19, 16, 3	18 r 4 — 5)94, 5, 44, 40, 4	16 r 3 — 5)83, 5, 33, 30, 3
49 r 1 — 2)99, 8, 19, 18, 1	18 r 3 — 4)75, 4, 35, 32, 3	15 r 2 — 5)77, 5, 27, 25, 2	18 r 1 — 2)37, 2, 17, 16, 1

Write the answer in the box.

What is 27 divided by 4?   6 r 3   Divide 78 by 5.   15 r 3

What is 46 divided by 3?   15 r 1   Divide 63 by 2.   31 r 1

Children may have difficulty finding quotients with
remainders. Have them perform long division until
the remaining value to be divided is less than the
divisor. That value is the remainder.

Division with remainders

Find each quotient.

$$
\begin{array}{r} 5\ r\ 4 \\ 6\overline{)34} \\ \underline{30} \\ 4 \end{array}
\qquad
\begin{array}{r} 7\ r\ 1 \\ 7\overline{)50} \\ \underline{49} \\ 1 \end{array}
$$

Find each quotient.

16 r 3 — 6)99, 6, 39, 36, 3	7 r 1 — 6)43, 42, 1	3 r 3 — 9)30, 27, 3	9 r 4 — 8)76, 72, 4
7 r 3 — 7)52, 49, 3	11 r 6 — 7)83, 7, 13, 7, 6	5 r 7 — 9)52, 45, 7	15 r 1 — 6)91, 6, 31, 30, 1
9 r 3 — 7)66, 63, 3	7 r 7 — 8)63, 56, 7	4 r 3 — 6)27, 24, 3	5 r 6 — 8)46, 40, 6
10 r 3 — 9)93, 9, 3	12 r 1 — 7)85, 7, 15, 14, 1	8 r 3 — 8)67, 64, 3	3 r 5 — 7)26, 21, 5

Write the answer in the box.

What is 87 divided by 7?   12 r 3   Divide 84 by 8.   10 r 4

What is 75 divided by 6?   12 r 3   Divide 73 by 9.   8 r 1

This page is similar to the previous page, but the
divisors are numbers greater than 5, so children
will need to know their times tables for numbers
greater than 5.

Real-life problems

Write the answer in the box.

Yasmin has $4.60 and she is given another $1.20.
How much money does she have?

$5.80

$$
\begin{array}{r} \$4.60 \\ +\ \$1.20 \\ \hline \$5.80 \end{array}
$$

David has 120 marbles.
He divides them equally among his 5 friends.
How many marbles
does each get?   24

$$
\begin{array}{r} 24 \\ 5\overline{)120} \\ \underline{10} \\ 20 \\ \underline{20} \\ 0 \end{array}
$$

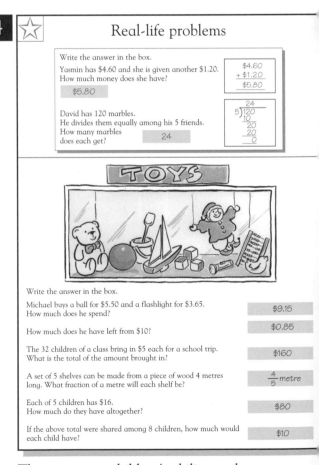

Write the answer in the box.

Michael buys a ball for $5.50 and a flashlight for $3.65.
How much does he spend? $9.15

How much does he have left from $10? $0.85

The 32 children of a class bring in $5 each for a school trip.
What is the total of the amount brought in? $160

A set of 5 shelves can be made from a piece of wood 4 metres
long. What fraction of a metre will each shelf be? $\frac{4}{5}$ metre

Each of 5 children has $16.
How much do they have altogether? $80

If the above total were shared among 8 children, how much would
each child have? $10

This page tests children's ability to choose
operations required to solve real-life problems,
mostly involving money. Discussing whether the
answer will be larger or smaller than the question
will help children decide what operation to use.

Real-life problems

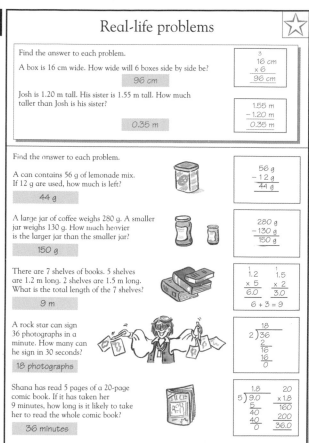

Find the answer to each problem.

A box is 16 cm wide. How wide will 6 boxes side by side be?

96 cm

$$\begin{array}{r} \overset{3}{16}\text{ cm} \\ \times\ 6 \\ \hline 96\text{ cm} \end{array}$$

Josh is 1.20 m tall. His sister is 1.55 m tall. How much taller than Josh is his sister?

0.35 m

$$\begin{array}{r} 1.55\text{ m} \\ -\ 1.20\text{ m} \\ \hline 0.35\text{ m} \end{array}$$

Find the answer to each problem.

A can contains 56 g of lemonade mix. If 12 g are used, how much is left?

44 g

$$\begin{array}{r} 56\text{ g} \\ -\ 12\text{ g} \\ \hline 44\text{ g} \end{array}$$

A large jar of coffee weighs 280 g. A smaller jar weighs 130 g. How much heavier is the larger jar than the smaller jar?

150 g

$$\begin{array}{r} 280\text{ g} \\ -\ 130\text{ g} \\ \hline 150\text{ g} \end{array}$$

There are 7 shelves of books. 5 shelves are 1.2 m long. 2 shelves are 1.5 m long. What is the total length of the 7 shelves?

9 m

$$\begin{array}{cc} 1.2 & 1.5 \\ \times\ 5 & \times\ 2 \\ \hline 6.0 & 3.0 \end{array}$$
$$6 + 3 = 9$$

A rock star can sign 36 photographs in a minute. How many can he sign in 30 seconds?

18 photographs

$$\begin{array}{r} 18 \\ 2\overline{)36} \\ \underline{2} \\ 16 \\ \underline{16} \\ 0 \end{array}$$

Shana has read 5 pages of a 20-page comic book. If it has taken her 9 minutes, how long is it likely to take her to read the whole comic book?

36 minutes

$$\begin{array}{cc} 1.8 & 20 \\ 5\overline{)9.0} & \times\ 1.8 \\ \underline{5} & \overline{160} \\ 40 & 200 \\ \underline{40} & \overline{36.0} \\ 0 \end{array}$$

This page continues with real-life problems, but with units other than money. To solve the third problem children must perform three operations.

Areas of rectangles and squares

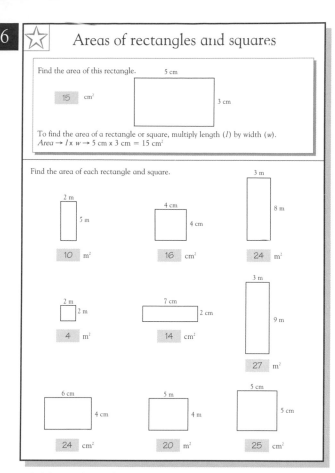

Find the area of this rectangle.

15 cm²

5 cm

3 cm

To find the area of a rectangle or square, multiply length (*l*) by width (*w*).
Area → *l* x *w* → 5 cm x 3 cm = 15 cm²

Find the area of each rectangle and square.

2 m / 5 m → **10** m²

4 cm / 4 cm → **16** cm²

3 m / 8 m → **24** m²

2 m / 2 m → **4** m²

7 cm / 2 cm → **14** cm²

3 m / 9 m → **27** m²

6 cm / 4 cm → **24** cm²

5 m / 4 m → **20** m²

5 cm / 5 cm → **25** cm²

Children should understand that area is measured in square units, such as cm². They will reach incorrect answers if they add sides instead of multiplying them, or try to find the area of a square by doubling the length of one side.

Problems involving time

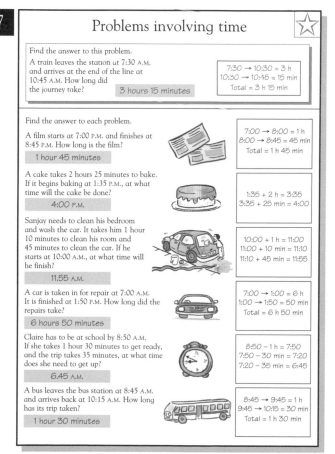

Find the answer to this problem.

A train leaves the station at 7:30 A.M. and arrives at the end of the line at 10:45 A.M. How long did the journey take?

3 hours 15 minutes

7:30 → 10:30 = 3 h
10:30 → 10:45 = 15 min
Total = 3 h 15 min

Find the answer to each problem.

A film starts at 7:00 P.M. and finishes at 8:45 P.M. How long is the film?

1 hour 45 minutes

7:00 → 8:00 = 1 h
8:00 → 8:45 = 45 min
Total = 1 h 45 min

A cake takes 2 hours 25 minutes to bake. If it begins baking at 1:35 P.M., at what time will the cake be done?

4:00 P.M.

1:35 + 2 h = 3:35
3:35 + 25 min = 4:00

Sanjay needs to clean his bedroom and wash the car. It takes him 1 hour 10 minutes to clean his room and 45 minutes to clean the car. If he starts at 10:00 A.M., at what time will he finish?

11.55 A.M.

10:00 + 1 h = 11:00
11:00 + 10 min = 11:10
11:10 + 45 min = 11:55

A car is taken in for repair at 7:00 A.M. It is finished at 1:50 P.M. How long did the repairs take?

6 hours 50 minutes

7:00 → 1:00 = 6 h
1:00 → 1:50 = 50 min
Total = 6 h 50 min

Claire has to be at school by 8:50 A.M. If she takes 1 hour 30 minutes to get ready, and the trip takes 35 minutes, at what time does she need to get up?

6.45 A.M.

8:50 − 1 h = 7:50
7:50 − 30 min = 7:20
7:20 − 35 min = 6:45

A bus leaves the bus station at 8:45 A.M. and arrives back at 10:15 A.M. How long has its trip taken?

1 hour 30 minutes

8:45 → 9:45 = 1 h
9:45 → 10:15 = 30 min
Total = 1 h 30 min

Children can reach the correct answers using a variety of methods. Sample methods are provided in the answers, but any method that children use to reach a correct answer is acceptable.

Bar graphs

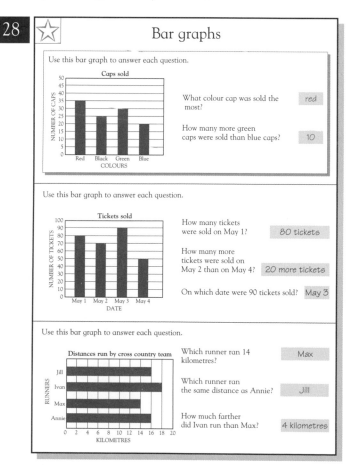

Use this bar graph to answer each question.

Caps sold

What colour cap was sold the most? **red**

How many more green caps were sold than blue caps? **10**

Use this bar graph to answer each question.

Tickets sold

How many tickets were sold on May 1? **80 tickets**

How many more tickets were sold on May 2 than on May 4? **20 more tickets**

On which date were 90 tickets sold? **May 3**

Use this bar graph to answer each question.

Distances run by cross country team

Which runner ran 14 kilometres? **Max**

Which runner ran the same distance as Annie? **Jill**

How much farther did Ivan run than Max? **4 kilometres**

This page requires children to read information, to look for specific information, and to manipulate the information they read on a bar graph. They may need to be reassured that horizontal bar graphs can be read in much the same way as vertical graphs.

Probability

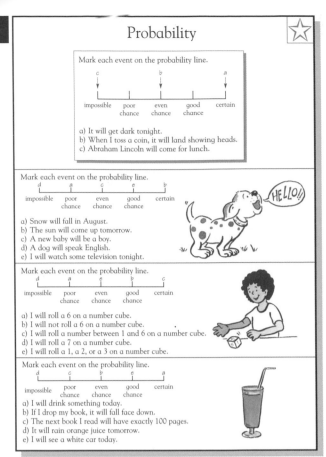

Mark each event on the probability line.

c → b → a →

impossible | poor chance | even chance | good chance | certain

a) It will get dark tonight.
b) When I toss a coin, it will land showing heads.
c) Abraham Lincoln will come for lunch.

Mark each event on the probability line.

d a c e b
impossible | poor chance | even chance | good chance | certain

a) Snow will fall in August.
b) The sun will come up tomorrow.
c) A new baby will be a boy.
d) A dog will speak English.
e) I will watch some television tonight.

HELLO!!

Mark each event on the probability line.

d a e b c
impossible | poor chance | even chance | good chance | certain

a) I will roll a 6 on a number cube.
b) I will not roll a 6 on a number cube.
c) I will roll a number between 1 and 6 on a number cube.
d) I will roll a 7 on a number cube.
e) I will roll a 1, a 2, or a 3 on a number cube.

Mark each event on the probability line.

d c b e a
impossible | poor chance | even chance | good chance | certain

a) I will drink something today.
b) If I drop my book, it will fall face down.
c) The next book I read will have exactly 100 pages.
d) It will rain orange juice tomorrow.
e) I will see a white car today.

In the first section, children should be able to identify events categorically. As the second section is based on mathematical probability, the answers are not subjective. There may be some discussion of answers for the third section.

Triangles

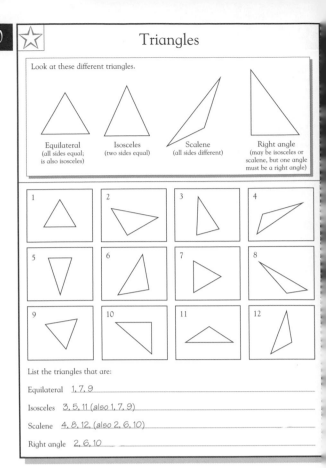

Look at these different triangles.

Equilateral (all sides equal; is also isosceles) | Isosceles (two sides equal) | Scalene (all sides different) | Right angle (may be isosceles or scalene, but one angle must be a right angle)

1 2 3 4
5 6 7 8
9 10 11 12

List the triangles that are:

Equilateral 1, 7, 9

Isosceles 3, 5, 11 (also 1, 7, 9)

Scalene 4, 8, 12, (also 2, 6, 10)

Right angle 2, 6, 10

This page will highlight any gaps in children's ability to recognize and name triangles. Make sure that children can identify triangles that have been rotated.

Expanded form

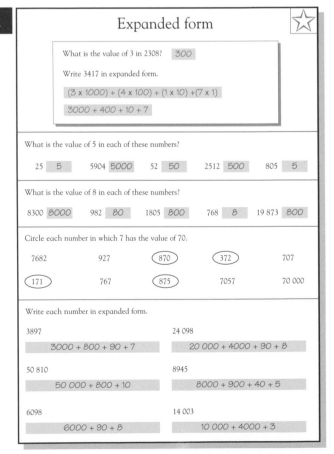

What is the value of 3 in 2308? 300

Write 3417 in expanded form.

(3 x 1000) + (4 x 100) + (1 x 10) + (7 x 1)

3000 + 400 + 10 + 7

What is the value of 5 in each of these numbers?

25 5   5904 5000   52 50   2512 500   805 5

What is the value of 8 in each of these numbers?

8300 8000   982 80   1805 800   768 8   19 873 800

Circle each number in which 7 has the value of 70.

7682   927   (870)   (372)   707

(171)   767   (875)   7057   70 000

Write each number in expanded form.

3897
3000 + 800 + 90 + 7

24 098
20 000 + 4000 + 90 + 8

50 810
50 000 + 800 + 10

8945
8000 + 900 + 40 + 5

6098
6000 + 90 + 8

14 003
10 000 + 4000 + 3

Errors may occur when children write numbers that include zeros in expanded form. When they work out the problems, they need not write 0 x 100 for a number such as 6098. However, for a number such as 50 815, they should write 50 x 1000.

Speed trials

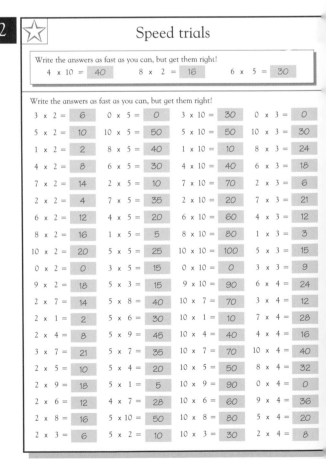

Write the answers as fast as you can, but get them right!

4 x 10 = 40   8 x 2 = 16   6 x 5 = 30

Write the answers as fast as you can, but get them right!

3 x 2 = 6	0 x 5 = 0	3 x 10 = 30	0 x 3 = 0
5 x 2 = 10	10 x 5 = 50	5 x 10 = 50	10 x 3 = 30
1 x 2 = 2	8 x 5 = 40	1 x 10 = 10	8 x 3 = 24
4 x 2 = 8	6 x 5 = 30	4 x 10 = 40	6 x 3 = 18
7 x 2 = 14	2 x 5 = 10	7 x 10 = 70	2 x 3 = 6
2 x 2 = 4	7 x 5 = 35	2 x 10 = 20	7 x 3 = 21
6 x 2 = 12	4 x 5 = 20	6 x 10 = 60	4 x 3 = 12
8 x 2 = 16	1 x 5 = 5	8 x 10 = 80	1 x 3 = 3
10 x 2 = 20	5 x 5 = 25	10 x 10 = 100	5 x 3 = 15
0 x 2 = 0	3 x 5 = 15	0 x 10 = 0	3 x 3 = 9
9 x 2 = 18	5 x 3 = 15	9 x 10 = 90	6 x 4 = 24
2 x 7 = 14	5 x 8 = 40	10 x 7 = 70	3 x 4 = 12
2 x 1 = 2	5 x 6 = 30	10 x 1 = 10	7 x 4 = 28
2 x 4 = 8	5 x 9 = 45	10 x 4 = 40	4 x 4 = 16
3 x 7 = 21	5 x 7 = 35	10 x 7 = 70	10 x 4 = 40
2 x 5 = 10	5 x 4 = 20	10 x 5 = 50	8 x 4 = 32
2 x 9 = 18	5 x 1 = 5	10 x 9 = 90	0 x 4 = 0
2 x 6 = 12	4 x 7 = 28	10 x 6 = 60	9 x 4 = 36
2 x 8 = 16	5 x 10 = 50	10 x 8 = 80	5 x 4 = 20
2 x 3 = 6	5 x 2 = 10	10 x 3 = 30	2 x 4 = 8

All the 3s

You will need to know these:

$1 \times 3 = 3$ $2 \times 3 = 6$ $3 \times 3 = 9$ $4 \times 3 = 12$ $5 \times 3 = 15$ $10 \times 3 = 30$

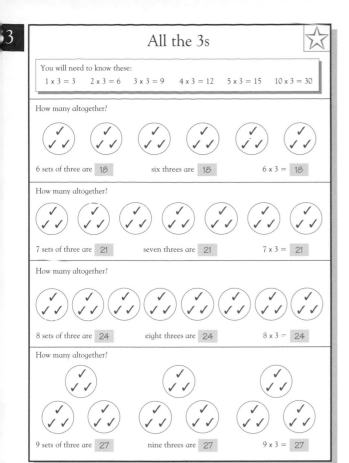

How many altogether?

6 sets of three are 18   six threes are 18 $6 \times 3 =$ 18

How many altogether?

7 sets of three are 21   seven threes are 21 $7 \times 3 =$ 21

How many altogether?

8 sets of three are 24   eight threes are 24 $8 \times 3 =$ 24

How many altogether?

9 sets of three are 27   nine threes are 27 $9 \times 3 =$ 27

All the 3s again

You should know all of the three times table by now.

$1 \times 3 = 3$ $2 \times 3 = 6$ $3 \times 3 = 9$ $4 \times 3 = 12$ $5 \times 3 = 15$
$6 \times 3 = 18$ $7 \times 3 = 21$ $8 \times 3 = 24$ $9 \times 3 = 27$ $10 \times 3 = 30$

Say these to yourself a few times.

Cover the three times table with a sheet of paper so you can't see the numbers.
Write the answers. Be as fast as you can, but get them right!

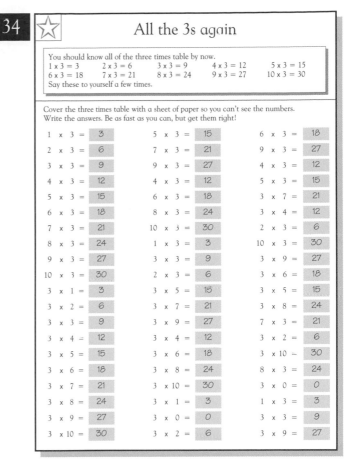

1 × 3 =	3	5 × 3 =	15	6 × 3 =	18
2 × 3 =	6	7 × 3 =	21	9 × 3 =	27
3 × 3 =	9	9 × 3 =	27	4 × 3 =	12
4 × 3 =	12	4 × 3 =	12	5 × 3 =	15
5 × 3 =	15	6 × 3 =	18	3 × 7 =	21
6 × 3 =	18	8 × 3 =	24	3 × 4 =	12
7 × 3 =	21	10 × 3 =	30	2 × 3 =	6
8 × 3 =	24	1 × 3 =	3	10 × 3 =	30
9 × 3 =	27	3 × 3 =	9	3 × 9 =	27
10 × 3 =	30	2 × 3 =	6	3 × 6 =	18
3 × 1 =	3	3 × 5 =	15	3 × 5 =	15
3 × 2 =	6	3 × 7 =	21	3 × 8 =	24
3 × 3 =	9	3 × 9 =	27	7 × 3 =	21
3 × 4 =	12	3 × 4 =	12	3 × 2 =	6
3 × 5 =	15	3 × 6 =	18	3 × 10 =	30
3 × 6 =	18	3 × 8 =	24	8 × 3 =	24
3 × 7 =	21	3 × 10 =	30	3 × 0 =	0
3 × 8 =	24	3 × 1 =	3	1 × 3 =	3
3 × 9 =	27	3 × 0 =	0	3 × 3 =	9
3 × 10 =	30	3 × 2 =	6	3 × 9 =	27

All the 4s

You should know these:

$1 \times 4 = 4$ $2 \times 4 = 8$ $3 \times 4 = 12$ $4 \times 4 = 16$ $5 \times 4 = 20$ $10 \times 4 = 40$

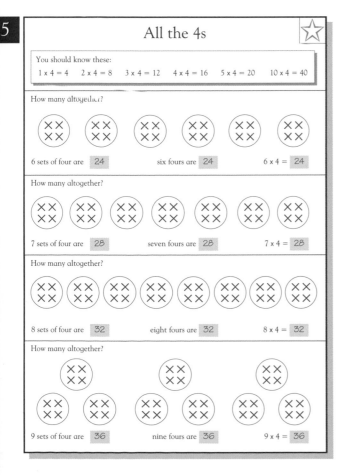

How many altogether?

6 sets of four are 24   six fours are 24 $6 \times 4 =$ 24

How many altogether?

7 sets of four are 28   seven fours are 28 $7 \times 4 =$ 28

How many altogether?

8 sets of four are 32   eight fours are 32 $8 \times 4 =$ 32

How many altogether?

9 sets of four are 36   nine fours are 36 $9 \times 4 =$ 36

All the 4s again

You should know all of the four times table by now.

$1 \times 4 = 4$ $2 \times 4 = 8$ $3 \times 4 = 12$ $4 \times 4 = 16$ $5 \times 4 = 20$
$6 \times 4 = 24$ $7 \times 4 = 28$ $8 \times 4 = 32$ $9 \times 4 = 36$ $10 \times 4 = 40$

Say these to yourself a few times.

Cover the four times table with a sheet of paper so you can't see the numbers.
Write the answers. Be as fast as you can, but get them right!

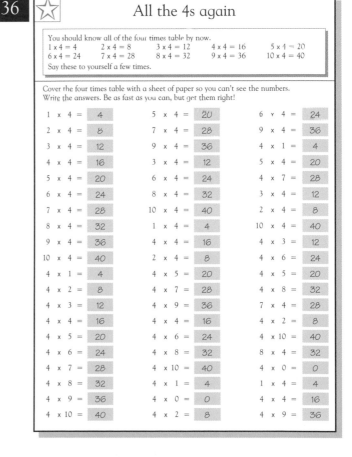

1 × 4 =	4	5 × 4 =	20	6 × 4 =	24
2 × 4 =	8	7 × 4 =	28	9 × 4 =	36
3 × 4 =	12	9 × 4 =	36	4 × 1 =	4
4 × 4 =	16	3 × 4 =	12	5 × 4 =	20
5 × 4 =	20	6 × 4 =	24	4 × 7 =	28
6 × 4 =	24	8 × 4 =	32	3 × 4 =	12
7 × 4 =	28	10 × 4 =	40	2 × 4 =	8
8 × 4 =	32	1 × 4 =	4	10 × 4 =	40
9 × 4 =	36	4 × 4 =	16	4 × 3 =	12
10 × 4 =	40	2 × 4 =	8	4 × 6 =	24
4 × 1 =	4	4 × 5 =	20	4 × 5 =	20
4 × 2 =	8	4 × 7 =	28	4 × 8 =	32
4 × 3 =	12	4 × 9 =	36	7 × 4 =	28
4 × 4 =	16	4 × 4 =	16	4 × 2 =	8
4 × 5 =	20	4 × 6 =	24	4 × 10 =	40
4 × 6 =	24	4 × 8 =	32	8 × 4 =	32
4 × 7 =	28	4 × 10 =	40	4 × 0 =	0
4 × 8 =	32	4 × 1 =	4	1 × 4 =	4
4 × 9 =	36	4 × 0 =	0	4 × 4 =	16
4 × 10 =	40	4 × 2 =	8	4 × 9 =	36

Speed trials ☆

You should know all of the 1, 2, 3, 4, 5, and 10 times tables by now, but how quickly can you do them?
Ask someone to time you as you do this page.
Remember, you must be fast but also correct.

4 x 2 = 8	6 x 3 = 18	9 x 5 = 45
8 x 3 = 24	3 x 4 = 12	8 x 10 = 80
7 x 4 = 28	7 x 5 = 35	7 x 2 = 14
6 x 5 = 30	3 x 10 = 30	6 x 3 = 18
8 x 10 = 80	1 x 2 = 2	5 x 4 = 20
8 x 2 = 16	7 x 3 = 21	4 x 5 = 20
5 x 3 = 15	4 x 4 = 16	3 x 10 = 30
9 x 4 = 36	6 x 5 = 30	2 x 2 = 4
5 x 5 = 25	4 x 10 = 40	1 x 3 = 3
7 x 10 = 70	6 x 2 = 12	0 x 4 = 0
0 x 2 = 0	5 x 3 = 15	10 x 5 = 50
4 x 3 = 12	8 x 4 = 32	9 x 2 = 18
6 x 4 = 24	0 x 5 = 0	8 x 3 = 24
3 x 5 = 15	2 x 10 = 20	7 x 4 = 28
4 x 10 = 40	7 x 2 = 14	6 x 5 = 30
7 x 2 = 14	8 x 3 = 24	5 x 10 = 50
3 x 3 = 9	9 x 4 = 36	4 x 0 = 0
2 x 4 = 8	5 x 5 = 25	3 x 2 = 6
7 x 5 = 35	7 x 10 = 70	2 x 8 = 16
9 x 10 = 90	5 x 2 = 10	1 x 9 = 9

☆ Some of the 6s

You should already know parts of the 6 times table because they are parts of the 1, 2, 3, 4, 5, and 10 times tables.
1 x 6 = 6   2 x 6 = 12   3 x 6 = 18
4 x 6 = 24   5 x 6 = 30   10 x 6 = 60
Find out if you can remember them quickly and correctly.

Cover the six times table with paper so you can't see the numbers.
Write the answers as quickly as you can.

What is three sixes?	18	What is ten sixes?	60
What is two sixes?	12	What is four sixes?	24
What is one six?	6	What is five sixes?	30

Write the answers as quickly as you can.

How many sixes make 12?	2	How many sixes make 6?	1
How many sixes make 30?	5	How many sixes make 18?	3
How many sixes make 24?	4	How many sixes make 60?	10

Write the answers as quickly as you can.

Multiply six by three.	18	Multiply six by ten.	60
Multiply six by two.	12	Multiply six by five.	30
Multiply six by one.	6	Multiply six by four.	24

Write the answers as quickly as you can.

4 x 6 = 24	2 x 6 = 12	10 x 6 = 60
5 x 6 = 30	1 x 6 = 6	3 x 6 = 18

Write the answers as quickly as you can.
A box contains six eggs. A man buys five boxes. How many eggs does he have?   30

A pack contains six sticks of gum.
How many sticks will there be in 10 packs?   60

The rest of the 6s ☆

You need to learn these:
6 x 6 = 36   7 x 6 = 42   8 x 6 = 48   9 x 6 = 54

This work will help you remember the 6 times table.

Complete these sequences.

6   12   18   24   30   36   42   48   54   60

5 x 6 = 30   so   6 x 6 = 30 plus another 6 = 36

18   24   30   36   42   48   54   60

6 x 6 = 36   so   7 x 6 = 36 plus another 6 = 42

6   12   18   24   30   36   42   48   54   60

7 x 6 = 42   so   8 x 6 = 42 plus another 6 = 48

6   12   18   24   30   36   42   48   54   60

8 x 6 = 48   so   9 x 6 = 48 plus another 6 = 54

6   12   18   24   30   36   42   48   54   60

Test yourself on the rest of the 6 times table.
Cover the above part of the page with a sheet of paper.

What is six sixes?	36	What is seven sixes?	42
What is eight sixes?	48	What is nine sixes?	54

8 x 6 = 48   7 x 6 = 42   6 x 6 = 36   9 x 6 = 54

☆ Practise the 6s

You should know all of the 6 times table now, but how quickly can you remember it?
Ask someone to time you as you do this page.
Remember, you must be fast but also correct.

1 x 6 = 6	2 x 6 = 12	7 x 6 = 42
2 x 6 = 12	4 x 6 = 24	3 x 6 = 18
3 x 6 = 18	6 x 6 = 36	9 x 6 = 54
4 x 6 = 24	8 x 6 = 48	6 x 4 = 24
5 x 6 = 30	10 x 6 = 60	1 x 6 = 6
6 x 6 = 36	1 x 6 = 6	6 x 2 = 12
7 x 6 = 42	3 x 6 = 18	6 x 8 = 48
8 x 6 = 48	5 x 6 = 30	0 x 6 = 0
9 x 6 = 54	7 x 6 = 42	6 x 3 = 18
10 x 6 = 60	9 x 6 = 54	5 x 6 = 30
6 x 1 = 6	6 x 3 = 18	6 x 7 = 42
6 x 2 = 12	6 x 5 = 30	2 x 6 = 12
6 x 3 = 18	6 x 7 = 42	6 x 9 = 54
6 x 4 = 24	6 x 9 = 54	4 x 6 = 24
6 x 5 = 30	6 x 2 = 12	8 x 6 = 48
6 x 6 = 36	6 x 4 = 24	10 x 6 = 60
6 x 7 = 42	6 x 6 = 36	6 x 5 = 30
6 x 8 = 48	6 x 8 = 48	6 x 0 = 0
6 x 9 = 54	6 x 10 = 60	6 x 1 = 6
6 x 10 = 60	6 x 0 = 0	6 x 6 = 36

Speed trials ☆

You should know all of the 1, 2, 3, 4, 5, 6, and 10 times tables by now, but how quickly can you remember them?
Ask someone to time you as you do this page.
Remember, you must be fast but also correct.

4 x 6 = 24	6 x 3 = 18	9 x 6 = 54
5 x 3 = 15	8 x 6 = 48	8 x 6 = 48
7 x 3 = 21	6 x 6 = 36	7 x 3 = 21
6 x 5 = 30	3 x 10 = 30	6 x 6 = 36
6 x 10 = 60	6 x 2 = 12	5 x 4 = 20
8 x 2 = 16	7 x 3 = 21	4 x 6 = 24
5 x 3 = 15	4 x 6 = 24	3 x 6 = 18
9 x 6 = 54	6 x 5 = 30	2 x 6 = 12
5 x 5 = 25	6 x 10 = 60	6 x 3 = 18
7 x 6 = 42	6 x 2 = 12	0 x 6 = 0
0 x 2 = 0	5 x 3 = 15	10 x 5 = 50
6 x 3 = 18	8 x 4 = 32	6 x 2 = 12
6 x 6 = 36	0 x 6 = 0	8 x 3 = 24
3 x 5 = 15	5 x 10 = 50	7 x 6 = 42
4 x 10 = 40	7 x 6 = 42	6 x 5 = 30
7 x 10 = 70	8 x 3 = 24	5 x 10 = 50
3 x 6 = 18	9 x 6 = 54	6 x 0 = 0
2 x 4 = 8	5 x 5 = 25	3 x 10 = 30
6 x 9 = 54	7 x 10 = 70	2 x 8 = 16
9 x 10 = 90	5 x 6 = 30	1 x 8 = 8

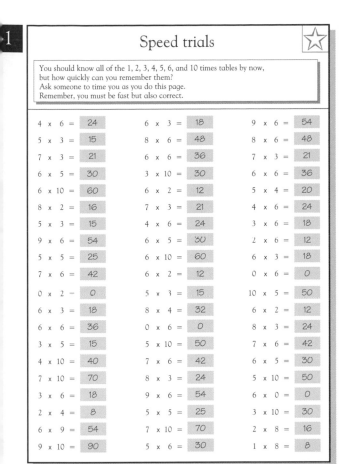

☆ Some of the 7s

You should already know parts of the 7 times table because they are parts of the 1, 2, 3, 4, 5, 6 and 10 times tables.
1 x 7 = 7   2 x 7 = 14   3 x 7 = 21   4 x 7 = 28
5 x 7 = 35   6 x 7 = 42   10 x 7 = 70
Find out if you can remember them quickly and correctly.

Cover the seven times table with paper and write the answers to these questions as quickly as you can.

What is three sevens? 21		What is ten sevens? 70
What is two sevens? 14		What is four sevens? 28
What is six sevens? 42		What is five sevens? 35

Write the answers as quickly as you can.

How many sevens make 14? 2	How many sevens make 42? 6
How many sevens make 35? 5	How many sevens make 21? 3
How many sevens make 28? 4	How many sevens make 70? 10

Write the answers as quickly as you can.

Multiply seven by three. 21	Multiply seven by ten. 70
Multiply seven by two. 14	Multiply seven by five. 35
Multiply seven by six. 42	Multiply seven by four. 28

Write the answers as quickly as you can.

4 x 7 = 28	2 x 7 = 14	10 x 7 = 70
5 x 7 = 35	1 x 7 = 7	3 x 7 = 21

Write the answers as quickly as you can.

A bag has seven candies. Ann buys five bags. How many candies does she have? 35

How many days are there in six weeks? 42

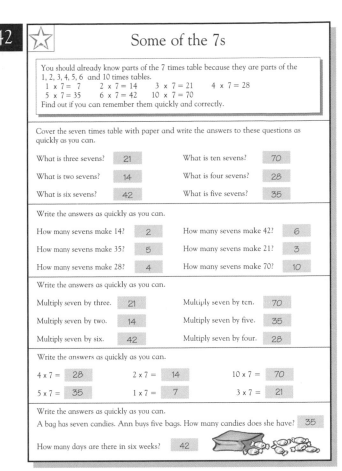

The rest of the 7s ☆

You should now know all of the 1, 2, 3, 4, 5, 6, and 10 times tables.
You need to learn only these parts of the seven times table.
7 x 7 = 49   8 x 7 = 56   9 x 7 = 63

This work will help you remember the 7 times table.

Complete these sequences.

7   14   21   28   35   42   49   56   63   70

6 x 7 = 42   so   7 x 7 = 42 plus another 7 = 49

21   28   35   42   49   56   63   70

7 x 7 = 49   so   8 x 7 = 49 plus another 7 = 56

7   14   21   28   35   42   49   56   63   70

8 x 7 = 56   so   9 x 7 = 56 plus another 7 = 63

7   14   21   28   35   42   49   56   63   70

Test yourself on the rest of the 7 times table.
Cover the section above with a sheet of paper.

What is seven sevens? 49   What is eight sevens? 56

What is nine sevens? 63   What is ten sevens? 70

8 x 7 = 56   7 x 7 = 49   9 x 7 = 63   10 x 7 = 70

How many days are there in eight weeks? 56

A package contains seven pens.
How many pens will there be in nine packets? 63

How many sevens make 56? 8

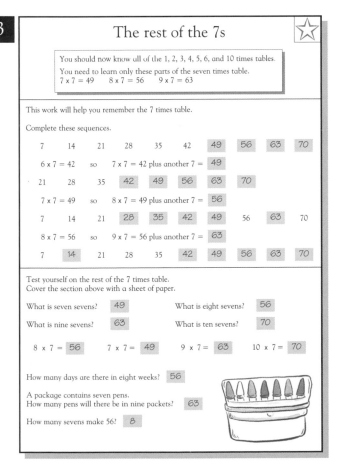

☆ Practise the 7s

You should know all of the 7 times table now, but how quickly can you remember it?
Ask someone to time you as you do this page.
Remember, you must be fast but also correct.

1 x 7 = 7	2 x 7 = 14	7 x 6 = 42
2 x 7 = 14	4 x 7 = 28	3 x 7 = 21
3 x 7 = 21	6 x 7 = 42	9 x 7 = 63
4 x 7 = 28	8 x 7 = 56	7 x 4 = 28
5 x 7 = 35	10 x 7 = 70	1 x 7 = 7
6 x 7 = 42	1 x 7 = 7	7 x 2 = 14
7 x 7 = 49	3 x 7 = 21	7 x 8 = 56
8 x 7 = 56	5 x 7 = 35	0 x 7 = 0
9 x 7 = 63	7 x 7 = 49	7 x 3 = 21
10 x 7 = 70	9 x 7 = 63	5 x 7 = 35
7 x 1 = 7	7 x 3 = 21	7 x 7 = 49
7 x 2 = 14	7 x 5 = 35	2 x 7 = 14
7 x 3 = 21	7 x 7 = 49	7 x 9 = 63
7 x 4 = 28	7 x 9 = 63	4 x 7 = 28
7 x 5 = 35	7 x 2 = 14	8 x 7 = 56
7 x 6 = 42	7 x 4 = 28	10 x 7 = 70
7 x 7 = 49	7 x 6 = 42	7 x 5 = 35
7 x 8 = 56	7 x 8 = 56	7 x 0 = 0
7 x 9 = 63	7 x 10 = 70	7 x 1 = 7
7 x 10 = 70	7 x 0 = 0	6 x 7 = 42

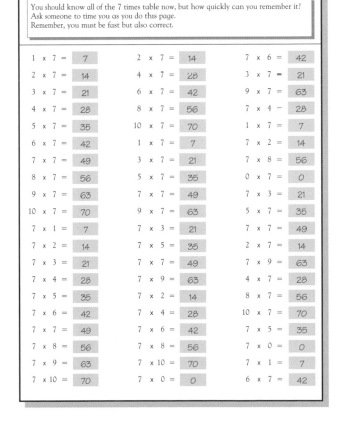

Speed trials

You should know all of the 1, 2, 3, 4, 5, 6, 7, and 10 times tables by now,
but how quickly can you remember them?
Ask someone to time you as you do this page.
Remember, you must be fast but also correct.

4 x 7 = 28	7 x 3 = 21	9 x 7 = 63
5 x 10 = 50	8 x 7 = 56	7 x 6 = 42
7 x 5 = 35	6 x 6 = 36	8 x 3 = 24
6 x 5 = 30	5 x 10 = 50	6 x 6 = 36
6 x 10 = 60	6 x 3 = 18	7 x 4 = 28
8 x 7 = 56	7 x 5 = 35	4 x 6 = 24
5 x 8 = 40	4 x 6 = 24	3 x 7 = 21
9 x 6 = 54	6 x 5 = 30	2 x 8 = 16
5 x 7 = 35	7 x 10 = 70	7 x 3 = 21
7 x 6 = 42	6 x 7 = 42	0 x 6 = 0
0 x 5 = 0	5 x 7 = 35	10 x 7 = 70
6 x 3 = 18	8 x 4 = 32	6 x 2 = 12
6 x 7 = 42	0 x 7 = 0	8 x 7 = 56
3 x 5 = 15	5 x 8 = 40	7 x 7 = 49
4 x 7 = 28	7 x 6 = 42	6 x 5 = 30
7 x 10 = 70	8 x 3 = 24	5 x 10 = 50
7 x 8 = 56	9 x 6 = 54	7 x 0 = 0
2 x 7 = 14	7 x 7 = 49	3 x 10 = 30
4 x 9 = 36	9 x 10 = 90	2 x 7 = 14
9 x 10 = 90	5 x 6 = 30	7 x 8 = 56

Some of the 8s

You should already know some of the 8 times table because it is part of the
1, 2, 3, 4, 5, 6, 7, and 10 times tables.

1 x 8 = 8	2 x 8 = 16	3 x 8 = 24	4 x 8 = 32
5 x 8 = 40	6 x 8 = 48	7 x 8 = 56	10 x 8 = 80

Find out if you can remember them quickly and correctly.

Cover the 8 times table with paper so you can't see the numbers.
Write the answers as quickly as you can.

What is three eights? 24	What is ten eights? 80
What is two eights? 16	What is four eights? 32
What is six eights? 48	What is five eights? 40

Write the answers as quickly as you can.

How many eights equal 16? 2	How many eights equal 40? 5
How many eights equal 32? 4	How many eights equal 24? 3
How many eights equal 56? 7	How many eights equal 48? 6

Write the answers as quickly as you can.

Multiply eight by three. 24	Multiply eight by ten. 80
Multiply eight by two. 16	Multiply eight by five. 40
Multiply eight by six. 48	Multiply eight by four. 32

Write the answers as quickly as you can.

6 x 8 = 48	2 x 8 = 16	10 x 8 = 80
5 x 8 = 40	7 x 8 = 56	3 x 8 = 24

Write the answers as quickly as you can.
A pizza has eight slices. John buys six pizzas.

How many slices does he have? 48

Which number multiplied by 8 gives the answer 56? 7

The rest of the 8s

You need to learn only these parts of the eight times table.
8 x 8 = 64   9 x 8 = 72

This work will help you remember the 8 times table.

Complete these sequences.

8   16   24   32   40   48   56   64   72   80

7 x 8 = 56   so   8 x 8 = 56 plus another 8 = 64

24   32   40   48   56   64   72   80

8 x 8 = 64   so   9 x 8 = 64 plus another 8 = 72

8   16   24   32   40   48   56   64   72   80

8   16   24   32   40   48   56   64   72   80

Test yourself on the rest of the 8 times table.
Cover the section above with a sheet of paper.

What is seven eights? 56	What is eight eights? 64
What is nine eights? 72	What is eight nines? 72

8 x 8 = 64   9 x 8 = 72   8 x 9 = 72   10 x 8 = 80

What number multiplied by 8 gives the answer 72? 9

A number multiplied by 8 gives the answer 80. What is the number? 10

David puts out building bricks in piles of 8.
How many bricks will there be in 10 piles? 80

What number multiplied by 5 gives the answer 40? 8

How many 8s make 72? 9

Practise the 8s

You should know all of the 8 times table now, but how quickly can you remember it?
Ask someone to time you as you do this page.
Be fast but also correct.

1 x 8 = 8	2 x 8 = 16	8 x 6 = 48
2 x 8 = 16	4 x 8 = 32	3 x 8 = 24
3 x 8 = 24	6 x 8 = 48	9 x 8 = 72
4 x 8 = 32	8 x 8 = 64	8 x 4 = 32
5 x 8 = 40	10 x 8 = 80	1 x 8 = 8
6 x 8 = 48	1 x 8 = 8	8 x 2 = 16
7 x 8 = 56	3 x 8 = 24	7 x 8 = 56
8 x 8 = 64	5 x 8 = 40	0 x 8 = 0
9 x 8 = 72	7 x 8 = 56	8 x 3 = 24
10 x 8 = 80	9 x 8 = 72	5 x 8 = 40
8 x 1 = 8	8 x 3 = 24	8 x 8 = 64
8 x 2 = 16	8 x 5 = 40	2 x 8 = 16
8 x 3 = 24	8 x 8 = 64	8 x 9 = 72
8 x 4 = 32	8 x 9 = 72	4 x 8 = 32
8 x 5 = 40	8 x 2 = 16	8 x 6 = 48
8 x 6 = 48	8 x 4 = 32	10 x 8 = 80
8 x 7 = 56	8 x 6 = 48	8 x 5 = 40
8 x 8 = 64	8 x 8 = 64	8 x 0 = 0
8 x 9 = 72	8 x 10 = 80	8 x 1 = 8
8 x 10 = 80	8 x 0 = 0	6 x 8 = 48

Speed trials

4 x 8 = 32	7 x 8 = 56	9 x 8 = 72
5 x 10 = 50	8 x 7 = 56	7 x 6 = 42
7 x 8 = 56	6 x 8 = 48	8 x 3 = 24
8 x 5 = 40	8 x 10 = 80	8 x 8 = 64
6 x 10 = 60	6 x 3 = 18	7 x 4 = 28
8 x 7 = 56	7 x 7 = 49	4 x 8 = 32
5 x 8 = 40	5 x 6 = 30	3 x 7 = 21
9 x 8 = 72	6 x 7 = 42	2 x 8 = 16
8 x 8 = 64	7 x 10 = 70	7 x 3 = 21
7 x 6 = 42	6 x 9 = 54	0 x 8 = 0
7 x 5 = 35	5 x 8 = 40	10 x 8 = 80
6 x 8 = 48	8 x 4 = 32	6 x 2 = 12
6 x 7 = 42	0 x 8 = 0	8 x 6 = 48
5 x 7 = 35	5 x 9 = 45	7 x 8 = 56
8 x 4 = 32	7 x 6 = 42	6 x 5 = 30
7 x 10 = 70	8 x 3 = 24	8 x 10 = 80
2 x 8 = 16	9 x 6 = 54	8 x 7 = 56
4 x 7 = 28	8 x 6 = 48	5 x 10 = 50
6 x 9 = 54	9 x 10 = 90	8 x 2 = 16
9 x 10 = 90	6 x 6 = 36	8 x 9 = 72

Some of the 9s

1 x 9 = 9	2 x 9 = 18	3 x 9 = 27	4 x 9 = 36	5 x 9 = 45
6 x 9 = 54	7 x 9 = 63	8 x 9 = 72	10 x 9 = 90	

Find out if you can remember them quickly and correctly.

Cover the nine times table so you can't see the numbers.
Write the answers as quickly as you can.

What is three nines?	27	What is ten nines?	90
What is two nines?	18	What is four nines?	36
What is six nines?	54	What is five nines?	45
What is seven nines?	63	What is eight nines?	72

Write the answers as quickly as you can.

How many nines equal 18?	2	How many nines equal 54?	6
How many nines equal 90?	10	How many nines equal 27?	3
How many nines equal 72?	8	How many nines equal 36?	4
How many nines equal 45?	5	How many nines equal 63?	7

Write the answers as quickly as you can.

Multiply nine by seven.	63	Multiply nine by ten.	90
Multiply nine by two.	18	Multiply nine by five.	45
Multiply nine by six.	54	Multiply nine by four.	36
Multiply nine by three.	27	Multiply nine by eight.	72

Write the answers as quickly as you can.

6 x 9 = 54	2 x 9 = 18	10 x 9 = 90
5 x 9 = 45	3 x 9 = 27	8 x 9 = 72
0 x 9 = 0	7 x 9 = 63	4 x 9 = 36

The rest of the 9s

This work will help you remember the 9 times table.
Complete these sequences.

9   18   27   36   45   54   63   72   81   90

8 x 9 = 72   so   9 x 9 = 72 plus another 9 = 81

27   36   45   54   63   72   81   90

9   18   27   36   45   54   63   72   81   90

9   18   27   36   45   54   63   72   81   90

Look for a pattern in the nine times table.

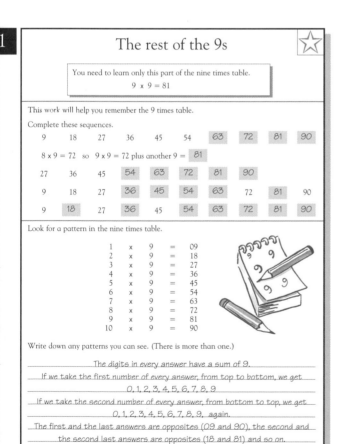

1	x	9	= 09
2	x	9	= 18
3	x	9	= 27
4	x	9	= 36
5	x	9	= 45
6	x	9	= 54
7	x	9	= 63
8	x	9	= 72
9	x	9	= 81
10	x	9	= 90

Write down any patterns you can see. (There is more than one.)

The digits in every answer have a sum of 9.
If we take the first number of every answer, from top to bottom, we get
0, 1, 2, 3, 4, 5, 6, 7, 8, 9
If we take the second number of every answer, from bottom to top, we get
0, 1, 2, 3, 4, 5, 6, 7, 8, 9, again.
The first and the last answers are opposites (09 and 90), the second and
the second last answers are opposites (18 and 81) and so on.

Encourage children to notice patterns. It does not
matter how they express these. One pattern is to
deduct 1 from the number being multiplied. This
gives the first digit of the answer. Then deduct this
first digit from 9 to get the second digit of the answer.

Practise the 9s

1 x 9 = 9	2 x 9 = 18	9 x 6 = 54
2 x 9 = 18	4 x 9 = 36	3 x 9 = 27
3 x 9 = 27	6 x 9 = 54	9 x 9 = 81
4 x 9 = 36	9 x 7 = 63	9 x 4 = 36
5 x 9 = 45	10 x 9 = 90	1 x 9 = 9
6 x 9 = 54	1 x 9 = 9	9 x 2 = 18
7 x 9 = 63	3 x 9 = 27	7 x 9 = 63
8 x 9 = 72	5 x 9 = 45	0 x 9 = 0
9 x 9 = 81	7 x 9 = 63	9 x 3 = 27
10 x 9 = 90	9 x 9 = 81	5 x 9 = 45
9 x 1 = 9	9 x 3 = 27	9 x 9 = 81
9 x 2 = 18	9 x 5 = 45	2 x 9 = 18
9 x 3 = 27	0 x 9 = 0	8 x 9 = 72
9 x 4 = 36	9 x 1 = 9	4 x 9 = 36
9 x 5 = 45	9 x 2 = 18	9 x 7 = 63
9 x 6 = 54	9 x 4 = 36	10 x 9 = 90
9 x 7 = 63	9 x 6 = 54	9 x 5 = 45
9 x 8 = 72	9 x 8 = 72	9 x 0 = 0
9 x 9 = 81	9 x 10 = 90	9 x 1 = 9
9 x 10 = 90	9 x 0 = 0	6 x 9 = 54

Speed trials

You should know all of the times tables by now, but how quickly can you remember them?
Ask someone to time you as you do this page.
Be fast and correct.

6 x 8 = 48	4 x 8 = 32	8 x 10 = 80
9 x 10 = 90	9 x 8 = 72	7 x 9 = 63
5 x 8 = 40	6 x 6 = 36	8 x 5 = 40
7 x 5 = 35	8 x 9 = 72	8 x 7 = 56
6 x 4 = 24	6 x 4 = 24	7 x 4 = 28
8 x 8 = 64	7 x 3 = 21	4 x 9 = 36
5 x 10 = 50	5 x 9 = 45	6 x 7 = 42
9 x 8 = 72	6 x 8 = 48	4 x 6 = 24
8 x 3 = 24	7 x 7 = 49	7 x 8 = 56
7 x 7 = 49	6 x 9 = 54	6 x 9 = 54
9 x 5 = 45	7 x 8 = 56	10 x 8 = 80
4 x 8 = 32	8 x 4 = 32	6 x 5 = 30
6 x 7 = 42	0 x 9 = 0	8 x 8 = 64
2 x 9 = 18	10 x 10 = 100	7 x 6 = 42
8 x 4 = 32	7 x 6 = 42	6 x 8 = 48
7 x 10 = 70	8 x 7 = 56	9 x 10 = 90
2 x 8 = 16	9 x 6 = 54	8 x 4 = 32
4 x 7 = 28	8 x 6 = 48	7 x 10 = 70
6 x 9 = 54	9 x 9 = 81	5 x 8 = 40
9 x 9 = 81	6 x 7 = 42	8 x 9 = 72

Times tables for division

Knowing the times tables can also help with division problems.
Look at these examples.
3 x 6 = 18 which means that 18 ÷ 3 = 6 and that 18 ÷ 6 = 3
4 x 5 = 20 which means that 20 ÷ 4 = 5 and that 20 ÷ 5 = 4
9 x 3 = 27 which means that 27 ÷ 3 = 9 and that 27 ÷ 9 = 3

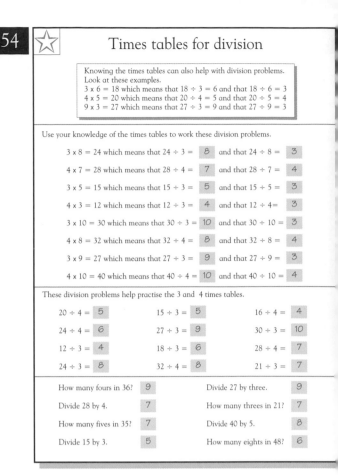

Use your knowledge of the times tables to work these division problems.

3 x 8 = 24 which means that 24 ÷ 3 = 8 and that 24 ÷ 8 = 3
4 x 7 = 28 which means that 28 ÷ 4 = 7 and that 28 ÷ 7 = 4
3 x 5 = 15 which means that 15 ÷ 3 = 5 and that 15 ÷ 5 = 3
4 x 3 = 12 which means that 12 ÷ 3 = 4 and that 12 ÷ 4= 3
3 x 10 = 30 which means that 30 ÷ 3 = 10 and that 30 ÷ 10 = 3
4 x 8 = 32 which means that 32 ÷ 4 = 8 and that 32 ÷ 8 = 4
3 x 9 = 27 which means that 27 ÷ 3 = 9 and that 27 ÷ 9 = 3
4 x 10 = 40 which means that 40 ÷ 4 = 10 and that 40 ÷ 10 = 4

These division problems help practise the 3 and 4 times tables.

20 ÷ 4 = 5	15 ÷ 3 = 5	16 ÷ 4 = 4
24 ÷ 4 = 6	27 ÷ 3 = 9	30 ÷ 3 = 10
12 ÷ 3 = 4	18 ÷ 3 = 6	28 ÷ 4 = 7
24 ÷ 3 = 8	32 ÷ 4 = 8	21 ÷ 3 = 7

How many fours in 36? 9	Divide 27 by three. 9
Divide 28 by 4. 7	How many threes in 21? 7
How many fives in 35? 7	Divide 40 by 5. 8
Divide 15 by 3. 5	How many eights in 48? 6

Times tables for division

This page will help you remember times tables by dividing by 2, 3, 4, 5, and 10.

20 ÷ 5 = 4   18 ÷ 3 = 6   60 ÷ 10 = 6

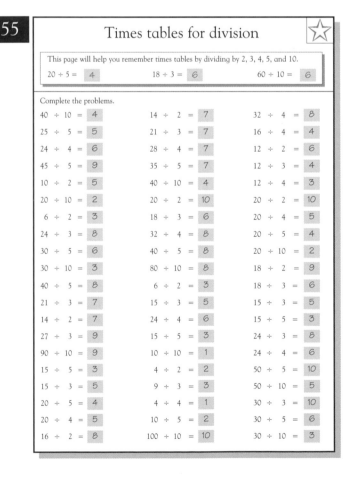

Complete the problems.

40 ÷ 10 = 4	14 ÷ 2 = 7	32 ÷ 4 = 8
25 ÷ 5 = 5	21 ÷ 3 = 7	16 ÷ 4 = 4
24 ÷ 4 = 6	28 ÷ 4 = 7	12 ÷ 2 = 6
45 ÷ 5 = 9	35 ÷ 5 = 7	12 ÷ 3 = 4
10 ÷ 2 = 5	40 ÷ 10 = 4	12 ÷ 4 = 3
20 ÷ 10 = 2	20 ÷ 2 = 10	20 ÷ 2 = 10
6 ÷ 2 = 3	18 ÷ 3 = 6	20 ÷ 4 = 5
24 ÷ 3 = 8	32 ÷ 4 = 8	20 ÷ 5 = 4
30 ÷ 5 = 6	40 ÷ 5 = 8	20 ÷ 10 = 2
30 ÷ 10 = 3	80 ÷ 10 = 8	18 ÷ 2 = 9
40 ÷ 5 = 8	6 ÷ 2 = 3	18 ÷ 3 = 6
21 ÷ 3 = 7	15 ÷ 3 = 5	15 ÷ 3 = 5
14 ÷ 2 = 7	24 ÷ 4 = 6	15 ÷ 5 = 3
27 ÷ 3 = 9	15 ÷ 5 = 3	24 ÷ 3 = 8
90 ÷ 10 = 9	10 ÷ 10 = 1	24 ÷ 4 = 6
15 ÷ 5 = 3	4 ÷ 2 = 2	50 ÷ 5 = 10
15 ÷ 3 = 5	9 ÷ 3 = 3	50 ÷ 10 = 5
20 ÷ 5 = 4	4 ÷ 4 = 1	30 ÷ 3 = 10
20 ÷ 4 = 5	10 ÷ 5 = 2	30 ÷ 5 = 6
16 ÷ 2 = 8	100 ÷ 10 = 10	30 ÷ 10 = 3

Times tables for division

This page will help you remember times tables by dividing by 2, 3, 4, 5, 6, and 10.

30 ÷ 6 = 5   12 ÷ 6 = 2   60 ÷ 10 = 6

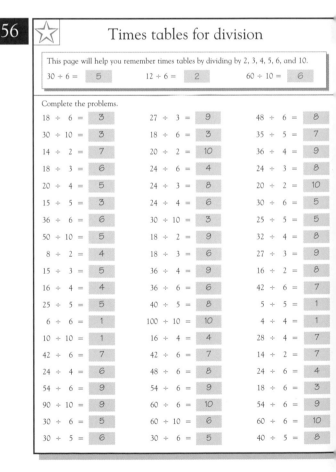

Complete the problems.

18 ÷ 6 = 3	27 ÷ 3 = 9	48 ÷ 6 = 8
30 ÷ 10 = 3	18 ÷ 6 = 3	35 ÷ 5 = 7
14 ÷ 2 = 7	20 ÷ 2 = 10	36 ÷ 4 = 9
18 ÷ 3 = 6	24 ÷ 6 = 4	24 ÷ 3 = 8
20 ÷ 4 = 5	24 ÷ 3 = 8	20 ÷ 2 = 10
15 ÷ 5 = 3	24 ÷ 4 = 6	30 ÷ 6 = 5
36 ÷ 6 = 6	30 ÷ 10 = 3	25 ÷ 5 = 5
50 ÷ 10 = 5	18 ÷ 2 = 9	32 ÷ 4 = 8
8 ÷ 2 = 4	18 ÷ 3 = 6	27 ÷ 3 = 9
15 ÷ 3 = 5	36 ÷ 4 = 9	16 ÷ 2 = 8
16 ÷ 4 = 4	36 ÷ 6 = 6	42 ÷ 6 = 7
25 ÷ 5 = 5	40 ÷ 5 = 8	5 ÷ 5 = 1
6 ÷ 6 = 1	100 ÷ 10 = 10	4 ÷ 4 = 1
10 ÷ 10 = 1	16 ÷ 4 = 4	28 ÷ 4 = 7
42 ÷ 6 = 7	42 ÷ 6 = 7	14 ÷ 2 = 7
24 ÷ 4 = 6	48 ÷ 6 = 8	24 ÷ 6 = 4
54 ÷ 6 = 9	54 ÷ 6 = 9	18 ÷ 6 = 3
90 ÷ 10 = 9	60 ÷ 6 = 10	54 ÷ 6 = 9
30 ÷ 6 = 5	60 ÷ 10 = 6	60 ÷ 6 = 10
30 ÷ 5 = 6	30 ÷ 6 = 5	40 ÷ 5 = 8

Times tables for division ☆

This page will help you remember times tables by dividing by 2, 3, 4, 5, 6, and 7.

14 ÷ 7 = 2　　　28 ÷ 7 = 4　　　70 ÷ 7 = 10

Complete the problems.

21 ÷ 7 = 3	18 ÷ 6 = 3	49 ÷ 7 = 7
35 ÷ 5 = 7	28 ÷ 7 = 4	35 ÷ 5 = 7
14 ÷ 2 = 7	24 ÷ 6 = 4	35 ÷ 7 = 5
18 ÷ 6 = 3	24 ÷ 4 = 6	24 ÷ 6 = 4
20 ÷ 5 = 4	24 ÷ 2 = 12	21 ÷ 3 = 7
15 ÷ 3 = 5	21 ÷ 7 = 3	70 ÷ 7 = 10
36 ÷ 4 = 9	42 ÷ 7 = 6	42 ÷ 7 = 6
56 ÷ 7 = 8	18 ÷ 3 = 6	32 ÷ 4 = 8
18 ÷ 2 = 9	49 ÷ 7 = 7	27 ÷ 3 = 9
15 ÷ 5 = 3	36 ÷ 4 = 9	16 ÷ 4 = 4
49 ÷ 7 = 7	36 ÷ 6 = 6	42 ÷ 6 = 7
25 ÷ 5 = 5	40 ÷ 5 = 8	45 ÷ 5 = 9
7 ÷ 7 = 1	70 ÷ 7 = 10	40 ÷ 4 = 10
63 ÷ 7 = 9	24 ÷ 3 = 8	24 ÷ 3 = 8
42 ÷ 7 = 6	42 ÷ 6 = 7	14 ÷ 7 = 2
24 ÷ 6 = 4	48 ÷ 6 = 8	24 ÷ 4 = 6
54 ÷ 6 = 9	54 ÷ 6 = 9	18 ÷ 3 = 6
28 ÷ 7 = 4	60 ÷ 6 = 10	56 ÷ 7 = 8
30 ÷ 6 = 5	63 ÷ 7 = 9	63 ÷ 7 = 9
35 ÷ 7 = 5	25 ÷ 5 = 5	48 ÷ 6 = 8

Times tables for division

This page will help you remember times tables by dividing by 2, 3, 4, 5, 6, 7, 8, and 9.

16 ÷ 8 = 2　　　35 ÷ 7 = 5　　　27 ÷ 9 = 3

Complete the problems.

42 ÷ 6 = 7	81 ÷ 9 = 9	56 ÷ 7 = 8
32 ÷ 8 = 4	56 ÷ 7 = 8	45 ÷ 5 = 9
14 ÷ 7 = 2	72 ÷ 9 = 8	35 ÷ 7 = 5
18 ÷ 9 = 2	24 ÷ 8 = 3	18 ÷ 9 = 2
63 ÷ 7 = 9	27 ÷ 9 = 3	21 ÷ 3 = 7
72 ÷ 9 = 8	72 ÷ 9 = 8	28 ÷ 7 = 4
72 ÷ 8 = 9	42 ÷ 6 = 7	64 ÷ 8 = 8
56 ÷ 7 = 8	27 ÷ 3 = 9	32 ÷ 8 = 4
18 ÷ 6 = 3	14 ÷ 7 = 2	27 ÷ 9 = 3
81 ÷ 9 = 9	36 ÷ 4 = 9	16 ÷ 8 = 2
63 ÷ 9 = 7	36 ÷ 6 = 6	42 ÷ 6 = 7
45 ÷ 5 = 9	48 ÷ 8 = 6	45 ÷ 9 = 5
54 ÷ 9 = 6	21 ÷ 7 = 3	40 ÷ 4 = 10
70 ÷ 7 = 10	24 ÷ 3 = 8	24 ÷ 8 = 3
42 ÷ 7 = 6	40 ÷ 8 = 5	63 ÷ 7 = 9
30 ÷ 5 = 6	45 ÷ 9 = 5	24 ÷ 6 = 4
54 ÷ 6 = 9	54 ÷ 6 = 9	18 ÷ 6 = 3
56 ÷ 8 = 7	42 ÷ 7 = 6	56 ÷ 8 = 7
30 ÷ 5 = 6	63 ÷ 9 = 7	63 ÷ 9 = 7
35 ÷ 7 = 5	50 ÷ 5 = 10	48 ÷ 8 = 6

Times tables practice grids ☆

This is a times tables grid.

X	3	4	5
7	21	28	35
8	24	32	40

Complete each times tables grid.

X	1	3	5	7	9
2	2	6	10	14	18
3	3	9	15	21	27

X	4	6
6	24	36
7	28	42
8	32	48

X	6	7	8	9	10
3	18	21	24	27	30
4	24	28	32	36	40
5	30	35	40	45	50

X	10	7	8	4
3	30	21	24	12
5	50	35	40	20
7	70	49	56	28

X	6	2	4	7
5	30	10	20	35
10	60	20	40	70

X	8	7	9	6
9	72	63	81	54
7	56	49	63	42

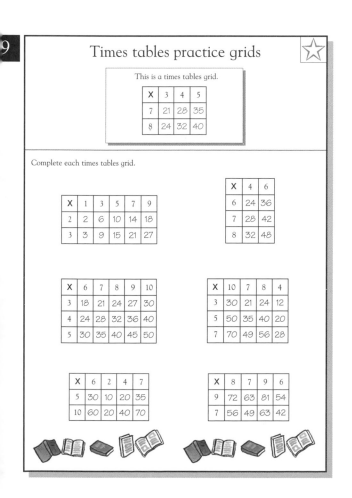

Times tables practice grids

Here are more times tables grids.

X	2	4	6
5	10	20	30
7	14	28	42

X	8	3	9	2
5	40	15	45	10
6	48	18	54	12
7	56	21	63	14

X	2	3	4	5
8	16	24	32	40
9	18	27	36	45

X	10	9	8	7
6	60	54	48	42
5	50	45	40	35
4	40	36	32	28

X	3	8
2	6	16
3	9	24
4	12	32
5	15	40
6	18	48
7	21	56

X	2	4	6	8
1	2	4	6	8
3	6	12	18	24
5	10	20	30	40
7	14	28	42	56
9	18	36	54	72
0	0	0	0	0

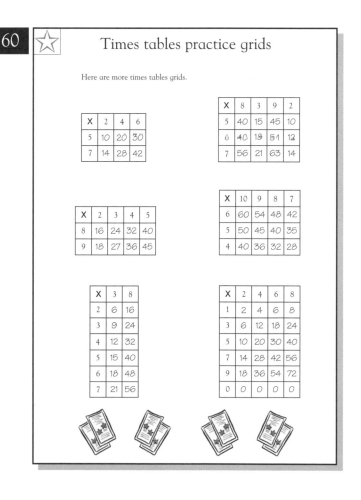

Times tables practice grids

Here are some other times tables grids.

X	8	9
7	56	63
8	64	72

X	9	8	7	6	5	4
9	81	72	63	54	45	36
8	72	64	56	48	40	32
7	63	56	49	42	35	28

X	2	5	9
4	8	20	36
7	14	35	63
8	16	40	72

X	2	3	4	5	7
4	8	12	16	20	28
6	12	18	24	30	42
8	16	24	32	40	56

X	3	5	7
2	6	10	14
8	24	40	56
6	18	30	42
0	0	0	0
4	12	20	28
7	21	35	49

X	8	7	9	6
7	56	49	63	42
9	72	63	81	54
0	0	0	0	0
10	80	70	90	60
8	64	56	72	48
6	48	42	54	36

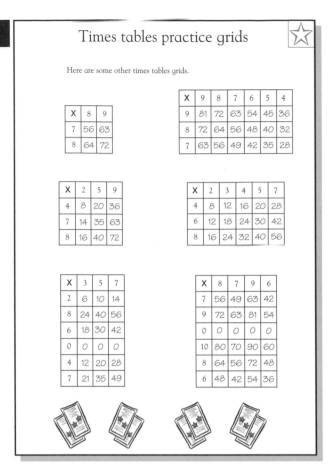

Speed trials

Try this final test.

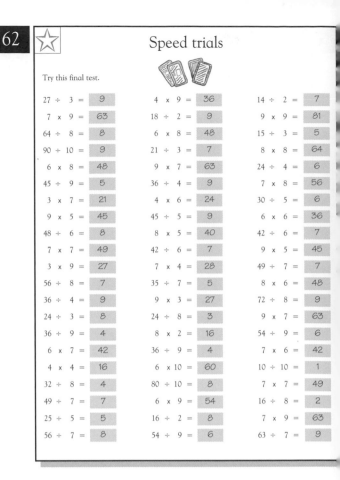

27 ÷ 3 = 9	4 x 9 = 36	14 ÷ 2 = 7
7 x 9 = 63	18 ÷ 2 = 9	9 x 9 = 81
64 ÷ 8 = 8	6 x 8 = 48	15 ÷ 3 = 5
90 ÷ 10 = 9	21 ÷ 3 = 7	8 x 8 = 64
6 x 8 = 48	9 x 7 = 63	24 ÷ 4 = 6
45 ÷ 9 = 5	36 ÷ 4 = 9	7 x 8 = 56
3 x 7 = 21	4 x 6 = 24	30 ÷ 5 = 6
9 x 5 = 45	45 ÷ 5 = 9	6 x 6 = 36
48 ÷ 6 = 8	8 x 5 = 40	42 ÷ 6 = 7
7 x 7 = 49	42 ÷ 6 = 7	9 x 5 = 45
3 x 9 = 27	7 x 4 = 28	49 ÷ 7 = 7
56 ÷ 8 = 7	35 ÷ 7 = 5	8 x 6 = 48
36 ÷ 4 = 9	9 x 3 = 27	72 ÷ 8 = 9
24 ÷ 3 = 8	24 ÷ 8 = 3	9 x 7 = 63
36 ÷ 9 = 4	8 x 2 = 16	54 ÷ 9 = 6
6 x 7 = 42	36 ÷ 9 = 4	7 x 6 = 42
4 x 4 = 16	6 x 10 = 60	10 ÷ 10 = 1
32 ÷ 8 = 4	80 ÷ 10 = 8	7 x 7 = 49
49 ÷ 7 = 7	6 x 9 = 54	16 ÷ 8 = 2
25 ÷ 5 = 5	16 ÷ 2 = 8	7 x 9 = 63
56 ÷ 7 = 8	54 ÷ 9 = 6	63 ÷ 7 = 9

Addition, multiplication, and division

Write the missing number in the box.
7 + ? = 7   3 x ? = 3
7 + 0 = 7   3 x 1 = 3

Write the missing number in the box.

4 + 0 = 4	12 x 1 = 12	1 x 9 = 9	6 + 0 = 6
3 + 12 = 15	17 + 8 = 25	11 + 8 = 19	9 + 17 = 26
4 + 5 = 9	12 + 5 = 17	35 ÷ 7 = 5	25 + 15 = 40
15 + 60 = 75	14 + 6 = 20	21 + 32 = 53	49 + 9 = 58
5 x 6 = 30	12 ÷ 4 = 3	50 ÷ 10 = 5	8 x 6 = 48
9 x 6 = 54	100 ÷ 20 = 5	63 x 10 = 630	36 ÷ 9 = 4

Rewrite each equation, and fill in the missing number.

3 x (6 x 4) = (3 x ?) x 4
3 x (6 x 4) = (3 x 6) x 4

(7 x 9) x 3 = 7 x (? x 3)
(7 x 9) x 3 = 7 x (9 x 3)

(2 x 5) x 9 = ? x (5 x 9)
(2 x 5) x 9 = 2 x (5 x 9)

8 x (8 x 7) = (8 x 8) x ?
8 x (8 x 7) = (8 x 8) x 7

5 x (10 + 3) = (5 x 10) + (? x 3)
5 x (10 + 3) = (5 x 10) + (5 x 3)

(8 + 6) x 7 = (8 x 7) + (6 x ?)
(8 + 6) x 7 = (8 x 7) + (6 x 7)

(3 + 7) x 2 = (? x 2) + (7 x 2)
(3 + 7) x 2 = (3 x 2) + (7 x 2)

9 x (5 + 12) = (? x 5) + (? x 12)
9 x (5 + 12) = (9 x 5) + (9 x 12)

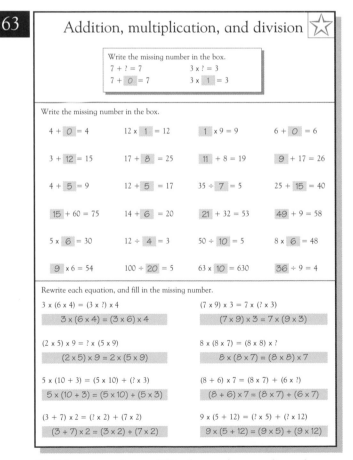

Children may have difficulty understanding the distributive property. Perform the operations to show them that 5 x (10 + 3) = (5 x 10) + (5 x 3).

Place value to 10 000

How many hundreds are there in 7000?   70   hundreds
(70 x 100 = 7000)

What is the value of the 9 in 694?   90   (because the 9 is in the tens column)

Write how many tens there are in:

400	40 tens	600	60 tens	900	90 tens
200	20 tens	1300	130 tens	4700	470 tens
4800	480 tens	1240	124 tens	1320	132 tens
2630	263 tens	5920	592 tens	4350	435 tens

What is the value of the 7 in these numbers?

76	70	720	700	137	7
7122	7000	7430	7000	724	700

What is the value of the 3 in these numbers?

3241	3000	2731	30	4623	3
4320	300	3999	3000	4372	300

Write how many hundreds there are in:

6400	64 hundreds	8500	85 hundreds
1900	19 hundreds	6200	62 hundreds
4600	46 hundreds	2400	24 hundreds

What is the value of the 8 in these numbers?

2148	8	9814	800	6384	80
8703	8000	1189	80	5428	8

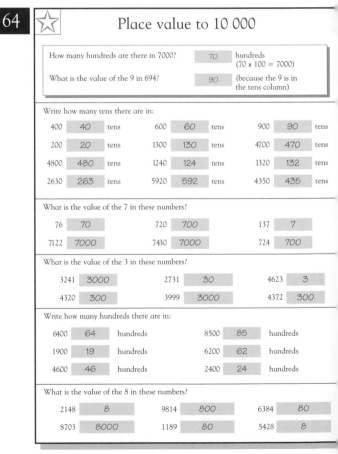

Explain to children that finding how many tens there are in a number is the same as dividing by 10. In the number 400, for example, there are 40 tens, because 400 divided by 10 is 40.

Multiplying and dividing by 10 ☆

Write the answer in the box.
37 x 10 = 370   58 ÷ 10 = 5.8

Write the product in the box.

94 x 10 = 940	13 x 10 = 130	37 x 10 = 370
36 x 10 = 360	47 x 10 = 470	54 x 10 = 540
236 x 10 = 2360	419 x 10 = 4190	262 x 10 = 2620
531 x 10 = 5310	674 x 10 = 6740	801 x 10 = 8010

Write the quotient in the box.

92 ÷ 10 = 9.2	48 ÷ 10 = 4.8	37 ÷ 10 = 3.7
18 ÷ 10 = 1.8	29 ÷ 10 = 2.9	54 ÷ 10 = 5.4
345 ÷ 10 = 34.5	354 ÷ 10 = 35.4	723 ÷ 10 = 72.3
531 ÷ 10 = 53.1	262 ÷ 10 = 26.2	419 ÷ 10 = 41.9

Find the missing factor.

23 x 10 = 230	75 x 10 = 750	99 x 10 = 990
48 x 10 = 480	13 x 10 = 130	25 x 10 = 250
52 x 10 = 520	39 x 10 = 390	27 x 10 = 270
62 x 10 = 620	86 x 10 = 860	17 x 10 = 170

Find the dividend.

47 ÷ 10 = 4.7	68 ÷ 10 = 6.8	124 ÷ 10 = 12.4
257 ÷ 10 = 25.7	362 ÷ 10 = 36.2	314 ÷ 10 = 31.4
408 ÷ 10 = 40.8	672 ÷ 10 = 67.2	809 ÷ 10 = 80.9
924 ÷ 10 = 92.4	327 ÷ 10 = 32.7	563 ÷ 10 = 56.3

Multiplying a number by 10 is the same as adding a 0 it. Dividing by 10 moves the decimal point one place to the left. Whole numbers (e.g. 58) can be written with a decimal point (58.0). In the last two sections, the inverse operation gives the answer.

☆ Ordering sets of measures

Write these measures in order, from least to greatest.

3100 km	24 km	1821 km	247 km	4 km	960 km
4 km	24 km	247 km	960 km	1821 km	3100 km

Write these measures in order, from least to greatest.

$526	$15 940	$1504	$826	$37 532
$526	$826	$1504	$15 940	$37 532

720 km	7200 km	27 410 km	15 km	247 km
15 km	247 km	720 km	7200 km	27 410 km

70 000 litres	650 litres	26 000 litres	6500 litres	7000 litres
650 litres	6500 litres	7000 litres	26 000 litres	70 000 litres

656 kg	9565 kg	22 942 kg	752 247 kg	1327 kg
656 kg	1327 kg	9565 kg	22 942 kg	752 247 kg

9520 yrs	320 yrs	4681 yrs	8940 yrs	20 316 yrs
320 yrs	4681 yrs	8940 yrs	9520 yrs	20 316 yrs

217 846 kg	75 126 kg	8 940 kg	14 632 kg	175 kg
175 kg	8940 kg	14 632 kg	75 126 kg	217 846 kg

9420 km	764 km	25 811 km	114 243 km	7240 km
764 km	7240 km	9420 km	25 811 km	114 243 km

$37 227	$1 365 240	$143 820	$950	$4212
$950	$4212	$37 227	$143 820	$1 365 240

24 091 m	59 473 m	1237 m	426 m	837 201 m
426 m	1237 m	24 091 m	59 473 m	837 201 m

47 632 g	847 g	9625 g	103 427 g	2330 g
847 g	2330 g	9625 g	47 632 g	103 427 g

7340 m	249 m	12 746 m	32 m	17 407 321 m
32 m	249 m	7340 m	12 746 m	17 407 321 m

You may need to help children identify the significant digit when sorting a group of numbers. In some cases, when the significant digits are the same, it will be necessary to compare the digits to the right of the significant digit.

Appropriate units of measure ☆

Choose the best units to measure the length of each item.

millimetres	centimetres	metres

desk	tooth	swimming pool
centimetres	millimetres	metres

Choose the best units to measure the length of each item.

centimetres	metres	kilometres

bed	bicycle	toothbrush	football field
centimetres	centimetres	centimetres	metres
shoe	driveway	sailboat	highway
centimetres	metres	metres	kilometres

The height of a door is about 2 metres .

The length of a pencil is about 17 centimetres .

The height of a flagpole is about 7 metres .

Choose the best units to measure the mass of each item.

grams	kilograms	tonnes

train	kitten	watermelon	tennis ball
tonnes	grams	kilograms	grams
shoe	bag of potatoes	elephant	washing machine
grams	kilograms	tonnes	kilograms

The mass of a hamburger is about 26 grams .

The mass of a bag of apples is about 1 kilogram .

The mass of a truck is about 4 tonnes .

Children might come up with their own examples of items that measure about 1 centimetre, 1 metre, and 1 kilometre, as well as items that have a mass about 1 gram, 1 kilogram, and 1 tonne. They can use these as benchmarks to find the appropriate unit.

☆ Identifying patterns

Continue each pattern.

Intervals of 6:	1	7	13	19	25	31	37
Intervals of 3:	27	24	21	18	15	12	9

Continue each pattern.

0	10	20	30	40	50	60
15	20	25	30	35	40	45
5	7	9	11	13	15	17
2	9	16	23	30	37	44
4	7	10	13	16	19	22
2	10	18	26	34	42	50

Continue each pattern.

44	38	32	26	20	14	8
33	29	25	21	17	13	9
27	23	19	15	11	7	3
56	48	40	32	24	16	8
49	42	35	28	21	14	7
28	25	22	19	16	13	10

Continue each pattern.

36	30	24	18	12	6	0
5	14	23	32	41	50	59
3	8	13	18	23	28	33
47	40	33	26	19	12	5
1	4	7	10	13	16	19

Point out that some of the patterns show an increase and some a decrease. Children should see what operation turns the first number into the second, and the second number into the third. They can then continue the pattern.

Recognizing multiples

Circle the multiples of 10.

14　　(20)　　25　　(30)　　47　　(60)

Circle the multiples of 6.

20　　(48)　　56　　(72)　　25　　35
1　　3　　(6)　　16　　26　　(36)

Circle the multiples of 7.

(14)　　24　　(35)　　27　　47　　(49)
(63)　　(42)　　52　　37　　64　　71

Circle the multiples of 8.

25　　31　　(48)　　84　　(32)　　(8)
18　　54　　(64)　　35　　(72)　　28

Circle the multiples of 9.

17　　(81)　　(27)　　35　　92　　106
(45)　　53　　(108)　　(90)　　33　　95
64　　(9)　　28　　(18)　　(36)　　98

Circle the multiples of 10.

15　　35　　(20)　　46　　(90)　　(100)
44　　37　　(30)　　29　　(50)　　45

Circle the multiples of 5.

(25)　　(110)　　(125)　　54　　(35)　　48
(45)　　33　　87　　98　　99　　(120)
43　　44　　(65)　　(55)　　21　　(20)

Circle the multiples of 4.

18　　(12)　　45　　66　　30　　(72)
(24)　　(36)　　58　　(68)　　(48)　　(60)
35　　29　　82　　74　　(84)　　94

Success on this page basically depends on a knowledge of multiplication tables. Where children experience difficulty, it may be necessary to reinforce multiplication tables.

Using information in tables

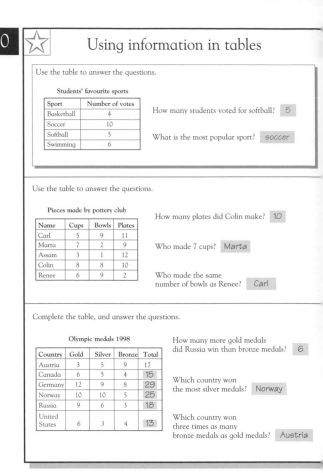

Use the table to answer the questions.

Students' favourite sports

Sport	Number of votes
Basketball	4
Soccer	10
Softball	5
Swimming	6

How many students voted for softball? 5

What is the most popular sport? soccer

Use the table to answer the questions.

Pieces made by pottery club

Name	Cups	Bowls	Plates
Carl	5	9	11
Marta	7	2	9
Assam	3	1	12
Colin	8	8	10
Renee	6	9	2

How many plates did Colin make? 10

Who made 7 cups? Marta

Who made the same number of bowls as Renee? Carl

Complete the table, and answer the questions.

Olympic medals 1998

Country	Gold	Silver	Bronze	Total
Austria	3	5	9	17
Canada	6	5	4	15
Germany	12	9	8	29
Norway	10	10	5	25
Russia	9	6	3	18
United States	6	3	4	13

How many more gold medals did Russia win than bronze medals? 6

Which country won the most silver medals? Norway

Which country won three times as many bronze medals as gold medals? Austria

On this page, children have to read, compare or manipulate information in a table. To answer the questions about the third table, children must first complete the final column.

Coordinate graphs

Write the coordinates for each point. Remember to write the coordinate for the x-axis first.

A　(2, 4)
B　(3, 2)
C　(5, 3)

Write the coordinates for each symbol.

▲　(2, 5)
■　(5, 5)
●　(1, 3)
★　(3, 2)
♣　(1, 1)

Place each of the points on the graph.

A　(2, 3)
B　(5, 4)
C　(2, 4)
D　(5, 3)
E　(4, 4)

Most errors on this page result from children using the incorrect order for coordinate pairs. Make sure children know that the x-coordinate is always written before the y-coordinate.

Fraction models

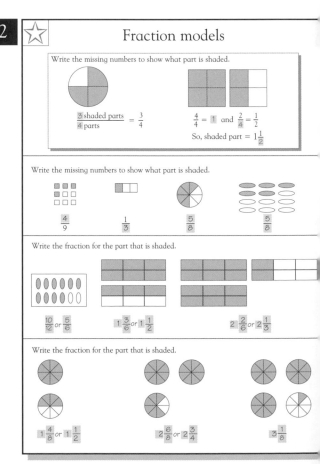

Write the missing numbers to show what part is shaded.

$\frac{3 \text{ shaded parts}}{4 \text{ parts}} = \frac{3}{4}$

$\frac{4}{4} = 1$ and $\frac{2}{4} = \frac{1}{2}$

So, shaded part $= 1\frac{1}{2}$

Write the missing numbers to show what part is shaded.

$\frac{4}{9}$　　$\frac{1}{3}$　　$\frac{5}{8}$　　$\frac{5}{8}$

Write the fraction for the part that is shaded.

$\frac{10}{12}$ or $\frac{5}{6}$　　$1\frac{3}{6}$ or $1\frac{1}{2}$　　$2\frac{2}{6}$ or $2\frac{1}{3}$

Write the fraction for the part that is shaded.

$1\frac{4}{8}$ or $1\frac{1}{2}$　　$2\frac{6}{8}$ or $2\frac{3}{4}$　　$3\frac{1}{8}$

Some children may need further explanation of the models of mixed numbers. Point out that when all the parts of a model are shaded, the model shows the number 1.

Converting fractions and decimals

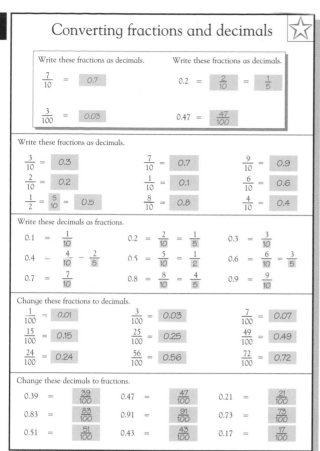

Write these fractions as decimals.

$\frac{7}{10}$ = 0.7

$\frac{3}{100}$ = 0.03

Write these fractions as decimals.

0.2 = $\frac{2}{10}$ = $\frac{1}{5}$

0.47 = $\frac{47}{100}$

Write these fractions as decimals.

$\frac{3}{10}$ = 0.3 $\frac{7}{10}$ = 0.7 $\frac{9}{10}$ = 0.9

$\frac{2}{10}$ = 0.2 $\frac{1}{10}$ = 0.1 $\frac{6}{10}$ = 0.6

$\frac{1}{2}$ = $\frac{5}{10}$ = 0.5 $\frac{8}{10}$ = 0.8 $\frac{4}{10}$ = 0.4

Write these decimals as fractions.

0.1 = $\frac{1}{10}$ 0.2 = $\frac{2}{10}$ = $\frac{1}{5}$ 0.3 = $\frac{3}{10}$

0.4 = $\frac{4}{10}$ = $\frac{2}{5}$ 0.5 = $\frac{5}{10}$ = $\frac{1}{2}$ 0.6 = $\frac{6}{10}$ = $\frac{3}{5}$

0.7 = $\frac{7}{10}$ 0.8 = $\frac{8}{10}$ = $\frac{4}{5}$ 0.9 = $\frac{9}{10}$

Change these fractions to decimals.

$\frac{1}{100}$ = 0.01 $\frac{3}{100}$ = 0.03 $\frac{7}{100}$ = 0.07

$\frac{15}{100}$ = 0.15 $\frac{25}{100}$ = 0.25 $\frac{49}{100}$ = 0.49

$\frac{24}{100}$ = 0.24 $\frac{56}{100}$ = 0.56 $\frac{72}{100}$ = 0.72

Change these decimals to fractions.

0.39 = $\frac{39}{100}$ 0.47 = $\frac{47}{100}$ 0.21 = $\frac{21}{100}$

0.83 = $\frac{83}{100}$ 0.91 = $\frac{91}{100}$ 0.73 = $\frac{73}{100}$

0.51 = $\frac{51}{100}$ 0.43 = $\frac{43}{100}$ 0.17 = $\frac{17}{100}$

A number line showing tenths with their decimal equivalents can help children. If they neglect to include the zeros when converting fractions such as $\frac{7}{100}$ to 0.07, ask them to convert the decimal back to the fraction to realize their error.

Factors of numbers from 31 to 65

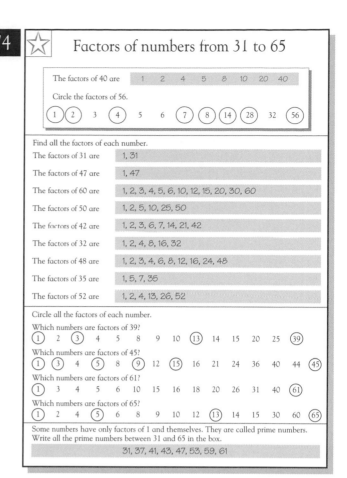

The factors of 40 are   1   2   4   5   8   10   20   40

Circle the factors of 56.

(1) (2) 3 (4) 5 6 (7) (8) (14) (28) 32 (56)

Find all the factors of each number.

The factors of 31 are   1, 31

The factors of 47 are   1, 47

The factors of 60 are   1, 2, 3, 4, 5, 6, 10, 12, 15, 20, 30, 60

The factors of 50 are   1, 2, 5, 10, 25, 50

The factors of 42 are   1, 2, 3, 6, 7, 14, 21, 42

The factors of 32 are   1, 2, 4, 8, 16, 32

The factors of 48 are   1, 2, 3, 4, 6, 8, 12, 16, 24, 48

The factors of 35 are   1, 5, 7, 35

The factors of 52 are   1, 2, 4, 13, 26, 52

Circle all the factors of each number.

Which numbers are factors of 39?

(1) 2 (3) 4 5 8 9 10 (13) 14 15 20 25 (39)

Which numbers are factors of 45?

(1) (3) 4 (5) 8 (9) 12 (15) 16 21 24 36 40 44 (45)

Which numbers are factors of 61?

(1) 3 4 5 6 10 15 16 18 20 26 31 40 (61)

Which numbers are factors of 65?

(1) 2 4 (5) 6 8 9 10 12 (13) 14 15 30 60 (65)

Some numbers have only factors of 1 and themselves. They are called prime numbers. Write all the prime numbers between 31 and 65 in the box.

31, 37, 41, 43, 47, 53, 59, 61

Children often miss some of the factors of large numbers. Encourage a systematic method to find factors. Remind children that 1 and the number itself are factors of a number. If necessary, discuss prime numbers with them.

Writing equivalent fractions

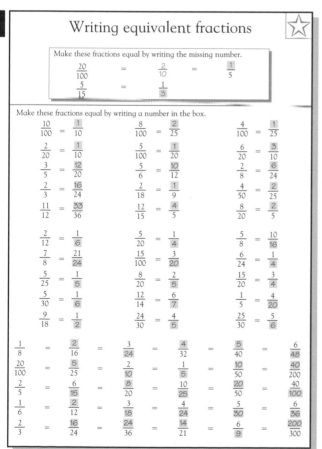

Make these fractions equal by writing the missing number.

$\frac{20}{100}$ = $\frac{2}{10}$ = $\frac{1}{5}$

$\frac{5}{15}$ = $\frac{1}{3}$

Make these fractions equal by writing a number in the box.

$\frac{10}{100}$ = $\frac{1}{10}$ $\frac{8}{100}$ = $\frac{2}{25}$ $\frac{4}{100}$ = $\frac{1}{25}$

$\frac{2}{20}$ = $\frac{1}{10}$ $\frac{5}{100}$ = $\frac{1}{20}$ $\frac{6}{20}$ = $\frac{3}{10}$

$\frac{3}{5}$ = $\frac{12}{20}$ $\frac{5}{6}$ = $\frac{10}{12}$ $\frac{2}{8}$ = $\frac{6}{24}$

$\frac{2}{3}$ = $\frac{16}{24}$ $\frac{2}{18}$ = $\frac{1}{9}$ $\frac{4}{50}$ = $\frac{2}{25}$

$\frac{11}{12}$ = $\frac{33}{36}$ $\frac{12}{15}$ = $\frac{4}{5}$ $\frac{8}{20}$ = $\frac{2}{5}$

$\frac{2}{12}$ = $\frac{1}{6}$ $\frac{5}{20}$ = $\frac{1}{4}$ $\frac{5}{8}$ = $\frac{10}{16}$

$\frac{7}{8}$ = $\frac{21}{24}$ $\frac{15}{100}$ = $\frac{3}{20}$ $\frac{6}{24}$ = $\frac{1}{4}$

$\frac{5}{25}$ = $\frac{1}{5}$ $\frac{8}{20}$ = $\frac{2}{5}$ $\frac{15}{20}$ = $\frac{3}{4}$

$\frac{5}{30}$ = $\frac{1}{6}$ $\frac{12}{14}$ = $\frac{6}{7}$ $\frac{1}{5}$ = $\frac{4}{20}$

$\frac{9}{18}$ = $\frac{1}{2}$ $\frac{24}{30}$ = $\frac{4}{5}$ $\frac{25}{30}$ = $\frac{5}{6}$

$\frac{1}{8}$ = $\frac{2}{16}$ = $\frac{3}{24}$ = $\frac{4}{32}$ = $\frac{5}{40}$ = $\frac{6}{48}$

$\frac{20}{100}$ = $\frac{5}{25}$ = $\frac{2}{10}$ = $\frac{1}{5}$ = $\frac{10}{50}$ = $\frac{40}{200}$

$\frac{2}{5}$ = $\frac{6}{15}$ = $\frac{8}{20}$ = $\frac{10}{25}$ = $\frac{20}{50}$ = $\frac{40}{100}$

$\frac{1}{6}$ = $\frac{2}{12}$ = $\frac{3}{18}$ = $\frac{4}{24}$ = $\frac{5}{30}$ = $\frac{6}{36}$

$\frac{2}{3}$ = $\frac{16}{24}$ = $\frac{24}{36}$ = $\frac{14}{21}$ = $\frac{6}{9}$ = $\frac{200}{300}$

If children have any problems, point out that fractions retain the same value if you multiply the numerator and denominator by the same number or divide the numerator and denominator by the same number.

Properties of polygons

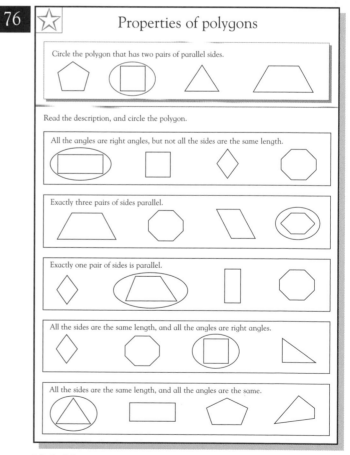

Circle the polygon that has two pairs of parallel sides.

Read the description, and circle the polygon.

All the angles are right angles, but not all the sides are the same length.

Exactly three pairs of sides parallel.

Exactly one pair of sides is parallel.

All the sides are the same length, and all the angles are right angles.

All the sides are the same length, and all the angles are the same.

If children answer questions incorrectly, make sure they understand the concepts of parallel lines, lengths of sides of a polygon, equal angles, and right angles.

Naming polygons

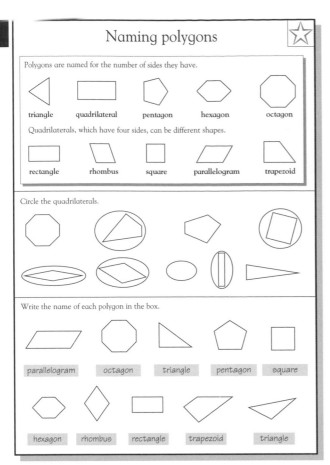

Polygons are named for the number of sides they have.

triangle | quadrilateral | pentagon | hexagon | octagon

Quadrilaterals, which have four sides, can be different shapes.

rectangle | rhombus | square | parallelogram | trapezoid

Circle the quadrilaterals.

Write the name of each polygon in the box.

parallelogram | octagon | triangle | pentagon | square

hexagon | rhombus | rectangle | trapezoid | triangle

The questions on this page require children to identify and name various polygons. Children may have difficulty differentiating among a square, a parallelogram, a rectangle, and a rhombus. Explain that they are all particular kinds of parallelograms.

Adding decimals

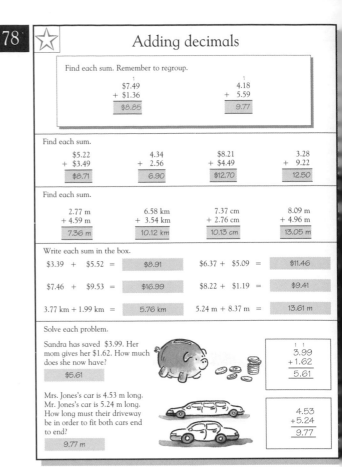

Find each sum. Remember to regroup.

```
   1                    1
 $7.49               4.18
+$1.36             + 5.59
 $8.85               9.77
```

Find each sum.

```
  $5.22      4.34      $8.21      3.28
+ $3.49    + 2.56    + $4.49    + 9.22
  $8.71      6.90     $12.70     12.50
```

Find each sum.

```
  2.77 m     6.58 km     7.37 cm     8.09 m
+ 4.59 m   + 3.54 km   + 2.76 cm   + 4.96 m
  7.36 m    10.12 km    10.13 cm    13.05 m
```

Write each sum in the box.

$3.39 + $5.52 = $8.91 $6.37 + $5.09 = $11.46

$7.46 + $9.53 = $16.99 $8.22 + $1.19 = $9.41

3.77 km + 1.99 km = 5.76 km   5.24 m + 8.37 m = 13.61 m

Solve each problem.

Sandra has saved $3.99. Her mom gives her $1.62. How much does she now have?

$5.61

```
  1 1
  3.99
+ 1.62
  5.61
```

Mrs. Jones's car is 4.53 m long. Mr. Jones's car is 5.24 m long. How long must their driveway be in order to fit both cars end to end?

9.77 m

```
  4.53
+ 5.24
  9.77
```

Children may place the decimal point incorrectly in sums that are presented horizontally (such as those in the third section). Have them rewrite the problems vertically, lining up the decimal points. Remind children to regroup when necessary.

Adding decimals

Find each sum. Remember to regroup.

```
   1                      1  1
 $4.96                 7.92 km
+$2.83               + 1.68 km
 $7.79                 9.60 km
```

Find each sum.

```
  8.94      $9.57      $7.96      5.73
+ 5.88    + $9.99    + $4.78    + 9.97
 14.82     $19.56     $12.74    15.70
```

```
  6.43 m     7.34 cm     8.62 km     3.04
+ 8.57 m   + 9.99 cm   + 8.08 km   + 5.76
 15.00 m    17.33 cm    16.70 km     8.80
```

Write each sum in the box.

$5.03 + $6.49 = $11.52   2.74 + 9.61 = 12.35

$8.32 + $9.58 = $17.90   1.29 + 4.83 = 6.12

5.26 km + 9.19 km = 14.45 km   2.04 m + 9.97 m = 12.01 m

Solve each problem.

Anna buys a can of soda for 45¢ and a sandwich for $1.39. How much does she pay?

$1.84

```
  1
  1.39
+ 0.45
  1.84
```

Mr. Bailey buys two wardrobes. One is 1.29 m wide and the other is 96 cm wide. How much space will they take up if he puts them side by side?

2.25 m

```
  1 1
  1.29
+ 0.96
  2.25
```

When the final decimal place of a sum is zero, it can be written, as in the second example, but it can also be omitted—unless the sum is an amount of dollars. To solve the final problem, children must realize that 96 cm is equivalent to 0.96 m.

Subtracting decimals

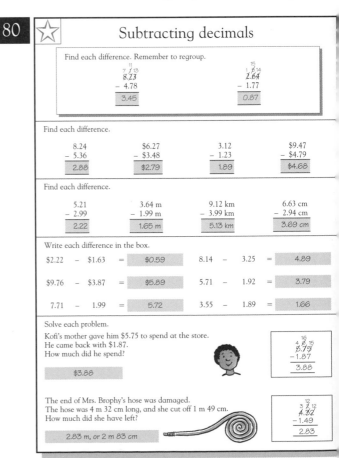

Find each difference. Remember to regroup.

```
  7 ⁷ 13            1 ⁷ 5 14
  8.23              2.64
- 4.78            - 1.77
  3.45              0.87
```

Find each difference.

```
  8.24      $6.27      3.12      $9.47
- 5.36    - $3.48    - 1.23    - $4.79
  2.88     $2.79      1.89      $4.68
```

Find each difference.

```
  5.21      3.64 m      9.12 km      6.63 cm
- 2.99    - 1.99 m    - 3.99 km    - 2.94 cm
  2.22     1.65 m      5.13 km      3.69 cm
```

Write each difference in the box.

$2.22 - $1.63 = $0.59   8.14 - 3.25 = 4.89

$9.76 - $3.87 = $5.89   5.71 - 1.92 = 3.79

7.71 - 1.99 = 5.72   3.55 - 1.89 = 1.66

Solve each problem.

Kofi's mother gave him $5.75 to spend at the store. He came back with $1.87. How much did he spend?

$3.88

```
  4 16
  5.75
- 1.87
  3.88
```

The end of Mrs. Brophy's hose was damaged. The hose was 4 m 32 cm long, and she cut off 1 m 49 cm. How much did she have left?

2.83 m, or 2 m 83 cm

```
  3 12
  4.32
- 1.49
  2.83
```

Some children are confused about subtracting decimals. Show them that once they line up the decimal points, they can simply subtract the digits lining up the decimal point of the answer as well.

Subtracting decimals ⭐

Find each difference. Remember to regroup.

$$\begin{array}{r} {\tiny 7\ 12}\\[-2pt] {\tiny 7\ \cancel{2}\ 11}\\[-2pt] \$8.31 \\ -\ \$2.94 \\ \hline \$5.37 \end{array} \qquad \begin{array}{r} {\tiny 5\ 13}\\[-2pt] {\tiny \cancel{6}.\cancel{2}3\ m}\\[-2pt] -\ 2.84\ m \\ \hline 3.39\ m \end{array}$$

Find each difference.

$5.31 − $1.89	8.24 − 2.87	7.23 − 3.44	$6.23 − $1.24	$4.11 − $1.12
$3.42	5.37	3.79	$4.99	$2.99

Find each difference.

8.14 m − 2.97 m	6.33 km − 2.94 km	9.11 cm − 1.32 cm	6.23 − 2.24	7.48 m − 3.49 m
5.17 m	3.39 km	7.79 cm	3.99	3.99 m

Write each difference in the box.

7.14 − 3.17 − **3.97** $3.39 − $1.47 = **$1.92**

8.51 − 6.59 = **1.92** $6.23 − $5.34 = **$0.89**

8.14 − 3.46 = **4.68**   7.42 m − 4.57 m = **2.85 m**

Solve each problem.

Suzanne goes to the park with $5.13 to spend. She buys a hot dog for $2.49. How much does she have left?   **$2.64**

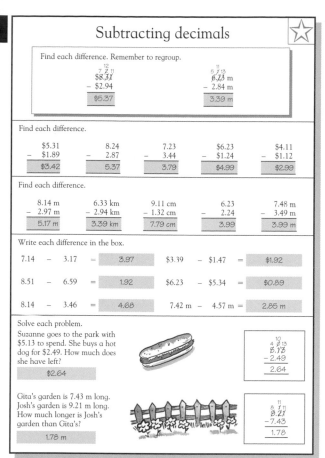

$$\begin{array}{r} {\tiny 4\ \cancel{0}\ 13}\\[-2pt] \cancel{5}.\cancel{1}\cancel{3} \\ -\ 2.49 \\ \hline 2.64 \end{array}$$

Gita's garden is 7.43 m long. Josh's garden is 9.21 m long. How much longer is Josh's garden than Gita's?   **1.78 m**

$$\begin{array}{r} {\tiny 8\ 11}\\[-2pt] {\tiny \cancel{9}.\cancel{2}1}\\[-2pt] -\ 7.43 \\ \hline 1.78 \end{array}$$

This page follows from the previous page. You may need to remind children that they can regroup across a decimal point in the same way as they would if the decimal point were not there.

⭐ Multiplying by one-digit numbers

Find each product. Remember to regroup.

$$\begin{array}{r} {\tiny 1\ 1}\\ 465 \\ \times\ 3 \\ \hline 1395 \end{array} \qquad \begin{array}{r} {\tiny 3}\\ 391 \\ \times\ 4 \\ \hline 1564 \end{array} \qquad \begin{array}{r} {\tiny 3\ 4}\\ 278 \\ \times\ 5 \\ \hline 1390 \end{array}$$

Find each product.

563 × 3	910 × 2	437 × 3	812 × 2
1689	1820	1311	1624
572 × 4	831 × 3	406 × 5	394 × 6
2288	2493	2030	2364

Find each product.

318 × 3	223 × 4	542 × 4	217 × 3
954	892	2168	651
127 × 4	275 × 5	798 × 6	365 × 6
508	1375	4788	2190
100 × 5	372 × 4	881 × 4	953 × 3
500	1488	3524	2859

Solve each problem.

A middle school has 255 students. A high school has 6 times as many students. How many children are there at the high school?   **1530 students**

$$\begin{array}{r} {\tiny 3\ 3}\\ 255 \\ \times\ 6 \\ \hline 1530 \end{array}$$

A train can carry 365 passengers. How many could it carry on

four trips?   **1460 passengers**

six trips?   **2190 passengers**

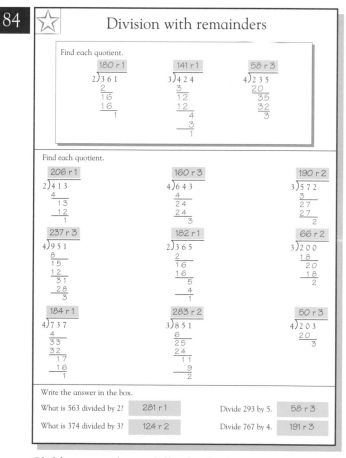

$$\begin{array}{r} {\tiny 2\ 2}\\ 365 \\ \times\ 4 \\ \hline 1460 \end{array} \qquad \begin{array}{r} {\tiny 3\ 3}\\ 365 \\ \times\ 6 \\ \hline 2190 \end{array}$$

Make sure children understand the convention of multiplication, i.e. multiply the ones first and work left. Problems on this page may result from gaps in knowledge of the 2, 3, 4, 5, and 6 times tables. Errors will also occur if children neglect to regroup.

Multiplying by one-digit numbers ⭐

Find each product. Remember to regroup.

$$\begin{array}{r} {\tiny 3\ 3}\\ 456 \\ \times\ 6 \\ \hline 2736 \end{array} \qquad \begin{array}{r} {\tiny 1\ 2}\\ 823 \\ \times\ 8 \\ \hline 6584 \end{array} \qquad \begin{array}{r} {\tiny 4\ 4}\\ 755 \\ \times\ 9 \\ \hline 6795 \end{array}$$

Find each product.

394 × 7	736 × 7	827 × 8	943 × 9
2758	5152	6616	8487
643 × 6	199 × 6	821 × 7	547 × 8
3858	1194	5747	4376
501 × 7	377 × 8	843 × 8	222 × 9
3507	3016	6744	1998
471 × 9	223 × 8	606 × 6	513 × 7
4239	1784	3636	3591
500 × 9	800 × 9	900 × 8	200 × 9
4500	7200	7200	1800

Solve each problem.

A crate holds 550 apples. How many apples are there in 8 crates?   **4400 apples**

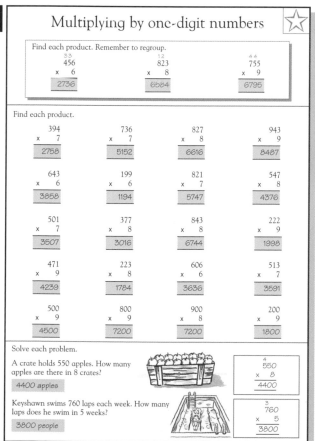

$$\begin{array}{r} {\tiny 4}\\ 550 \\ \times\ 8 \\ \hline 4400 \end{array}$$

Keyshawn swims 760 laps each week. How many laps does he swim in 5 weeks?   **3800 people**

$$\begin{array}{r} {\tiny 3}\\ 760 \\ \times\ 5 \\ \hline 3800 \end{array}$$

Problems encountered will be similar to the previous page. Gaps in knowledge of the 6, 7, 8, and 9 times table will result in children's errors.

⭐ Division with remainders

Find each quotient.

$$\begin{array}{r} 180\ r\ 1 \\ 2\overline{)361} \\ \underline{2} \\ 16 \\ \underline{16} \\ 1 \end{array} \qquad \begin{array}{r} 141\ r\ 1 \\ 3\overline{)424} \\ \underline{3} \\ 12 \\ \underline{12} \\ 4 \\ \underline{3} \\ 1 \end{array} \qquad \begin{array}{r} 58\ r\ 3 \\ 4\overline{)235} \\ \underline{20} \\ 35 \\ \underline{32} \\ 3 \end{array}$$

Find each quotient.

$$\begin{array}{r} 206\ r\ 1 \\ 2\overline{)413} \\ \underline{4} \\ 13 \\ \underline{12} \\ 1 \end{array} \qquad \begin{array}{r} 160\ r\ 3 \\ 4\overline{)643} \\ \underline{4} \\ 24 \\ \underline{24} \\ 3 \end{array} \qquad \begin{array}{r} 190\ r\ 2 \\ 3\overline{)572} \\ \underline{3} \\ 27 \\ \underline{27} \\ 2 \end{array}$$

$$\begin{array}{r} 237\ r\ 3 \\ 4\overline{)951} \\ \underline{8} \\ 15 \\ \underline{12} \\ 31 \\ \underline{28} \\ 3 \end{array} \qquad \begin{array}{r} 182\ r\ 1 \\ 2\overline{)365} \\ \underline{2} \\ 16 \\ \underline{16} \\ 5 \\ \underline{4} \\ 1 \end{array} \qquad \begin{array}{r} 66\ r\ 2 \\ 3\overline{)200} \\ \underline{18} \\ 20 \\ \underline{18} \\ 2 \end{array}$$

$$\begin{array}{r} 184\ r\ 1 \\ 4\overline{)737} \\ \underline{4} \\ 33 \\ \underline{32} \\ 17 \\ \underline{16} \\ 1 \end{array} \qquad \begin{array}{r} 283\ r\ 2 \\ 3\overline{)851} \\ \underline{6} \\ 25 \\ \underline{24} \\ 11 \\ \underline{9} \\ 2 \end{array} \qquad \begin{array}{r} 50\ r\ 3 \\ 4\overline{)203} \\ \underline{20} \\ 3 \end{array}$$

Write the answer in the box.

What is 563 divided by 2?   **281 r 1**   Divide 293 by 5.   **58 r 3**

What is 374 divided by 3?   **124 r 2**   Divide 767 by 4.   **191 r 3**

Children may have difficulty finding quotients with remainders. Have them perform long division until the remaining value to be divided is less than the divisor. That value is the remainder.

Division with remainders

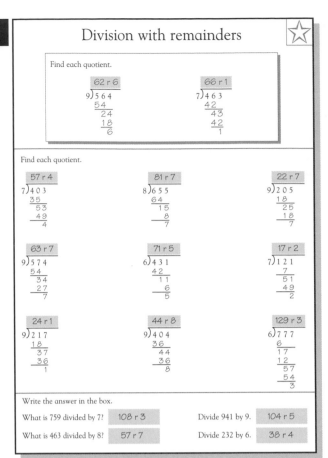

Find each quotient.

$$62 \text{ r } 6$$
$$9\overline{)564}$$
$$\underline{54}$$
$$24$$
$$\underline{18}$$
$$6$$

$$66 \text{ r } 1$$
$$7\overline{)463}$$
$$\underline{42}$$
$$43$$
$$\underline{42}$$
$$1$$

Find each quotient.

$$57 \text{ r } 4$$
$$7\overline{)403}$$
$$\underline{35}$$
$$53$$
$$\underline{49}$$
$$4$$

$$81 \text{ r } 7$$
$$8\overline{)655}$$
$$\underline{64}$$
$$15$$
$$\underline{8}$$
$$7$$

$$22 \text{ r } 7$$
$$9\overline{)205}$$
$$\underline{18}$$
$$25$$
$$\underline{18}$$
$$7$$

$$63 \text{ r } 7$$
$$9\overline{)574}$$
$$\underline{54}$$
$$34$$
$$\underline{27}$$
$$7$$

$$71 \text{ r } 5$$
$$6\overline{)431}$$
$$\underline{42}$$
$$11$$
$$\underline{6}$$
$$5$$

$$17 \text{ r } 2$$
$$7\overline{)121}$$
$$\underline{7}$$
$$51$$
$$\underline{49}$$
$$2$$

$$24 \text{ r } 1$$
$$9\overline{)217}$$
$$\underline{18}$$
$$37$$
$$\underline{36}$$
$$1$$

$$44 \text{ r } 8$$
$$9\overline{)404}$$
$$\underline{36}$$
$$44$$
$$\underline{36}$$
$$8$$

$$129 \text{ r } 3$$
$$6\overline{)777}$$
$$\underline{6}$$
$$17$$
$$\underline{12}$$
$$57$$
$$\underline{54}$$
$$3$$

Write the answer in the box.

What is 759 divided by 7?   108 r 3

Divide 941 by 9.   104 r 5

What is 463 divided by 8?   57 r 7

Divide 232 by 6.   38 r 4

This page is similar to the previous page, but the divisors are numbers greater than 5. Children will need to know their 6, 7, 8 and 9 times tables.

Real-life problems

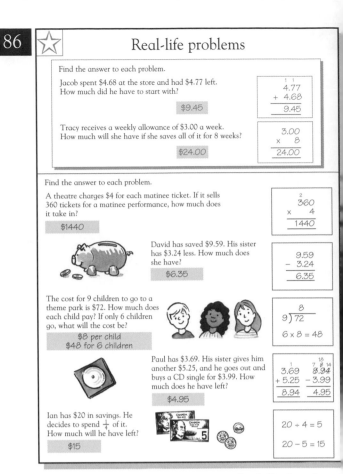

Find the answer to each problem.

Jacob spent $4.68 at the store and had $4.77 left. How much did he have to start with?

$9.45

$$\begin{array}{r} 1\ 1 \\ 4.77 \\ +\ 4.68 \\ \hline 9.45 \end{array}$$

Tracy receives a weekly allowance of $3.00 a week. How much will she have if she saves all of it for 8 weeks?

$24.00

$$\begin{array}{r} 3.00 \\ \times\ \ \ 8 \\ \hline 24.00 \end{array}$$

Find the answer to each problem.

A theatre charges $4 for each matinee ticket. If it sells 360 tickets for a matinee performance, how much does it take in?

$1440

$$\begin{array}{r} 2 \\ 360 \\ \times\ \ \ 4 \\ \hline 1440 \end{array}$$

David has saved $9.59. His sister has $3.24 less. How much does she have?

$6.35

$$\begin{array}{r} 9.59 \\ -\ 3.24 \\ \hline 6.35 \end{array}$$

The cost for 9 children to go to a theme park is $72. How much does each child pay? If only 6 children go, what will the cost be?

$8 per child
$48 for 6 children

$$8$$
$$9\overline{)72}$$
$$6 \times 8 = 48$$

Paul has $3.69. His sister gives him another $5.25, and he goes out and buys a CD single for $3.99. How much does he have left?

$4.95

$$\begin{array}{r} 1 \\ 3.69 \\ +\ 5.25 \\ \hline 8.94 \end{array}$$

$$\begin{array}{r} 7\ 18 \\ \cancel{8}.\cancel{9}4 \\ -\ 3.99 \\ \hline 4.95 \end{array}$$

Ian has $20 in savings. He decides to spend $\frac{1}{4}$ of it. How much will he have left?

$15

$$20 \div 4 = 5$$
$$20 - 5 = 15$$

This page requires children to apply skills they have learned. If they are unsure about what operation to use, discuss whether they expect the answer to be larger or smaller. This can help them decide whether to add, subtract, multiply or divide.

Real-life problems

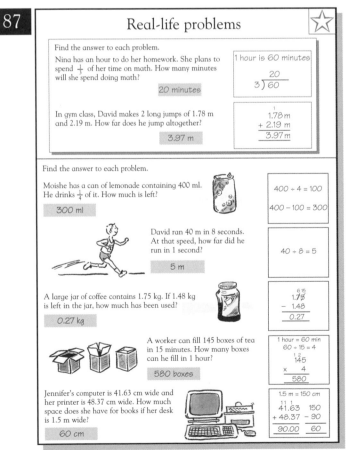

Find the answer to each problem.

Nina has an hour to do her homework. She plans to spend $\frac{1}{3}$ of her time on math. How many minutes will she spend doing math?

20 minutes

1 hour is 60 minutes

$$20$$
$$3\overline{)60}$$

In gym class, David makes 2 long jumps of 1.78 m and 2.19 m. How far does he jump altogether?

3.97 m

$$\begin{array}{r} 1 \\ 1.78 \text{ m} \\ +\ 2.19 \text{ m} \\ \hline 3.97 \text{ m} \end{array}$$

Find the answer to each problem.

Moishe has a can of lemonade containing 400 ml. He drinks $\frac{1}{4}$ of it. How much is left?

300 ml

$$400 \div 4 = 100$$
$$400 - 100 = 300$$

David ran 40 m in 8 seconds. At that speed, how far did he run in 1 second?

5 m

$$40 \div 8 = 5$$

A large jar of coffee contains 1.75 kg. If 1.48 kg is left in the jar, how much has been used?

0.27 kg

$$\begin{array}{r} 6\ 15 \\ 1.\cancel{7}\cancel{5} \\ -\ 1.48 \\ \hline 0.27 \end{array}$$

A worker can fill 145 boxes of tea in 15 minutes. How many boxes can he fill in 1 hour?

580 boxes

1 hour = 60 min
$$60 \div 15 = 4$$

$$\begin{array}{r} 1\ 2 \\ 145 \\ \times\ \ \ 4 \\ \hline 580 \end{array}$$

Jennifer's computer is 41.63 cm wide and her printer is 48.37 cm wide. How much space does she have for books if her desk is 1.5 m wide?

60 cm

1.5 m = 150 cm

$$\begin{array}{r} 1\ 1 \\ 41.63 \\ +\ 48.37 \\ \hline 90.00 \end{array}$$
$$\begin{array}{r} 150 \\ -\ 90 \\ \hline 60 \end{array}$$

This page deals with units other than money. As on the previous page, children have to decide what operation to use. Note that solving the final problem requires two operations.

Perimeters of squares and rectangles

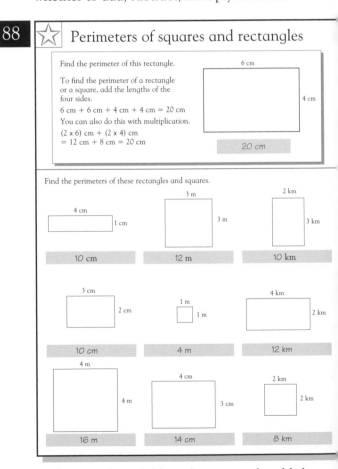

Find the perimeter of this rectangle.

To find the perimeter of a rectangle or a square, add the lengths of the four sides.

6 cm + 6 cm + 4 cm + 4 cm = 20 cm

You can also do this with multiplication.

(2 × 6) + (2 × 4) cm
= 12 cm + 8 cm = 20 cm

6 cm · 4 cm

20 cm

Find the perimeters of these rectangles and squares.

4 cm · 1 cm → 10 cm

3 m · 3 m → 12 m

2 km · 3 km → 10 km

3 cm · 2 cm → 10 cm

1 m · 1 m → 4 m

4 km · 2 km → 12 km

4 m · 4 m → 16 m

4 cm · 3 cm → 14 cm

2 km · 2 km → 8 km

Make sure that children do not simply add the lengths of two sides of a figure rather than all four sides. You may want to help children realize that the perimeter of a square can be found by multiplying the length of one side by 4.

Problems involving time

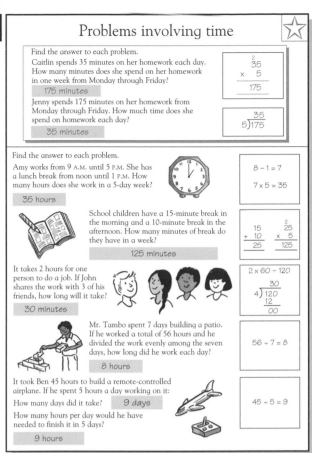

Find the answer to each problem.
Caitlin spends 35 minutes on her homework each day. How many minutes does she spend on her homework in one week from Monday through Friday?

$$\begin{array}{r} \overset{2}{35} \\ \times\ 5 \\ \hline 175 \end{array}$$

175 minutes

Jenny spends 175 minutes on her homework from Monday through Friday. How much time does she spend on homework each day?

$$5\overline{)175}$$

35 minutes

Find the answer to each problem.

Amy works from 9 A.M. until 5 P.M. She has a lunch break from noon until 1 P.M. How many hours does she work in a 5-day week?

$8 - 1 = 7$
$7 \times 5 = 35$

35 hours

School children have a 15-minute break in the morning and a 10-minute break in the afternoon. How many minutes of break do they have in a week?

$$\begin{array}{r} 15 \\ +\ 10 \\ \hline 25 \end{array} \qquad \begin{array}{r} \overset{2}{25} \\ \times\ 5 \\ \hline 125 \end{array}$$

125 minutes

It takes 2 hours for one person to do a job. If John shares the work with 3 of his friends, how long will it take?

$2 \times 60 = 120$

$$\begin{array}{r} 30 \\ 4\overline{)120} \\ 12 \\ \hline 00 \end{array}$$

30 minutes

Mr. Tambo spent 7 days building a patio. If he worked a total of 56 hours and he divided the work evenly among the seven days, how long did he work each day?

$56 \div 7 = 8$

8 hours

It took Ben 45 hours to build a remote-controlled airplane. If he spent 5 hours a day working on it:

How many days did it take?　**9 days**

$45 \div 5 = 9$

How many hours per day would he have needed to finish it in 5 days?

9 hours

For the second problem, children should realize that a school week is 5 days. For the third problem, check that children divide by 4 rather than 3.

Using bar graphs

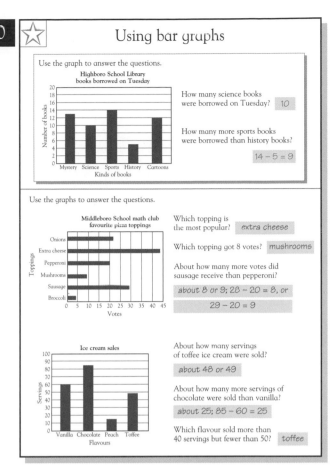

Use the graph to answer the questions.

Highboro School Library books borrowed on Tuesday

How many science books were borrowed on Tuesday?　**10**

How many more sports books were borrowed than history books?

14 – 5 = 9

Use the graphs to answer the questions.

Middleboro School math club favourite pizza toppings

Which topping is the most popular?　**extra cheese**

Which topping got 8 votes?　**mushrooms**

About how many more votes did sausage receive than pepperoni?

about 8 or 9; 28 – 20 = 8, or
29 – 20 = 9

Ice cream sales

About how many servings of toffee ice cream were sold?

about 48 or 49

About how many more servings of chocolate were sold than vanilla?

about 25; 85 – 60 = 25

Which flavour sold more than 40 servings but fewer than 50?　**toffee**

On this page, children have to find specific entries, compare or manipulate information read from a bar graph. Some children may need to be reassured that a horizontal bar graph can be read in much the same way as a vertical bar graph.

Congruency

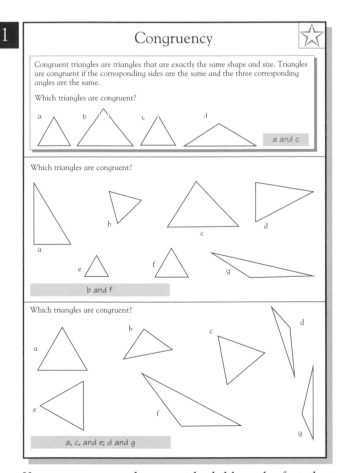

Congruent triangles are triangles that are exactly the same shape and size. Triangles are congruent if the corresponding sides are the same and the three corresponding angles are the same.

Which triangles are congruent?

a　　b　　c　　d

a and c

Which triangles are congruent?

b and f

Which triangles are congruent?

a, c, and e; d and g

You may want to discuss with children the fact that a triangle with congruent corresponding sides also has congruent corresponding angles.

Lines of symmetry

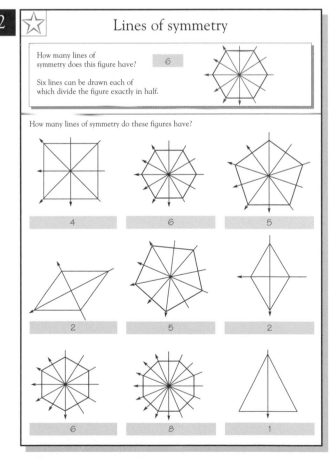

How many lines of symmetry does this figure have?　**6**

Six lines can be drawn each of which divide the figure exactly in half.

How many lines of symmetry do these figures have?

4　　**6**　　**5**

2　　**5**　　**2**

6　　**8**　　**1**

Make sure that children understand that the lines of symmetry of the figures on this page could be between opposite vertices, between the mid-points of opposite sides, or between vertices and mid-points of their opposite sides.

Writing equivalent number sentences ☆

Write a multiplication sentence that goes with 24 ÷ 6 = 4.
6 × 4 = 24 or 4 × 6 = 24
Write a related subtraction sentence for 5 + 12 = 17.
17 − 5 = 12 or 17 − 12 = 5

Write a related subtraction sentence for each sentence.

25 + 12 = 37   37 − 25 = 12 or 37 − 12 = 25

35 + 8 = 43   43 − 35 = 8 or 43 − 8 = 35

13 + 9 = 22   22 − 9 = 13 or 22 − 13 = 9

Write a related addition sentence for each sentence.

35 − 24 = 11   11 + 24 = 35 or 24 + 11 = 35

82 − 23 = 59   23 + 59 = 82 or 59 + 23 = 82

45 − 20 = 25   25 + 20 = 45 or 20 + 25 = 45

Write a related multiplication sentence for each sentence.

36 ÷ 4 = 9   4 × 9 = 36 or 9 × 4 = 36

32 ÷ 2 = 16   16 × 2 = 32 or 2 × 16 = 32

72 ÷ 9 = 8   8 × 9 = 72 or 9 × 8 = 72

Write a related division sentence for each sentence.

8 × 6 = 48   48 ÷ 8 = 6 or 48 ÷ 6 = 8

7 × 12 = 84   84 ÷ 7 = 12 or 84 ÷ 12 = 7

9 × 5 = 45   45 ÷ 9 = 5 or 45 ÷ 5 = 9

If children answer any questions incorrectly, have them check their answers to find out if they have written sentences that do not express facts.

☆ Multiplying and dividing

Write the answer in the box.
26 × 10 = 260   26 × 100 = 2600
400 ÷ 10 = 40   400 ÷ 100 = 4

Write the product in the box.

33 × 10 = 330   21 × 10 = 210   42 × 10 = 420

94 × 100 = 9400   36 × 100 = 3600   81 × 100 = 8100

416 × 10 = 4160   204 × 10 = 2040   513 × 10 = 5130

767 × 100 = 76 700   821 × 100 = 82 100   245 × 100 = 24 500

Write the quotient in the box.

120 ÷ 10 = 12   260 ÷ 10 = 26   470 ÷ 10 = 47

300 ÷ 100 = 3   800 ÷ 100 = 8   400 ÷ 100 = 4

20 ÷ 10 = 2   30 ÷ 10 = 3   70 ÷ 10 = 7

500 ÷ 100 = 5   100 ÷ 100 = 1   900 ÷ 100 = 9

Write the number that has been multiplied by 100.

59 × 100 = 5900   714 × 100 = 71 400

721 × 100 = 72 100   234 × 100 = 23 400

11 × 100 = 1100   470 × 100 = 47 000

84 × 100 = 8400   441 × 100 = 44 100

Write the number that has been divided by 100.

200 ÷ 100 = 2   800 ÷ 100 = 8

2100 ÷ 100 = 21   1800 ÷ 100 = 18

8600 ÷ 100 = 86   2100 ÷ 100 = 21

1000 ÷ 100 = 10   5900 ÷ 100 = 59

Children should realize that multiplying a whole number by 10 or 100 means writing one or two zeros at the end of it. To divide a multiple of 10 by 10, take the final zero off the number. The two final sections require use of the inverse operation.

Ordering sets of measures ☆

Write these amounts in order, from least to greatest.

70 cm	300 mm	2 km	6 m	500 mm
300 mm	500 mm	70 cm	6 m	2 km

Write these amounts in order, from least to greatest.

500¢	$4.00	$5.50	350¢	640¢
350¢	$4.00	500¢	$5.50	640¢
2 ml	1 litre	12 ml	2 litres	10 ml
2 ml	10 ml	12 ml	1 litre	2 litres
125 min	2 h	3½ h	200 min	¾ h
¾ h	2 h	125 min	200 min	3½ h
2500 m	2 km	1000 cm	20 m	1000 m
1000 cm	20 m	1000 m	2 km	2500 m
$240	3500¢	$125.00	4600¢	$50.00
3500¢	4600¢	$50.00	$125.00	$240
1 m	9 cm	24 mm	72 mm	7 cm
24 mm	7 cm	72 mm	9 cm	1 m
6 ml	8 litres	3 litres	1 ml	4 ml
1 ml	4 ml	6 ml	3 litres	8 litres
2 h	75 min	1½ h	100 min	150 min
75 min	1½ h	100 min	2 h	150 min
44 mm	4 cm	4 m	4 km	40 cm
4 cm	44 mm	40 cm	4 m	4 km
4 m	36 cm	2 mm	20 cm	2 m
2 mm	20 cm	36 cm	2 m	4 m

Most errors will result from a lack of understanding of the relationship between measures written using different units. Look out for confusion between large numbers of small units and small numbers of large units, such as 350¢ and $4.00.

☆ Decimal models

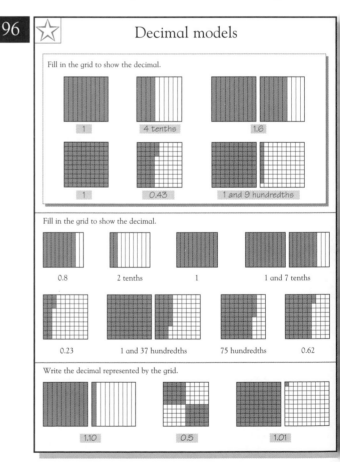

Fill in the grid to show the decimal.

1   4 tenths   1.6

1   0.43   1 and 9 hundredths

Fill in the grid to show the decimal.

0.8   2 tenths   1   1 and 7 tenths

0.23   1 and 37 hundredths   75 hundredths   0.62

Write the decimal represented by the grid.

1.10   0.5   1.01

Children may have difficulty understanding that the zero in a number such as 1.09 is needed. If they write such a number incorrectly, show them that their answer actually represents a different number.

97 Identifying patterns

Continue each pattern.

Steps of 2:	$\frac{1}{2}$	$2\frac{1}{2}$	$4\frac{1}{2}$	$6\frac{1}{2}$	$8\frac{1}{2}$	$10\frac{1}{2}$
Steps of 5:	3.5	8.5	13.5	18.5	23.5	28.5

Continue each pattern.

$5\frac{1}{2}$	$10\frac{1}{2}$	$15\frac{1}{2}$	$20\frac{1}{2}$	$25\frac{1}{2}$	$30\frac{1}{2}$
$1\frac{1}{4}$	$3\frac{1}{4}$	$5\frac{1}{4}$	$7\frac{1}{4}$	$9\frac{1}{4}$	$11\frac{1}{4}$
$8\frac{1}{3}$	$9\frac{1}{3}$	$10\frac{1}{3}$	$11\frac{1}{3}$	$12\frac{1}{3}$	$13\frac{1}{3}$
$55\frac{3}{4}$	$45\frac{3}{4}$	$35\frac{3}{4}$	$25\frac{3}{4}$	$15\frac{3}{4}$	$5\frac{3}{4}$
$42\frac{1}{2}$	$38\frac{1}{2}$	$34\frac{1}{2}$	$30\frac{1}{2}$	$26\frac{1}{2}$	$22\frac{1}{2}$
7.5	6.5	5.5	4.5	3.5	2.5
28.4	25.4	22.4	19.4	16.4	13.4
81.6	73.6	65.6	57.6	49.6	41.6
6.3	10.3	14.3	18.3	22.3	26.3
12.1	13.1	14.1	15.1	16.1	17.1
14.6	21.6	28.6	35.6	42.6	49.6
$11\frac{1}{2}$	$10\frac{1}{2}$	$9\frac{1}{2}$	$8\frac{1}{2}$	$7\frac{1}{2}$	$6\frac{1}{2}$
8.4	11.4	14.4	17.4	20.4	23.4
$7\frac{3}{4}$	$13\frac{3}{4}$	$19\frac{3}{4}$	$25\frac{3}{4}$	$31\frac{3}{4}$	$37\frac{3}{4}$
57.5	48.5	39.5	30.5	21.5	12.5

Although the patterns here are formed by adding or subtracting whole numbers, the items in each are mixed numbers or decimals. The operation that turns the first number into the second, and the second into the third can be used to continue the pattern.

98 Products with odd and even numbers

Find the products of these numbers.

3 and 4 The product of 3 and 4 is 12. 6 and 8 The product of 6 and 8 is 48.

Find the products of these odd and even numbers.

5 and 6	The product of 5 and 6 is 30.	3 and 2	The product of 3 and 2 is 6.
7 and 4	The product of 7 and 4 is 28.	8 and 3	The product of 8 and 3 is 24.
6 and 3	The product of 6 and 3 is 18.	2 and 9	The product of 2 and 9 is 18.
10 and 3	The product of 10 and 3 is 30.	12 and 5	The product of 12 and 5 is 60.

What do you notice about your answers? The product of odd and even numbers is always an even number.

Find the products of these odd numbers.

5 and 7	The product of 5 and 7 is 35.	3 and 9	The product of 3 and 9 is 27.
5 and 11	The product of 5 and 11 is 55.	7 and 3	The product of 7 and 3 is 21.
9 and 5	The product of 9 and 5 is 45.	11 and 7	The product of 11 and 7 is 77.
13 and 3	The product of 13 and 3 is 39.	1 and 5	The product of 1 and 5 is 5.

What do you notice about your answers? The product of two odd numbers is always an odd number.

Find the products of these even numbers.

2 and 4	The product of 2 and 4 is 8.	4 and 6	The product of 4 and 6 is 24.
6 and 2	The product of 6 and 2 is 12.	4 and 8	The product of 4 and 8 is 32.
10 and 2	The product of 10 and 2 is 20.	4 and 10	The product of 4 and 10 is 40.
6 and 10	The product of 6 and 10 is 60.	6 and 8	The product of 6 and 8 is 48.

What do you notice about your answers? The product of two even numbers is always an even number.

Can you write a rule for the products with odd and even numbers?

The product of two numbers will always be even unless both numbers are odd.

Children may need help answering the questions on what they notice about the products. Accept any rule about products that children write as long as it indicates that they have grasped the concept.

99 Squares of numbers

Find the square of 2.

2 x 2 = 4

What is the area of this square?

2 cm, 2 cm

2 x 2 = 4
Area = 4 cm²

Find the square of these numbers.

3	3 x 3 = 9	1	1 x 1 = 1	6	6 x 6 = 36
7	7 x 7 = 49	8	8 x 8 = 64	5	5 x 5 = 25
9	9 x 9 = 81	4	4 x 4 = 16	10	10 x 10 = 100

Now try these.

13	13 x 13 = 169	20	20 x 20 = 400	40	40 x 40 = 1600
11	11 x 11 = 121	12	12 x 12 = 144	30	30 x 30 = 900

What are the areas of these squares?

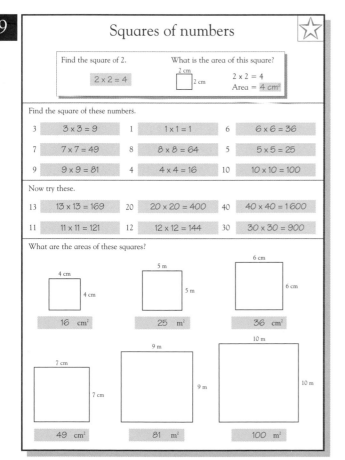

4 cm, 4 cm: 16 cm²

5 m, 5 m: 25 m²

6 cm, 6 cm: 36 cm²

7 cm, 7 cm: 49 cm²

9 m, 9 m: 81 m²

10 m, 10 m: 100 m²

Make sure that children understand that area is given in square units. You may want to add lines to divide the square in the example into quarters, to show 4 square centimetres. Check that they are in fact squaring the numbers, and not multiplying by two.

100 Factors of numbers from 66 to 100

The factors of 66 are 1 2 3 6 11 22 33 66

Circle the factors of 94. (1) (2) 28 32 43 (47) 71 86 (94)

Write the factors of each number in the box.

The factors of 70 are 1, 2, 5, 7, 10, 14, 35, 70

The factors of 85 are 1, 5, 17, 85

The factors of 69 are 1, 3, 23, 69

The factors of 83 are 1, 83

The factors of 75 are 1, 3, 5, 15, 25, 75

The factors of 96 are 1, 2, 3, 4, 6, 8, 12, 16, 24, 32, 48, 96

The factors of 63 are 1, 3, 7, 9, 21, 63

The factors of 99 are 1, 3, 9, 11, 33, 99

The factors of 72 are 1, 2, 3, 4, 6, 8, 9, 12, 18, 24, 36, 72

Circle the factors of 68.
(1) (2) 3 (4) 5 6 7 8 9 11 12 (17) (34) 35 62 (68)

Circle the factors of 95.
(1) 2 3 4 (5) 15 16 17 (19) 24 37 85 90 (95) 96

Circle the factors of 88.
(1) (2) 3 (4) 5 6 (8) 10 (11) 15 (22) 25 27 (44) 87 (88)

Circle the factors of 73.
(1) 2 4 5 6 8 9 10 12 13 14 15 30 60 (73)

A prime number only has two factors, 1 and itself.
Write all the prime numbers between 66 and 100 in the box.

67, 71, 73, 79, 83, 89, 97

Children often miss some of the factors of large numbers. Encourage a systematic method of finding factors. Children may forget that 1 and the number itself are factors of a number. If necessary, discuss prime numbers with children.

Renaming fractions

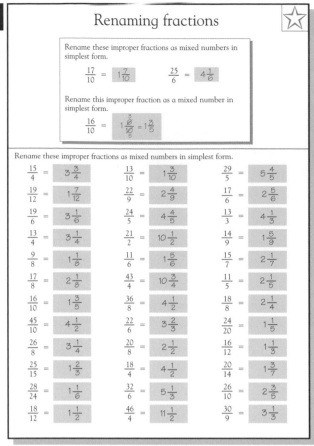

Rename these improper fractions as mixed numbers in simplest form.

$$\frac{17}{10} = 1\frac{7}{10} \qquad \frac{25}{6} = 4\frac{1}{6}$$

Rename this improper fraction as a mixed number in simplest form.

$$\frac{16}{10} = 1\frac{\cancel{6}^{3}}{\cancel{10}_{5}} = 1\frac{3}{5}$$

Rename these improper fractions as mixed numbers in simplest form.

$\frac{15}{4} = 3\frac{3}{4}$	$\frac{13}{10} = 1\frac{3}{10}$	$\frac{29}{5} = 5\frac{4}{5}$
$\frac{19}{12} = 1\frac{7}{12}$	$\frac{22}{9} = 2\frac{4}{9}$	$\frac{17}{6} = 2\frac{5}{6}$
$\frac{19}{6} = 3\frac{1}{6}$	$\frac{24}{5} = 4\frac{4}{5}$	$\frac{13}{3} = 4\frac{1}{3}$
$\frac{13}{4} = 3\frac{1}{4}$	$\frac{21}{2} = 10\frac{1}{2}$	$\frac{14}{9} = 1\frac{5}{9}$
$\frac{9}{8} = 1\frac{1}{8}$	$\frac{11}{6} = 1\frac{5}{6}$	$\frac{15}{7} = 2\frac{1}{7}$
$\frac{17}{8} = 2\frac{1}{8}$	$\frac{43}{4} = 10\frac{3}{4}$	$\frac{11}{5} = 2\frac{1}{5}$
$\frac{16}{10} = 1\frac{3}{5}$	$\frac{36}{8} = 4\frac{1}{2}$	$\frac{18}{8} = 2\frac{1}{4}$
$\frac{45}{10} = 4\frac{1}{2}$	$\frac{22}{6} = 3\frac{2}{3}$	$\frac{24}{20} = 1\frac{1}{5}$
$\frac{26}{8} = 3\frac{1}{4}$	$\frac{20}{8} = 2\frac{1}{2}$	$\frac{16}{12} = 1\frac{1}{3}$
$\frac{25}{15} = 1\frac{2}{3}$	$\frac{18}{4} = 4\frac{1}{2}$	$\frac{20}{14} = 1\frac{3}{7}$
$\frac{28}{24} = 1\frac{1}{6}$	$\frac{32}{6} = 5\frac{1}{3}$	$\frac{26}{10} = 2\frac{3}{5}$
$\frac{18}{12} = 1\frac{1}{2}$	$\frac{46}{4} = 11\frac{1}{2}$	$\frac{30}{9} = 3\frac{1}{3}$

To change improper fractions to mixed numbers, children should divide the numerator by the denominator and place the remainder over the denominator. Help them simplify answers by finding common factors for the numerator and denominator.

Ordering sets of decimals

Write these decimals in order, from least to greatest.

0.45	0.21	2.07	1.45	3.62	2.17
0.21	0.45	1.45	2.07	2.17	3.62

Write these decimals in order, from least to greatest.

5.63	2.14	5.6	3.91	1.25	4.63
1.25	2.14	3.91	4.63	5.6	5.63
9.39	0.24	7.63	8.25	7.49	9.40
0.24	7.49	7.63	8.25	9.39	9.40
1.05	2.36	1.09	2.41	7.94	1.50
1.05	1.09	1.50	2.36	2.41	7.94
3.92	5.63	2.29	4.62	5.36	2.15
2.15	2.29	3.92	4.62	5.36	5.63
28.71	21.87	27.18	21.78	28.17	27.81
21.78	21.87	27.18	27.81	28.17	28.71

Write these measures in order, from least to greatest.

$56.25	$32.40	$11.36	$32.04	$55.26	$36.19
$11.36	$32.04	$32.40	$36.19	$55.26	$56.25
94.21 km	87.05 km	76.91 km	94.36 km	65.99 km	110.75 km
65.99 km	76.91 km	87.05 km	94.21 km	94.36 km	110.75 km
$26.41	$47.23	$26.14	$35.23	$49.14	$35.32
$26.14	$26.41	$35.23	$35.32	$47.23	$49.14
19.51 m	16.15 m	15.53 m	12.65 m	24.24 m	16.51 m
12.65 m	15.53 m	16.15 m	16.51 m	19.51 m	24.24 m
7.35 l	8.29 l	5.73 l	8.92 l	10.65 l	4.29 l
4.29 l	5.73 l	7.35 l	8.29 l	8.92 l	10.65 l

Children should take special care when they order sets that include numbers with similar digits that have different place values. Make sure that they understand how place value defines a number: for example, 6.959 is less than 7.1

Symmetry

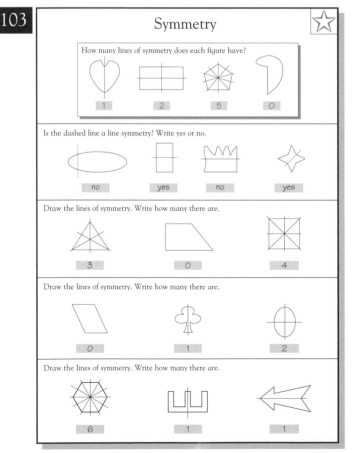

How many lines of symmetry does each figure have?

1 2 5 0

Is the dashed line a line symmetry? Write yes or no.

no yes no yes

Draw the lines of symmetry. Write how many there are.

3 0 4

Draw the lines of symmetry. Write how many there are.

0 1 2

Draw the lines of symmetry. Write how many there are.

6 1 1

Children may have difficulty understanding that a line of symmetry in a pentagon passes through the mid-point of a side and the opposite vertex. Place a pocket mirror upright along a line of symmetry to show how the reflection completes the figure.

Comparing areas

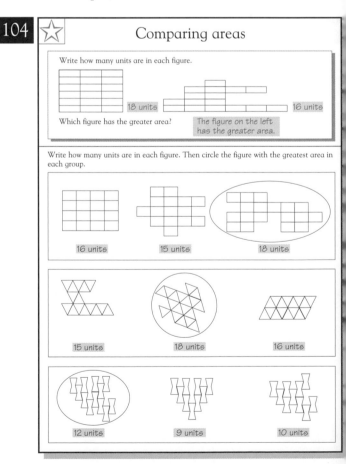

Write how many units are in each figure.

18 units 16 units

Which figure has the greater area? The figure on the left has the greater area.

Write how many units are in each figure. Then circle the figure with the greatest area in each group.

16 units 15 units 18 units

15 units 18 units 16 units

12 units 9 units 10 units

Children may not realize that they can compare the areas of irregular figures. Make sure that they take care to count the units in each figure, rather than incorrectly assuming that the longest or tallest figure has the greater area.

Probability

Use the table to answer the questions.

Pairs of socks in Mr. O' Neill's drawer

colour	number
red	2
blue	5
green	3
yellow	2
black	6

If Mr. O' Neill picks a pair of socks without looking, which colour is he most likely to pick? **black**

Which colour is Mr. O' Neill as likely to pick as red? **yellow**

Use the table to answer the questions.

Marbles in Margaret's bag

orange	blue	white	yellow
𝍠𝍠𝍠	𝍠𝍠	𝍠𝍠	𝍠𝍠𝍠𝍠

If Margaret picks a marble without looking, is she more likely to pick an orange marble or a yellow marble? **yellow**

Which colour is she least likely to pick? **blue**

Use the graph to answer the questions.

Jellybeans in a jar

If you pick a jellybean without looking, which colour will you most probably pick? **red**

Are you more likely to pick a pink jellybean or a yellow jellybean? **yellow**

Which colour jellybean are you as likely to pick as an orange one? **green**

Children must read the tally table and the bar graph to compare the numbers of items. Make sure they understand that there is an equal probability of picking either of two items if there is the same number of each.

Column addition

Find these sums.

```
  11              1 2 1
 $327           1374 km
 $644           2362 km
 $923           1690 km
+$455         + 4216 km
 $2349          9642 km
```

Find these sums.

539 m	206 m	481 m	735 m
965 m	812 m	604 m	234 m
774 m	619 m	274 m	391 m
+ 347 m	+ 832 m	+ 976 m	+ 863 m
2625 m	2469 m	2335 m	2223 m
746 kg	817 kg	944 kg	763 kg
201 kg	591 kg	835 kg	861 kg
432 kg	685 kg	391 kg	608 kg
+ 309 kg	+ 245 kg	+ 105 kg	+ 671 kg
1688 kg	2338 kg	2275 kg	2903 kg
6329 m	5243 m	6431 m	8690 m
3251 m	2845 m	7453 m	5243 m
2642 m	1937 m	4650 m	6137 m
+ 4823 m	+ 5610 m	+ 3782 m	+ 5843 m
17 045 m	15 637 m	22 316 m	25 913 m
$4721	$3654	$8172	$4352
$1711	$5932	$1475	$3920
$8342	$6841	$7760	$8439
+ $2365	+ $4736	+ $8102	+ $1348
$17 139	$21 163	$25 509	$18 059
1573 km	4902 km	3756 km	8010 km
6231 km	7547 km	1150 km	7793 km
2112 km	8463 km	5535 km	1641 km
+ 2141 km	+ 6418 km	+ 3852 km	+ 7684 km
12 057 km	27 330 km	14 293 km	25 128 km

This page requires children to perform basic addition. However, with a larger number of addends, there is a greater possibility of neglecting to regroup correctly.

Column addition

Find these sums.

```
  1 1 1           2 2 1
 3461 km         $3645
 2100 km         $4231
 3522 km         $8560
 4159 km         $7213
+ 3614 km       + $9463
 16 856 km       $33 112
```

Find these sums.

3144 m	2510 m	3276 m	1475 m
2345 m	1734 m	1593 m	2653 m
8479 m	5421 m	6837 m	2765 m
1004 m	3205 m	1769 m	3742 m
+ 6310 m	+ 2365 m	+ 3846 m	+ 5905 m
21 282 m	15 235 m	17 321 m	16 540 m
$1480	$4527	$3063	$8741
$6366	$8309	$8460	$6334
$1313	$6235	$2712	$3231
$3389	$4487	$3756	$6063
+ $4592	+ $4065	+ $5650	+ $4096
$17 140	$27 623	$23 641	$28 465
8644 km	3823 km	8636 km	8618 km
3353 km	9275 km	8986 km	3453 km
6400 km	3669 km	5367 km	4404 km
5768 km	2998 km	6863 km	4361 km
+ 1092 km	+ 7564 km	+ 3605 km	+ 5641 km
25 257 km	27 329 km	33 457 km	26 477 km
$3742	$8596	$2739	$8463
$2785	$5430	$6517	$5641
$7326	$8379	$6014	$9430
$1652	$2943	$7115	$8204
+ $5753	+ $1081	+ $2704	+ $6326
$21 258	$26 429	$25 089	$38 064

This page is similar to the previous one, but children must find the sum of a larger number of addends.

Adding fractions

Write the sum in simplest form.

$$\frac{1}{8} + \frac{3}{8} = \frac{4}{8} = \frac{1}{2} \qquad \frac{3}{5} + \frac{3}{5} = \frac{6}{5} = 1\frac{1}{5}$$

Write the sum in simplest form.

$$\frac{1}{3} + \frac{1}{3} = \frac{2}{3} \qquad\qquad \frac{2}{9} + \frac{4}{9} = \frac{6}{9} = \frac{2}{3}$$

$$\frac{1}{4} + \frac{1}{4} = \frac{2}{4} = \frac{1}{2} \qquad\qquad \frac{5}{7} + \frac{1}{7} = \frac{6}{7}$$

$$\frac{2}{3} + \frac{2}{3} = \frac{4}{3} = 1\frac{1}{3} \qquad\qquad \frac{1}{12} + \frac{3}{12} = \frac{4}{12} = \frac{1}{3}$$

$$\frac{3}{7} + \frac{5}{7} = \frac{8}{7} = 1\frac{1}{7} \qquad\qquad \frac{5}{11} + \frac{9}{11} = \frac{14}{11} = 1\frac{3}{11}$$

$$\frac{2}{5} + \frac{4}{5} = \frac{6}{5} = 1\frac{1}{5} \qquad\qquad \frac{5}{18} + \frac{4}{18} = \frac{9}{18} = \frac{1}{2}$$

$$\frac{5}{16} + \frac{7}{16} = \frac{12}{16} = \frac{3}{4} \qquad\qquad \frac{5}{9} + \frac{5}{9} = \frac{10}{9} = 1\frac{1}{9}$$

$$\frac{3}{8} + \frac{5}{8} = \frac{8}{8} = 1 \qquad\qquad \frac{4}{15} + \frac{7}{15} = \frac{11}{15}$$

$$\frac{7}{13} + \frac{8}{13} = \frac{15}{13} = 1\frac{2}{13} \qquad\qquad \frac{2}{5} + \frac{1}{5} = \frac{3}{5}$$

$$\frac{5}{16} + \frac{7}{16} = \frac{12}{16} = \frac{3}{4} \qquad\qquad \frac{1}{6} + \frac{5}{6} = \frac{6}{6} = 1$$

$$\frac{9}{10} + \frac{7}{10} = \frac{16}{10} = \frac{8}{5} = 1\frac{3}{5} \qquad \frac{3}{4} + \frac{3}{4} = \frac{6}{4} = \frac{3}{2} = 1\frac{1}{2}$$

$$\frac{4}{5} + \frac{3}{5} = \frac{7}{5} = 1\frac{2}{5} \qquad\qquad \frac{1}{8} + \frac{5}{8} = \frac{6}{8} = \frac{3}{4}$$

$$\frac{7}{12} + \frac{5}{12} = \frac{12}{12} = 1 \qquad\qquad \frac{3}{10} + \frac{7}{10} = \frac{10}{10} = \frac{6}{5} = 1\frac{1}{5}$$

$$\frac{3}{11} + \frac{5}{11} = \frac{8}{11} \qquad\qquad \frac{9}{15} + \frac{11}{15} = \frac{20}{15} = \frac{4}{3} = 1\frac{1}{3}$$

$$\frac{8}{14} + \frac{5}{14} = \frac{13}{14} \qquad\qquad \frac{1}{20} + \frac{6}{20} = \frac{7}{20}$$

Some children may incorrectly add both the numerators and the denominators. Demonstrate that only the numerators should be added when the fractions have the same denominators: $\frac{1}{2} + \frac{1}{2}$ equals $\frac{2}{2}$ or 1, not $\frac{2}{4}$.

Adding fractions

Write the sum in simplest form.

$\frac{1}{12} + \frac{3}{4} = \frac{1}{12} + \frac{9}{12} = \frac{10}{12} = \frac{5}{6}$

$\frac{3}{5} + \frac{7}{10} = \frac{6}{10} + \frac{7}{10} = \frac{13}{10} = 1\frac{3}{10}$

Write the sum in simplest form.

$\frac{1}{6} + \frac{2}{3} = \frac{1}{6} + \frac{4}{6} = \frac{5}{6}$

$\frac{1}{3} + \frac{2}{6} = \frac{2}{6} + \frac{2}{6} = \frac{4}{6} = \frac{2}{3}$

$\frac{8}{12} + \frac{5}{24} = \frac{16}{24} + \frac{5}{24} = \frac{21}{24} = \frac{7}{8}$

$\frac{5}{7} + \frac{7}{14} = \frac{10}{14} + \frac{7}{14} = \frac{17}{14} = 1\frac{3}{14}$

$\frac{5}{6} + \frac{9}{12} = \frac{10}{12} + \frac{9}{12} = \frac{19}{12} = 1\frac{7}{12}$

$\frac{4}{5} + \frac{3}{10} = \frac{8}{10} + \frac{3}{10} = \frac{11}{10} = 1\frac{1}{10}$

$\frac{3}{8} + \frac{5}{24} = \frac{9}{24} + \frac{5}{24} = \frac{14}{24} = \frac{7}{12}$

$\frac{4}{9} + \frac{2}{3} = \frac{4}{9} + \frac{6}{9} = \frac{10}{9} = 1\frac{1}{9}$

$\frac{7}{8} + \frac{3}{16} = \frac{14}{16} + \frac{3}{16} = \frac{17}{16} = 1\frac{1}{16}$

$\frac{3}{10} + \frac{7}{20} = \frac{6}{20} + \frac{7}{20} = \frac{13}{20}$

$\frac{7}{12} + \frac{7}{36} = \frac{21}{36} + \frac{7}{36} = \frac{28}{36} = \frac{7}{9}$

$\frac{6}{10} + \frac{7}{30} = \frac{18}{30} + \frac{7}{30} = \frac{25}{30} = \frac{5}{6}$

$\frac{7}{12} + \frac{5}{6} = \frac{7}{12} + \frac{10}{12} = \frac{17}{12} = 1\frac{5}{12}$

$\frac{9}{25} + \frac{1}{5} = \frac{9}{25} + \frac{5}{25} = \frac{14}{25}$

$\frac{6}{16} + \frac{1}{4} = \frac{6}{16} + \frac{4}{16} = \frac{10}{16} = \frac{5}{8}$

$\frac{5}{15} + \frac{5}{30} = \frac{10}{30} + \frac{5}{30} = \frac{15}{30} = \frac{1}{2}$

$\frac{7}{8} + \frac{1}{2} = \frac{7}{8} + \frac{4}{8} = \frac{11}{8} = 1\frac{3}{8}$

$\frac{2}{3} + \frac{7}{15} = \frac{10}{15} + \frac{7}{15} = \frac{17}{15} = 1\frac{2}{15}$

$\frac{5}{14} + \frac{9}{28} = \frac{10}{28} + \frac{9}{28} = \frac{19}{28}$

$\frac{3}{33} + \frac{5}{11} = \frac{3}{33} + \frac{15}{33} = \frac{18}{33} = \frac{6}{11}$

On this page, children must rename fractions so that both addends have the same denominator. They should also be aware that they must simplify the sum when necessary.

Subtracting fractions

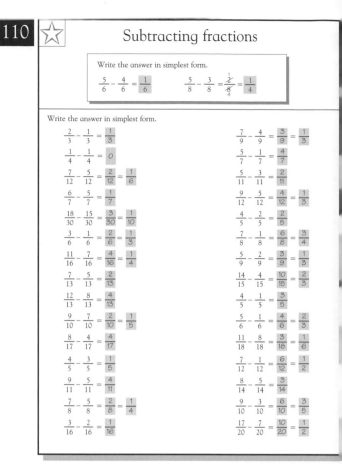

Write the answer in simplest form.

$\frac{5}{6} - \frac{4}{6} = \frac{1}{6}$

$\frac{5}{8} - \frac{3}{8} = \frac{2}{8} = \frac{1}{4}$

Write the answer in simplest form.

$\frac{2}{3} - \frac{1}{3} = \frac{1}{3}$

$\frac{1}{4} - \frac{1}{4} = 0$

$\frac{7}{12} - \frac{5}{12} = \frac{2}{12} = \frac{1}{6}$

$\frac{6}{7} - \frac{5}{7} = \frac{1}{7}$

$\frac{18}{30} - \frac{15}{30} = \frac{3}{30} = \frac{1}{10}$

$\frac{3}{6} - \frac{1}{6} = \frac{2}{6} = \frac{1}{3}$

$\frac{11}{16} - \frac{7}{16} = \frac{4}{16} = \frac{1}{4}$

$\frac{7}{13} - \frac{5}{13} = \frac{2}{13}$

$\frac{12}{13} - \frac{8}{13} = \frac{4}{13}$

$\frac{9}{10} - \frac{7}{10} = \frac{2}{10} = \frac{1}{5}$

$\frac{8}{17} - \frac{4}{17} = \frac{4}{17}$

$\frac{4}{5} - \frac{3}{5} = \frac{1}{5}$

$\frac{9}{11} - \frac{5}{11} = \frac{4}{11}$

$\frac{7}{8} - \frac{5}{8} = \frac{2}{8} = \frac{1}{4}$

$\frac{3}{16} - \frac{2}{16} = \frac{1}{16}$

$\frac{7}{9} - \frac{4}{9} = \frac{3}{9} = \frac{1}{3}$

$\frac{5}{7} - \frac{1}{7} = \frac{4}{7}$

$\frac{5}{11} - \frac{3}{11} = \frac{2}{11}$

$\frac{9}{12} - \frac{5}{12} = \frac{4}{12} = \frac{1}{3}$

$\frac{4}{5} - \frac{2}{5} = \frac{2}{5}$

$\frac{7}{8} - \frac{1}{8} = \frac{6}{8} = \frac{3}{4}$

$\frac{5}{9} - \frac{2}{9} = \frac{3}{9} = \frac{1}{3}$

$\frac{14}{15} - \frac{4}{15} = \frac{10}{15} = \frac{2}{3}$

$\frac{4}{5} - \frac{1}{5} = \frac{3}{5}$

$\frac{5}{6} - \frac{1}{6} = \frac{4}{6} = \frac{2}{3}$

$\frac{11}{18} - \frac{8}{18} = \frac{3}{18} = \frac{1}{6}$

$\frac{7}{12} - \frac{1}{12} = \frac{6}{12} = \frac{1}{2}$

$\frac{8}{14} - \frac{5}{14} = \frac{3}{14}$

$\frac{9}{10} - \frac{3}{10} = \frac{6}{10} = \frac{3}{5}$

$\frac{17}{20} - \frac{7}{20} = \frac{10}{20} = \frac{1}{2}$

On this page, children subtract fractions that have the same denominators. If they neglect to simplify their answers, help them find common factors in the numerator and denominator.

Subtracting fractions

Write the answer in simplest form.

$\frac{3}{4} - \frac{1}{12} = \frac{9}{12} - \frac{1}{12} = \frac{8}{12} = \frac{2}{3}$

$\frac{3}{5} - \frac{4}{10} = \frac{6}{10} - \frac{4}{10} = \frac{2}{10} = \frac{1}{5}$

Write the answer in simplest form.

$\frac{5}{6} - \frac{9}{12} = \frac{10}{12} - \frac{9}{12} = \frac{1}{12}$

$\frac{6}{14} - \frac{9}{28} = \frac{12}{28} - \frac{9}{28} = \frac{3}{28}$

$\frac{7}{8} - \frac{6}{16} = \frac{14}{16} - \frac{6}{16} = \frac{8}{16} = \frac{1}{2}$

$\frac{1}{2} - \frac{5}{12} = \frac{6}{12} - \frac{5}{12} = \frac{1}{12}$

$\frac{6}{16} - \frac{1}{4} = \frac{6}{16} - \frac{4}{16} = \frac{2}{16} = \frac{1}{8}$

$\frac{7}{9} - \frac{7}{36} = \frac{28}{36} - \frac{7}{36} = \frac{21}{36} = \frac{7}{12}$

$\frac{8}{12} - \frac{3}{24} = \frac{16}{24} - \frac{3}{24} = \frac{13}{24}$

$\frac{7}{8} - \frac{1}{2} = \frac{7}{8} - \frac{4}{8} = \frac{3}{8}$

$\frac{5}{7} - \frac{1}{21} = \frac{15}{21} - \frac{1}{21} = \frac{14}{21} = \frac{2}{3}$

$\frac{3}{4} - \frac{3}{20} = \frac{15}{20} - \frac{3}{20} = \frac{12}{20} = \frac{3}{5}$

$\frac{8}{21} - \frac{2}{7} = \frac{8}{21} - \frac{6}{21} = \frac{2}{21}$

$\frac{6}{10} - \frac{7}{30} = \frac{18}{30} - \frac{7}{30} = \frac{11}{30}$

$\frac{1}{3} - \frac{2}{6} = \frac{2}{6} - \frac{2}{6} = 0$

$\frac{5}{15} - \frac{5}{30} = \frac{10}{30} - \frac{5}{30} = \frac{5}{30} = \frac{1}{6}$

$\frac{8}{9} - \frac{2}{3} = \frac{8}{9} - \frac{6}{9} = \frac{2}{9}$

$\frac{6}{7} - \frac{7}{14} = \frac{12}{14} - \frac{7}{14} = \frac{5}{14}$

$\frac{2}{5} - \frac{4}{15} = \frac{6}{15} - \frac{4}{15} = \frac{2}{15}$

$\frac{3}{10} - \frac{3}{20} = \frac{6}{20} - \frac{3}{20} = \frac{3}{20}$

$\frac{7}{12} - \frac{2}{6} = \frac{7}{12} - \frac{4}{12} = \frac{3}{12} = \frac{1}{4}$

$\frac{14}{18} - \frac{5}{9} = \frac{14}{18} - \frac{10}{18} = \frac{4}{18} = \frac{2}{9}$

$\frac{1}{2} - \frac{3}{8} = \frac{4}{8} - \frac{3}{8} = \frac{1}{8}$

$\frac{3}{5} - \frac{6}{15} = \frac{9}{15} - \frac{6}{15} = \frac{3}{15} = \frac{1}{5}$

On this page, children must write both fractions with the same denominator before subtracting. If necessary, point out that fractions have the same value as long as you multiply the numerator and denominator by the same number.

Multiplying

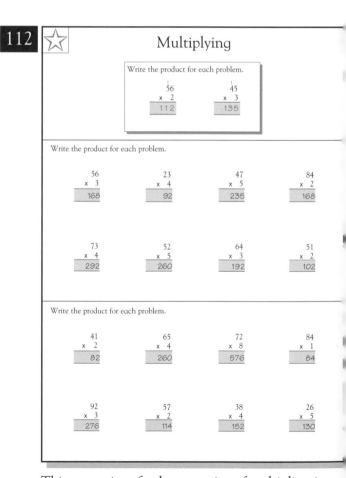

Write the product for each problem.

```
  56        45
×  2      ×  3
 112       135
```

Write the product for each problem.

```
  56        23        47        84
×  3      ×  4      ×  5      ×  2
 168        92       235       168


  73        52        64        51
×  4      ×  5      ×  3      ×  2
 292       260       192       102
```

Write the product for each problem.

```
  41        65        72        84
×  2      ×  4      ×  8      ×  1
  82       260       576        84


  92        57        38        26
×  3      ×  2      ×  4      ×  5
 276       114       152       130
```

This page gives further practice of multiplication.

Multiplying ☆

Write the product for each problem.

$$\begin{array}{r}{}^6\\39\\\times\ 7\\\hline 273\end{array}\qquad\begin{array}{r}{}^6\\68\\\times\ 8\\\hline 544\end{array}$$

Write the product for each problem.

$$\begin{array}{r}87\\\times\ 8\\\hline 696\end{array}\quad\begin{array}{r}76\\\times\ 8\\\hline 608\end{array}\quad\begin{array}{r}99\\\times\ 9\\\hline 891\end{array}\quad\begin{array}{r}85\\\times\ 8\\\hline 680\end{array}$$

$$\begin{array}{r}88\\\times\ 5\\\hline 440\end{array}\quad\begin{array}{r}67\\\times\ 6\\\hline 402\end{array}\quad\begin{array}{r}94\\\times\ 9\\\hline 846\end{array}\quad\begin{array}{r}89\\\times\ 7\\\hline 623\end{array}$$

Write the product for each problem.

$$\begin{array}{r}87\\\times\ 9\\\hline 783\end{array}\quad\begin{array}{r}46\\\times\ 7\\\hline 322\end{array}\quad\begin{array}{r}58\\\times\ 9\\\hline 522\end{array}\quad\begin{array}{r}73\\\times\ 8\\\hline 584\end{array}$$

$$\begin{array}{r}95\\\times\ 7\\\hline 665\end{array}\quad\begin{array}{r}58\\\times\ 8\\\hline 464\end{array}\quad\begin{array}{r}78\\\times\ 7\\\hline 546\end{array}\quad\begin{array}{r}96\\\times\ 9\\\hline 864\end{array}$$

This page gives further practice of multiplication as on the previous page. Make sure that children do not neglect to regroup when necessary.

Dividing by one-digit numbers

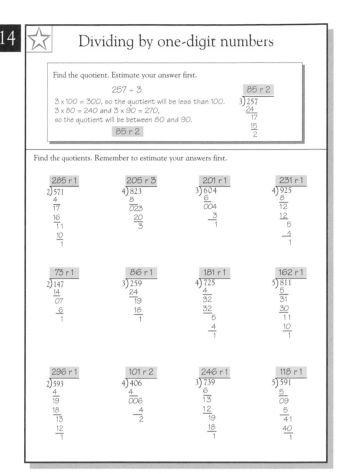

Find the quotient. Estimate your answer first.

$257 \div 3$

$3 \times 100 = 300$, so the quotient will be less than 100.
$3 \times 80 = 240$ and $3 \times 90 = 270$,
so the quotient will be between 80 and 90.

85 r 2

$$\begin{array}{r}85\ r\ 2\\3)\overline{257}\\\underline{24}\\17\\\underline{15}\\2\end{array}$$

Find the quotients. Remember to estimate your answers first.

285 r 1
$$\begin{array}{r}2)\overline{571}\\4\\\overline{17}\\16\\\overline{11}\\10\\\overline{1}\end{array}$$

205 r 3
$$\begin{array}{r}4)\overline{823}\\8\\\overline{023}\\20\\\overline{3}\end{array}$$

201 r 1
$$\begin{array}{r}3)\overline{604}\\6\\\overline{004}\\3\\\overline{1}\end{array}$$

231 r 1
$$\begin{array}{r}4)\overline{925}\\8\\\overline{12}\\12\\\overline{5}\\4\\\overline{1}\end{array}$$

73 r 1
$$\begin{array}{r}2)\overline{147}\\14\\\overline{07}\\6\\\overline{1}\end{array}$$

86 r 1
$$\begin{array}{r}3)\overline{259}\\24\\\overline{19}\\18\\\overline{1}\end{array}$$

181 r 1
$$\begin{array}{r}4)\overline{725}\\4\\\overline{32}\\32\\\overline{5}\\4\\\overline{1}\end{array}$$

162 r 1
$$\begin{array}{r}5)\overline{811}\\5\\\overline{31}\\30\\\overline{11}\\10\\\overline{1}\end{array}$$

296 r 1
$$\begin{array}{r}2)\overline{593}\\4\\\overline{19}\\18\\\overline{13}\\12\\\overline{1}\end{array}$$

101 r 2
$$\begin{array}{r}4)\overline{406}\\4\\\overline{006}\\4\\\overline{2}\end{array}$$

246 r 1
$$\begin{array}{r}3)\overline{739}\\6\\\overline{13}\\12\\\overline{19}\\18\\\overline{1}\end{array}$$

118 r 1
$$\begin{array}{r}5)\overline{591}\\5\\\overline{09}\\5\\\overline{41}\\40\\\overline{1}\end{array}$$

Children may have difficulty finding quotients with remainders. Have them perform long division until the remaining value to be divided is less than the divisor. That value is the remainder.

Dividing by one-digit numbers ☆

Find the quotient. Estimate your answer first.

$845 \div 8$

$8 \times 100 = 800$, so the quotient will be more than 100.
$8 \times 110 = 880$, so the quotient will be between 100 and 110.

105 r 5

$$\begin{array}{r}105\ r\ 5\\8)\overline{845}\\8\\\overline{04}\\0\\\overline{45}\\40\\\overline{5}\end{array}$$

Find the quotients. Remember to estimate your answers first.

138 r 5
$$\begin{array}{r}6)\overline{833}\\6\\\overline{23}\\18\\\overline{53}\\48\\\overline{5}\end{array}$$

66 r 3
$$\begin{array}{r}7)\overline{465}\\42\\\overline{45}\\42\\\overline{3}\end{array}$$

117 r 5
$$\begin{array}{r}8)\overline{941}\\8\\\overline{14}\\8\\\overline{61}\\56\\\overline{5}\end{array}$$

90 r 2
$$\begin{array}{r}9)\overline{812}\\81\\\overline{02}\end{array}$$

80 r 6
$$\begin{array}{r}7)\overline{566}\\56\\\overline{06}\end{array}$$

71 r 2
$$\begin{array}{r}7)\overline{499}\\49\\\overline{09}\\7\\\overline{2}\end{array}$$

66 r 4
$$\begin{array}{r}8)\overline{532}\\48\\\overline{52}\\48\\\overline{4}\end{array}$$

40 r 1
$$\begin{array}{r}8)\overline{321}\\32\\\overline{01}\end{array}$$

90 r 5
$$\begin{array}{r}7)\overline{635}\\63\\\overline{05}\end{array}$$

40 r 5
$$\begin{array}{r}9)\overline{365}\\36\\\overline{05}\end{array}$$

99 r 4
$$\begin{array}{r}6)\overline{598}\\54\\\overline{58}\\54\\\overline{4}\end{array}$$

20 r 4
$$\begin{array}{r}9)\overline{184}\\18\\\overline{04}\end{array}$$

This page is similar to the previous page, but the divisors are numbers greater than 5. Children will need to know their 6, 7, 8, and 9 times tables.

Real-life problems

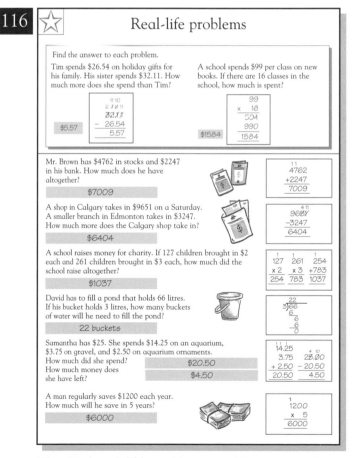

Find the answer to each problem.

Tim spends $26.54 on holiday gifts for his family. His sister spends $32.11. How much more does she spend than Tim?

$5.57

$$\begin{array}{r}{}^{1\ 1\ 10}\\3\cancel{2}.\cancel{1}\cancel{1}\\-\ 26.54\\\hline 5.57\end{array}$$

A school spends $99 per class on new books. If there are 16 classes in the school, how much is spent?

$1584

$$\begin{array}{r}99\\\times\ 16\\\hline 594\\990\\\hline 1584\end{array}$$

Mr. Brown has $4762 in stocks and $2247 in his bank. How much does he have altogether?

$7009

$$\begin{array}{r}{}^{1\ 1}\\4762\\+2247\\\hline 7009\end{array}$$

A shop in Calgary takes in $9651 on a Saturday. A smaller branch in Edmonton takes in $3247. How much more does the Calgary shop take in?

$6404

$$\begin{array}{r}{}^{4\ 11}\\96\cancel{5}\cancel{1}\\-3247\\\hline 6404\end{array}$$

A school raises money for charity. If 127 children brought in $2 each and 261 children brought in $3 each, how much did the school raise altogether?

$1037

$$\begin{array}{r}127\\\times\ 2\\\hline 254\end{array}\quad\begin{array}{r}261\\\times\ 3\\\hline 783\end{array}\quad\begin{array}{r}254\\+783\\\hline 1037\end{array}$$

David has to fill a pond that holds 66 litres. If his bucket holds 3 litres, how many buckets of water will he need to fill the pond?

22 buckets

$$\begin{array}{r}22\\3)\overline{66}\\6\\\overline{6}\\6\\\overline{0}\end{array}$$

Samantha has $25. She spends $14.25 on an aquarium, $3.75 on gravel, and $2.50 on aquarium ornaments. How much did she spend? How much money does she have left?

$20.50

$4.50

$$\begin{array}{r}{}^{1\ 1\ 1}\\14.25\\3.75\\+\ 2.50\\\hline 20.50\end{array}\quad\begin{array}{r}{}^{4\ 10}\\2\cancel{5}.00\\-20.50\\\hline 4.50\end{array}$$

A man regularly saves $1200 each year. How much will he save in 5 years?

$6000

$$\begin{array}{r}{}^1\\1200\\\times\ 5\\\hline 6000\end{array}$$

The third and fifth problems on this page require multiple steps to reach the correct answers. If children have difficulty, help them plan out methods to solve the problems.

Real-life problems

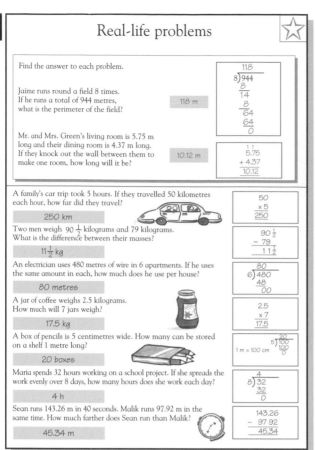

Find the answer to each problem.

Jaime runs round a field 8 times.
If he runs a total of 944 metres,
what is the perimeter of the field?

118 m

$$\begin{array}{r} 118 \\ 8\overline{)944} \\ \underline{8} \\ 14 \\ \underline{8} \\ 64 \\ \underline{64} \\ 0 \end{array}$$

Mr. and Mrs. Green's living room is 5.75 m
long and their dining room is 4.37 m long.
If they knock out the wall between them to
make one room, how long will it be?

10.12 m

$$\begin{array}{r} {}^{1\,1} \\ 5.75 \\ + 4.37 \\ \hline 10.12 \end{array}$$

A family's car trip took 5 hours. If they travelled 50 kilometres
each hour, how far did they travel?

250 km

$$\begin{array}{r} 50 \\ \times 5 \\ \hline 250 \end{array}$$

Two men weigh $90\frac{1}{2}$ kilograms and 79 kilograms.
What is the difference between their masses?

$11\frac{1}{2}$ kg

$$\begin{array}{r} 90\frac{1}{2} \\ - 79 \\ \hline 11\frac{1}{2} \end{array}$$

An electrician uses 480 metres of wire in 6 apartments. If he uses
the same amount in each, how much does he use per house?

80 metres

$$\begin{array}{r} 80 \\ 6\overline{)480} \\ \underline{48} \\ 00 \end{array}$$

A jar of coffee weighs 2.5 kilograms.
How much will 7 jars weigh?

17.5 kg

$$\begin{array}{r} 2.5 \\ \times 7 \\ \hline 17.5 \end{array}$$

A box of pencils is 5 centimetres wide. How many can be stored
on a shelf 1 metre long?

20 boxes

1 m = 100 cm $\quad \begin{array}{r} 20 \\ 5\overline{)100} \\ \underline{100} \\ 0 \end{array}$

Maria spends 32 hours working on a school project. If she spreads the
work evenly over 8 days, how many hours does she work each day?

4 h

$$\begin{array}{r} 4 \\ 8\overline{)32} \\ \underline{32} \\ 0 \end{array}$$

Sean runs 143.26 m in 40 seconds. Malik runs 97.92 m in the
same time. How much farther does Sean run than Malik?

45.34 m

$$\begin{array}{r} 143.26 \\ - 97.92 \\ \hline 45.34 \end{array}$$

Children will need to know that there are 100
centimetres in a metre to solve the fifth problem on
this page.

Problems involving time

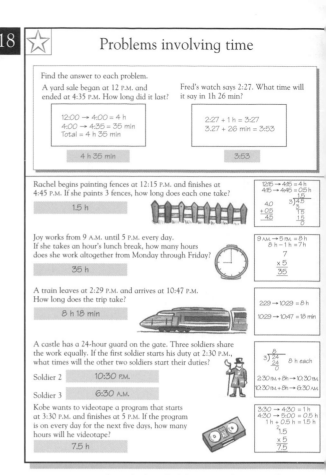

Find the answer to each problem.

A yard sale began at 12 P.M. and
ended at 4:35 P.M. How long did it last?

12:00 → 4:00 = 4 h
4:00 → 4:35 = 35 min
Total = 4 h 35 min

4 h 35 min

Fred's watch says 2:27. What time will
it say in 1h 26 min?

2:27 + 1 h = 3:27
3:27 + 26 min = 3:53

3:53

Rachel begins painting fences at 12:15 P.M. and finishes at
4:45 P.M. If she paints 3 fences, how long does each one take?

1.5 h

12:15 → 4:15 = 4 h
4:15 → 4:45 = 0.5 h
4.0
+ 0.5
4.5

$\begin{array}{r} 1.5 \\ 3\overline{)4.5} \\ \underline{3} \\ 15 \\ \underline{15} \end{array}$

Joy works from 9 A.M. until 5 P.M. every day.
If she takes an hour's lunch break, how many hours
does she work altogether from Monday through Friday?

35 h

9 A.M. → 5 P.M. = 8 h
8 h − 1 h = 7 h
$\begin{array}{r} 7 \\ \times 5 \\ \hline 35 \end{array}$

A train leaves at 2:29 P.M. and arrives at 10:47 P.M.
How long does the trip take?

8 h 18 min

2:29 → 10:29 = 8 h
10:29 → 10:47 = 18 min

A castle has a 24-hour guard on the gate. Three soldiers share
the work equally. If the first soldier starts his duty at 2:30 P.M.,
what times will the other two soldiers start their duties?

Soldier 2   **10:30 P.M.**

Soldier 3   **6:30 A.M.**

$\begin{array}{r} 8 \\ 3\overline{)24} \\ \underline{24} \end{array}$ 8 h each

2:30 P.M. + 8 h → 10:30 P.M.
10:30 P.M. + 8 h → 6:30 A.M.

Kobe wants to videotape a program that starts
at 3:30 P.M. and finishes at 5 P.M. If the program
is on every day for the next five days, how many
hours will he videotape?

7.5 h

3:30 → 4:30 = 1 h
4:30 → 5:00 = 0.5 h
1 h + 0.5 h = 1.5 h
$\begin{array}{r} 1.5 \\ \times 5 \\ \hline 7.5 \end{array}$

You may need to help children understand time
periods so that they can manage the questions
more easily. For example, borrowing an hour in a
subtraction problem is the same as borrowing
60 minutes.

Looking at graphs

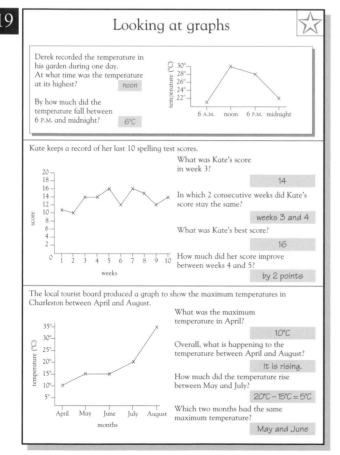

Derek recorded the temperature in
his garden during one day.
At what time was the temperature
at its highest?   **noon**

By how much did the
temperature fall between
6 P.M. and midnight?   **6°C**

Kate keeps a record of her last 10 spelling test scores.

What was Kate's score
in week 3?   **14**

In which 2 consecutive weeks did Kate's
score stay the same?   **weeks 3 and 4**

What was Kate's best score?   **16**

How much did her score improve
between weeks 4 and 5?   **by 2 points**

The local tourist board produced a graph to show the maximum
temperatures in Charleston between April and August.

What was the maximum
temperature in April?   **10°C**

Overall, what is happening to the
temperature between April and August?   **It is rising.**

How much did the temperature rise
between May and July?   **20°C − 15°C = 5°C**

Which two months had the same
maximum temperature?   **May and June**

On this page, children are required to find two or
more pieces of information on a graph. They then
have to compare or find the difference in value.
In the first question, make sure that children
understand the meaning of consecutive.

Place value for whole numbers

Write the value of 7 in 573 in standard form and word form.
70   **seventy**

What happens to the value of 247 if you change the 2 to a 3?
The value of the number increases by 100.

Write the value of the 6 in these numbers in standard form and word form.

26	162	36 904	12 612
6	**60**	**6000**	**600**
six	**sixty**	**six thousand**	**six hundred**

Circle the numbers that have a 7 with a value of seventy.

457 682   (67 974)   870 234   372 987

(177 079)   (767 777)   (79 875)   16 757

Write what happens to the value of each number.

Change the 6 in 3586 to 3.   **The value of the number decreases by 3.**

Change the 9 in 1921 to 8.   **The value of the number decreases by 100.**

Change the 7 in 7246 to 9.   **The value of the number increases by 2000.**

Change the 1 in 817 to 9.   **The value of the number increases by 80.**

Change the 5 in 50 247 to 1.   **The value of the number decreases by 40 000.**

Change the 2 in 90 205 to 9.   **The value of the number increases by 700.**

Children may need help completing the final
section of the page. If so, help them work through
the first question of the section. Have children
write the new number for each question before
trying to find the answer.

Place value for decimals

Write the value of 5 in 7.53 in standard form and word form.
0.5   5 tenths

What happens to the value of 2.48 if you change the 8 to a 1?
The value of the number decreases by 0.07.

Write the value of the 9 in these numbers in standard form and written form.

2.9	0.19	975.04	9.12
0.9	0.09	900	9
9 tenths	9 hundredths	9 hundred	nine

0.89	591.65	19.85	3.96
0.09	90	9	0.9
9 hundredths	ninety	nine	9 tenths

Write what happens to the value of each number.

Change the 8 in 35.86 to 7.   The value of the number decreases by 0.1.

Change the 2 in 1.02 to 6.   The value of the number increases by 0.04.

Change the 3 in 3460 to 9.   The value of the number increases by 6000.

Change the 1 in 8.17 to 6.   The value of the number increases by 0.5.

Change the 5 in 8.35 to 1.   The value of the number decreases by 0.04.

Circle the numbers that have an 8 with a value of 8 tenths.
457.68   (1.8)   8.09   (35.85)   388.1

Circle the numbers that have a 5 with a value of 5 hundredths.
550.7   (5.25)   (99.95)   16.53   (68.95)

Circle the numbers that have a 3 with a value of 3 tenths.
3603.3   0.93   32.45   (5.33)   23.53

This page is similar to the previous one, but involves decimals rather than whole numbers. For the second section of questions, it may help children to write the new numbers and then find the difference between them and the original numbers.

Reading tally charts

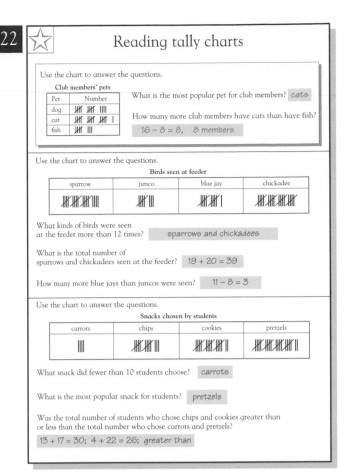

Use the chart to answer the questions.

Club members' pets

Pet	Number
dog	JHT JHT IIII
cat	JHT JHT JHT I
fish	JHT III

What is the most popular pet for club members? cats

How many more club members have cats than have fish?
16 − 8 = 8,   8 members

Use the chart to answer the questions.

Birds seen at feeder

sparrow	junco	blue jay	chickadee
JHT JHT JHT IIII	JHT III	JHT JHT I	JHT JHT JHT JHT

What kinds of birds were seen at the feeder more than 12 times?   sparrows and chickadees

What is the total number of sparrows and chickadees seen at the feeder?   19 + 20 = 39

How many more blue jays than juncos were seen?   11 − 8 = 3

Use the chart to answer the questions.

Snacks chosen by students

carrots	chips	cookies	pretzels
IIII	JHT JHT III	JHT JHT JHT II	JHT JHT JHT JHT II

What snack did fewer than 10 students choose?   carrots

What is the most popular snack for students?   pretzels

Was the total number of students who chose chips and cookies greater than or less than the total number who chose carrots and pretzels?
13 + 17 = 30; 4 + 22 = 26; greater than

If children have difficulty reading tally charts, show them that they can count by 5s for groups of tallies that are crossed out.

Volumes of cubes

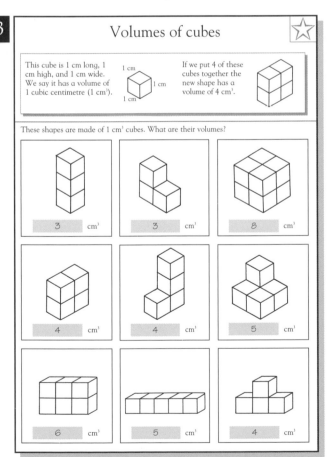

This cube is 1 cm long, 1 cm high, and 1 cm wide. We say it has a volume of 1 cubic centimetre (1 cm³).

If we put 4 of these cubes together the new shape has a volume of 4 cm³.

These shapes are made of 1 cm³ cubes. What are their volumes?

3 cm³   3 cm³   8 cm³

4 cm³   4 cm³   5 cm³

6 cm³   5 cm³   4 cm³

To find the volume of some of the shapes on this page, children must visualize in order to determine how many blocks cannot be seen in the illustrations. In the third and sixth shapes there is one block that is not shown.

Acute and obtuse angles

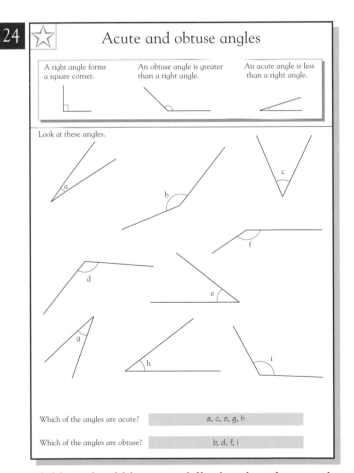

A right angle forms a square corner.

An obtuse angle is greater than a right angle.

An acute angle is less than a right angle.

Look at these angles.

Which of the angles are acute?   a, c, e, g, h

Which of the angles are obtuse?   b, d, f, i

Children should have no difficulty identifying each angle if they compare it to a right angle.

Acute and obtuse angles

This angle measures 45°.

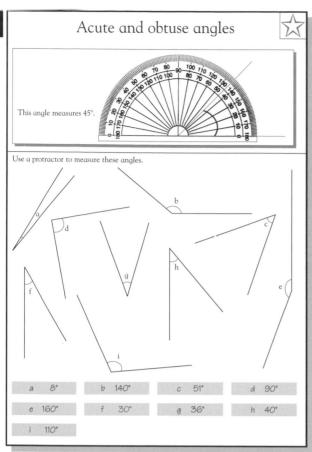

Use a protractor to measure these angles.

a 8°	b 140°	c 51°	d 90°
e 160°	f 30°	g 36°	h 40°
i 110°			

If children make errors on this page, the most likely reasons are that they have placed the protractor inaccurately above the vertex of the angle or that they have read the protractor from the wrong direction.

Addition fact families

Circle the number sentence that is in the same fact family.

12 − 5 = 7 5 + 7 = 12	12 − 4 = 8	(7 + 5 = 12)	12 + 12 = 24
10 − 8 = 2 8 + 2 = 10	8 − 6 = 2	(2 + 8 = 10)	8 − 2 = 6

Circle the number sentence that is in the same fact family.

7 + 8 = 15 8 + 7 = 15	7 + 5 = 12	(15 − 8 = 7)	8 − 7 = 1
17 − 6 = 11 11 + 6 = 17	(17 − 11 = 6)	17 + 6 = 23	5 + 6 = 11
14 − 5 = 9 14 − 9 = 5	9 − 3 = 6	14 + 9 = 23	(5 + 9 = 14)
9 + 7 = 16 7 + 9 = 16	(16 − 9 = 7)	16 + 7 = 23	9 − 7 = 2
19 − 9 = 10 19 − 10 = 9	9 + 3 = 12	(9 + 10 = 19)	18 − 8 = 10
4 + 7 = 11 11 − 4 = 7	11 + 4 = 15	(7 + 4 = 11)	7 + 7 = 14

Write the fact family for each group of numbers.

5, 6, 11	6, 10, 4	5, 13, 8
5 + 6 = 11	6 + 4 = 10	5 + 8 = 13
6 + 5 = 11	4 + 6 = 10	8 + 5 = 13
11 − 6 = 5	10 − 6 = 4	13 − 8 = 5
11 − 5 = 6	10 − 4 = 6	13 − 5 = 8

Children should understand that subtraction "undoes" addition. You may want to use counters to show the addition fact families.

Odds and evens

Write the answer in the box.

3 + 3 = 6   4 + 6 = 10   7 + 3 = 10   2 + 6 = 8

Add the even numbers to the even numbers.

4 + 8 = 12	12 + 6 = 18	10 + 6 = 16	8 + 14 = 22
20 + 14 = 34	14 + 12 = 26	16 + 10 = 26	30 + 20 = 50
14 + 16 = 30	18 + 6 = 24	22 + 8 = 30	20 + 40 = 60

What do you notice about each answer?   All the answers are even numbers.

Add the odd numbers to the odd numbers.

7 + 9 = 16	5 + 7 = 12	11 + 5 = 16	9 + 5 = 14
7 + 7 = 14	9 + 3 = 12	15 + 5 = 20	13 + 7 = 20
11 + 3 = 14	17 + 9 = 26	15 + 9 = 24	13 + 15 = 28

What do you notice about each answer?   All the answers are even numbers.

Add the odd numbers to the even numbers.

3 + 8 = 11	9 + 12 = 21	5 + 18 = 23	7 + 14 = 21
11 + 4 = 15	13 + 10 = 23	15 + 6 = 21	21 + 4 = 25
7 + 20 = 27	13 + 30 = 43	11 + 16 = 27	17 + 6 = 23

What do you notice about each answer?   All the answers are odd numbers.

Add the even numbers to the odd numbers.

6 + 7 = 13	8 + 5 = 13	10 + 9 = 19	2 + 17 = 19
10 + 29 = 39	14 + 3 = 17	8 + 13 = 21	12 + 5 = 17
14 + 7 = 21	8 + 51 = 59	16 + 9 = 25	30 + 17 = 47

What do you notice about each answer?   All the answers are odd numbers.

Children should notice that adding two even numbers results in an even number and adding two odd numbers results in an odd number. Adding an odd and an even number gives an odd number. The order in which numbers are added is not important.

Word problems

Write the answer in the box.
I multiply a number by 6 and the answer is 24.
What number did I begin with? 4

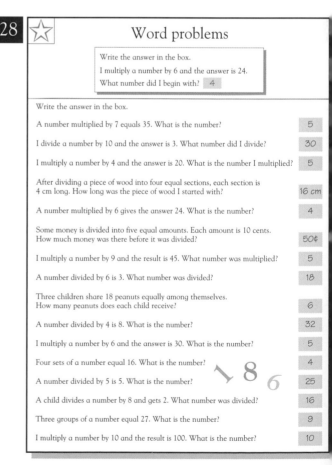

Write the answer in the box.

A number multiplied by 7 equals 35. What is the number?	5
I divide a number by 10 and the answer is 3. What number did I divide?	30
I multiply a number by 4 and the answer is 20. What is the number I multiplied?	5
After dividing a piece of wood into four equal sections, each section is 4 cm long. How long was the piece of wood I started with?	16 cm
A number multiplied by 6 gives the answer 24. What is the number?	4
Some money is divided into five equal amounts. Each amount is 10 cents. How much money was there before it was divided?	50¢
I multiply a number by 9 and the result is 45. What number was multiplied?	5
A number divided by 6 is 3. What number was divided?	18
Three children share 18 peanuts equally among themselves. How many peanuts does each child receive?	6
A number divided by 4 is 8. What is the number?	32
I multiply a number by 6 and the answer is 30. What is the number?	5
Four sets of a number equal 16. What is the number?	4
A number divided by 5 is 5. What is the number?	25
A child divides a number by 8 and gets 2. What number was divided?	16
Three groups of a number equal 27. What is the number?	9
I multiply a number by 10 and the result is 100. What is the number?	10

Some children find these sorts of problems difficult even if they are good with times tables and division. Many of the problems require children to perform the inverse operation. Have children check their answers to make sure they are correct.

Word problems

Write the answer in the box.

A child is given four dimes. How much money does she have altogether? 40¢

Write the answer in the box.

A box contains 6 eggs. How many boxes would I need to buy to have 18 eggs? 3

When Peter multiplies his apartment number by 3, the result is 75. What is his apartment number? 25

A boy is given three bags of candy. There are 20 pieces in each bag. How many pieces of candy does the boy have in total? 60

One photograph costs $1.80. How much will two photographs cost? $3.60

Four lifeboats carry a total of 100 people. How many people are in each boat? 25

A dog buries 20 bones on Monday, 30 bones on Tuesday, and 40 bones on Wednesday. How many bones has the dog buried altogether? 90

A shepherd had 200 sheep but 70 were lost in a snowstorm. How many sheep does the shepherd have left? 130

Three women win the lottery and share $900 equally among themselves. How much does each woman receive? $300

A truck contains 50 barrels of oil. It delivers 27 barrels to one garage. How many barrels are left on the truck? 23

A car trip is supposed to be 70 kilometres long but the car breaks down half-way. How far has the car gone when it breaks down? 35 km

Andrej has a collection of 150 baseball cards. He sells 30 of them to a friend. How many cards does he have left? 120

A teacher has 32 children in her class. 13 children are out with the flu. How many children are left in class? 19

Children will need to think carefully about how they will solve each problem. If they have difficulty, talk each problem through with them.

Multiples

Circle the multiples of 3.

4   7   (9)   14   20   (24)

Circle the multiples of 3.

4	7	10	(15)	(21)	(30)	35	50
2	4	(6)	8	10	(12)	14	16
1	(3)	5	7	(9)	11	13	(15)
2	5	8	11	14	17	20	23
5	10	(15)	20	25	(30)	35	40
0	(3)	(6)	(9)	(12)	(15)	(18)	(21)
10	20	(30)	40	50	(60)	70	80
5	8	11	14	17	20	23	26
2	7	13	17	(21)	25	(33)	(60)

Circle the multiples of 4.

2	7	11	15	19	23	(28)	31
2	(4)	6	(8)	10	(12)	14	(16)
1	3	5	7	9	11	13	15
3	6	9	(12)	15	18	21	(24)
(4)	(12)	14	18	22	(24)	(28)	34
5	10	15	(20)	25	30	35	(40)
3	5	(12)	17	(24)	26	(32)	(80)
1	5	9	13	18	(20)	(60)	(100)
10	(20)	30	(40)	50	(60)	70	(80)

Children may not know the rule for finding a multiple of 3: if the digits of a number add up to a multiple of 3, then the number itself is a multiple of 3. For example, 2 + 7 = 9, which is a multiple of 3, so 27 is a multiple of 3 (and so is 72).

Factors

Write the factors of each number.

6   1, 2, 3, 6   8   1, 2, 4, 8

Write the factors of each number.

4	1, 2, 4	10	1, 2, 5, 10	14	1, 2, 7, 14
9	1, 3, 9	3	1, 3	12	1, 2, 3, 4, 6, 12
7	1, 7	15	1, 3, 5, 15	17	1, 17
5	1, 5	20	1, 2, 4, 5, 10, 20	19	1, 19
2	1, 2	24	1, 2, 3, 4, 6, 8, 12, 24	11	1, 11
13	1, 13	30	1, 2, 3, 5, 6, 10, 15, 30	16	1, 2, 4, 8, 16

Write the factors of each number.

1	1	4	1, 2, 4	16	1, 2, 4, 8, 16
25	1, 5, 25	36	1, 2, 3, 4, 6, 9, 12, 18, 36	49	1, 7, 49
64	1, 2, 4, 8, 16, 32, 64	81	1, 3, 9, 27, 81	100	1, 2, 4, 5, 10, 20, 25, 50, 100

Do you notice anything about the number of factors each of the numbers has?
Each number has an odd number of factors.

Do you know the name for these special numbers?   These are squares.

Write the factors of each number.

2	1, 2	3	1, 3	5	1, 5
7	1, 7	11	1, 11	13	1, 13
17	1, 17	19	1, 19	23	1, 23
29	1, 29	31	1, 31	37	1, 37

Do you notice anything about the number of factors each of the numbers has?
The factors of each number are 1 and the number itself.

Do you know the name for these special numbers?   These are prime numbers.

Children may neglect to include 1 and the number itself as factors of a number. For larger numbers, they may not include all the factors in their answers. Point out that 1 is not a prime number.

Fractions

Write the answer in the box.

$1\frac{1}{2} + \frac{1}{4} = 1\frac{3}{4}$ $2\frac{1}{2} + 3\frac{1}{2} = 6$ $1\frac{1}{4} + 2\frac{1}{2} = 3\frac{3}{4}$

Write the answer in the box.

$2\frac{1}{4} + 1\frac{1}{4} = 3\frac{1}{2}$ $1\frac{1}{2} + 1\frac{1}{2} = 3$ $1\frac{1}{4} + \frac{1}{4} = 1\frac{1}{2}$

$3\frac{1}{2} + 1 = 4\frac{1}{2}$ $3\frac{1}{2} + 1\frac{1}{4} = 4\frac{3}{4}$ $2\frac{1}{4} + 4 = 6\frac{1}{4}$

$4\frac{1}{2} + 1\frac{1}{4} = 5\frac{3}{4}$ $2\frac{1}{2} + 1\frac{1}{2} = 4$ $5 + 1\frac{1}{2} = 6\frac{1}{2}$

$3\frac{1}{4} + 1\frac{1}{2} = 4\frac{3}{4}$ $2 + 3\frac{1}{2} = 5\frac{1}{2}$ $7 + \frac{1}{2} = 7\frac{1}{2}$

$3 + \frac{1}{4} = 3\frac{1}{4}$ $4\frac{1}{4} + \frac{1}{4} = 4\frac{1}{2}$ $5 + 4\frac{1}{2} = 9\frac{1}{2}$

Write the answer in the box.

$1\frac{1}{3} + 2\frac{1}{3} = 3\frac{2}{3}$ $3\frac{1}{3} + 4\frac{2}{3} = 8$ $1\frac{2}{3} + 5 = 6\frac{2}{3}$

$3\frac{2}{3} + 2 = 5\frac{2}{3}$ $4\frac{1}{3} + 1\frac{2}{3} = 6$ $2\frac{2}{3} + 1\frac{2}{3} = 4\frac{1}{3}$

$1\frac{2}{3} + 1\frac{2}{3} = 3\frac{1}{3}$ $4\frac{1}{3} + 2\frac{1}{3} = 6\frac{2}{3}$ $3 + 2\frac{1}{3} = 5\frac{1}{3}$

$6 + 2\frac{2}{3} = 8\frac{2}{3}$ $2\frac{1}{3} + 3\frac{2}{3} = 6$ $3\frac{1}{3} + 1\frac{1}{3} = 4\frac{2}{3}$

$5\frac{2}{3} + 2\frac{2}{3} = 8\frac{1}{3}$ $7 + \frac{1}{3} = 7\frac{1}{3}$ $2\frac{2}{3} + 5\frac{2}{3} = 8\frac{1}{3}$

Write the answer in the box.

$2\frac{1}{5} + 2\frac{2}{5} = 4\frac{3}{5}$ $3\frac{1}{5} + 2\frac{3}{5} = 5\frac{4}{5}$ $1\frac{4}{5} + 6 = 7\frac{4}{5}$

$3\frac{1}{5} + 3\frac{2}{5} = 6\frac{3}{5}$ $4 + 2\frac{2}{5} = 6\frac{2}{5}$ $5\frac{3}{5} + 1\frac{1}{5} = 6\frac{4}{5}$

$\frac{3}{5} + \frac{3}{5} = 1\frac{1}{5}$ $3\frac{2}{5} + \frac{4}{5} = 4\frac{1}{5}$ $3\frac{1}{5} + \frac{2}{5} = 3\frac{4}{5}$

It is technically correct if children add $\frac{1}{4}$ and $\frac{1}{4}$ to get $\frac{2}{4}$, but they should be encouraged to simplify this to $\frac{1}{2}$. Some children may not simplify improper fractions that are part of a mixed number (such as $3\frac{6}{5}$). Show them how to do this.

Fractions and decimals ☆

Write each fraction as a decimal.

$1\frac{1}{10}$ = 1.1 $1\frac{2}{10}$ = 1.2 $1\frac{7}{10}$ = 1.7

Write each decimal as a fraction.

2.5 = $2\frac{1}{2}$ 1.9 = $1\frac{9}{10}$ 3.2 = $3\frac{2}{10}$

Write each fraction as a decimal.

$2\frac{1}{2}$ 2.5 $3\frac{1}{10}$ 3.1 $4\frac{3}{10}$ 4.3 $1\frac{1}{2}$ 1.5

$5\frac{1}{10}$ 5.1 $2\frac{3}{10}$ 2.3 $8\frac{1}{10}$ 8.1 $5\frac{1}{2}$ 5.5

$7\frac{8}{10}$ 7.8 $2\frac{4}{10}$ 2.4 $6\frac{1}{2}$ 6.5 $8\frac{1}{2}$ 8.5

$7\frac{6}{10}$ 7.6 $9\frac{1}{2}$ 9.5 $6\frac{7}{10}$ 6.7 $10\frac{1}{2}$ 10.5

Write each decimal as a fraction.

3.2 $3\frac{2}{10}$ 4.5 $4\frac{1}{2}$ 1.7 $1\frac{7}{10}$ 1.2 $1\frac{1}{2}$

6.5 $6\frac{1}{2}$ 2.7 $2\frac{7}{10}$ 5.2 $5\frac{2}{10}$ 5.5 $5\frac{1}{2}$

7.2 $7\frac{2}{10}$ 8.5 $8\frac{1}{2}$ 9.7 $9\frac{7}{10}$ 10.2 $10\frac{2}{10}$

11.5 $11\frac{1}{2}$ 12.7 $12\frac{7}{10}$ 13.2 $13\frac{2}{10}$ 14.5 $14\frac{1}{2}$

15.7 $15\frac{7}{10}$ 16.2 $16\frac{2}{10}$ 17.5 $17\frac{1}{2}$ 18.7 $18\frac{7}{10}$

Write each fraction as a decimal.

$\frac{1}{2}$ = 0.5 $\frac{2}{10}$ = 0.2 $\frac{3}{10}$ = 0.3

Write each decimal as a fraction.

0.5 = $\frac{1}{2}$ 0.2 = $\frac{2}{10}$ 0.7 = $\frac{7}{10}$

If children have difficulty, you may want to use a number line showing fractions and decimals.

Real-life problems

Write the answer in the box.

A number multiplied by 8 is 56. What is the number?   7

I divide a number by 9 and the result is 6. What is the number?   54

Write the answer in the box.

A number multiplied by 6 is 42. What is the number?   7

I divide a number by 4 and the result is 7. What is the number?   28

I divide a number by 8 and the result is 6. What number did I begin with?   48

A number multiplied by itself gives the answer 25. What is the number?   5

I divide a number by 7 and the result is 7. What number did I begin with?   49

A number multiplied by itself gives the answer 49. What is the number?   7

When I multiply a number by 7 I end up with 56. What number did I begin with?   8

Seven times a number is 63. What is the number?   9

What do I have to multiply 8 by to get the result 72?   9

Nine times a number is 81. What is the number?   9

When 6 is multiplied by a number the result is 42. What number was 6 multiplied by?   7

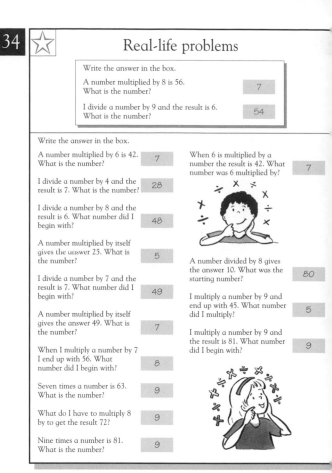

A number divided by 8 gives the answer 10. What was the starting number?   80

I multiply a number by 9 and end up with 45. What number did I multiply?   5

I multiply a number by 9 and the result is 81. What number did I begin with?   9

Some children find these sorts of problems difficult even if they are good with times tables and division. Many of the problems require children to perform the inverse operation. Have them check their answers to make sure they are correct.

Symmetry ☆

The dotted line is a mirror line. Complete each shape.

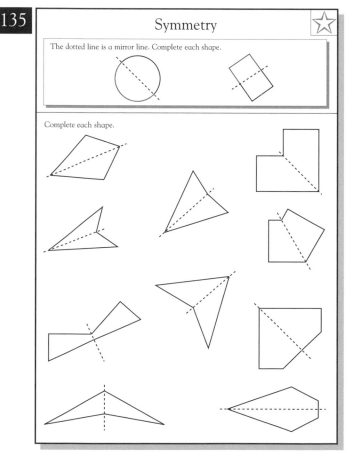

Complete each shape.

If children have difficulties with these shapes, let them use a mirror. Even if they are confident, let them check the shapes they have drawn with a mirror when they finish.

Fractions and decimals

Write each fraction as a decimal.

$\frac{1}{2}$ = 0.5 $\frac{1}{10}$ = 0.1

Write each decimal as a fraction.

0.25 = $\frac{1}{4}$ 0.4 = $\frac{4}{10}$

Write each fraction as a decimal.

$\frac{1}{10}$ 0.1 $\frac{1}{2}$ 0.5 $\frac{3}{10}$ 0.3 $\frac{5}{10}$ 0.5

$\frac{2}{10}$ 0.2 $\frac{9}{10}$ 0.9 $\frac{6}{10}$ 0.6 $\frac{1}{10}$ 0.1

$\frac{2}{10}$ 0.2 $\frac{3}{10}$ 0.3 $\frac{4}{10}$ 0.4 $\frac{5}{10}$ 0.5

$\frac{6}{10}$ 0.6 $\frac{7}{10}$ 0.7 $\frac{8}{10}$ 0.8 $\frac{9}{10}$ 0.9

Write each decimal as a fraction.

0.8 $\frac{8}{10}$ 0.5 $\frac{5}{10}$ 0.3 $\frac{3}{10}$ 0.4 $\frac{2}{5}$

0.25 $\frac{1}{4}$ 0.7 $\frac{7}{10}$ 0.2 $\frac{1}{5}$ 0.75 $\frac{3}{4}$

0.2 $\frac{2}{10}$ 0.6 $\frac{6}{10}$ 0.5 $\frac{1}{2}$ 0.8 $\frac{4}{5}$

0.1 $\frac{1}{10}$ 0.4 $\frac{4}{10}$ 0.6 $\frac{3}{5}$ 0.9 $\frac{9}{10}$

Write the answer in the box.

Which two of the fractions above are the same as 0.5? $\frac{5}{10}$, $\frac{1}{2}$

Which two of the fractions above are the same as 0.8? $\frac{8}{10}$, $\frac{4}{5}$

Which two of the fractions above are the same as 0.6? $\frac{6}{10}$, $\frac{3}{5}$

Which two of the fractions above are the same as 0.2? $\frac{2}{10}$, $\frac{1}{5}$

Which two of the fractions above are the same as 0.4? $\frac{4}{10}$, $\frac{2}{5}$

Children should realize that $\frac{1}{10}$ is equivalent to 0.1. If necessary, help them understand that $\frac{2}{10}$ is equivalent to 0.2, and so on. Children also need to know the decimal equivalents of $\frac{1}{4}$ and $\frac{3}{4}$.

Fractions of shapes

Shade $\frac{3}{5}$ of each shape.

Shade $\frac{4}{5}$ of each shape.

Shade the fraction shown of each shape.

$\frac{4}{10}$

$\frac{8}{10}$

$\frac{3}{10}$

$\frac{7}{10}$

$\frac{6}{10}$

$\frac{9}{10}$

Children may shade in any combination of the sections as long as the shaded area represents the correct fraction.

Fractions

Colour $\frac{3}{4}$ of each shape.

Colour $\frac{2}{3}$ of each shape.

Colour $\frac{3}{4}$ of each shape.

Children may shade in any combination of the sections as long as the shaded area represents the correct fraction.

Reading timetables

	Frostburg	Elmhurst	Badger Farm	Winchester
Redline bus	8:00	8:05	8:15	8:25
Blueline bus	8:05	No stop	8:12	8:20
City taxi	8:30	8:35	8:45	8:55
Greenline bus	8:07	No stop	No stop	8:15

The timetable shows the times it takes to travel using different transport companies between Frostburg and Winchester.

Write the answer in the box.

How long does the Redline bus take between Frostburg and Winchester? → 25 minutes

When does the Blueline bus arrive at Badger Farm? → 8:12

Where does the Greenline bus not stop? → Elmhurst

Where is City taxi at 8.35? → Elmhurst

Does the Blueline bus stop at Elmhurst? → No

How long does the Redline bus take to travel between Badger Farm and Winchester? → 10 minutes

Which is the fastest trip between Frostburg and Winchester? → Greenline bus

Which service arrives at five minutes to nine? → City taxi

How long does City taxi take between Frostburg and Badger Farm? → 15 minutes

Where is the Blueline bus at twelve minutes past eight? → Badger farm

Children should find this exercise fairly straightforward. If they have difficulty, help them read across the rows and down the columns to find the information they need.

Averages

Write the average of this row in the box.

4	2	2	2	6	3	2

The average is 3.

Write the average of each row in the box.

2	3	7	4	2	7	2	5	4
7	4	5	4	8	5	3	4	5
5	3	5	3	5	2	4	5	4
7	5	9	7	2	4	8	6	6
4	3	4	3	4	3	4	7	4
1	4	2	7	3	8	2	5	4
3	2	1	2	2	3	2	1	2
8	3	6	3	8	2	8	2	5

Write the average of each row in the box.

4	8	6	3	9	6	6	6
5	9	2	6	9	1	3	5
6	3	8	6	1	5	6	5
3	8	6	7	5	9	4	6
1	8	3	4	2	6	4	4
9	5	8	7	4	7	9	7
1	3	2	3	1	2	2	2
6	3	7	4	5	8	2	5

If necessary, remind children that the average of a set of quantities is the sum of the quantities divided by the total number of quantities.

Multiplying larger numbers by ones ☆

Write the product for each problem.

¹³	¹ ³¹
529	1 273
x 4	x 5
2116	**6365**

Write the product for each problem.

724	831	126	455
x 2	x 3	x 3	x 4
1448	**2493**	**378**	**1820**

161	282	349	253
x 4	x 5	x 5	x 6
644	**1410**	**1745**	**1518**

328	465	105	562
x 6	x 6	x 4	x 4
1968	**2790**	**420**	**2248**

Write the product for each problem.

4261	1582	3612	4284
x 3	x 3	x 4	x 4
12 783	**4746**	**14 448**	**17 136**

5907	1263	1303	1467
x 5	x 5	x 6	x 6
29 535	**6315**	**7818**	**8802**

6521	8436	1599	3761
x 6	x 6	x 6	x 6
39 126	**50 616**	**9594**	**22 566**

5837	6394	8124	3914
x 4	x 5	x 6	x 6
23 348	**31 970**	**48 744**	**23 484**

Children should understand the convention of multiplication problems, i.e. to multiply the ones first and work left, carrying when necessary. Problems on this page will highlight gaps in knowledge of 2, 3, 4, 5, and 6 times tables.

☆ Multiplying larger numbers by ones

Write the product for each problem.

¹⁴	¹ ⁷⁴
417	2185
x 7	x 9
2919	**19 665**

Write the product for each problem.

419	604	715	327
x 7	x 7	x 8	x 7
2933	**4228**	**5720**	**2289**

425	171	682	246
x 8	x 9	x 8	x 8
3400	**1539**	**5456**	**1968**

436	999	319	581
x 8	x 9	x 9	x 9
3488	**8991**	**2871**	**5229**

Write the product for each problem.

4331	2816	1439	2617
x 7	x 7	x 8	x 8
30 317	**19 712**	**11 512**	**20 936**

3104	4022	3212	2591
x 8	x 8	x 9	x 9
24 832	**32 176**	**28 908**	**23 319**

1710	3002	2468	1514
x 9	x 8	x 7	x 8
15 390	**24 016**	**17 276**	**12 112**

4624	2993	3894	4361
x 7	x 8	x 8	x 9
32 368	**23 944**	**31 152**	**39 249**

Any problems encountered on this page will be similar to those of the previous page. Gaps in the child's knowledge of 7, 8, and 9 times tables will be highlighted here.

Real-life multiplication problems ☆

There are 157 apples in a box.
How many will there be in three boxes?

¹²
157
x 3
471

471 apples

A stamp album can hold 550 stamps.
How many stamps will 5 albums hold?

2750 stamps

550
x 5
2750

A train can take 425 passengers.
How many can it take in four trips?

1700 passengers

425
x 4
1700

Mr Jenkins puts $256 a month into the bank.
How much will he have put in after six months?

$1536

256
x 6
1536

A theatre can seat 5524 people. If a play runs for 7 days, what is the maximum number of people who will be able to see it?

38 668 people

5 524
x 7
38 668

A car costs $9956. How much will it cost a company to buy nine cars for its people?

$89 604

9 956
x 9
89 604

Installing a new window for a house costs $435. How much will it cost to install 8 windows of the same size?

$3480

435
x 8
3480

An airplane flies at a steady speed of 550 kilometres per hour. How far will it travel in 7 hours?

3850 km/h

550
x 7
3850

This page provides an opportunity for children to apply their skills of multiplication to real-life problems. As with previous multiplication work, gaps in their knowledge of multiplication facts will be highlighted here.

☆ Area of rectangles and squares

Find the area of this rectangle.

To find the area of a rectangle or square, we multiply length (l) by width (w).

Area = **800 cm²**

¹
32
x 25
160
+640
800 cm²

(w) 25 cm
(l) 32 cm

Find the area of these rectangles and squares.
You may need to do your work on a separate sheet.

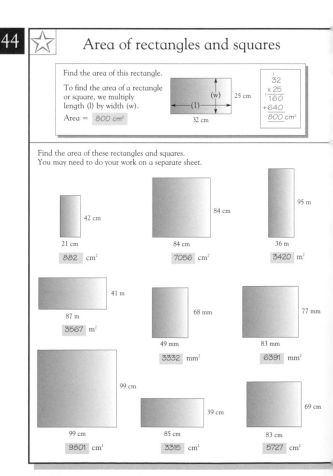

42 cm
21 cm
882 cm²

84 cm
84 cm
7056 cm²

95 m
36 m
3420 m²

41 m
87 m
3567 m²

68 mm
49 mm
3332 mm²

77 mm
83 mm
6391 mm²

99 cm
99 cm
9801 cm²

39 cm
85 cm
3315 cm²

69 cm
83 cm
5727 cm²

Children may confuse area and perimeter, and add the sides together instead of multiplying the two sides to arrive at the area. If any answers are wrong, check the long multiplication, and if necessary, revise the method.

Perimeter of shapes ☆

Find the perimeter of this rectangle.

To find the perimeter of a rectangle or square, we add the two lengths and the two widths together.

12.4 cm
27.3 cm

1 1
27.3 cm
27.3 cm
12.4 cm
+ 12.4 cm
79.4 cm

79.4 cm

Find the perimeter of these rectangles and squares.
You may need to do your work on a separate sheet.

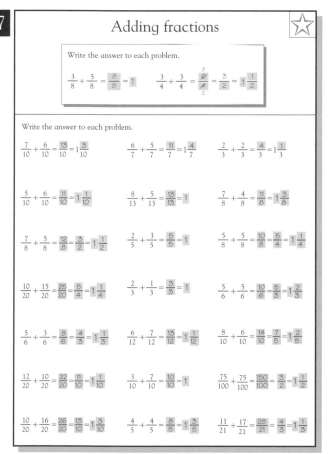

29.8 cm
20.4 cm
47.2 cm
154 cm

64.7 cm
20.4 cm
81.6 cm

36.8 cm

64.7 cm
258.8 cm

22.9 cm
119.4 cm

37.2 cm
47.8 cm

37.2 cm
148.8 cm
93.2 cm
282 cm

96.3 cm

50.5 cm
37.9 cm

50.5 cm
202 cm
65.2 cm
206.2 cm
24.8 cm
242.2 cm

On this page and the next, the most likely problem will be confusion with the area work done on the previous page. Remind children to add the four sides together.

Adding fractions

Work out the answer to the problem.

$$\frac{1}{5} + \frac{3}{5} = \frac{4}{5} \qquad \frac{4}{9} + \frac{2}{9} = \frac{6}{9} = \frac{2}{3}$$

Remember to reduce to simplest form if you need to.

Work out the answer to each sum. Reduce to simplest form if you need to.

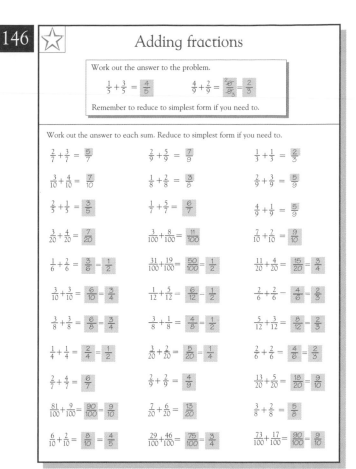

$\frac{2}{7} + \frac{3}{7} = \frac{5}{7}$ $\frac{2}{9} + \frac{5}{9} = \frac{7}{9}$ $\frac{1}{3} + \frac{1}{3} = \frac{2}{3}$

$\frac{3}{10} + \frac{4}{10} = \frac{7}{10}$ $\frac{1}{8} + \frac{2}{8} = \frac{3}{8}$ $\frac{2}{9} + \frac{3}{9} = \frac{5}{9}$

$\frac{2}{5} + \frac{1}{5} = \frac{3}{5}$ $\frac{1}{7} + \frac{5}{7} = \frac{6}{7}$ $\frac{4}{9} + \frac{1}{9} = \frac{5}{9}$

$\frac{3}{20} + \frac{4}{20} = \frac{7}{20}$ $\frac{3}{100} + \frac{8}{100} = \frac{11}{100}$ $\frac{7}{10} + \frac{2}{10} = \frac{9}{10}$

$\frac{1}{6} + \frac{2}{6} = \frac{3}{6} = \frac{1}{2}$ $\frac{31}{100} + \frac{19}{100} = \frac{50}{100} = \frac{1}{2}$ $\frac{11}{20} + \frac{4}{20} = \frac{15}{20} = \frac{3}{4}$

$\frac{3}{10} + \frac{3}{10} = \frac{6}{10} = \frac{3}{4}$ $\frac{1}{12} + \frac{5}{12} = \frac{6}{12} = \frac{1}{2}$ $\frac{2}{6} + \frac{2}{6} = \frac{4}{6} = \frac{2}{3}$

$\frac{3}{8} + \frac{3}{8} = \frac{6}{8} = \frac{3}{4}$ $\frac{3}{8} + \frac{1}{8} = \frac{4}{8} = \frac{1}{2}$ $\frac{5}{12} + \frac{3}{12} = \frac{8}{12} = \frac{2}{3}$

$\frac{1}{4} + \frac{1}{4} = \frac{2}{4} = \frac{1}{2}$ $\frac{3}{20} + \frac{2}{20} = \frac{5}{20} = \frac{1}{4}$ $\frac{2}{6} + \frac{2}{6} = \frac{4}{6} = \frac{2}{3}$

$\frac{2}{7} + \frac{4}{7} = \frac{6}{7}$ $\frac{2}{9} + \frac{2}{9} = \frac{4}{9}$ $\frac{13}{20} + \frac{5}{20} = \frac{18}{20} = \frac{9}{10}$

$\frac{81}{100} + \frac{9}{100} = \frac{90}{100} = \frac{9}{10}$ $\frac{7}{20} + \frac{6}{20} = \frac{13}{20}$ $\frac{3}{8} + \frac{2}{8} = \frac{5}{8}$

$\frac{6}{10} + \frac{2}{10} = \frac{8}{10} = \frac{4}{5}$ $\frac{29}{100} + \frac{46}{100} = \frac{75}{100} = \frac{3}{4}$ $\frac{73}{100} + \frac{17}{100} = \frac{90}{100} = \frac{9}{10}$

Difficulty in reducing the sum to its simplest form points to a weakness in finding common factors of the numerator and denominator. Children can reduce the answer in stages, first looking at whether 2 is a common factor, then 3, and so on.

Adding fractions ☆

Write the answer to each problem.

$$\frac{3}{8} + \frac{5}{8} = \frac{8}{8} = 1 \qquad \frac{3}{4} + \frac{3}{4} = \frac{6}{4} = \frac{3}{2} = 1\frac{1}{2}$$

Write the answer to each problem.

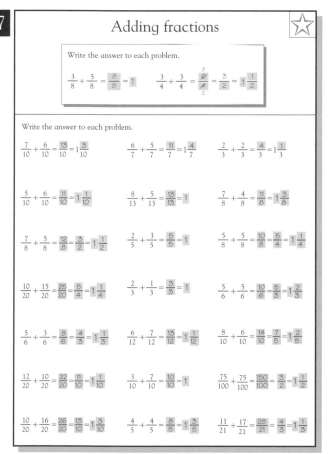

$\frac{7}{10} + \frac{6}{10} = \frac{13}{10} = 1\frac{3}{10}$ $\frac{6}{7} + \frac{5}{7} = \frac{11}{7} = 1\frac{4}{7}$ $\frac{2}{3} + \frac{2}{3} = \frac{4}{3} = 1\frac{1}{3}$

$\frac{5}{10} + \frac{6}{10} = \frac{11}{10} = 1\frac{1}{10}$ $\frac{8}{13} + \frac{5}{13} = \frac{13}{13} = 1$ $\frac{7}{8} + \frac{4}{8} = \frac{11}{8} = 1\frac{3}{8}$

$\frac{7}{8} + \frac{5}{8} = \frac{12}{8} = \frac{3}{2} = 1\frac{1}{2}$ $\frac{2}{5} + \frac{3}{5} = \frac{5}{5} = 1$ $\frac{5}{8} + \frac{5}{8} = \frac{10}{8} = \frac{5}{4} = 1\frac{1}{4}$

$\frac{10}{20} + \frac{15}{20} = \frac{25}{20} = \frac{5}{4} = 1\frac{1}{4}$ $\frac{2}{3} + \frac{1}{3} = \frac{3}{3} = 1$ $\frac{5}{6} + \frac{5}{6} = \frac{10}{6} = \frac{5}{3} = 1\frac{2}{3}$

$\frac{5}{6} + \frac{3}{6} = \frac{8}{6} = \frac{4}{3} = 1\frac{1}{3}$ $\frac{6}{12} + \frac{7}{12} = \frac{13}{12} = 1\frac{1}{12}$ $\frac{8}{10} + \frac{6}{10} = \frac{14}{10} = \frac{7}{5} = 1\frac{2}{5}$

$\frac{12}{20} + \frac{10}{20} = \frac{22}{20} = \frac{11}{10} = 1\frac{1}{10}$ $\frac{3}{10} + \frac{7}{10} = \frac{10}{10} = 1$ $\frac{75}{100} + \frac{75}{100} = \frac{150}{100} = \frac{3}{2} = 1\frac{1}{2}$

$\frac{10}{20} + \frac{16}{20} = \frac{26}{20} = \frac{13}{10} = 1\frac{3}{10}$ $\frac{4}{5} + \frac{4}{5} = \frac{8}{5} = 1\frac{3}{5}$ $\frac{11}{21} + \frac{17}{21} = \frac{28}{21} = \frac{4}{3} = 1\frac{1}{3}$

If children leave the answer as a fraction or do not reduce it, they are completing only one of the two steps to finding the simplest form. Have them first write the answer as a mixed number, and then reduce the fraction part.

Subtracting fractions

Write the answer to each problem.

$$\frac{4}{5} - \frac{2}{5} = \frac{2}{5} \qquad \frac{8}{9} - \frac{5}{9} = \frac{3}{9} = \frac{1}{3}$$

Reduce to simplest form if you need to.

Write the answer to each problem. Reduce to simplest form if you need to.

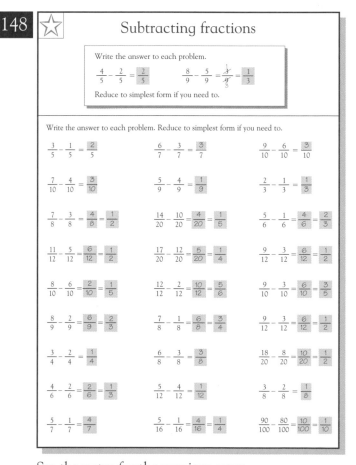

$\frac{3}{5} - \frac{1}{5} = \frac{2}{5}$ $\frac{6}{7} - \frac{3}{7} = \frac{3}{7}$ $\frac{9}{10} - \frac{6}{10} = \frac{3}{10}$

$\frac{7}{10} - \frac{4}{10} = \frac{3}{10}$ $\frac{5}{9} - \frac{4}{9} = \frac{1}{9}$ $\frac{2}{3} - \frac{1}{3} = \frac{1}{3}$

$\frac{7}{8} - \frac{3}{8} = \frac{4}{8} = \frac{1}{2}$ $\frac{14}{20} - \frac{10}{20} = \frac{4}{20} = \frac{1}{5}$ $\frac{5}{6} - \frac{1}{6} = \frac{4}{6} = \frac{2}{3}$

$\frac{11}{12} - \frac{5}{12} = \frac{6}{12} = \frac{1}{2}$ $\frac{17}{20} - \frac{12}{20} = \frac{5}{20} = \frac{1}{4}$ $\frac{9}{12} - \frac{3}{12} = \frac{6}{12} = \frac{1}{2}$

$\frac{8}{10} - \frac{6}{10} = \frac{2}{10} = \frac{1}{5}$ $\frac{12}{12} - \frac{2}{12} = \frac{10}{12} = \frac{5}{6}$ $\frac{9}{10} - \frac{3}{10} = \frac{6}{10} = \frac{3}{5}$

$\frac{8}{9} - \frac{2}{9} = \frac{6}{9} = \frac{2}{3}$ $\frac{7}{8} - \frac{1}{8} = \frac{6}{8} = \frac{3}{4}$ $\frac{9}{12} - \frac{3}{12} = \frac{6}{12} = \frac{1}{2}$

$\frac{3}{4} - \frac{2}{4} = \frac{1}{4}$ $\frac{6}{8} - \frac{3}{8} = \frac{3}{8}$ $\frac{18}{20} - \frac{8}{20} = \frac{10}{20} = \frac{1}{2}$

$\frac{4}{6} - \frac{2}{6} = \frac{2}{6} = \frac{1}{3}$ $\frac{5}{12} - \frac{4}{12} = \frac{1}{12}$ $\frac{3}{8} - \frac{2}{8} = \frac{1}{8}$

$\frac{5}{7} - \frac{1}{7} = \frac{4}{7}$ $\frac{5}{16} - \frac{1}{16} = \frac{4}{16} = \frac{1}{4}$ $\frac{90}{100} - \frac{80}{100} = \frac{10}{100} = \frac{1}{10}$

See the notes for the previous page.

Showing decimals

Write the decimals on the number line.

0.4, 0.5, 0.6, 0.8, 0.9, 0.25, 0.45, 0.63

0	0.25	0.45	0.63		1
	0.1 0.2 0.3 0.4 0.5 0.6 0.7 0.8 0.9				

Write the decimals on the number line.

0.56, 0.2, 0.87, 0.45, 0.98, 0.6, 0.1

0	0.25	0.5	0.75	1
	0.1 0.2 0.45 0.56 0.6 0.87 0.98			

Write the decimals on the number line.

1.41, 1.8, 1.3, 1.98, 1.68, 1.2

1	1.25	1.5	1.75	2
	1.2 1.3 1.41 1.68 1.8 1.98			

Write these decimals on the number line.

2.5, 3.75, 2.25, 3.1, 3.68, 4.2

2		3		4
	2.25 2.5	3.1	3.68 3.75	4.2

If children are confused as to where to place the hundredths, have them first fill in all of the tenths on the number line. Then ask them to find those tenths between which the hundredths fall.

Conversions: length

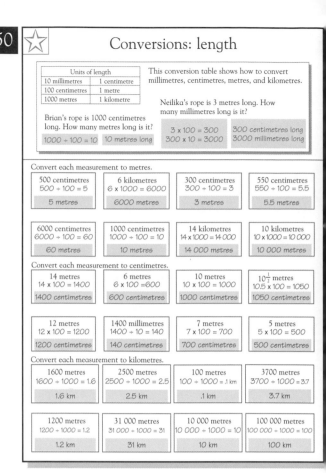

Units of length	
10 millimetres	1 centimetre
100 centimetres	1 metre
1000 metres	1 kilometre

This conversion table shows how to convert millimetres, centimetres, metres, and kilometres.

Neilika's rope is 3 metres long. How many millimetres long is it?

Brian's rope is 1000 centimetres long. How many metres long is it?

$1000 \div 100 = 10$ 10 metres long

$3 \times 100 = 300$ 300 centimetres long
$300 \times 10 = 3000$ 3000 millimetres long

Convert each measurement to metres.

500 centimetres $500 \div 100 = 5$ **5 metres**	6 kilometres $6 \times 1000 = 6000$ **6000 metres**	300 centimetres $300 \div 100 = 3$ **3 metres**	550 centimetres $550 \div 100 = 5.5$ **5.5 metres**
6000 centimetres $6000 \div 100 = 60$ **60 metres**	1000 centimetres $1000 \div 100 = 10$ **10 metres**	14 kilometres $14 \times 1000 = 14\,000$ **14 000 metres**	10 kilometres $10 \times 1000 = 10\,000$ **10 000 metres**

Convert each measurement to centimetres.

14 metres $14 \times 100 = 1400$ **1400 centimetres**	6 metres $6 \times 100 = 600$ **600 centimetres**	10 metres $10 \times 100 = 1000$ **1000 centimetres**	$10\frac{1}{2}$ metres $10.5 \times 100 = 1050$ **1050 centimetres**
12 metres $12 \times 100 = 1200$ **1200 centimetres**	1400 millimetres $1400 \div 10 = 140$ **140 centimetres**	7 metres $7 \times 100 = 700$ **700 centimetres**	5 metres $5 \times 100 = 500$ **500 centimetres**

Convert each measurement to kilometres.

1600 metres $1600 \div 1000 = 1.6$ **1.6 km**	2500 metres $2500 \div 1000 = 2.5$ **2.5 km**	100 metres $100 \div 1000 = .1$ km **.1 km**	3700 metres $3700 \div 1000 = 3.7$ **3.7 km**
1200 metres $1200 \div 1000 = 1.2$ **1.2 km**	31 000 metres $31\,000 \div 1000 = 31$ **31 km**	10 000 metres $10\,000 \div 1000 = 10$ **10 km**	100 000 metres $100\,000 \div 1000 = 100$ **100 km**

If children are confused whether to multiply or divide, ask them if the new unit is a longer or shorter unit. If the unit is longer, there will be fewer of them, so division would be the appropriate operation.

Conversions: capacity

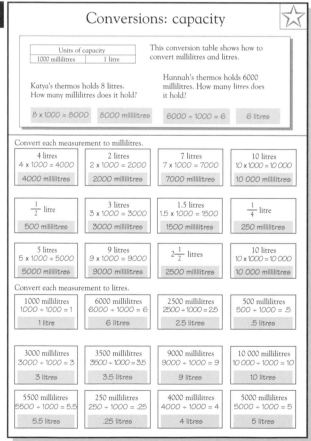

Units of capacity	
1000 millilitres	1 litre

This conversion table shows how to convert millilitres and litres.

Katya's thermos holds 8 litres. How many millilitres does it hold?

Hannah's thermos holds 6000 millilitres. How many litres does it hold?

$8 \times 1000 = 8000$ 8000 millilitres

$6000 \div 1000 = 6$ 6 litres

Convert each measurement to millilitres.

4 litres $4 \times 1000 = 4000$ **4000 millilitres**	2 litres $2 \times 1000 = 2000$ **2000 millilitres**	7 litres $7 \times 1000 = 7000$ **7000 millilitres**	10 litres $10 \times 1000 = 10\,000$ **10 000 millilitres**
$\frac{1}{2}$ litre **500 millilitres**	3 litres $3 \times 1000 = 3000$ **3000 millilitres**	1.5 litres $1.5 \times 1000 = 1500$ **1500 millilitres**	$\frac{1}{4}$ litre **250 millilitres**
5 litres $5 \times 1000 = 5000$ **5000 millilitres**	9 litres $9 \times 1000 = 9000$ **9000 millilitres**	$2\frac{1}{2}$ litres **2500 millilitres**	10 litres $10 \times 1000 = 10\,000$ **10 000 millilitres**

Convert each measurement to litres.

1000 millilitres $1000 \div 1000 = 1$ **1 litre**	6000 millilitres $6000 \div 1000 = 6$ **6 litres**	2500 millilitres $2500 \div 1000 = 2.5$ **2.5 litres**	500 millilitres $500 \div 1000 = .5$ **.5 litres**
3000 millilitres $3000 \div 1000 = 3$ **3 litres**	3500 millilitres $3500 \div 1000 = 3.5$ **3.5 litres**	9000 millilitres $9000 \div 1000 = 9$ **9 litres**	10 000 millilitres $10\,000 \div 1000 = 10$ **10 litres**
5500 millilitres $5500 \div 1000 = 5.5$ **5.5 litres**	250 millilitres $250 \div 1000 = .25$ **.25 litres**	4000 millilitres $4000 \div 1000 = 4$ **4 litres**	5000 millilitres $5000 \div 1000 = 5$ **5 litres**

See the comments for the previous page.

Rounding money

Round to the nearest dollar.

$3.95 rounds to **$4**

$2.25 rounds to **$2**

Round to the nearest ten dollars.

$15.50 rounds to **$20**

$14.40 rounds to **$10**

Round to the nearest dollar.

$2.60 rounds to **$3** $8.49 rounds to **$8** $3.39 rounds to **$3**

$9.55 rounds to **$10** $1.75 rounds to **$2** $4.30 rounds to **$4**

$7.15 rounds to **$7** $6.95 rounds to **$7** $2.53 rounds to **$3**

Round to the nearest ten dollars.

$37.34 rounds to **$40** $21.75 rounds to **$20** $85.03 rounds to **$90**

$71.99 rounds to **$70** $66.89 rounds to **$70** $52.99 rounds to **$50**

$55.31 rounds to **$60** $12.79 rounds to **$10** $15.00 rounds to **$20**

Round to the nearest hundred dollars.

$307.12 rounds to **$300** $175.50 rounds to **$200** $115.99 rounds to **$100**

$860.55 rounds to **$900** $417.13 rounds to **$400** $650.15 rounds to **$700**

$739.10 rounds to **$700** $249.66 rounds to **$200** $367.50 rounds to **$400**

If children have difficulty, have them decide which are the two nearest hundred dollars, and which is closest to the number.

Estimating sums of money

Round to the leading digit. Estimate the sum.

$3.26 → $3
+ $4.82 → + $5
is about $8

$68.53 → $70
+ $34.60 → + $30
is about $100

Round to the leading digit. Estimate the sum.

$52.61 → $50
+ $27.95 → + $30
is about $80

$19.20 → $20
+ $22.13 → + $20
is about $40

$70.75 → $70
+ $12.49 → + $10
is about $80

$701.34 → $700
+ $100.80 → + $100
is about $800

$339.50 → $300
+ $422.13 → + $400
is about $700

$160.07 → $200
+ $230.89 → + $200
is about $400

$25.61 → $30
+ $72.51 → + $70
is about $100

$61.39 → $60
+ $19.50 → + $20
is about $80

$18.32 → $20
+ $13.90 → + $10
is about $30

$587.35 → $600
+ 251.89 → + $300
is about $900

$109.98 → $100
+ $210.09 → + $200
is about $300

$470.02 → $500
+ $203.17 → + $200
is about $700

Round to the leading digit. Estimate the sum.

$75.95 + $17.95 → $100

$41.67 + $20.35 → $60

$49.19 + $38.70 → $90

$784.65 + $101.05 → $900

$516.50 + $290.69 → $800

$58.78 + $33.25 → $90

$82.90 + $11.79 → $90

$90.09 + $14.50 → $100

In section 2, children need to estimate by rounding mentally. If they have trouble, have them write the rounded numbers above the originals, and then add them.

Estimating differences of money

Round the numbers to the leading digit. Estimate the differences.

$8.75 → $9
− $5.10 → − $5
is about $4

$61.47 → $60
− $35.64 → − $40
is about $20

Round the numbers to the leading digit. Estimate the differences.

$17.90 → $20
− $12.30 → − $10
is about $10

$6.40 → $6
− $3.75 → − $4
is about $2

$87.45 → $90
− $54.99 → − $50
is about $40

$34.90 → $30
− $12.60 → − $10
is about $20

$8.68 → $9
− $4.39 → − $4
is about $5

$363.24 → $400
− $127.66 → − $100
is about $300

$78.75 → $80
− $24.99 → − $20
is about $60

$64.21 → $60
− $28.56 → − $30
is about $30

$723.34 → $700
− $487.12 → − $500
is about $200

Round the numbers to the leading digit. Estimate the differences.

$8.12 − $1.35
→ $8 − $1 = $7

$49.63 − $27.85
→ $50 − $30 = $20

$7.50 − $3.15
→ $8 − $3 = $5

$85.15 − $42.99
→ $90 − $40 = $50

$5.85 − $4.75
→ $6 − $5 = $1

$634.60 − $267.25
→ $600 − $300 = $300

$37.35 − $16.99
→ $40 − $20 = $20

$842.17 − $169.54
→ $800 − $200 = $600

$56.95 − $20.58
→ $60 − $20 = $40

$628.37 − $252.11
→ $600 − $300 = $300

See the comments for the previous page.

Estimating sums and differences

Round the numbers to the leading digit. Estimate the sum or difference.

3576 → 4000
+ 1307 → +1000
is about 5000

198 248 → 200 000
− 116 431 → − 100 000
is about 100 000

Round the numbers to the leading digit. Estimate the sum or difference.

685 → 700
+ 489 → + 500
is about 1200

21 481 → 20 000
− 12 500 → − 10 000
is about 10 000

7834 → 8 000
+ 3106 → + 3 000
is about 11 000

682 778 → 700 000
+ 130 001 → + 100 000
is about 800 000

58 499 → 60 000
− 22 135 → − 20 000
is about 40 000

902 276 → 900 000
− 615 999 →− 600 000
is about 300 000

46 801 → 50 000
+ 34 700 → + 30 000
is about 80 000

9734 → 10 000
− 8306 → − 8 000
is about 2 000

65 606 → 70 000
+ 85 943 → + 90 000
is about 160 000

5218 → 5000
− 3673 → − 4000
is about 1000

745 → 700
+ 451 → + 500
is about 1200

337 297 → 300 000
− 168 931 →− 200 000
is about 100 000

Write < or > for each problem.

329 + 495 > 800

11 569 − 6146 < 6000

563 − 317 < 300

8193 − 6668 > 1000

41 924 − 12 445 < 50 000

634 577 + 192 556 > 800 000

18 885 + 12 691 > 30 000

713 096 − 321 667 < 400 000

In section 2, children need to think about their estimates more carefully if the estimate is very close to the number on the right side of the equation. Have them look at the digits in the next place to to adjust their estimates up or down.

Conversion tables

Draw a table to convert dollars to cents.

$	cents
1	100
2	200
3	300

Complete the conversion chart below.

Weeks	Days
1	7
2	14
3	21
4	28
5	35
6	42
7	49
8	56
9	63
10	70

Sunday
Monday
Tuesday
Wednesday
Thursday
Friday
Saturday

If there are 60 minutes in 1 hour, make a conversion chart for up to 10 hours.

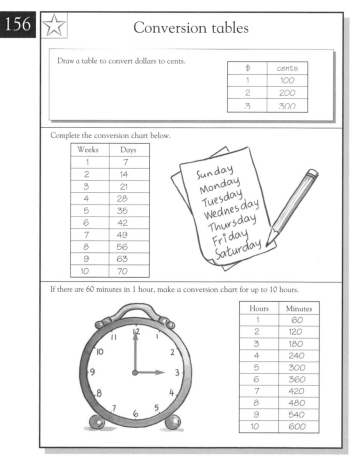

Hours	Minutes
1	60
2	120
3	180
4	240
5	300
6	360
7	420
8	480
9	540
10	600

Children will grasp that they are dealing in multiples of 7 and later, 60. Any problems will be due to weaknesses in times tables or from missing numbers as they work down the chart. Encourage care and concentration.

Extra Practice

Answer Section
with Parents' Notes

This section provides answers for the Extra Practice section on pages 158–201. There are also notes for each page, indicating the skills being developed, pointing out potential issues, or providing ideas for extra activities and ways to help children.

Children will get plenty of practice in solving problems and applying the four operations (+, −, x, and ÷). Children are expected to be able to represent the problems symbolically and communicate the mathematical process clearly. If children really understand the math, they will be able to reason critically and explain their reasoning.

Occasionally, you may find that a particular problem is slightly beyond your child's capabilities. Offer as much help and support as needed, and encourage them to reason out the solutions to the best of their abilities.

Around the home, provide opportunities for practical use of measuring equipment and appropriate tools, such as calculators, watches, timetables, and weighing scales. This will help children to visualize situations when answering math problems.

Build your child's confidence with words of praise. If they are getting answers wrong, encourage them to return to try again another time. Good luck, and remember to have fun!

★ Reading and writing numbers

These are large numbers, be careful how you read and write them.

Write the number in words.

6124 Six thousand one hundred twenty-four

5102 Five thousand one hundred two

7034 Seven thousand thirty-four

1638 One thousand six hundred thirty-eight

7400 Seven thousand four hundred

2805 Two thousand eight hundred five

3967 Three thousand nine hundred sixty-seven

7452 Seven thousand four hundred fifty-two

Write the number.

One thousand forty-nine	1049
Nine hundred eighty-four	984
Four hundred seventeen	417
Four hundred seventy-six	476
One hundred six	106
Three thousand ninety-seven	3097
One thousand six hundred twenty-four	1624
One thousand three	1003

A comma is not normally used to separate the thousands and hundreds, and children should learn not to use one in that position. When a number has more than four digits, a space is used (e.g., 34 232).

Completing sequences ★

Some answers have negative values.

Complete each sequence.

12	24	36	48	60	72	84	96
24	32	40	48	56	64	72	80
18	27	36	45	54	63	72	81
45	50	55	60	65	70	75	80
−40	−35	−30	25	−20	−15	−10	−5
−18	−15	−12	−9	−6	−3	0	3
−36	−32	−28	−24	−20	−16	−12	−8
−70	−60	−50	−40	−30	−20	−10	0
63	52	41	30	19	8	−3	−14
80	71	62	53	44	35	26	17
26	21	16	11	6	1	−4	−9
8	−12	−16	−20	−24	−28	−32	−36
13	26	39	52	65	78	91	104
−31	−25	−19	−13	−7	−1	5	11
12	18	24	30	36	42	48	54

Complete this sequence but be careful, this is a bit trickier.

2	4	8	16	32	64	128

Children should begin by looking at the numbers already given and working out the "gaps," after that they should be able to continue the sequences. The sequences with negative numbers will be a little more challenging.

★ Odd and even

Write the odd numbers that are missing in each sequence.

3	5	7	9	11	13
17	19	21	23	25	27
41	43	45	47	49	51
79	81	83	85	87	89

Write the even numbers that are missing in each sequence.

8	10	12	14	16	18
26	28	30	32	34	36
50	52	54	56	58	60
92	94	96	98	100	102

Strike out the numbers that are **not** odd.

650   179   231

538   792

705   163   196

Strike out the numbers that are **not** even.

979   488   297

406   135

584   753   322

Circle the correct answer.

Adding two odd numbers together will always give an   odd number   (even number)

Adding two even numbers together will always give an   odd number   (even number)

It is important children realize all even numbers can be divided by 2 without a remainder. Recognizing even numbers will also help in later work on factors.

Adding and subtracting 10, 100 ★

Try to answer these questions as quickly as possible—but still be correct!

58 + 10 = 68	71 + 10 = 81	92 + 10 = 102	46 + 10 = 56
10 + 31 = 41	10 + 19 = 29	10 + 42 = 52	10 + 56 = 66
73 + 10 = 83	66 + 10 = 76	82 + 10 = 92	79 + 10 = 89
100 + 48 = 148	100 + 67 = 167	100 + 39 = 139	100 + 14 = 114
76 + 100 = 176	98 + 100 = 198	34 + 100 = 134	9 + 100 = 109
100 + 42 = 142	66 + 100 = 166	100 + 56 = 156	31 + 100 = 131

Write the answers.

76 − 10 = 66	93 − 10 = 83	48 − 10 = 38	60 − 10 = 50
113 − 10 = 103	156 − 10 = 146	231 − 10 = 221	400 − 10 = 390
261 − 10 = 251	200 − 10 = 190	403 − 10 = 393	601 − 10 = 591
250 − 100 = 150	134 − 100 = 34	700 − 100 = 600	106 − 100 = 6
327 − 100 = 227	708 − 100 = 608	1000 − 100 = 900	853 − 100 = 753
564 − 100 = 464	100 − 100 = 0	1242 − 100 = 1142	1067 − 100 = 967

By this stage children should be able to add and subtract 10 and 100 with ease.

★ Multiplying by 10 and 100

Try to answer these questions as quickly as possible—but still be correct!

3 x 10 = 30	7 x 10 = 70	9 x 10 = 90	10 x 10 = 100
12 x 10 = 120	0 x 10 = 0	14 x 10 = 140	1 x 10 = 10
15 x 10 = 150	17 x 10 = 170	21 x 10 = 210	30 x 10 = 300
10 x 2 = 20	10 x 6 = 60	10 x 0 = 0	10 x 8 = 80
10 x 13 = 130	10 x 24 = 240	10 x 50 = 500	10 x 22 = 220
10 x 15 = 150	10 x 36 = 360	10 x 100 = 1000	10 x 6 = 60

Write the answers.

2 x 100 = 200	4 x 100 = 400	6 x 100 = 600	11 x 100 = 1100
0 x 100 = 0	5 x 100 = 500	14 x 100 = 1400	15 x 100 = 1500
1 x 100 = 100	7 x 100 = 700	9 x 100 = 900	19 x 100 = 1900
100 x 8 = 800	100 x 14 = 1400	100 x 3 = 300	100 x 10 = 1000
100 x 18 = 1800	100 x 23 = 2300	100 x 61 = 6100	100 x 32 = 3200
100 x 0 = 0	100 x 55 = 5500	100 x 82 = 8200	100 x 16 = 1600

Write the answers.

$\frac{1}{2}$ x 10 = 5　　$\frac{1}{5}$ x 10 = 2　　100 x $\frac{1}{2}$ = 50　　$\frac{1}{5}$ x 100 = 20

Multiplying whole numbers by 10 and 100 will be important when the time comes to multiply with decimals. Always be careful when multiplying anything by 0 as children sometimes find it hard to understand this will result in nothing!

Dividing by 10 and 100 ★

Divide each number by 10.

20 2	50 5	90 9	10 1	100 10
30 3	60 6	70 7	80 8	40 4

Write the answer.

60 ÷ 10 = 6	80 ÷ 10 = 8	10 ÷ 10 = 1	40 ÷ 10 = 4
70 ÷ 10 = 7	20 ÷ 10 = 2	90 ÷ 10 = 9	50 ÷ 10 = 5

Divide each amount by 10.

120 ¢ 12 ¢	170 cm 17 cm	200 mL 20 mL	90 ¢ 9 ¢
250 cm 25 cm	400 kg 40 kg	110 m 11 m	30 litres 3 litres
50 km 5 km	180 m 18 m	500 kg 50 kg	230 g 23 g

Write the answer.

140 kg ÷ 10 = 14 kg	70 ¢ ÷ 10 = 7 ¢	80 g ÷ 10 = 8 g
280 m ÷ 10 = 28 m	330 ¢ ÷ 10 = 33 ¢	560 m ÷ 10 = 56 m
400 kg ÷ 10 = 40 kg	780 g ÷ 10 = 78 g	20 mL ÷ 10 = 2 mL

Divide each number by 100.

400　4　　　600　6　　　800　8　　　100　1

Write the answers.

4500 ÷ 100 = 45　　　2800 ÷ 100 = 28　　　6400 ÷ 100 = 64

Dividing by 10 and 100 can be a little trickier for children although they should be confident when the answers result in whole numbers. Children need to be careful when converting between units such as 30 litres divided by 10.

★ Ordering decimals

Write each row in order, beginning with the smallest number.

0.4	0.1	0.5	0.2	0.9	0.1	0.2	0.4	0.5	0.9
0.8	1.0	0.1	0.3	0.6	0.1	0.3	0.6	0.8	1.0
2.3	1.3	2.1	3.1	3.2	1.3	2.1	2.3	3.1	3.2

Write each row in order, beginning with the smallest value.

2.6 m	1.9 m	2.3 m	2.0 m	1.8 m	1.8 m	1.9 m	2.0 m	2.3 m	2.6 m
12.8 kg	4.8 kg	20.0 kg	6.3 kg	9.7 kg	4.8 kg	6.3 kg	9.7 kg	12.8 kg	20.0 kg
5.2 g	2.5 g	5.0 g	2.0 g	2.2 g	2.0 g	2.2 g	2.5 g	5.0 g	5.2 g

Write each row in order, beginning with the smallest number.

2.31	3.12	1.32	1.23	2.13	1.23	1.32	2.13	2.31	3.12
8.75	7.85	7.58	8.57	5.78	5.78	7.58	7.85	8.57	8.75
4.63	6.34	6.43	4.36	3.64	3.64	4.36	4.63	6.34	6.43

Write each row in order, beginning with the smallest value.

4.72 km	7.05 km	6.31 km	4.02 km	8.13 km
4.02 km	4.72 km	6.31 km	7.05 km	8.13 km
12.45 cm	10.86 cm	14.64 cm	9.07 cm	11.64 cm
9.07 cm	10.86 cm	11.64 cm	12.45 cm	14.64 cm
16.67 kg	15.67 kg	15.76 kg	17.56 kg	16.76 kg
15.67 kg	15.76 kg	16.67 kg	16.76 kg	17.56 kg

Children need to see decimals as an extension of the number system they are already used to, e.g., tens, hundreds, and thousands. In time they should become used to terms such as "tenths," "hundredths," and "thousandths."

Rounding ★

Round each amount to the nearest 10.

46 50	59 60	42 40	85 90	34 30
9 10	27 30	91 90	53 50	88 90

Round each amount to the nearest 100.

126 100	141 100	139 100	184 200	155 200
212 200	268 300	193 200	237 200	165 200
112 100	350 300	278 300	490 500	135 100
466 500	885 900	327 300	70 100	751 800
206 200	650 700	180 200	263 300	505 500

Round each amount to the nearest whole number.

0.85 1	1.34 1	2.51 3	2.02 2	1.05 1
3.56 4	2.75 3	4.19 4	2.38 2	4.52 5
6.4 6	8.3 8	12.1 12	8.2 8	4.9 5
6.5 7	11.7 12	3.6 4	8.8 9	10.5 11
3.45 3	2.06 2	3.01 3	4.08 4	5.09 5

At this stage rounding should be fairly straightforward as long as children remember the rule about the "half position" being rounded upward, such as 6.5 becoming 7.

166

Comparing numbers

Circle the larger number or amount each time.

0.5 or 0.3	0.5 kg or **600 g**	**$\frac{1}{2}$** or 0.3
1.2 or **2.1**	**70 cm** or 0.5 m	**$2.40** or 189 ¢
5.6 m or **600 cm**	0.3 or **0.4**	$1.90 or **$5.00**

Circle the smaller number or amount each time.

0.8 or **$\frac{1}{2}$**	3.5 m or **290 cm**	4.2 or **2.4**
3.5 or 5.3	625 cm or **6.2 m**	**130 g** or 1.2 kg
3.5 litres or **$3\frac{1}{4}$ litres**	$3.50 or **250 ¢**	**65 cm** or 1 m

Circle the larger number or amount each time.

6 x 7 or 40	**2 x 12** or 22	**double 150** or 295
3.5 km or half of 5 km	**3 x 8** or 6 x 3	$2.50 or **300 ¢**
400 mL or **0.5 L**	**40 x 2** or 10 x 7	**4 m** or 54 cm

Circle the smaller number or amount each time.

6 kg or **53 g**	6.72 or **6.27**	**$7.00** or 1000 ¢
12 km or **half of 14 km**	**4.01** or 4.1	2 km or **1600 m**
2.65 km or **2.56 km**	7.54 m or **7.45 m**	**3.6 m** or 400 cm

Circle the larger number each time.

10 x 11 or **12 x 10**	**8 x 7** or 6 x 9	7 x 4 or **6 x 5**
4 x 11 or 6 x 7	6 x 4 or **9 x 3**	11 x 3 or **9 x 8**
5 x 8 or 7 x 5	**6 x 6** or 8 x 4	**10 x 5** or 5 x 5

166

Much of this work revolves around children being able to successfully change between units, in other words, understanding that in order to work some answers, information such as "100 cm in a metre" will be essential.

167

Units of measurement

These are the units we might use sometimes.
millimetres (mm), centimetres (cm), metres (m), grams (g), kilograms (kg), millilitres (mL), litres (L), kilometres (km)

Write the most sensible unit to measure each of these.

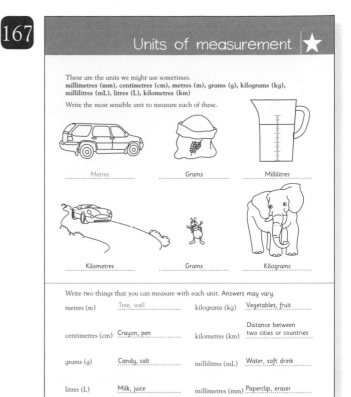

Metres

Grams

Millilitres

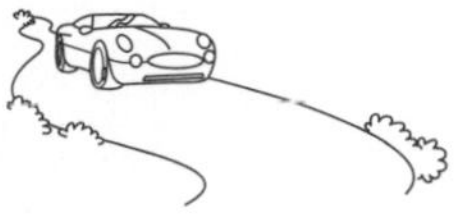
Kilometres

Grams

Kilograms

Write two things that you can measure with each unit. Answers may vary.

metres (m)	Tree, wall	kilograms (kg)	Vegetables, fruit
centimetres (cm)	Crayon, pen	kilometres (km)	Distance between two cities or countries
grams (g)	Candy, salt	millilitres (mL)	Water, soft drink
litres (L)	Milk, juice	millimetres (mm)	Paperclip, eraser

167

These questions give practice in choosing the most appropriate units with which to measure. Children should have been introduced to units such as centimetres and kilograms but may not have much practical experience of using them.

168

Fractions

What is half ($\frac{1}{2}$) of each amount? (US)

$3.00 $1.50	$5.00 $2.50	6 kg 3 kg	3 g 1.5 g	60 m 30 m
$1.20 $0.60	$1.50 $0.75	12 mL 6 mL	$2.50 $1.25	6 m 3 m

What is two-thirds ($\frac{2}{3}$) of each amount?

12 m 8 m	21 kg 14 kg	15 g 10 g	$6.00 $4.00	30 m 20 m
18 g 12 g	$3.00 $2.00	21 km 14 km	24 kg 16 kg	15 m 10 m

What is a quarter ($\frac{1}{4}$) of each amount?

$1.00 $0.25	60 cm 15 cm	2 m 0.5 m	48 g 12 g	$4.00 $1.00
120 cm 30 cm	80 g 20 g	12 kg 3 kg	32 ¢ 8 ¢	56 g 14 g

What is one-fifth ($\frac{1}{5}$) of each amount?

20 ¢ 4 ¢	50 ¢ 10 ¢	10 ¢ 2 ¢	25 cm 5 cm	$20.00 $4.00
60 cm 12 cm	10 m 2 m	40 km 8 km	35 g 7 g	45 kg 9 kg

What is two-fifths ($\frac{2}{5}$) of each amount?

30 ¢ 12 ¢	$20.00 $8.00	10 cm 4 cm	5 m 2 m	20 mm 8 mm
40 ¢ 16 ¢	50 g 20 g	60 kg 24 kg	55 ¢ 22 ¢	25 ¢ 10 ¢

168

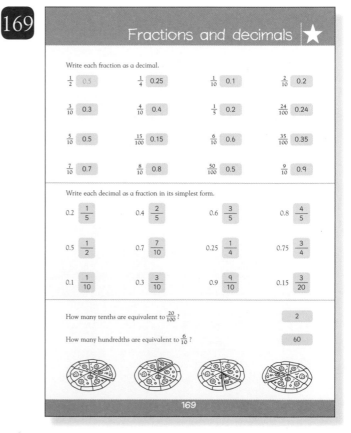

By now children should be familiar with the common fractions such as $\frac{1}{2}$, $\frac{1}{4}$, and $\frac{3}{4}$. Fifths and tenths will be less familiar but will become so. With fractions such as $\frac{2}{3}$, encourage children to first work out $\frac{1}{3}$ and then double it.

169

Fractions and decimals

Write each fraction as a decimal.

$\frac{1}{2}$ 0.5	$\frac{1}{4}$ 0.25	$\frac{1}{10}$ 0.1	$\frac{2}{10}$ 0.2
$\frac{3}{10}$ 0.3	$\frac{4}{10}$ 0.4	$\frac{1}{5}$ 0.2	$\frac{24}{100}$ 0.24
$\frac{5}{10}$ 0.5	$\frac{15}{100}$ 0.15	$\frac{6}{10}$ 0.6	$\frac{35}{100}$ 0.35
$\frac{7}{10}$ 0.7	$\frac{8}{10}$ 0.8	$\frac{50}{100}$ 0.5	$\frac{9}{10}$ 0.9

Write each decimal as a fraction in its simplest form.

0.2 $\frac{1}{5}$	0.4 $\frac{2}{5}$	0.6 $\frac{3}{5}$	0.8 $\frac{4}{5}$
0.5 $\frac{1}{2}$	0.7 $\frac{7}{10}$	0.25 $\frac{1}{4}$	0.75 $\frac{3}{4}$
0.1 $\frac{1}{10}$	0.3 $\frac{3}{10}$	0.9 $\frac{9}{10}$	0.15 $\frac{3}{20}$

How many tenths are equivalent to $\frac{20}{100}$? 2

How many hundredths are equivalent to $\frac{6}{10}$? 60

169

Children should know the connection between fractions and decimals and be able to interchange them with ease, especially tenths and hundredths. Note that they may not have been formally taught this conversion.

★ Keeping skills sharp

Which of these is the same as 20 305? Circle the correct answer.

Twenty thousand three hundred fifty   Twenty-three thousand five

(Twenty thousand three hundred five)   Twenty thousand thirty-five

Complete each sequence.

18	14	10	6	2	-2	-6	-10

-14	-9	-4	1	6	11	16	21

12	10	8	6	4	2	0	-2

Write the answers.

45	100	100	78
x 10	x 27	x 0.5	x 100
450	2700	50	7800

Find the answer to each problem.

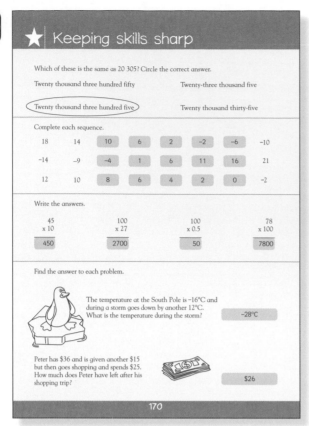

The temperature at the South Pole is −16°C and during a storm goes down by another 12°C. What is the temperature during the storm?   -28°C

Peter has $36 and is given another $15 but then goes shopping and spends $25. How much does Peter have left after his shopping trip? $26

170

Keeping skills sharp ★

Place the amounts in order, starting with the smallest.

| $6.50 | 560 ¢ | $6.05 | $65.00 | 680 ¢ | $5.06 |
| $5.06 | 560 ¢ | $6.05 | $6.50 | 680 ¢ | $65.00 |

These are some of the ingredients for a cake.

Round each amount to the nearest whole gram.

14.2 g of salt   14 g of salt

225.3 g of flour   225 g of flour

130.4 g of cherries   130 g of cherries

90.7 g of almonds   91 g of almonds

A class usually has 33 children but two-thirds are away on a trip.
How many children did not go on the trip?   11

How many tenths are equivalent to one half?   5

How many thirds are equivalent to one whole?   3

How many quarters are equivalent to 2?   8

Write each decimal as a fraction.

0.5 $\frac{1}{2}$ 0.2 $\frac{2}{10}$ 0.75 $\frac{3}{4}$ 0.9 $\frac{9}{10}$

Write each fraction as a decimal.

$\frac{4}{10}$ 0.4 $\frac{7}{10}$ 0.7 $\frac{37}{100}$ 0.37 $\frac{12}{100}$ 0.12

171

This page along with page 171 acts as revision and a reminder of the work in the previous pages. It can be given as a test if required.

★ Adding

Write the answers.

46 + 20 = 66	21 + 30 = 51	54 + 40 = 94	53 + 10 = 63
73 + 30 = 103	69 + 40 = 109	45 + 70 = 115	95 + 20 = 115
67 + 50 = 117	70 + 60 = 130	90 + 90 = 180	40 + 80 = 120
49 + 13 = 62	52 + 18 = 70	62 + 12 = 74	37 + 16 = 53
46 + 32 = 78	53 + 27 = 80	38 + 43 = 81	74 + 17 = 91
76 + 28 = 104	44 + 66 = 110	12 + 73 = 85	55 + 23 = 78

Write the answers.

73	56	39	52	51
+ 15	+ 17	+ 24	+ 38	+ 26
88	73	63	90	77

25	67	48	90	85
+ 45	+ 44	+ 28	+ 23	+ 17
70	111	76	113	102

Write the answers.

$8 + $80 + $4 = $92 $45 + $25 + $15 = $85

60 cm + 6 cm + 12 cm = 78 cm   12 ¢ + 24 ¢ + 36 ¢ = 72 ¢

32 cm + 64 cm + 8 cm = 104 cm   35 ¢ + 45 ¢ + 16 ¢ = 96 ¢

21 cm + 20 cm + 19 cm = 60 cm   12 ¢ + 13 ¢ + 14 ¢ = 39 ¢

172

Subtracting ★

Write the answers.

40 − 12 = 28	50 − 17 = 33	60 − 11 = 49	80 − 19 = 61
90 − 18 = 72	30 − 10 = 20	100 − 15 = 85	60 − 45 = 15
26 − 14 = 12	39 − 16 = 23	42 − 11 = 31	63 − 22 = 41
76 − 34 = 42	96 − 45 = 51	54 − 40 = 14	59 − 28 = 31
46 − 17 = 29	52 − 16 = 36	73 − 19 = 54	25 − 17 = 8
34 − 18 = 16	48 − 29 = 19	40 − 26 = 14	81 − 44 = 37

Write the answers.

35	41	57	63	44
− 12	− 20	− 25	− 41	− 34
23	21	32	22	10

27	32	54	70	36
− 19	− 14	− 26	− 37	− 17
8	18	28	33	19

Write the answers.

47 cm − 34 cm = 13 cm   59 ¢ − 28 ¢ = 31 ¢   70 m − 32 m = 38 m

$40 − $26 = $14   61 ¢ − 34 ¢ = 27 ¢   73 cm − 48 cm = 25 cm

64 m − 49 m = 15 m   53 ¢ − 49 ¢ = 4 ¢   25 ¢ − 24 ¢ = 1 ¢

21 ¢ − 17 ¢ = 4 ¢   41 ¢ − 38 ¢ = 3 ¢ $98 − $45 = $53

173

Children should have methods of working addition problems in both their vertical and horizontal forms. As children become more proficient at math, they should see the importance of reaching the answer speedily.

As with addition on the previous page, children should by now be able to work out these problems both quickly and accurately.

★ Multiples

Circle the multiples of 9.

4   19   29   (18)

39   (36)   (27)

(90)   (108)

Circle the multiples of 8.

(8)   26   (16)   34

(32)   55   54

(64)   50

Circle the multiples of 7.

(21)   24   (35)   37

(42)   46   (70)

(14)   39

Circle the numbers that are multiples of both 7 and 9.

35   36   49   42

28   56   (63)

45   42

Circle the numbers that are multiples of both 6 and 8.

12   18   (24)   40

8   (48)   60

80   (96)

Circle the numbers that are multiples of both 4 and 8.

4   (8)   12   36

20   (24)   30

(40)   (48)

Circle the numbers that are multiples of both 5 and 10.

5   (10)   15   (40)

(30)   35   25

55   (60)

Circle the numbers that are multiples of both 4 and 6.

4   6   (12)   8

20   32   (24)

(48)   22

A good understanding of multiples can be seen as a way of reinforcing times tables knowledge but is also a useful thing within its own right. Multiples will also be helpful when working with factors at a later stage.

Factors ★

Factors are numbers that divide exactly into another number.
For example, factors of 6 are 1, 2, 3, and 6.

Write the factors of each number.

4   1, 2, and 4   5   1 and 5   6   1, 2, 3, and 6

7   1 and 7   8   1, 2, 4, and 8   9   1, 3, and 9

10   1, 2, 5, and 10   12   1, 2, 3, 4, 6, and 12   14   1, 2, 7, and 14

15   1, 3, 5, and 15   16   1, 2, 4, 8, and 16   17   1 and 17

26   1, 2, 13, and 26   21   1, 3, 7, and 21   22   1, 2, 11, and 22

23   1 and 23   27   1, 3, 9, and 27   25   1, 5, and 25

20   1, 2, 4, 5, 10, and 20   24   1, 2, 3, 4, 6, 8, 12, and 24

36   1, 2, 3, 4, 6, 9, 12, 18, and 36   28   1, 2, 4, 7, 14, and 28

30   1, 2, 3, 5, 6, 10, 15, and 30   32   1, 2, 4, 8, 16, and 32

Of which number are these factors?

(1, 3, 9)   9   (1, 3, 5, 15)   15   (1, 2, 4, 8)   8

What do you notice about the factors of these numbers?

4   9   16   25   36

49   81   64   100

They have an odd number of factors.

What do you notice about the factors of these numbers?

3   5   7   11   13

17   19   23   29

They each have only two factors.

Understanding factors is a very useful skill and really helps children who have a deep knowledge of times tables now. The number of factors a number has will play an important part in high school mathematics.

★ Times tables 5, 6, 7, 8, and 9

Can you be correct and quick?
Write the answers.

3 x 6 = 18	4 x 7 = 28	3 x 8 = 24	4 x 9 = 36
10 x 6 = 60	7 x 7 = 49	1 x 8 = 8	0 x 9 = 0
6 x 0 = 0	7 x 10 = 70	8 x 8 = 64	7 x 9 = 63
0 x 6 = 0	5 x 9 = 45	8 x 9 = 72	9 x 0 = 0
6 x 9 = 54	7 x 8 = 56	6 x 8 = 48	9 x 5 = 45
6 x 4 = 24	7 x 6 = 42	8 x 0 = 0	9 x 9 = 81
1 x 6 = 6	1 x 7 = 7	5 x 8 = 40	9 x 6 = 54
2 x 6 = 12	0 x 7 = 0	8 x 4 = 32	2 x 9 = 18
6 x 6 = 36	7 x 5 = 35	8 x 7 = 56	9 x 8 = 72
5 x 6 = 30	2 x 7 = 14	2 x 8 = 16	3 x 9 = 27
8 x 6 = 48	3 x 7 = 21	10 x 8 = 80	5 x 0 = 0
6 x 7 = 42	7 x 9 = 63	8 x 5 = 40	9 x 10 = 90

Write the answers.

3 x 5 = 15	1 x 5 = 5	0 x 5 = 0	5 x 3 = 15
10 x 5 = 50	6 x 5 = 30	2 x 5 = 10	8 x 5 = 40
5 x 5 = 25	5 x 9 = 45	5 x 4 = 20	5 x 7 = 35

By this age children should have a good knowledge of the times tables. Although they may not find learning the times tables interesting, the knowledge will help them gain confidence in many mathematical areas.

Multiplying ★

Write the answers.

35 x 3 = 105	42 x 3 = 126	38 x 5 = 190	74 x 3 = 222
69 x 2 = 138	71 x 3 = 213	56 x 4 = 224	73 x 3 = 219
67 x 4 = 268	58 x 2 = 116	14 x 6 = 84	23 x 6 = 138
44 x 3 = 132	52 x 6 = 312	46 x 3 = 138	32 x 4 = 128

Write the answers.

29 x 3	36 x 4	45 x 5	54 x 6	62 x 7
87	144	225	324	434
71 x 4	86 x 3	93 x 4	73 x 5	64 x 2
284	258	372	365	128
59 x 4	43 x 5	23 x 6	38 x 4	40 x 6
236	215	138	152	240
56 x 3	63 x 4	76 x 2	41 x 5	67 x 7
168	252	152	205	469
78 x 8	89 x 10	37 x 5	48 x 6	59 x 7
624	890	185	288	413

Most schools will teach multiplication in both horizontal and vertical forms and children should have been given strategies to work problems in different ways.

★ Dividing with remainders

Write the answers. Some of these answers may have remainders.

27 ÷ 4 = 6 r3	24 ÷ 4 = 6	47 ÷ 4 = 11 r3	44 ÷ 4 = 11
29 ÷ 3 = 9 r2	14 ÷ 3 = 4 r2	17 ÷ 3 = 5 r2	21 ÷ 3 = 7
12 ÷ 7 = 1 r5	56 ÷ 7 = 8	77 ÷ 7 = 11	23 ÷ 7 = 3 r2
15 ÷ 5 = 3	6 ÷ 5 = 1 r1	12 ÷ 5 = 2 r2	34 ÷ 5 = 6 r4
10 ÷ 8 = 1 r2	57 ÷ 8 = 7 r1	84 ÷ 8 = 10 r4	24 ÷ 8 = 3
48 ÷ 6 = 8	38 ÷ 6 = 6 r2	44 ÷ 6 = 7 r2	19 ÷ 6 = 3 r1
90 ÷ 9 = 10	52 ÷ 9 = 5 r7	70 ÷ 9 = 7 r7	40 ÷ 9 = 4 r4
70 ÷ 10 = 7	100 ÷ 10 = 10	130 ÷ 10 = 13	26 ÷ 10 = 2 r6
44 ÷ 11 = 4	120 ÷ 11 = 10 r10	82 ÷ 11 = 7 r5	211 ÷ 11 = 19 r2

Write the answers.

$$2)\overline{19} = 9\,r1 \quad -18 \quad \overline{1}$$
$$2)\overline{23} = 11\,r1 \quad -22 \quad \overline{1}$$
$$2)\overline{41} = 20\,r1 \quad -40 \quad \overline{1}$$
$$2)\overline{30} = 15 \quad -30 \quad \overline{0}$$
$$2)\overline{26} = 13 \quad -26 \quad \overline{0}$$

$$3)\overline{32} = 10\,r2 \quad -30 \quad \overline{2}$$
$$3)\overline{41} = 13\,r2 \quad -39 \quad \overline{2}$$
$$3)\overline{13} = 4\,r1 \quad -12 \quad \overline{1}$$
$$3)\overline{17} = 5\,r2 \quad -15 \quad \overline{2}$$
$$3)\overline{21} = 7 \quad -21 \quad \overline{0}$$

Recognizing that things don't always work out exactly is interesting for children and division with remainders is an example. It is usual to use an "r" to indicate the remainder, but children may have been taught another way.

More dividing ★

Write the answers. Some of these answers may have remainders.

$$8)\overline{48} = 6 \quad -48 \quad \overline{0}$$
$$9)\overline{57} = 6\,r3 \quad -54 \quad \overline{3}$$
$$6)\overline{32} = 5\,r2 \quad -30 \quad \overline{2}$$
$$11)\overline{77} = 7 \quad -77 \quad \overline{0}$$
$$10)\overline{90} = 9 \quad -90 \quad \overline{0}$$

$$4)\overline{41} = 10\,r1 \quad -40 \quad \overline{1}$$
$$4)\overline{5} = 1\,r1 \quad -4 \quad \overline{1}$$
$$7)\overline{56} = 8 \quad -56 \quad \overline{0}$$
$$5)\overline{27} = 5\,r2 \quad -25 \quad \overline{2}$$
$$7)\overline{28} = 4\,r4 \quad -28 \quad \overline{4}$$

Write the answers.

18 ÷ 3 = 6	26 ÷ 9 = 2 r8	53 ÷ 2 = 26 r1	76 ÷ 10 = 7 r6
49 ÷ 7 = 7	41 ÷ 10 = 4 r1	14 ÷ 8 = 1 r6	75 ÷ 6 = 12 r3
69 ÷ 7 = 9 r6	37 ÷ 8 = 4 r5	7 ÷ 7 = 1	78 ÷ 11 = 7 r1

What is the remainder each time?

6 divided by 5 — 1	28 divided by 10 — 8	17 divided by 11 — 6
42 divided by 6 — 0	50 divided by 11 — 6	25 divided by 8 — 1
53 divided by 6 — 5	19 divided by 7 — 5	26 divided by 3 — 2
100 divided by 9 — 1	87 divided by 2 — 1	60 divided by 7 — 4

This page provides further practice with division with remainders. At a later stage children will be shown how to convert the remainder into a fraction.

★ Choosing the operation

Which operation makes the number sentence correct?

14 ÷ 2 = 7	25 + 2 = 27	32 ÷ 4 = 8
15 x 3 = 45	2 x 20 = 40	50 + 10 = 60
12 + 12 = 24	16 x 2 = 32	40 ÷ 8 = 5
6 x 2 = 12	6 ÷ 2 = 3	14 ÷ 7 = 2
40 + 10 = 50	14 − 5 = 9	12 + 6 = 18
20 ÷ 2 = 10	36 + 12 = 48	4 x 5 = 20
7 x 8 = 56	10 ÷ 10 = 1	34 ÷ 2 = 17
50 + 10 = 60	56 ÷ 7 = 8	100 − 60 = 40
40 − 8 = 32	72 + 2 = 74	30 ÷ 3 = 10
50 − 20 = 30	2 ÷ 2 = 1	24 ÷ 6 = 4
42 ÷ 6 = 7	24 ÷ 12 = 2	32 − 20 = 12
1 + 2 = 3	21 x 3 = 63	12 − 12 = 0
10 + 5 = 15	16 − 2 = 14	14 x 3 = 42
60 ÷ 3 = 20	60 ÷ 10 = 6	35 ÷ 7 = 5

These questions test how well children are thinking beyond the straightforward questions. They should be able to recognize the number sentence and see which operation to use to make the sentence true.

Real-life problems ★

Use the box for your working out if needed.

A package contains 12 chocolate cookies. Barbara buys four packages for a party. How many cookies will Barbara have?

$$\begin{array}{r} 12 \\ \times 4 \\ \hline 48 \end{array}$$

48 cookies

Ann runs 2000 metres around the school field each day for five days. How far has Ann run in total over the five days?

10 000 metres

Songs can be downloaded from a website for 50 ¢ each. Kenny has $1.70 to spend on downloads. How many songs can Kenny download and how much will he have left?

3 songs and 20 ¢ left

Harris shares 50 bananas equally between 8 monkeys and gives the remainder to a giraffe. How many bananas does the giraffe receive?

2 bananas

Mark has $20. He shares this with his two sisters and gives the remainder to charity. How much does Mark give to charity?

$2

Children earn $15 a week delivering newspapers. Three children put their weekly earnings together. How much do the children have in total?

$45

Once again children will need to have the ability to sort out "what needs to be done." When a strategy has been developed, the next step is to carefully, quickly, and accurately work out the answer.

★ Money

Write the answers.

30 ¢ + 50 ¢ = 80 ¢	25 ¢ + 35 ¢ = 60 ¢	50 ¢ + 70 ¢ = 120 ¢
15 ¢ + 25 ¢ = 40 ¢	12 ¢ + 17 ¢ = 29 ¢	23 ¢ + 40 ¢ = 63 ¢
42 ¢ + 13 ¢ = 55 ¢	60 ¢ + 29 ¢ = 89 ¢	32 ¢ + 17 ¢ = 49 ¢
18 ¢ + 23 ¢ = 41 ¢	54 ¢ + 17 ¢ = 71 ¢	45 ¢ + 18 ¢ = 63 ¢
34 ¢ + 26 ¢ = 60 ¢	52 ¢ + 18 ¢ = 70 ¢	67 ¢ + 16 ¢ = 83 ¢
25 ¢ + 27 ¢ = 52 ¢	48 ¢ + 56 ¢ = 104 ¢	72 ¢ + 19 ¢ = 91 ¢
60 ¢ – 15 ¢ = 45 ¢	70 ¢ – 50 ¢ = 20 ¢	85 ¢ – 35 ¢ = 50 ¢
40 ¢ – 12 ¢ = 28 ¢	32 ¢ – 11 ¢ = 21 ¢	50 ¢ – 27 ¢ = 23 ¢
75 ¢ – 32 ¢ = 43 ¢	56 ¢ – 19 ¢ = 37 ¢	95 ¢ – 65 ¢ = 30 ¢

Round to the nearest dollar.

$2.34 $2.00	$15.25 $15.00	$0.78 $1.00
$1.50 $2.00	$3.50 $4.00	$5.01 $5.00
$1.20 $1.00	$1.80 $2.00	$2.65 $3.00
$0.37 $0	$0.84 $1.00	$6.20 $6.00
$1.54 $2.00	$2.60 $3.00	$4.50 $5.00
$4.65 $5.00	$1.90 $2.00	$2.30 $2.00
$18.00 $18.00	$12.00 $12.00	$17.42 $17.00

Although many children have been taught both horizontal and vertical methods for addition and subtraction, some schools only teach the vertical (column) method. Children will need to re-write these questions in that form.

Money problems ★

Use the box for working out if you need to.

John earns $12 a week gardening for a neighbour. He works for six weeks. How much has John earned in the six weeks? **$72**

$$\begin{array}{r} 12 \\ \times 6 \\ \hline 72 \end{array}$$

Jo has saved $15 to spend on her vacation. Her vacation will last two weeks. How much will Jo spend each week if she spends the same amount each week? **$7.50**

Yasir saves 25 ¢ coins to spend on toys. He has saved twenty 25 ¢ coins. How much has Yasir saved? **$5**

It costs Esther $5.50 a week to buy food for her dog. How much will the dog's food cost in total for eight weeks? **$44**

Konrad is given $10 to spend at a fair and actually spends $8.45. How much does Konrad have left? **$1.55**

Mirka saves $6 a month for a new mp3 player. How much will Mirka have saved after one year? **$72**

Children should be able to see fairly easily what is required by way of working out and then carry out the problem quickly and accurately.

★ Units of measurement

Write each length in metres.

8 km 8000 m	15 km 15 000 m	60 km 60 000 m	100 km 100 000 m
2.5 km 2500 m	1.34 km 1340 m	6.13 km 6130 m	12.7 km 12 700 m
7.056 km 7056 m	1.008 km 1008 m	5.030 km 5030 m	8.44 km 8440 m

Write each length in centimetres.

2 m 200 cm	12 m 1200 cm	50 m 5000 cm	9.2 m 920 cm
2.1 m 210 cm	5.5 m 550 cm	4.85 m 485 cm	1.94 m 194 cm
9.06 m 906 cm	6.04 m 604 cm	0.65 m 65 cm	2.07 m 207 cm

Write each weight in grams.

7 kg 7000 g	18 kg 18 000 g	23 kg 23 000 g	2.1 kg 2100 g
8.4 kg 8400 g	12.7 kg 12 700 g	3.9 kg 3900 g	5.98 kg 5980 g
9.56 kg 9560 g	2.06 kg 2060 g	1.08 kg 1080 g	0.67 kg 670 g

Write each weight in kilograms.

50 g 0.05 kg	180 g 0.180 kg	4 g 0.004 kg	39 g 0.039 kg
546 g 0.546 kg	3005 g 3.005 kg	14 000 g 14 kg	20 000 g 20 kg
1500 g 1.5 kg	700 g 0.7 kg	7905 g 7.905 kg	3456 g 3.456 kg

Write each amount in litres.

900 mL 0.9 L	100 mL 0.1 L	2450 mL 2.45 L	4780 mL 4.78 L

The metric units of measurements are commonly used in everyday life, and children should be given practice with them.

Measuring problems ★

Use the box for your working out.

The workmen have laid 562 m of blacktop for a new path. The path has to be 640 m long. How much further do the workmen need to go? **78 m**

$$\begin{array}{r} 640 \\ -562 \\ \hline 78 \end{array}$$

Eleanor has to put 20 litres of orange juice into 40 glasses. How much should Eleanor put in each glass? **half a litre**

Matt needs 450 grams of flour for a cake recipe but only has 400 grams. How much more flour does Matt need? **50 grams**

Richard has to cut a length of wood to be exactly 53 centimetres long. He begins with a piece of wood 60 centimetres long. How much wood does Richard need to cut off? **7 cm**

A large parcel weighs 8 kg. Parcels cost $1.30 per kg to post. How much will the parcel cost to post? **$10.40**

A family travels by car from Matheson City to Elliot Lake. The distance between the cities is about 136 kilometres. After 72 kilometres, the car runs out of gas. How much farther is there still to go? **64 km**

A tortoise can travel 25 centimetres in 5 minutes. If the tortoise can keep up the same speed, how far will it travel in one hour? **300 cm**

These questions give more practice in deciding which operation is needed. As children grow older, more and more math will depend upon them being able to "see the problem" and then using the best method to solve it.

★ Keeping skills sharp

Three children put their money together to buy some flowers.

$2.55 $1.80 $3.20

How much money do they have in total to spend on flowers?

$7.55

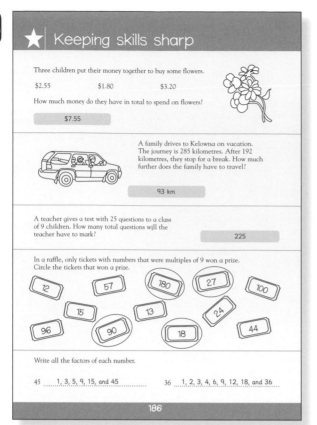

A family drives to Kelowna on vacation. The journey is 285 kilometres. After 192 kilometres, they stop for a break. How much further does the family have to travel?

93 km

A teacher gives a test with 25 questions to a class of 9 children. How many total questions will the teacher have to mark?

225

In a raffle, only tickets with numbers that were multiples of 9 won a prize. Circle the tickets that won a prize.

12   57   180   27   100
15   13   24
96   90   18   44

Write all the factors of each number.

45   1, 3, 5, 9, 15, and 45   36   1, 2, 3, 4, 6, 9, 12, 18, and 36

This test reinforces the skills learned so far. It can be repeated as often as appropriate but should be used mainly to highlight areas where children are doing well and those where further practice is necessary.

Keeping skills sharp ★

A builder puts bricks in piles of 12. A load of 100 bricks is delivered. How many piles will the builder make and how many bricks will be left over?

8 piles and 4 left over.

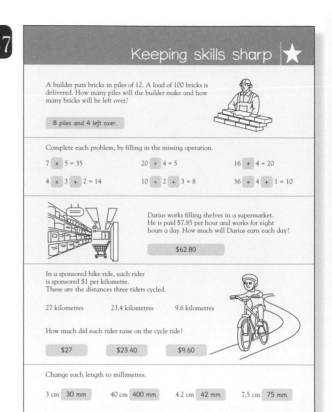

Complete each problem, by filling in the missing operation.

7 [x] 5 = 35   20 [÷] 4 = 5   16 [÷] 4 = 20

4 [x] 3 [+] 2 = 14   10 [÷] 2 [+] 3 = 8   36 [÷] 4 [+] 1 = 10

Darius works filling shelves in a supermarket. He is paid $7.85 per hour and works for eight hours a day. How much will Darius earn each day?

$62.80

In a sponsored bike ride, each rider is sponsored $1 per kilometre. These are the distances three riders cycled.

27 kilometres   23.4 kilometres   9.6 kilometres

How much did each rider raise on the cycle ride?

$27 $23.40 $9.60

Change each length to millimetres.

3 cm   30 mm   40 cm   400 mm   4.2 cm   42 mm   7.5 cm   75 mm

---

★ Reading timetables

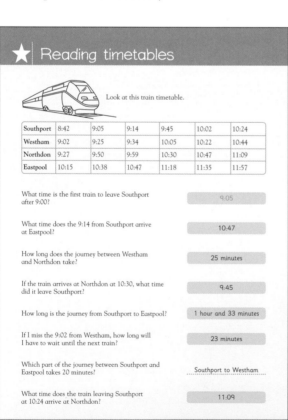 Look at this train timetable.

Southport	8:42	9:05	9:14	9:45	10:02	10:24
Westham	9:02	9:25	9:34	10:05	10:22	10:44
Northdon	9:27	9:50	9:59	10:30	10:47	11:09
Eastpool	10:15	10:38	10:47	11:18	11:35	11:57

What time is the first train to leave Southport after 9:00?

9:05

What time does the 9:14 from Southport arrive at Eastpool?

10:47

How long does the journey between Westham and Northdon take?

25 minutes

If the train arrives at Northdon at 10:30, what time did it leave Southport?

9:45

How long is the journey from Southport to Eastpool?

1 hour and 33 minutes

If I miss the 9:02 from Westham, how long will I have to wait until the next train?

23 minutes

Which part of the journey between Southport and Eastpool takes 20 minutes?

Southport to Westham

What time does the train leaving Southport at 10:24 arrive at Northdon?

11:09

Children see many timetables as they grow up, from TV menus of programs to movie times. The skills are usually straightforward but the more practice the better.

Time problems ★

Darius and Amy go to the movie theatre to watch a movie. The movie begins at 7:15 and lasts two and a half hours. What time does the movie end?

9:45

It will take a delivery lady 55 minutes to go from the warehouse to a customer. The delivery has to be made by 10:00 a.m. What is the latest time the lady can leave the warehouse?

9:05 a.m.

Each half of a soccer match lasts 45 minutes. The first half of a match had four minutes added for injuries. The second half had 3 minutes added for injuries. How long was the match in total?

97 minutes

Barbara is going on a fast ferry. The journey takes 4 hours and 20 minutes. If the ferry leaves at 8:30 a.m., what time will it arrive?

12:50 p.m.

Kasim is very fussy about how long to boil his egg. He likes his egg boiled for exactly 210 seconds. How long is 210 seconds in minutes and seconds?

3 minutes and 30 seconds

In the morning, Olly wakes up at 8:00 a.m. He spends 8 minutes getting dressed, 20 minutes having breakfast, 5 minutes washing and cleaning his teeth, and he is then ready to go to school. At what time is Olly ready to go to school?

8:33 a.m.

An exam is supposed to last one and a half hours but Clara finishes it with 12 minutes to spare. How long does Clara take to complete the exam?

1 hour and 18 minutes

By now children should be very confident with using various clock types to tell the time but may need practice in working with time, such as finding out "how much longer?" or "when will we arrive?"

★ Measuring weight

1000 grams (g) are the same as 1 kilogram (kg).

Write the answers.

4 kg = 4000 g   6 kg = 6000 g   8 kg = 8000 g

9 kg = 9000 g   10 kg = 10 000 g   12 kg = 12 000 g

2000 g = 2 kg   3000 g = 3 kg   5000 g = 5 kg

1000 g = 1 kg   7000 g = 7 kg   10 000 g = 10 kg

Match the object to its weight. Draw a line.

- 20 mg
- 200 g
- 3 kg

Match the object to its weight. Draw a line.

- 120 g
- 1 kg
- 15 g

Children may need help in working out these questions. Encourage them to estimate weights before actually measuring.

Measuring volume ★

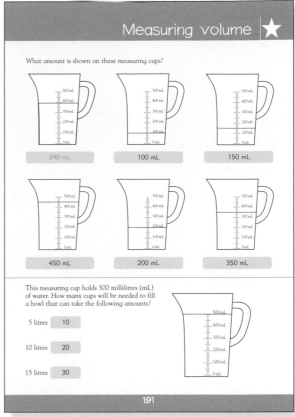

What amount is shown on these measuring cups?

390 mL   100 mL   150 mL

450 mL   200 mL   350 mL

This measuring cup holds 500 millilitres (mL) of water. How many cups will be needed to fill a bowl that can take the following amounts?

5 litres 10

10 litres 20

15 litres 30

This activity continues to support children as they work with metric units of measuring the volume of liquids.

★ Graphs

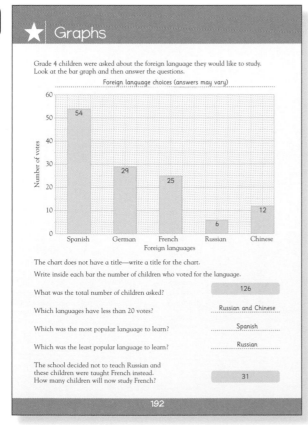

Grade 4 children were asked about the foreign language they would like to study. Look at the bar graph and then answer the questions.

Foreign language choices (answers may vary)

Number of votes: Spanish 54, German 29, French 25, Russian 6, Chinese 12

The chart does not have a title—write a title for the chart.

Write inside each bar the number of children who voted for the language.

What was the total number of children asked?   126

Which languages have less than 20 votes?   Russian and Chinese

Which was the most popular language to learn?   Spanish

Which was the least popular language to learn?   Russian

The school decided not to teach Russian and these children were taught French instead. How many children will now study French?   31

Children will know that it is good practice to label a graph with a title and a heading for the two axis. The chosen title may vary from the suggestion above.

More graphs ★

David is going to record his test scores over one term. These are David's scores out of 20.

Week	1	2	3	4	5	6	7	8	9	10	11	12
Score	12	7	13	12	11	14	14	16	13	17	18	20

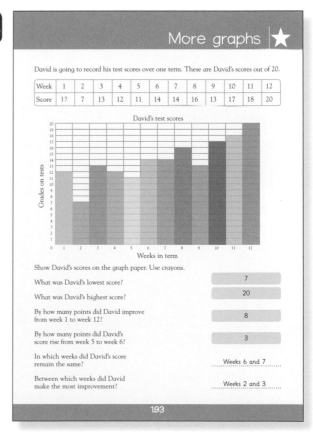

David's test scores

Show David's scores on the graph paper. Use crayons.

What was David's lowest score?   7

What was David's highest score?   20

By how many points did David improve from week 1 to week 12?   8

By how many points did David's score rise from week 5 to week 6?   3

In which weeks did David's score remain the same?   Weeks 6 and 7

Between which weeks did David make the most improvement?   Weeks 2 and 3

Graphs appear in many forms and this is another example of a type that children may encounter. Children should be used to "reading" information in whatever format particular tables or diagrams are presented.

★ Perimeters

What is the perimeter of each shape?

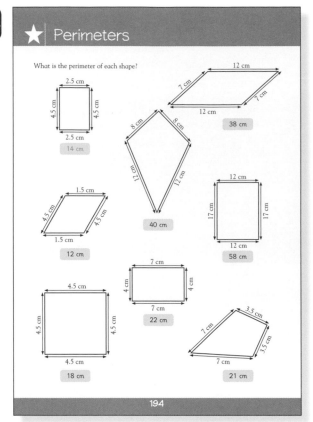

The perimeter is the distance around the outside of a shape, and children should cope well as long as they add or multiply carefully. Children should know a square has four equal sides and so should multiply one side by four.

Symmetry ★

Is the dotted line a line of symmetry?

Complete each drawing.

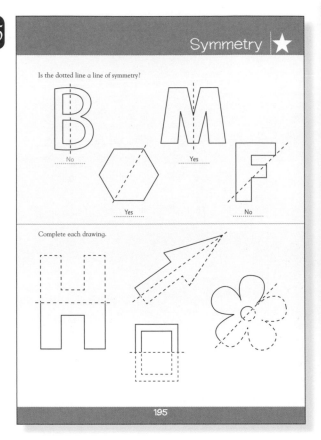

Symmetry is often a fun activity for children. By this stage, children are unlikely to need a mirror to help them work out if a shape is symmetrical or what the other side of a shape should look like to complete the symmetry.

★ Angles

Use a protractor to carefully measure each angle.

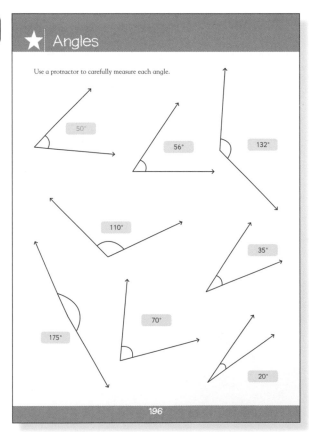

Protractors can vary in design—the traditional ones will have two possibilities for an "answer." Ask children to measure carefully and also tell you whether the angle is acute, right, or obtuse. Check their familiarity with these terms.

More angles ★

Use a protractor to measure more angles.

Now use your protractor to draw these same angles.

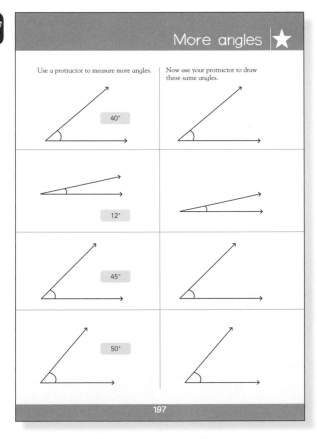

Although children do not usually draw angles with a protractor at this level, encourage them to try, and help them out if needed.

★ Quadrilaterals ★

Look at the shapes. Name two differences between a square and a rectangle.

A rectangle does not have all sides the same.

A square is a regular shape.

Look at the shapes. Name two differences between a rectangle and a trapezoid.

A trapezoid has no right angles.

A rectangle has two sets of parallel lines.

Look at the shapes. Name two similarities between a rhombus and a square.

They both have all sides of the same length.

They both have two sets of parallel lines.

Look at the shapes. Name two similarities between a rectangle and a parallelogram.

They both have two sets of parallel lines.

They both have two pairs of sides of the same length.

Children should be familiar with all of these quadrilaterals and their properties. This activity checks that they are confident in quickly recalling the shape names and noticing the difference in the shapes.

Properties of 3-D shapes ★

Look at the shapes.

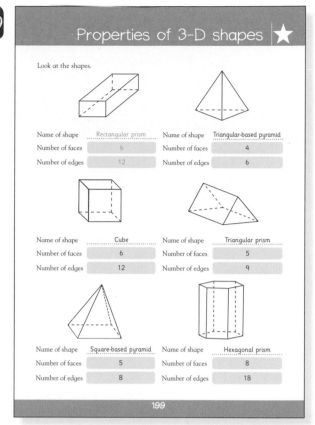

Name of shape Rectangular prism	Name of shape Triangular-based pyramid
Number of faces 6	Number of faces 4
Number of edges 12	Number of edges 6
Name of shape Cube	Name of shape Triangular prism
Number of faces 6	Number of faces 5
Number of edges 12	Number of edges 9
Name of shape Square-based pyramid	Name of shape Hexagonal prism
Number of faces 5	Number of faces 8
Number of edges 8	Number of edges 18

Although not covered on this page, children should know that faces can be flat or curved and that an edge happens when two faces meet.

★ Keeping skills sharp

Barbara finds out her rail journey will take 3 hours 25 minutes. If Barbara's train journey begins at 9:42 a.m., what time will it end?

1:07 p.m.

A playing field is 320 m long and 250 m across. What is the perimeter of the field?

1140 m

Ann runs these distances to get fitter.

1300 m   2000 m   2300 m   3600 m

What is Ann's mean (average) distance?

2300 m

Give the remainder each time.

20 divided by 3 2   14 divided by 5 4   13 divided by 6 1

24 ÷ 4 = 0   30 ÷ 4 = 2   17 ÷ 2 = 1

How many edges does a triangular prism have?   9

What shape am I?

I am a quadrilateral.

I have opposite sides parallel.

Only the opposite angles are equal.   Parallelogram

The final two pages are a third test that children can use to find out how well they have understood the work so far.

Keeping skills sharp ★

A bricklayer builds a wall around a garden. This is a plan of the garden.

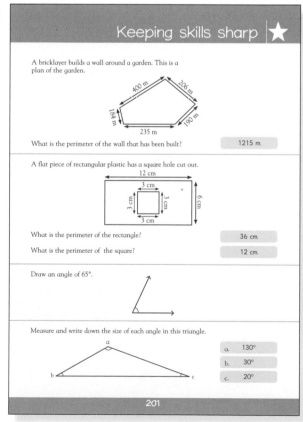

What is the perimeter of the wall that has been built?   1215 m

A flat piece of rectangular plastic has a square hole cut out.

What is the perimeter of the rectangle?   36 cm

What is the perimeter of the square?   12 cm

Draw an angle of 65°.

Measure and write down the size of each angle in this triangle.

a.   130°

b.   30°

c.   20°

DK
Senior Editor Deborah Lock
Art Director Martin Wilson
Publishing Director Sophie Mitchell
Pre-production Francesca Wardell
Jacket Designer Martin Wilson
Canadian Editor Barbara Campbell
Canadian Math Consultant Marilyn Wilson

DK Delhi
Editorial Monica Saigal, Tanya Desai
Design Pallavi Narain, Dheeraj Arora,
Tanvi Nathyal, Jyotsna Khosla
DTP Designer Anita Yadav

Expanded Canadian Edition, 2013
DK Publishing is represented in Canada by
Tourmaline Editions Inc.
662 King Street West, Suite 304
Toronto, Ontario M5V 1M7

Published in Great Britain in 2013
by Dorling Kindersley Limited
Copyright © 2005, 2013 Dorling Kindersley Limited
A Penguin Company
13 14 15 10 9 8 7 6 5 4 3 2 1
001-187485-August 2013

Library and Archives Canada Cataloguing in Publication
Math made easy : grade 4, ages 9-10 /
Canadian math consultant,
Marilyn Wilson. -- Expanded Canadian ed.
ISBN 978-1-55363-205-4
1. Mathematics--Problems, exercises, etc.
2. Mathematics--Study and teaching (Elementary).
I. Wilson, Marilyn
QA107.2.M3885 2013   510.76   C2012-908197-3

DK books are available at special discounts when
purchased in bulk for corporate sales, sales promotions,
premiums, fund-raising, or educational use.
For details, please contact specialmarkets@tourmaline.ca.

Printed and bound in China by L. Rex Printing Co., Ltd.

All images © Dorling Kindersley.
For further information see: www.dkimages.com
Discover more at
www.dk.com